Lecture Notes of the Institute
for Computer Sciences, Social Informatics
and Telecommunications Engineering   109

Phan Cong Vinh   Nguyen Manh Hung
Nguyen Thanh Tung   Junichi Suzuki (Eds.)

Context-Aware Systems and Applications

First International Conference, ICCASA 2012
Ho Chi Minh City, Vietnam, November 26-27, 2012
Revised Selected Papers

Volume Editors

Phan Cong Vinh
Nguyen Manh Hung
Nguyen Thanh Tung
Nguyen Tat Thanh University
Ho Chi Minh City, Vietnam
E-mail: {pcvinh, htnmhung, nttung}@ntt.edu.vn

Junichi Suzuki
University of Massachusetts
Boston, MA 02125-3393, USA
E-mail: jxs@cs.umb.edu

ISSN 1867-8211   e-ISSN 1867-822X
ISBN 978-3-642-36641-3   e-ISBN 978-3-642-36642-0
DOI 10.1007/978-3-642-36642-0
Springer Heidelberg Dordrecht London New York

Library of Congress Control Number: 2013931511

CR Subject Classification (1998):
H.3.3-5, H.4.1-3, H.5.1-5, I.2.1, I.2.4, I.2.10, C.2.2, C.2.4, K.4.4, I.5.1-4

Typesetting: Camera-ready by author, data conversion by Scientific Publishing Services, Chennai, India

Printed on acid-free paper

Springer is part of Springer Science+Business Media (www.springer.com)

Preface

The aim of the First International Conference on Context-Aware Systems and Applications (ICCASA) was to provide an international forum to discuss recently booming research issues—context-aware systems, which are primarily inspired by the human autonomic nervous system—as well as to bring researchers and practitioners together to further develop and to apply them to real-world problems. Context-awareness is one of the hot topics in ICT currently undergoing rapid advancements and emerging on the spot as one of the priority research areas. We hope that ICCASA plays an important role in encouraging researchers not only to advance theories but also to develop application techniques of context-awareness.

This was the first conference in the series and the first time that it was held in Ho Chi Minh City, Vietnam. ICCASA 2012 sponsored by Create-NET, Vietnam National Foundation for Science and Technology Development (NAFOSTED), Vietnam Ministry of Education and Training (MOET), and MIR-Labs was a place for highly original ideas about how context-aware systems are going to shape networked computing systems of the future.

The Program Committee received over 100 submissions from 20 countries and each paper was reviewed by at least three expert reviewers. We chose 34 papers after intensive discussions held among the Program Committee members. We really appreciate the excellent reviews and lively discussions of the Program Committee members and external reviewers in the review process. This year we chose two prominent invited speakers, Son Vuong from the University of British Columbia, Canada, and Phan Cong Vinh from Nguyen Tat Thanh University, Vietnam. The abstracts of their talks are included in these proceedings.

ICCASA 2012 was jointly organized by The European Alliance for Innovation (EAI) and Nguyen Tat Thanh University (NTTU). This conference could not have been organized without the strong support from the staff members of both organizations. We would especially like to thank Imrich Chlamtac (University of Trento and Create-NET), Åza Swedin (EAI), Elisa Mendini (EAI), and Erica Polini (EAI) for their great help in organizing the conference. We also appreciate the gentle guidance and help from the Advisory Chairs Banh Tien Long (MOET), Bui Van Ga (MOET), Nguyen Minh Hong (Vietnam Ministry of Information and Communications), and Phan Thanh Binh (Ho Chi Minh City Vietnam Natioanl University).

November 2012

Phan Cong Vinh
Nguyen Manh Hung
Nguyen Thanh Tung
Jun Suzuki

Organization

Steering Committee

Imrich Chlamtac	Create-Net and University of Trento, Italy
Phan Cong Vinh	NTTU, Vietnam
Emil Vassev	Lero at University of Limerick, Ireland
Jun Suzuki	UMass, USA
Kuan-Ching Li	Providenc University, Taiwan

Advisory Committee

Bui Van Ga	Ministry of Education and Training, Vietnam
Nguyen Minh Hong	Ministry of Information and Communications, Vietnam
Banh Tien Long	Ministry of Education and Training, Vietnam
Phan Thanh Binh	HCMVNU, Vietnam

General Co-chairs

Nguyen Manh Hung	NTTU, Vietnam
Phan Cong Vinh	NTTU, Vietnam

Organizing Co-chairs

Nguyen Van Luong	NTTU, Vietnam
Nguyen Tuan Anh	NTTU, Vietnam
Nguyen Van Sanh	Mahidol University, Thailand
Le Huy Ba	NTTU, Vietnam

Publication Co-chairs

Bui Duy Tan	NTTU, Vietnam
Vuong Xuan Chi	NTTU, Vietnam

Publicity Co-chairs

Pham Van Dat	NTTU, Vietnam
Nguyen Hoang Loc	NTTU, Vietnam

International Liaison Co-chairs

Le Quang Khanh	NTTU, Vietnam
Vu Ngoc Hai	NTTU, Vietnam

Local Arrangements Co-chairs

Thai Thi Thanh Thao	NTTU, Vietnam
Nguyen Minh Khai	NTTU, Vietnam
Vu Thi Nguyet Vien	NTTU, Vietnam
Nguyen Trong Tuan	NTTU, Vietnam
Do Nguyen Anh Thu	NTTU, Vietnam
Luong Thi Tien	NTTU, Vietnam
Le Thi Thuy Duong	NTTU, Vietnam
Hoang Tung	NTTU, Vietnam

Web Co-chairs

Thai Thi Thanh Thao	NTTU, Vietnam
Thai Truc Nhi	NTTU, Vietnam

Program Committee Co-chairs

Phan Cong Vinh	NTTU, Vietnam
Nguyen Thanh Tung	IU-HNVNU, Vietnam
Jun Suzuki	UMass, USA

Program Committee

Antonio Manzalini	Telecom Italia Future Center, Italy
Ashiq Anjum	Bristol Institute of Technology, UK
Corrado Moiso	Telecom Italia Future Center, Italy
Cem Safak Sahin	BAE Systems, USA
Costin Badica	University of Craiova, Romania
Cristian-Gyozo Haba	"Gheorghe Asachi" Technical University of Iasi, Romania
Dongkyun Kim	KISTI, South Korea
Emil Vassev	Lero at University of Limerick, Ireland
Eugenio Almeida	National Institute for Space Research (INPE), Brazil
George C. Alexandropoulos	Athens Information Technology, Greece
Hiroshi Wada	NICTA, Australia
Jonathan Bowen	London South Bank University, UK
Marco Aldinucci	University of Turin, Italy
Massimiliano Rak	Second University of Naples, Italy
Massimo Villari	University of Messina, Italy

Nedal Ababneh   WiSAR Lab (LYIT), France
Paolo Bellavista   DEIS - University of Bologna, Italy
Quan Thanh Tho   Ho Chi Minh City University of Technology,
                         Vietnam
Radu Calinescu   Aston University, UK
Sherif Abdelwahed   Mississippi State University, USA
Tiziana Calamoneri   "Sapienza" University of Rome, Italy
Tran Viet   Institute of Informatics, SAS, Slovakia
Vladimir Vlassov   KTH Royal Institute of Technology, Sweden
Yaser Jararweh   Jordan University of Science and Technology,
                         Jordan

Additional Reviewers

Alina Patelli   Aston University, UK
Huynh Thi Thanh Binh   Hanoi University of Science and Technology,
                         Vietnam
Ngo Thanh Long   Le Qui Don University, Vietnam
Nguyen Thanh Binh   Ho Chi Minh City University of Technology,
                         Vietnam
Nguyen Tran Minh Khue   Ho Chi Minh City University of Information
                         Technology, Vietnam
Nguyen Van Phuc   NTTU, Vietnam
Phan Trung Huy   Hanoi University of Science and Technology,
                         Vietnam

Sponsors

Create-NET
Vietnam National Foundation for Science and Technology Development
(NAFOSTED)
Vietnam Ministry of Education and Training (MOET)
MIR-Labs

Table of Contents

Context-Aware Systems

Context-Aware Technologies

Related Topics of Context-Awareness

Activity-Based Entities Relationship in Monitoring Context Awareness

Nor Azlina Aziz Fadzillah, Nasiroh Omar, and Siti Zaleha Zainal Abidin

University Technology MARA,
40450 Shah Alam, Malaysia
norazlina@perlis.uitm.edu.my, nasiroh@tmsk.uitm.edu.my,
sitizaleha533@salam.uitm.edu.my

Abstract. Communication and collaboration among members in virtual workspace are becoming more complex and challenging. Users are invisible and they are merely represented by their tasks in align with resources. In order to maintain effective communication among users, monitoring context awareness in a collaborative space is crucial. A vital aspect of awareness is associated with coordinating work practices by displaying and monitoring virtual users' actions. This paper focuses on user activities in five dominant domains for the purpose of understanding phenomena in contextual awareness. Activities and their relationships are explored to produce an activity-based entities relationship in monitoring context awareness.

Keywords: Collaborative workspace, context-awareness, entities relationship, activities, monitoring.

1 Introduction

Collaboration involves groups of people working together to achieve certain goals. It relies on the ability to work either virtual or physical of the on-going and seamless transition between individual and collaborative task [1]. In network collaborative virtual environment (NCVE), each collaborator holds a specific job function such as manager, supervisor, administrator, secretary and day-to-day operation workers [2]. It involves common people behavior such as eye contact, gaze duration and touch, which are invisible in the virtual world [1].

Today, the requirements for context-aware software, are more and more difficult to handle such as limited connectivity, hardware heterogeneity, and changes in user preferences [3]. Users are either less aware of others using the software or they are less comfortable posting because they do not know who is using the system [4]. They note that all users feel that sharing their locations or events context to other people in the system is important.

The context awareness applications usually make use of human computer interaction. When the interaction occurs, people tend to ignore whether the information is understood by others. People who are sharing their tasks do not know what others exactly do and what their task or work progress during the conversation in NCVE. In addition, misunderstanding emerges when people do not have the same background knowledge [5].

P.C. Vinh et al. (Eds.): ICCASA 2012, LNICST 109, pp. 1–9, 2013.

This paper is intended to explore and understand phenomena in contextual awareness. The relationships between user, task and resources will determine the entities involved in workspace environment. All entities and their relationships will be explored in order to determine the monitoring process of user task in the collaborative workspace.

2   Context Aware Entities

Collaborative virtual environment is used to support collaborative work between geographically separated and between collocated collaborators [6]. All collaborators should aware and understand the activities of others which provide contexts of their activities. A context is open and dynamic concepts which represent the activities performed in a workspace. It can be used to facilitate the communication in human-computer interaction. This context is used to ensure that user contributions are relevant to the group's activity [7]. It is important to recognise the context within the group and evaluate user actions with respect to group activities, progress and goals.

Workspace awareness aids coordination of tasks and resources, and assists transitions between user and shared activities [8]. Most activities involve *user*, *human computer interface* and *middleware* (Figure 1). *User* involves user needs, preferences and expertise [9]. Whereas, *human computer interface* is concerned on how people interact with computing technology [10]. At the architectural level, a *middleware* provides platform for *human computer interface* [11]. The *middleware* should consider both elements and mechanisms used in gathering awareness information in collaborative workspace [8].

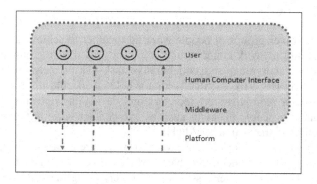

Fig. 1. General view of collaborative workspace

Our previous study has revealed eight elements that mostly associated with context-awareness research namely *domain, activity of user, context object, locations, type of communication, type of context, digital elements* and *models* [12]. Within these elements, *activity of user* should be focused in order to capture monitoring process and their relationships in the contextual awareness.

Most context-aware collaborative workspaces compose of *user*, *resources* and *task* [12]. In order to understand the process of collaborative communication, the user should be aware of who is online, what they are doing, and what their plans are [12], [13],[14]. When initiating a communication, it is important to be aware of the context that the inculator is operating in, and to establish a common understanding of the context [5]. Communication involves user relation, location and time [15], [16], [17]. Context-based workspace awareness can also be supported by computer technology [18]. Users should be assured that their partners have the same relevant information, device, media, and tools.

In addition, user activities play an important role in a shared-workspace collaboration [3], [19]. An activity is always user-centric and has some goals [20]. It can be defined as awareness of collaborators' work that supports performance in complex tasks [14]. Awareness of activities at different levels either individual, group or organizational, requires different information [3]. It also implies people's plan and understandings, knowledge of what one's collaborators are doing, and identifying, coordinating, and carrying out different types of task [21]. The next section investigates user activities in five dominant domains that use contextual awareness as part of the system.

3   Exploring Monitoring User Activities

The monitoring process is one of the main activities in the workspace. Designing efficient monitoring tools for online collaborative environments is certainly a complex task [18],[22]. A critical aspect of awareness is the associated coordinate work practices of displaying and monitoring actions [23]. This aspect concerns on how colleagues easily monitor the action which influent their work. Monitoring activities or practices in collaborative system is an important feature which allows user to obtain historical data and user's interactions in the collocated working environments [24], [25], [26].

Our analysis of activity awareness in the collaborative workspace was based on five dominant domains; education, context-based workspace, communication, visualization and business. The domains represent the activities during the collaboration in order to extract the contextual media used, how the media are monitored and the communication types involved among users (Table 1).

Based on Table 1, it is found that monitoring is important in collaborative learning because it gives vital information and allows user to take immediate corrective actions [27]. It also helps user dealing with the collaborative tools to accurately monitor multiple communication channels, make quick and effective decisions, and reply to critical messages [28]. For example, monitoring contextual activities in e-learning gives high learnability, low number of errors and no unrecoverable errors [29].

Table 1. Summary of the selected samples in monitoring user activities

Domain	Contextual Media	Contextual Activities	Type of communication
Learning	• Dialog box [18] • Color coded system [18] [30] [31] • Text chat box [30] • Whiteboard[30] • Tagging [32] • Group chat [22], [33]	• Change of color [18] [30] [31] • Comments [18] • Lesson Calendar [33] • Graph [22]	• Face to face [18] • One-to-one [14] [31] • Peer-to-peer [22] • Teamwork [18] [30]
Context-Based Workspace	• Status bar [27] • Audio [34] • Colored line-border [27] • Text editor [35] • Word [36]	• Change of color [27] • Drawing task [34] • Calendar [35] • Clicking on a word [36]	• One-to-one [27] [34] [36] • Teamwork [35]
Communication	• Keyword [28] • Text annotation [37] • Video chatting [38] • Chat [39]	• Highlight keyword [28] • Speech-to-text [28] • Voice [28] • Comment [37] [38] • Share activity button [39] • Onlline/offline filter [39]	• One-to-one [25] [37] • Group [38] [39]
Visualizing Approach	• Time tracking [29] • Finger-rays [40] • Blog, Twitter, Youtube [41]	• Colored points [29] • Line chart [29] [41] • Bar chart [29] [41] • Multitouch [40]	• One-to-one [41] • One-to-many [41] • Peer-to-peer [29],[40]
Business	• Image [42] • Member verification [43]	• Rating-based ranking [42] • System monitor panel [43] • Streaming controller modules [43]	• One-to-one [42] • Group [43]

Studies have revealed that contextual activities such as color coded system, colored-line border, chat box and keyword, can be used to monitor contextual awareness between users [18] [30] [31] [27]. In addition, images and suggestion lists help significantly in business activities [42].   Moreover, messages are easier to be used in communication activities [28].

However, there are still some issues for monitoring the contextual activities. Gutwin et al. [34] categorizes three limitations in visualizing user activities. First, display areas must be visible to all users to be useful since the awareness information is hidden in many scenarios (e.g., both small screen and large-screen setting). Second, visual information about activities may be difficult to see if the action is small or workspace is cluttered. Third, the observer must attend to the awareness display in order to notice changes in the display.

Furthermore, many factors such as system signals, user queries and attached devices could burden system performance [44]. In order to increase the performance, a mechanism is needed to distribute activity awareness to relevant contacts and allow users to control with whom they share their activity [39]. The next section proposes activity-based entities relationship for context aware monitoring mechanism to understand the contextual awareness phenomena.

4   Activity-Based Entities Relationship

An activity composes of many entities and their connections. The activities need to be monitored to ensure that the goals are achieved. The monitoring process is usually based on type of communication, synchronous work session, monitoring interface and evaluation. Based on the requirements, context aware elements have been proposed [12] as depicted in Figure 2.

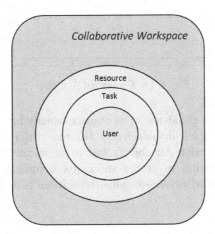

Fig. 2. Context-aware elements

The communication involves one-to-one or a group of users. The users will communicate via network in a virtual environment to accomplish their goal. People who are sharing their tasks require details information of what others exactly do and what are their task progressions or work in the collaborative workspace [12]. For example, during the conversation, user A will communicate with user B (Figure 3). Both users should observe their environment and activities. They should respond and understand the action taken during the work progress to achieve the goals. This action would require contextual media to access and update their task.

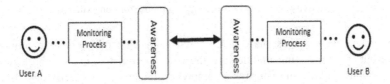

Fig. 3. The user interaction in contextual awareness activities

The contextual media are used to interact and convey messages among users. Examples of contextual media include online calendars, color coded system, dialog box, message, word, and text annotation. The media are monitored by an object that consists of user, task and resources (Figure 4). The communication between objects is governed by monitoring process that is supported by appropriate technologies.

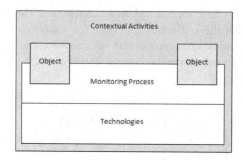

Fig. 4. The Contextual Activities

The communication in collaborative workspace usually involves a group of users from different domain. Each domain has a different activities and goals but may use similar contextual media. All objects will communicate with each other and it needs a monitoring process to ensure successful communication. Based on the contextual activities, an activity-based entities relationship is proposed for a group of users (Figure 5).

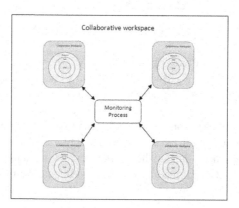

Fig. 5. An activity-based entities monitoring model for contextual awareness

The relationship shows that even though each object has its own monitoring process but the underlying middleware must be coordinated and synchronized in a single generalize platform to portray a comprehensive group work activities.

5   Conclusion

As the collaborative work faces uncertainty and complexity due to location, time and cultural differences among users, monitoring users' activities are difficult for completing their work tasks. This paper has explored user contextual activities in five dominant domains in order to analyze the monitoring process on how information is shared and monitored in the collaborative workspace. We examined the awareness activities and extracted the contextual media involved in each domain. Through this investigation, we found that the monitoring process help users to access and response to the taken action. Following this investigation, we proposed entities relationship for contextual awareness. Based on the relationship, our future work will investigate further on suitable underlying middleware that provide coordination and synchronization that are able to provide an aid in knowledge creation, transfer and sharing task among users especially in collaborative workspace.

Acknowledgements. The authors would like to thank Ministry of Higher Education (FRGS Grant) and University Technology MARA Malaysia for the financial support.

References

1. Tromp, J.G., Steed, A., Wilson, J.R.: Systematic usability evaluation and design issues for collaborative virtual environments. Presence: Teleoperators & Virtual Environments 12(3), 241–267 (2003)
2. Idrus, Z., et al.: Roles of users in interactive networked collaborative environment (2011)
3. Parra, C., Blanc, X., Duchien, L.: Context awareness for dynamic service-oriented product lines. Carnegie Mellon University (2009)
4. Ganoe, C.H., et al.: Mobile awareness and participation in community-oriented activities. ACM (2010)
5. Poteet, S., et al.: Miscommunications and context awareness (2009)
6. Churchill, E.F., Snowdon, D.: Collaborative Virtual Environments: an introductory review of issues and systems. Virtual Reality 3(1), 3–15 (1998)
7. Dourish, P., Bellotti, V.: Awareness and coordination in shared workspaces. ACM (1992)
8. Gutwin, C., Greenberg, S.: Workspace awareness for groupware. ACM (1996)
9. Göker, A., Myrhaug, H.I.: User context and personalisation (2002)
10. Olson, G.M., Olson, J.S.: Human-computer interaction: Psychological aspects of the human use of computing. Annual Review of Psychology 54(1), 491–516 (2003)
11. García, P., et al.: MOVE: component groupware foundations for collaborative virtual environments. ACM (2002)
12. Fadzillah, N., Omar, N., Abidin, S.: Application-based context-awareness in collaborative workspaces: A review. IEEE (2012)
13. Gutwin, C., Greenberg, S., Roseman, M.: Supporting awareness of others in groupware. ACM (1996)
14. Carroll, J.M., et al.: Notification and awareness: synchronizing task-oriented collaborative activity. International Journal of Human-Computer Studies 58(5), 605–632 (2003)

15. Kappel, G., et al.: Customisation for ubiquitous web applications: a comparison of approaches. International Journal of Web Engineering and Technology 1(1), 79–111 (2003)

16. Kleinrock, L.: Nomadicity: anytime, anywhere in a disconnected world. Mobile Networks and Applications 1(4), 351–357 (1996)

17. Schwinger, W., et al.: Context-awareness in mobile tourism guides–A comprehensive survey. Rapport Technique. Johannes Kepler University Linz (2005)

18. Hurtado, C., Guerrero, L.A.: Enhancement of Collaborative Learning Activities using Portable Devices in the Classroom. Journal of Universal Computer Science 17(2), 332–347 (2011)

19. Abowd, G., et al.: Towards a better understanding of context and context-awareness. Springer (1999)

20. Schaub, F., et al.: Towards context adaptive privacy decisions in ubiquitous computing. IEEE (2012)

21. Farooq, U., et al.: Activity awareness in collaboratories (2008)

22. Juan, A.A., et al.: Developing an information system for monitoring student's activity in online collaborative learning. IEEE (2008)

23. Monitor, W.A.S.I.: The Awareness Network, To Whom Should I Display My Actions? And, Whose Actions Should I Monitor? IEEE Transactions on Software Engineering 37(3), 325 (2011)

24. Babic, F., et al.: A logging mechanism for acquisition of real data from different collaborative systems for analytical purposes. IEEE (2010)

25. Hindmarsh, J., et al.: Object-focused interaction in collaborative virtual environments. ACM Transactions on Computer-Human Interaction (TOCHI) 7(4), 477–509 (2000)

26. Fraser, M., et al.: Supporting awareness and interaction through collaborative virtual interfaces (1999)

27. Bardram, J.E., Hansen, T.R.: Context-based workplace awareness. Computer Supported Cooperative Work (CSCW) 19(2), 105–138 (2010)

28. Finomore Jr., V., et al.: Effects of a Network-Centric Multi-Modal Communication tool on a Communication Monitoring task. SAGE Publications (2010)

29. Govaerts, S., Verbert, K., Klerkx, J., Duval, E.: Visualizing Activities for Self-reflection and Awareness. In: Luo, X., Spaniol, M., Wang, L., Li, Q., Nejdl, W., Zhang, W. (eds.) ICWL 2010. LNCS, vol. 6483, pp. 91–100. Springer, Heidelberg (2010)

30. Xiao, L.: A Shared Rationale Space for Supporting Knowledge Awareness in Collaborative Learning Activities: An Empirical Study. IEEE (2011)

31. Duval, E.: Attention please! Learning analytics for visualization and recommendation (2011)

32. Carroll, J.M., et al.: Supporting activity awareness in computer-mediated collaboration. IEEE (2011)

33. Chronopoulos, T., Hatzilygeroudis, I.: An intelligent system for monitoring and supervising lessons in LAMS. IEEE (2010)

34. Gutwin, C., et al.: Chalk sounds: the effects of dynamic synthesized audio on workspace awareness in distributed groupware. ACM (2011)

35. Steinfield, C., Jang, C.Y., Pfaff, B.: Supporting virtual team collaboration: the TeamSCOPE system (1999)

36. Lanza, M., Hattori, L., Guzzi, A.: Supporting collaboration awareness with real-time visualization of development activity. IEEE (2010)

37. Harrison, C., Amento, B.: CollaboraTV: Using asynchronous communication to make TV social again. In: Interactive TV: A Shared Experience, Adjunct Proceedings of EuroITV, Amsterdam, pp. 218–222 (2007)
38. Kadav, A., et al.: Improving the online video chat experience. Ergonomics and Health Aspects of Work with Computers, 199–208 (2011)
39. Houben, S., et al.: Co-activity manager: integrating activity-based collaboration into the desktop interface. ACM (2012)
40. Ardaiz, O., et al.: Virtual collaborative environments with distributed multitouch support (2010)
41. Popescu, E., Cioiu, D.: Instructor Support for Monitoring and Visualizing Students' Activity in a Social Learning Environment. IEEE (2012)
42. Boutemedjet, S., Ziou, D.: Using Images in Context-Aware Recommender Systems (2010)
43. Chunwijitra, S., et al.: Design of Suitable Meeting Management Model for WebELS Meeting to Meet the Business Situations (2011)
44. Lee, S., Park, S.: A study on issues in context-aware systems based on a survey and service scenarios. IEEE (2009)

Context-Aware User Preferences in Systems for Pervasive Computing and Social Networking

Elizabeth Papadopoulou, Sarah Gallacher, Nick K. Taylor, M. Howard Williams, and Fraser Blackmun

School of Math & Computer Sciences, Heriot-Watt University,
Edinburgh EH14 4AS, UK
{E.Papadopoulou,S.Gallacher,N.K.Taylor,M.H.Williams,
F.R.Blackmun}@hw.ac.uk

Abstract. Context-aware user preferences play an important role in adapting the behaviour of pervasive systems to satisfy the individual user in different contexts. Most of the pervasive system prototypes that have been developed, incorporate context-aware user preferences, capturing them in an appropriate form and using them to personalize the behaviour of the prototype. However, the rapid rise in use of social networking systems has created a new possibility – that of combining this type of system with pervasive systems to create a new type of system with the benefits of both. The challenge lies in finding how to integrate these two different paradigms in a seamless way to create such a system. This introduces new challenges for the context-dependent user preferences for both individuals and communities. This paper describes briefly some of the ideas, especially as they relate to context-aware user preferences.

Keywords: Context-aware, user preferences, learning, personalization, pervasive systems, social networking.

1 Introduction

Pervasive computing and social networking are two separate paradigms that are of great importance to current and future systems.

The first of these, pervasive computing, is concerned with the problems arising from the rapid growth in the number of devices in the environment surrounding the user, and the overwhelming number of services available to her. A major aim of pervasive computing is to provide the essential support that a user needs to help her communicate with and interact with this increasingly complex environment. This includes interaction with and control of devices and services while protecting her from the underlying complexity in doing so [1]. Many prototypes have been produced to experiment with the ideas of pervasive computing (e.g. Adaptive House [2], Ubisec [3], GAIA [4], MavHome [5], Things That Think (TTT) [6], Daidalos [7]).

In order to be acceptable to the end-user, a pervasive system must be able to adapt its behaviour to take account of the needs and preferences of individual users. Since the user cannot be expected to provide the system with the information to do so, the

P.C. Vinh et al. (Eds.): ICCASA 2012, LNICST 109, pp. 10–17, 2013.

approach generally adopted is for systems to monitor the user's behaviour and infer the user preferences from it. However, this task is both complex and challenging. Indeed one of the major challenges facing the developers of pervasive systems is to build up a subset of user preferences which, although incomplete, is sufficiently useful that it can provide a level of adaptive behaviour that is acceptable to the user.

An example of a pervasive system platform that operates in this way is that developed in the Persist project [8]. This was based on the use of Personal Smart Spaces for the development of pervasive systems. The prototype platform developed is founded on the notions of context-awareness and of personalisation based on user monitoring and learning to establish and refine context-dependent user preferences. The prototype has been used to demonstrate the ideas and to experiment with them.

The second paradigm, social networking, is one that has been hugely successful. Facebook has become a household name and systems such as LinkedIn, YouTube, Flickr, Skype, etc. have all become very popular with a very large user base. Social networking itself has been advancing rapidly and the latest developments in this area involve the incorporation of user context into such systems. The main focus has been on user location, and systems such as FourSquare rely entirely on this.

However, a new challenge lies in bringing together these two different paradigms, social networking and pervasive computing, in a fully integrated fashion. This would mean that the user could interact with friends and contacts via the social networking functionality as well as with services and devices in her environment through the pervasive functionality in a seamless manner. This has particular advantages for context and personalization which can be used to support both.

This paper describes some of our current research in this area. The next section describes some aspects of the Persist pervasive system platform while section 3 discusses briefly the issue of combining social networking and pervasive capabilities, especially with respect to context-dependent user preferences. Section 4 concludes on the state of implementation.

2   Pervasive Computing and Persist

The approach developed in the Persist project for handling pervasive behaviour is based on the notion of a Personal Smart Space (PSS). A PSS consists of a collection of devices belonging to a single owner (user or organisation) that are connected to form an ad hoc network. This may be mobile (in the case of a person who may move around with her PSS) or fixed (in the case of a fixed smart space, e.g. a smart home).

When one PSS encounters one or more other PSSs, they may interact with one another. This involves a PSS identifying itself to the other PSSs, subject to the constraints of user privacy. They may then proceed to share information or even third party services with other PSSs. This is described in more detail in [8].

Using the concept of Personal Smart Spaces the Persist project built a pervasive system prototype to demonstrate some of the capabilities that this can provide. This was based on an architecture consisting of five layers, as illustrated in Fig. 1.

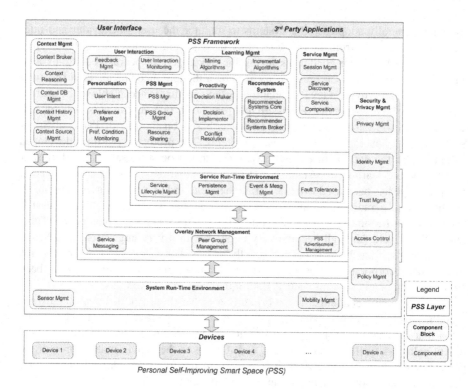

Fig. 1. The high level architecture of a Personal Smart Space

Central to this system is the notion of context-aware personalization. By this we mean the adaptation of the behaviour of a system to meet the needs and preferences of an individual user. This is an essential feature of the Persist platform. To achieve this two separate mechanisms are used. The first of these is based on user preferences. Each user has a set of user preferences associated with them which are used to tailor system behaviour to meet these preferences. In particular this is used to tailor individual services on behalf of the user. This functionality is provided by the Preference Manager and the Preference Condition Monitor in the Personalisation subsystem.

The second mechanism that is used in Persist is based on models of User Intent. In this case models are constructed over time of the sequences of actions performed by the user and typical recurring sequences are identified. These are then used to predict future actions that the user may wish to take. This is handled by the User Intent component of the Personalisation subsystem.

These two mechanisms predict actions which the system should take in order to personalize its behaviour in a way that might help the user. However, overall control of such actions is handled by the Proactivity subsystem which takes the final decision as to whether an action should be performed or not, and resolves any conflicts that may arise between the actions proposed by these two mechanisms.

Learning also has a key role to play in the Persist system. In order to capture these user preference rules, the Persist platform monitors the actions taken by the user and stores these together with the state of selected context attributes at the time of the action. Two forms of machine learning are then used to extract and refine user preferences. The one is an offline datamining algorithm which is used to analyse the whole data set. This is slow and only used at convenient times (e.g. at night). The other is an incremental algorithm which is applied only to the latest subset of the data. This is much faster and is applied when needed (e.g. when the actions predicted by the preference rules lead to a conflict). The overall process is illustrated in Fig. 2.

Although the main elements of context used in the preference rules were the symbolic location of the user and some categorization of time/day, we also experimented with other sensors, including ones that determined the user's current state in terms of sitting, standing, walking, etc.

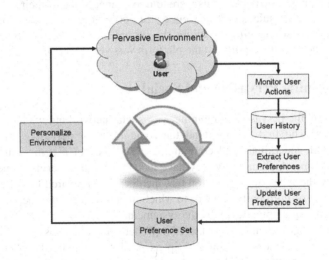

Fig. 2. Process of building and updating the set of context-dependent user preferences

As can be seen from Fig. 1, the issues of Privacy and Security are treated very seriously in the Persist system. In the case of the context-dependent user preferences, three strategies are employed to protect the information on the user, viz.

(1) The user preference rules are held by the Preference Management component of the system, which provides two routes to them. The first is a GUI which the user can access to view and, if necessary, change preferences. The second is the route provided to all other system and third party software which wants to use preferences. In the latter case the software calls the Preference Manager, which evaluates the appropriate rules whenever required, returning any action that results from this evaluation. The component cannot return the preference rule itself. Thus no component can obtain unauthorized access to this information through this route.

(2) In addition to this basic protection mechanism, the Persist system also supports multiple identities. Thus a user can select different identities to use with different services. Once again user preferences are used to assist the user in the process of

selecting identifiers. This has the added advantage that this selection process is context-aware. Thus the system may select different identities for the same third party service in different contexts. This helps to protect the real identity of a user when using different services.

(3) The final protection mechanism investigated for the Persist platform involves the use of privacy policies. Here the user must specify a set of privacy policy rules that specify what information can be given to what services and under what conditions.

To assess the effectiveness of our approach to context-aware user preferences, an experiment was conducted to learn viewing preferences for television. This was based on the fact that viewing preferences at home might be different from those at work. Twenty four volunteers took part and used the prototype to select television channels to watch on various plasma screens at different locations in our building. After an initial learning phase, the participants were told to change some of their selections and repeat the exercise. Results show an accuracy of 100% after two circuits of the initial learning phase. After changing selections the system took up to five circuits to learn the changes. The overall response to the platform was very positive.

3   Combining Pervasive and Social

In order to combine pervasive computing with social networking we have made two major changes. The first is to extend the basic ideas of pervasive computing to incorporate both individuals and communities. The idea of a community can be a fairly complex one. A community may have its own criteria in terms of membership, it may specify the types of information that members are prepared to share with each other and the set of third party services to which members may have access, it may be created manually or automatically by the system, and so on.

The second major change is to the PSS. Where the PSS was created to handle pervasive systems, a more general concept is needed to handle the combination of pervasive computing with social networking. For this purpose the concept of PSS has been extended to that of a Cooperating Smart Space (CSS) which has some of the properties of a PSS but also includes functionality for social networking. This is described in detail in [10].

The most important extension affecting context-aware preferences introduced in the CSS is the notion of community preferences. Just as individual users may have preferences associated with them, communities too may have preferences. For example, suppose that one creates a community of first year Computer Science students at a university. This community may have a particular preference for where to meet for lunch on a weekday at university, or for getting together on a Wednesday afternoon to play/watch football.

The main challenge here is how to derive these community preferences. On the one hand they could be obtained by extracting the individual preferences from the preference sets of each of its members and analyzing them to look for clusters. On the other hand, one may aggregate the history data from all its members and analyze this to extract preferences that apply to the whole group.

Another mechanism for obtaining preferences is by inheritance. Within any community one may also have sub-communities – subsets of the membership of the parent community who are linked together for some purpose. A sub-community may inherit preferences from the parent community as well as having its own unique preferences.

More generally, the preferences of individual users will be updated whenever the system discovers new preferences or changes to existing ones. The same applies to the management of community preferences. One major problem is that of how to deal with conflicts – such as those that may arise when the individual user preference results in a different outcome from that of a community preference.

Another important issue relating to communities which needs to be taken into account concerns how these are created. One obvious way of creating a community is for a user to set this up. However, a more challenging problem is for the system to identify potential communities dynamically. This involves analyzing the data relating to a set of CSSs and looking for clusters based on their attributes.

To illustrate the power of such a system, consider the following extract from the set of scenarios used to illustrate the behaviour of such a system:

Scene 1: Harry is a new student who has just arrived at Heriot-Watt University (HWU). He is alerted to important communities that he is strongly encouraged to join, particularly the "Freshers" community that all new students can join. On joining the Freshers community Harry inherits several community preferences. One such preference is the preferred venue to buy lunch on campus. He is also automatically added to a "Computer Science" community for the degree course he is taking.

Scene 2: That evening Harry attends a Freshers' event called the "Proactive Disco". It is a community based disco that takes into account the individual user preferences relating to music of all the people currently dancing on the dance floor (identified using sensor technology) and decides what music tracks to play.

Scene 3: Harry is leaving his dorm room to attend his first lecture. His CSS identifies his intent to attend the lecture and the navigation service is automatically started to direct Harry to the lecture room. On his way Harry's CSS identifies another person nearby who also has the intent of attending the same lecture. Since they share intents and since the other person's mood is 'happy', Harry's CSS suggests an introduction which he accepts. Harry's CSS shows him a picture of the other person and tells Harry his name is Tom. They begin to chat as they walk together to the lecture.

4   Implementing a Pervasive Social Networking System

The set of requirements that has emerged for this type of system is much more extensive than that for a pervasive system such as the Persist system. The Societies project [9] is building on the work done in Persist to create a platform that combines pervasive computing and social networking in a seamless way, and which exhibits both types of behaviour. This is based on a rather different architecture that can deal with this combination of functionalities. For example, the issue of scalability takes on new significance when communities can end up with thousands of users. Similarly, the way in which context-dependent user preferences are handled becomes more complex – with strategies employed to learn both individual and community preferences and to arbitrate between them when necessary.

To assess user reaction to these ideas, we conducted two evaluations. In the first a group of volunteers was given a storyboard presentation illustrating the behaviour of the platform and questioned on their reactions to aspects of the system.

In the second a physical experiment was set up with a version of the platform so that volunteers could experience the type of behaviour at first hand, and once again they were questioned on their reactions.

The conclusions from this exercise relevant to this paper were:

(a) The participants found the idea of the system taking decisions on their behalf more acceptable after experiencing the system than before it. In answer to the question "Would you allow the system to take decisions on your behalf ..." 47% responded positively before the experiment while 77% responded positively after it.

(b) Asked about whether they would mind if the system monitored them in order to obtain improved user preferences, only 7% responded negatively.

The first prototype of the Societies platform is nearing completion. It is based on Android phones linking to the cloud for the main processing and storage requirements. The system will be exposed to different types of users and its performance evaluated in three separate user trials in the last quarter of 2012/first quarter of 2013. These are:

(1) Student trial, in which a number of students will be given the platform to use over an extended period.

(2) Disaster management trial, in which the system will be employed by real disaster management end users.

(3) Enterprise trial, in which the system will be used by industrial users for typical situations in commerce and industry, including conference type applications.

More details of this can be found at http://wiki.ict-societies.eu.

Acknowledgement. Besides thanking the European Commission for their support for the PERSIST and SOCIETIES projects, the authors also wish to thank colleagues in the two projects without whom this paper would not have been possible. Apart from funding these two projects, the European Commission has no responsibility for the content of this paper.

References

1. Satyanarayanan, M.: Pervasive computing: vision and challenges. IEEE PCM 8(4), 10–17 (2001)
2. Mozer, M.C.: Lessons from an Adaptive House. In: Cook, D., Das, R. (eds.) Smart Environments: Technologies, Protocols and Applications, pp. 273–294 (2004)

3. Groppe, J., Mueller, W.: Profile Management Technology for Smart Customizations in Private Home Applications. In: 16th Int. Workshop on Database and Expert Systems Applications (DEXA 2005), pp. 226–230 (2005)
4. Kindberg, T., Barton, J.: A web-based nomadic computing system. Computer Networks 35, 443–456 (2001)
5. Youngblood, M.G., Holder, L.B., Cook, D.J.: Managing Adaptive Versatile Environments. In: 3rd IEEE Int. Conf on Pervasive Computing and Communications (PerCom 2005), pp. 351–360 (2005)
6. Mistry, P., Maes, P.: Sixth Sense: A Wearable Gestural Interface. In: International Conference on Computer Graphics and Interactive Techniques, Yokohama, Article 11 (2009)
7. Williams, M.H., Taylor, N.K., Roussaki, I., Robertson, P., Farshchian, B., Doolin, K.: Developing a Pervasive System for a Mobile Environment. In: eChallenges 2006 – Exploiting the Knowledge Economy, pp. 1695–1702. IOS Press (2006)
8. Crotty, M., Taylor, N., Williams, H., Frank, K., Roussaki, I., Roddy, M.: A Pervasive Environment Based on Personal Self-improving Smart Spaces. In: Gerhäuser, H., Hupp, J., Efstratiou, C., Heppner, J. (eds.) AmI 2008. CCIS, vol. 32, pp. 58–62. Springer, Heidelberg (2009)
9. Gallacher, S., Papadopoulou, E., Taylor, N.K., Blackmun, F.R., Williams, M.H., Roussaki, I., Kalatzis, N., Liampotis, N., Zhang, D.: Personalisation in a System Combining Pervasiveness and Social Networking. In: 1st Workshop on Social Interactive Media Networking and Applications (SIMNA 2011), ICCCN 20, Hawaii (2011)
10. Gallacher, S., Papadopoulou, E., Taylor, N.K., Blackmun, F.R., Williams, M.H.: Intelligent Systems that Combine Pervasive Computing and Social Networking. In: Proc. Ninth International Conference on Ubiquitous Intelligence and Computing (IEEE UIC 2012), pp. 151–158. IEEE Computer Society (2012)

Context-Aware Security Solutions for Cyber Physical Systems

Kaiyu Wan[1] and Vangalur Alagar[2]

[1] Xi'an Jiaotong-Liverpool University, Suzhou, Jiangsu, China
`kaiyu.wan@xjtlu.edu.cn`
[2] Concordia University, Montreal, Canada
`alagar@cs.concordia.ca`

Abstract. The integration of physical systems and processes with networked computing has led to the emergence of a new generation of engineered systems, called Cyber-Physical Systems (CPS). These systems are large networked systems of systems, in which a component system may itself be a grid. In this paper we survey the current state of the art of CPS, identify the issues surrounding security control, and investigate the extent to which context information may be used to improve security and survivability of CPS.

Keywords: cyber-physical systems, secure control, context-awareness, security architecture.

1 Introduction

Cyber-Physical Systems (CPS) [3] integrate computing and communication in a super-large scale in order that its capabilities will include controlling and monitoring the physical world in which it is embedded. These systems are large networked systems of systems, in which a component system (also called site) may be a grid, or a real-time reactive system, or a system that provides ubiquitous computing environment. A direct link between two CPS components is itself a network, because each component might be a grid and several links exist between these two grids. The largeness, the heterogeneity in computing, communication platforms, and resources having domain specific properties make CPS hard to comprehend, design, and operate. The NSF program description [6] states the grand view that CPS initiative is "to transform our world with systems that respond more quickly, are more precise, work in dangerous and inaccessible environments, and provide large scale distributed services." The strategic application domains of CPS [6] include monitoring and managing large-scale physical infrastructures (demand-driven power distribution, environmental monitoring and protection, and water systems management), health care (perpetual life assistance for disabled, high confidence medical aid to remote areas), transportation (congestion control, safe evacuations), and defense systems (avionics). In all these applications there is a need to provide timely services at every *context* of service request. Since service requests may be generated by (non-technical)

P.C. Vinh et al. (Eds.): ICCASA 2012, LNICST 109, pp. 18–29, 2013.

humans and physical devices (that are no longer dumb) the system must be intelligent enough to either provide or refuse services at different contexts, while assuring *safety* and *security*. Breach of security or lack of security might force the system to violate safety properties. Many of the CPS applications are safety-critical. Failure to provide services at the right contexts or providing services to unauthorized entities in any context can result in irreparable harm to the physical world surrounding it. This is the motivation for us to identify security issues in CPS and investigate the role of context-awareness in improving the extent of CPS security. We have structured the paper as follows: In Section 2 we make precise the notion of critical assets and bring it out the relevance of context. In Section 3 we motivate the need for a context representation and situation evaluation. In Section 4 we formalize the notion of context-awareness, using the context representation. In Section 5 we describe a generic context-aware security architecture and explain how context-awareness can be effective for CPS security. In Section 6 we comment on certain aspects of CPS security where context-awareness may not be relevant, and conclude the paper with a brief summary of our ongoing work.

2   Critical Assets

We use the term *asset* in a generic sense to denote an entity that is relevant and essential to CPS operation. All entities required for perception of the environment, computation of CPS processes and control units, and communication between CPS sites are assets. An asset might be a resource, or a physical device, or a controller, or a switch, or a protocol. In order that CPS operations progress without failure and CPS survives external and internal attacks it is essential to *secure* the assets. We label an asset *critical* if its quality degradation adversely affects the physical world surrounding it, and also mitigates to other system assets disrupting the operational goals of the system. It is absolute that critical assets are protected during their life time.

The two basic questions are 'who labels a resource as critical?' and 'how critical assets are to be classified'. The criticality level can be assessed only by an expert in the resource domain. A risk model is necessary to assess the critical level of an asset, and measure the damage caused by its unreliable performance or untimely availability. So, the answer to the first question is 'resource experts label critical resources'. As an example, an expert in the water sector domain might conclude that an interference with the operation of water treatment equipment is highly risky because it will cause chemical imbalance in drinking water, which in turn is catastrophic to the clients of that water company. So, the domain expert will label the water treatment equipment as a critical asset. In answering the second question we contend that a resource expert might classify a resource as *highly critical* in one context and *not critical* in some other context. As an example, a control engineer might conclude that if the control system software in a power plant is tampered by unauthorized personnel, it is likely to alter drastically the behavior of power distribution, causing blackouts. So, 'control system software' should be labeled as a critical asset. However, the control engineer with data from the marketing team might conclude that in some regions blackout might be tolerable, whereas in many other regions it will not be acceptable. So, the control system software may be labeled *highly critical* in the regions where blackouts are unacceptable, and labeled *not critical* in the regions where blackouts are tolerable. In general, the resource domain experts should classify assets and determine their criticality levels in different contexts. Based upon this classification, security policies may be enforced in a context-aware security architecture to secure the critical assets in CPS. For the sake of definiteness let us assume $\{CL = most\ critical\ (mc)$, *critical* (cc), *average critical* (ac), and *not critical* (nc)$\}$ is the set of labels used by domain experts to label resources.

3   Context-Dependence

The life-cycle of an asset has several states. An asset might be *discovered*, or *produced*, or *procured*, or *requested*, or *idle*, or *allocated*, or *delivered*. In each state several contexts might exist and the asset needs to be secured in these contexts. It is impossible to identify all possible contexts in each state. However, the application domain expert should be able to identify the *situations* in each state where the asset should be tightly controlled. Situations may be formulated as *rules*. Business rules and legal rules governing asset states are known to the application domain expert, they can be put together as a framework to constrain the situations. Any context that validates a situation then becomes a context of interest. Thus, searching for contexts of interest and formulating situation constraints are related to one another.

Context information is *heterogeneous* and *multi-dimensional*. As an example, water is an ubiquitous asset. A business rule of a water sector company might be *"water may not be sold to a client who is located in a zone Z either because the company is not permitted to supply water in zone Z or the water quality does not meet the standards of zone Z"*. As another example, copper mined in a location is a local asset. The legal rule *"copper may not be made available in cities within 100 km from the mine"* constrains the asset allocation. As a final example, consider nuclear power asset. In many countries strict laws might forbid or restrict the sale and use of this asset. These examples suggest that (1) locality (region), type of asset, and quality information are the heterogeneous and multi-dimensional context information, and (2) actual contexts for allocating the assets should satisfy the business and legal rules (situations). Therefore, context information must be structured in such a way that situations can be evaluated at the contexts.

Context, as a first class entity, has been studied in many disciplines, including linguistics, philosophy, and AI. However its importance in ubiquitous computing is unmatched by other disciplines. In computing, context was made popular by the seminal works of Dey [4] and Winograd [9]. A formal context representation and context calculus was developed by Wan [7]. Wan [8] gives a survey of contexts, logic of contexts, and context calculus. It is this notation and ideas that we briefly sketch below and use it to formalize context-awareness. A *context space* is defined for an application in a domain and contexts are constructed within that space. A context space includes a finite set of *dimensions* and a *type* associated with each dimension. The typed values are called *tags* along each dimension. The asset manager chooses the context space by defining the dimensions and tags that are necessary to safeguard the asset access, and regulate asset distribution. Such dimensions are usually hidden in the rules governing asset states. A set of generic dimensions and the tag types, suggested in Wan [8] are WHO, $WHAT$, $WHERE$, $WHEN$, and WHY. Their meanings and the tag types associated with them are given below.

- WHO: This dimension is used to specify the owner of the asset, or the role of the client requesting the asset. Its type is either *String* or *enumeratedset*.
- $WHAT$: This dimension is used to specify the type of asset available or requested. Its type is *String*.
- $WHERE$: The target location where the asset is to be delivered. Its type is either *String* or *enumeratedset*.
- $WHEN$: The time when the asset is to be delivered. Its type is either *String* or an *Abstractdatatype*.
- WHY: The purpose for requesting the asset. The type is either *String* or *enumeratedset*.

Depending on the asset domain it is possible that additional dimensions may be included in context information. Domain-specific ontologies are to be made available for fine grained specifications and use of contexts. As an example, with the help of ontology dimension names such as 'LOCATION' and 'WHERE' might be considered as synonyms, and will share the same tag type. The toolkit developed by Wan [7] includes a context representation, relational semantics for contexts, and a context calculus. This toolkit expects a context sensing unit to transform the raw context information into the context notation $[D_1 : v_1, D_2 : v_2, \ldots, d_n : v_n]$, where v_i is the value sensed in dimension D_i. An example of a context in this representation is $c = [WHERE : mysite, WHEN : 11/20/2012, WHO : Alice, WHAT : Proal]$, the setting in which either *Alice* has the asset *Proal* (as asset owner) or *Alice* requests the asset *Proal* (as asset requester). The context calculus allows contexts to be composed, compared, and decomposed using relational operators. It allows a formal evaluation of situations at a context. We had suggested that the domain experts, with the help of business executives, first determine the situations for asset states, and next discover the contexts hidden in the rules. Therefore, it is justified to assume that a situation is encoded as a logical formula p on the dimension names and other variables. A given situation may be valid in many different contexts. Given a context c, in order to check that a situation p is true in context c, the dimension names in p are bound to the tag values in the definition of context c and p is evaluated. An example situation is the predicate $can\_deliver == (\mid x - WHERE \mid < 100) \land (d_2 < 3 + WHEN)$, where $\mid \ldots \mid$ denotes the distance expression and $(3 + WHEN)$ means within 3 days of specified time. When evaluated at c, we will get the expression ($| x - mysite | < 100$) $\land$ ($d_2 < 11/23/2012$). Given values for the location variable x and date variable d_2 this expression will evaluate to either true or false.

3.1 Context-Dependent Labeling of Assets

In CPS it is hard to foresee all possible instances (contexts) when an asset will be accessed or requested. However, given the attributes of the asset the resource domain expert should have a knowledge about the situations governing its use. Each situation is encoded as a predicate[1]. We assign the same criticality label to an asset at all contexts that satisfy the situation predicate. To formalize this notation we define $\mathcal{OB}$, the set of objects in the system, $\mathcal{SU}$, the set of subjects in the system, $\mathcal{RO}$, the set of roles that subjects are allowed to play, $\mathcal{AS} \subset \mathcal{OB}$, the set of assets, $\mathcal{SI}$, the set of situations, and $\mathcal{CO}$, the set of contexts. The function

$$L : \mathcal{AS} \times \mathcal{SI} \to CL$$

assigns for $o \in \mathcal{AS}$ and $p \in \mathcal{SI}$, the label $l \in CL$. That is, $L(o,p) = l$. For $p \neq p'$, $L(o,p) \neq L(o,p')$. For $c \in CO$ and $p \in SI$ we write $\mathbf{vc}(c,p)$ to denote the validity condition that p is true in context c. So, the asset $o \in AS$ has the label $L(o,p) \in CL$ in context c if $\mathbf{vc}(c,p)$ holds. As the system dynamics changes, contexts might change which in turn might dynamically relabel an asset. To deal with dynamic contexts, the toolkit [7] is integrated into the security architecture shown in Figure 1. Thus, the architecture is *context-aware*.

3.2 Representation of Context-Dependent Access Control Policies

In [1] we have discussed a context-dependent grant-access policy with regard to managing identity of subjects in transaction-based systems. We adapt this approach for the purpose of CPS. Let $\mathcal{AC}$ denote a finite set of actions. We define access policies by functions. The function AS assigns to an individual $s \in \mathcal{SU}$ a set of signed actions, called *access rights*, on an object $o \in OB$. We write $+a \in AS(s,o,c)$, to affirm that the subject s is allowed to perform action $a \in \mathcal{AC}$ on object o in context c, and write $-a \in AS(s,o,c)$ to affirm that the subject s is not permitted to perform action a on the object o. Policies may exist for providing access rights to groups of objects and subjects. The function SG gives for a subject s the groups $SG(s)$ to which the subject s belongs. The function AG assigns to a group $g \in \mathcal{GR}$ a set of rights on an object $o \in OB$. If $+a \in AG(g,o,c)$ then every entity in g is allowed to perform action a on object o in context c. If $-a \in AG(g,o,c)$ then no entity in g is allowed to perform action a on object o in context c. Roles might be defined in the system such that an entity may assume a role in a certain context. Function SR gives for each individual subject $s \in S$, the set $SR(s,c)$ of roles assumed by s in context c.

---

[1] In general a temporal logic may be used. For simplicity we restrict to predicate logic framework.

The function AR defines for each role $r \in R$ in context c, the set $AR(r, o, c)$ of rights that r has on the object o in that context. We define the grant policy as a function SP, which for a subject s in context c grants or denies access to object o. We use the notation $\mathbf{vc}(c, p)$ to denote that the policy p (written as situation predicate) is valid in context c.

1. [P1:] *s is an individual subject*   The subject s is granted to perform the actions explicitly allowed for it on the object o in context c if there exists no policy in context c that overrules that privilege .

$$SP(s, o, c) \;=\; if\ \mathbf{vc}(c, p)\ then\ AS(s, o, c)\ else\ \emptyset$$

2. [P2:] *s has a set of roles but is not a member of a group*   The subject s is granted the right to perform an action a on an object o in context c if at least one of the roles in $SR(s) \neq \emptyset$ is authorized to access o and none of them is denied to access o in context c.

$$SP(s, o, c) \;=\; \{+a \mid p_r(a, s, o) \wedge a \in \mathcal{AC} \wedge r \in SR(s)\},$$

where
$p_r(a, s, o) \equiv \mathbf{vc}(c, p) \;\wedge\; +a \in AR(r, o, c) \;\wedge\; \sim \exists r' \in SR(s) \bullet (-a \in AR(r', o, c))$.

3. [P3:] *s has no roles and belongs to one or more groups*   In context c the subject s belonging to the groups in $SG(s)$ is granted to perform an action a on an object o, if at least one of the groups in $SG(s)$ is authorized to access o in context c and none of the groups in $SG(s)$ is denied to access it in context c.

$$SP(s, o, c) \;=\; \{+a \mid p_g(a, s, o) \wedge a \in \mathcal{AC} \wedge g \in SG(s)\},$$

where
$p_g(a, s, o) \equiv \mathbf{vc}(c, p) \;\wedge\; +a \in AG(g, o, c) \;\wedge\; \sim \exists g' \in SG(s) \bullet (-a \in AG(g', o, c))$.

4. [P4:] *s has a set of roles and belongs to one or more groups*   Using the predicates defined in the previous two steps we define

$$SP(s, o, c) \;=\; \{+a \mid +a \in (p_r(a, s, o) \cap p_g(a, s, o)) \wedge r \in SR(s) \wedge g \in SG(s)\}$$

If A and B are arbitrary sets of subjects then the subjects in the set $A \cup B$ has permissions $(\bigcup_{s \in A} SP(s, o, c)) \cap (\bigcup_{s \in B} SP(s, o, c))$, and the subjects in the set $A \cap B$ has permissions $(\bigcup_{s \in A} SP(s, o, c)) \cup (\bigcup_{s \in B} SP(s, o, c))$.

4   Modeling Context-Awareness

Awareness induces the system elements to become proactive. We say the system is *self-aware* if it knows its full list of active users, assets used, policies in force, and process states. Thus, self-awareness may be characterized by (1) a set of *Users* who are active subjects in the system, (2) a set of active *Assets*, (3) a set of *Permissions*, namely access policy controlling access to assets, and (4) a statement of *Purpose*, an application-specific key-word defining the set of application specific tasks. Self-awareness is also called internal awareness. The internal awareness is thus a set of contexts built upon the four dimensions *User, Asset, Permission, Purpose*. Let $UC = \{UC_1, \ldots, UC_m\}$ be the set of user categories, and $DC = \{DC_1, \ldots, DC_k\}$ be the set of asset categories which are to be protected. We regard UC_i's and DC_js as dimensions. Let PC denote the purpose dimension and PM denote the *Permissions* dimension. Assume that the tag set along each UC_i is the set of user names, the tag set along each DC_i can be the set of identifiers to assets, the tag set for PC is $\{Legal, Administrative, Marketing\}$, and references to the grant policies are tags for dimension PM. Contexts with these dimension/tag sets are *Internal Security Contexts* (ISC). Based on the initial state of the system a set of ISC contexts can be constructed. As system evolves, ISC contexts will undergo modifications. A context of type ISC provides awareness information to protect the internal states of the system. An example of ISC context is $[UC_1 : u, DC_2 : j, PC : Communication]$, meaning that client u with role UC_1 is allowed access to the asset referenced by j in category DC_2 for communication purposes.

We say the system is *context-aware* if it knows the potential set of clients seeking to access it, the physical devices with which it has to interact in its environment and their statuses, and information fed to it through a sensor network connected to it. Context-awareness is also called external awareness. From the policies governing the system interaction with its environment external-awareness contexts can be constructed. Such policies includes privacy rules, obligation rules, and other exceptions. We call this context set *External Security Contexts* (ESC). An example of ESC context is $[WHO : Alice, WHAT : file, RLOC : Shanghai, WHY : Medical]$. It is the setting where *Alice* is accessing the resource *file* from the remote location *Shanghai* for *Medical* purposes. CPS nodes use context-awareness are sharpening *perception* and *adaptation*. Based upon the recent context-aware information received the system reasons about the appropriate action to be taken in a timely manner.

5 Context-Aware Security Features for CPS

In this section we address *trustworthiness, security architecture*, and *secure asset flow* as the three issues for which context-awareness can provide safe solutions. These three are among the many challenges and claims raised in [2].

5.1 Trustworthiness

Cardénas et. al [2] emphasize the importance of trustworthiness notion and trust management schemes for CPS components. They state '*if trustworthiness metric of a component deviates significantly from the trust that is associated with the component, then the component may be regarded as insecure and its contribution toward the operation of CPS may be restricted or discarded.* Trustworthiness is a system property [5] and needs to be verified by independent trusted authorities. The trustworthiness claims include one or more of the set { *safety features*, *security features*, *reliability features*, *guaranteed availability features*, and *accountability features*} . Accountability feature might reveal the independent authorities (contact numbers/emails) who can be contacted for verifying the trustworthy claims. A trusted authority (TA) has the knowledge and skills to verify these claims and provide a *ranking* (security level acceptance) for the system. So, we assume that a CPS has one or more TAs who will evaluate the system at each CPS site and award a ranking for it. The evaluation procedure is as outlined in the Orange book for *Trusted Computing Systems* except that it is context-dependent. A site may see the ranking of other CPS sites by browsing the directories kept by the TAs. By comparing its ranking with the ranking of other sites, a site might decide to get products and services only with those sites whose security rankings are either equal to or above its ranking. In particular, if site i requests an asset o from a site j in context c then the following must be true:

- $ranking(j, c) \geq ranking(i, c)$
- the asset o is released to site i together with (1) the context-dependent criticality level $L(o, p)$ (determined at site j), (2) the situation predicate p, and (2) the context-dependent grant function $SP(s, o, c)$, $s \in SR$.

The certificate from TA will make explicit the context in which the site was evaluated and the context of validity of the certificate itself. Hence site j must have its local policy adapted in order to use the asset received from site i; Otherwise, security may not be guaranteed for site i.

5.2 Security Architecture

In this section we emphasize the role of context-awareness for security, not specific algorithms for enforcing security. A generic context-aware architecture is shown in Figure 1. The architecture can be easily specialized to build more specific applications. Usually a ring of defenses exist to protect SCADA networking systems. A strong fire-wall protection is built to safeguard the SCADA network from both the internal corporate network and the Internet. Keeping this in mind we have introduced a fire-wall for the security architecture.

The toolkit in Figure 1 has the context space database containing the dimensions and their tag sets. It constructs contexts according to the syntax explained in Section 3, implements context operators [7], and evaluates situations in different contexts. As an example, in the expression $[TIME : d_1, WHO : Alice, WHAT : filetransfer, WHERE : Shanghai, WHEN : d_2, WHY : Auditing] \downarrow \{WHO, WHAT, WHY\}$ the operator $\downarrow$ is selection operator, its left operand is a context and its right operand is a set of contexts. The semantics of selection is 'extract from the context (left operand) the subcontext whose dimensions match those in the set (right operand)'. Thus, the above expression evaluates to $[WHO : Alice, WHAT : filetransfer, WHY : Auditing]$. In general, formal expressions for evaluating situations in context expressions can be

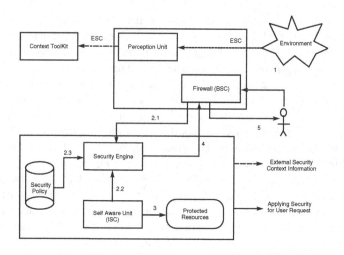

Fig. 1. Generic Architecture for Context-aware Security

written down. As an example, if c_1, c_2 and c_3 are three contexts, X is a set of contexts, and p is a situation predicate, the expression $\mathbf{vc}((c_1 \ominus c_2) \sqcap c_3) \downarrow X, p)$ requires the evaluation of the context from the expression $(c_1 \ominus c_2) \sqcap c_3) \downarrow X$ and then evaluating p in the resulting context. Such operations are necessary for managing mobile contexts and reasoning contextual behavior. The toolkit supports other units, such as 'Security Policy' unit, in the architecture wherever context information is required. In addition, context toolkit and protected assets are loosely coupled so that adding or removing of new assets and modifying their respective access policies can be achieved in a transparent manner. The security policy base is usually pre-defined by system administrators and may change periodically. The perception unit can be either a sensor network that monitor the environment or simply a user interface. The self-aware unit monitors the internal states in the system and maintains a history of state changes. The security engine applies security policies internally to data and operations, and at the fire-wall level for authentication of user requests. The labels shown in the figure roughly indicate the sequence of interactions: [1.] Stimulus from the environment processed by the 'Perception Unit' to construct external contexts. [2.1.] Fire-wall forwards stimulus after applying boundary security context. [2.2.] Security engine collects internal security context information from internal system states. [2.3.] Security engine refers to security policy base. [3.] Security engine applies security policy relevant to security contexts to protected assets. [4.] Security engine sends the result to the environment through fire-wall. [5.] Fire-wall filters the response using boundary security context and forwards the result to the environment.

This architecture can be used to deter and prevent the compromise of assets local to a CPS site, such as data resources, actuators or other physical devices. A collection of mobile sensors can be deployed to detect intruders and take preventive action. The prudent defensive action is the gradual shutdown of the actuator, when a threat is detected. By preventing external attack on physical devices we are improving *availability* and eliminating *denial of service*. In order to prevent *deception attacks* (prevent false information from being sent from sensors and controllers, which happen when sensors or controllers are themselves compromised) we need to strengthen ESC unit. This is a challenging problem.

5.3   Secure Asset Flow

The security of the asset transferred from one site to another CPS site cannot be guaranteed to be secure unless the network through which it is sent is made secure. Unfortunately, the traditional methods used for network security is not sufficient to assure the networked CPS sites. It is necessary to isolate CPS network from corporate IT networks and the Internet, surround CPS with several defense rings, and further inject it with strict security measures. Under this assumption, we discuss the following flow policy for CPS assets.

When a site j receives a request for asset 0 from a site i, it will validate the certificate of site i and verify the eligibility condition $ranking(j) \geq ranking(i)$. Once these are verified, the asset together with its context-dependent criticality level, and the context-dependent grant function for o both as determined at site j will be sent to site i. The asset may be transferred through a set of CPS sites. That is, $j = j_0, j_1, \ldots, j_k = i$ may be the CPS network path through which the asset is transferred. We call this an asset flow. Assets that flow are the cyber assets, such as data, control information, corporate policies, encryption keys, and protocols. The primary sources of threats to a flow are organizational threats from employees of the organization who manage the different sites on the flow path, control and other assets that enable the flow, and outside attackers. Even the best flow security can be invalidated by a poor people system. The human assets who manage a CPS network will include IT professionals, control engineers, security experts, and many non-experts. They are usually dispersed over different application domain or departments within an organization. People might be careless at best or untrustworthy at best in order that a security breach might arise. Context-awareness might help to prevent some of these security lapses. Some employees may use illegitimate means and violate local policies to access the information which is not legitimately required in their job related tasks. Context-dependent policy enforcements and authorizations will prevent such incidents. Some of the security lapses might be "unintentional" or "accidental". As an example, the information left on the screen of a computer can be seen by another employee who is not authorized to know it. Context-aware motion detection systems can catch such incidents and force remedial actions. Some actions include automatic log-outs whenever the system is left idle, and "warning" employees about their behavioral code. Another kind of threat is that employees who have authorized access to an asset violate the trust instituted in them. This problem is serious in a networked system such as CPS which operates in a decentralized fashion. To minimize this kind of abuse, we had suggested that the asset together with its context-dependent criticality level, and the context-dependent grant function for o as determined at the host site be transmitted. The security at any site through which the asset passes should enforce its local policies that do not violate the intended access rights imposed by the host site. Another kind of threat is the attack sponsored by collaboration among a group of employees. Towards defending this kind of attack we had given an expression for calculating access rights for arbitrary sets of subjects in Section 3.2. Rotating employees to work in different departments under different contexts, and audit trails may also deter this kind of threat.

We contend that ESC context can be used effectively at every site in the flow path. The node j_r that receives from its predecessor node j_{r-1} not only the asset but also the context information which is the *union* of all context information from site j_0 to site j_{r-1}. That context is the ESC for safe keeping and safely forwarding the asset to the next site in the flow path. Since "purpose" is a ESC context is domain information, the security level clearance of the asset at a site is also domain-dependent. Consequently, the transmission channel (flow path) through which the request is sent must have a security clearance higher than or equal to that assigned for the asset. Moreover, site j_r sending the asset to site j_{r+1} should have the security clearance for sending it, and site j_{r+1} must have the security clearance to receive the asset. Assume that security levels for subjects are modeled by function S we impose three constraints for a secure flow from subject s_1 in site j_r to subject s_2 at site j_{r+1} while sending asset o along a channel σ. It is essential that the situation p for executing each action below should satisfy the context c of the action. That is, $\mathbf{vc}(c, p)$ must be true.

- [secure channel for asset o]: If $L(o, p) \leq L(\sigma, p)$, then in context c the channel σ is secure for asset o in context c.
- [s_1 can write on σ]: If $write + \ \in\ SP(s_1, o, c)$ and $S(s_1, p) \leq L(\sigma, p)$, then the subject s_1 can write o on channel σ.
- [s_2 can read on σ]: If $read + \ \in\ SP(s_2, o, c)$ and $S(s_2, p) \geq L(\sigma, p)$, then the subject s_2 can read o from channel σ.

6   Conclusion

Cardénas et. al [2] have put forth a list of open problems for CPS security, and Weiss [10] eloquently has brought out the security loopholes in existing electric power grids. The two conclusions that we derive from these studies are (1) there exists no study yet in weaving tightly context-awareness and security solutions for studying CPS security, and (2) technological solutions for CPS security, even if they are found, may not be realizable soon because of the non-coordination of efforts between control engineers, IT sector, government organization, and industry partners. Our research effort is mainly directed at technically feasible context-aware solutions for CPS. The security architecture proposed in this paper is for every CPS node. Context-based labeling of critical assets, context-dependent trustworthiness, and context-aware asset flow are ingrained at different levels of this architecture. Thus, CPS network will have a network of context-aware security architectures. Time is a specific instance of context. As an example the context $[TIME : 10 : 30]$ is the clock time $10 : 30$. The predicate $10 < TIME < 11$ evaluates to true in this context. Relative times can be modeled by a context with two dimensions, and time duration can be modeled using the 'directed range operator $\rightarrowtail$' [8].

Acknowledgments. This research is supported by Research Grants from National Natural Science Foundation of China (Project Number 61103029), Natural Science Foundation of Jiangsu Province, China, and Natural Sciences and Engineering Research Council, Canada.

References

1. Alagar, V., Wan, K.: Context Based Enforcement of Authorization for Privacy and Security in Identity Management. In: de Leeuw, E., Fischer-Hübner, S., Tseng, J., Borking, J. (eds.) Policies and Research in Identity Management. IFIP, vol. 261, pp. 25–37. Springer, Boston (2008)
2. Cardénas, A.A., Amin, S., Sastry, S.: Secure Control: Towards Survivable Cyber-Physical Systems. In: 28th International Conference on Distributed Computing Systems Workshops, ICDCS 2008, pp. 495–500 (June 2008)
3. Cyber-Physical Systems: Executive Summary, CPS Steering Group (2008), http://varma.ece.cmu.edu/summit/CPS-Executive-Summary.pdf
4. Dey, A.K., Abowd, G.D.: A Conceptual Framework and a Toolkit for Supporting Rapid Prototyping of Context-aware Applications. Human-Computer Interaction 16(2-4), 7–166 (2001)
5. Mohammad, M., Alagar, V.: A Formal Approach for the Specification and Verification of Trustworthy Component-Based Systems. Journal of Systems and Software 84, 77–104 (2011)
6. USA NSF Program Solicitation NSF-08-611 (2008)
7. Wan, K.: Lucx: Lucid Enriched with Context. Ph.d thesis, Concordia University, Montreal, Canada (January 2006)
8. Wan, K.: A Brief History of Context. International Journal of Computer Science Issues 6(2) (November 2009)
9. Winograd, T.: Architectures for Context. Human-Computer Interaction (HCI) 16(2), 401–419 (2001)
10. Weiss, J.M.: Control Systems Cyber Security - The Need for Appropriate Regulations to Assure the Cyber Security of Electric Grid. Testimony before The Committee on Homeland Security (October 2007), http://chsdemocrats.house.gov/SiteDocuments/20071017164638-60716.pdf

3D Interaction Assistance in Virtual Reality: A Semantic Reasoning Engine for Context-Awareness

Yannick Dennemont, Guillaume Bouyer, Samir Otmane, and Malik Mallem

IBISC Laboratory, Evry University, France
{yannick.dennemont,guillaumme.bouyer,samir.otmane,malik.mallem}@ibisc.fr

Abstract. This work focuses on 3D interaction assistance by adding adaptivity depending on the tasks, the objectives, and the general interaction context. An engine to reach context-awareness has been implemented in Prolog+CG which uses Conceptual Graphs (CGs) based on an ontology. CGs descriptions of the available sensors and actuators in our scene manager (Virtools) allow the engine to take decisions and send them through Open Sound Control (OSC). Measurements and adaptations corresponding to specific tools uses are decided from rules handled by the engine. This project is a step towards Intelligent Virtual Environments, which proposes a hybrid solution by adding a separate semantic reasoning to classic environments. The first experiment automatically manages few modalities depending on the distance to objects, user movement, available tools, etc. Gestures are used both as an engine direct control and as an interpretation of user activity.

Keywords: Interaction Techniques, Context-awareness, Knowledge Representation Formalism and Methods,Virtual reality.

1 Interaction Adaptation: Toward Context-Awareness

Tasks in immersive virtual environments are associated to 3D interaction (3DI) techniques and devices (e.g. selection of 3D objects with a flystick using ray-casting or virtual hand). As tasks and environments become more and more complex, these techniques can no longer be the same for every applications. A solution can be to adapt the interaction [5] to the needs and the context in order to improve usability, for example to:

- choose other techniques ("specificity") or make techniques variations ("flavor")[18];
- add or manage modalities[12][4][18];
- perform automatically parts of the task [7].

These adaptations can be done manually by the developer or the user, or automatically by the system: this is "adaptive" or "context-aware" 3DI . This open issue enables to:

P.C. Vinh et al. (Eds.): ICCASA 2012, LNICST 109, pp. 30–40, 2013.

- speed up the interaction [7];
- diminish the cognitive load (as in ubiquitous computing);
- tailor the interaction [22] [18];
- add or manage interaction possibilities [4].

In order to go beyond basic interaction, adaptive systems can first provide recognitions from raw data (on an activity recognition layer, Figure 1). But to achieve a better adaptivity, more content is needed: the context. A formal and well recognized definition is [10]: *Context is any information that can be used to characterize the situation of an entity. An entity is a person, place, or object that is considered relevant to the interaction between a user and an application, including the user and applications themselves.* Thus, an ideal system for 3DI assistance is context-aware as *it uses context to provide relevant information and/or services to the user, where relevancy depends on the user's task.*

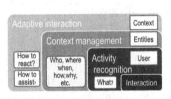
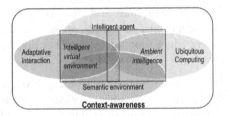

Fig. 1. Different layers to reach adaptive interaction

Fig. 2. Different families of context-aware applications

Context-awareness emerged from intelligent systems [6]. Some drawbacks were due to fully abstract reasoning or user exclusion. Intelligent assistance systems can be split in two trends. Systems tend to stress user assistance on well defined context (e.g. [4]) or to stress context identification that leads to direct adaptations for each situation (e.g. [9][11]). Context-awareness has different focuses (Figure 2), yet there is a shared ideal list of properties to handle [1]:

- Heterogeneity and mobility of context;
- Relationships and dependencies between context;
- Timeliness: access to past and future states;
- Imperfection: data can be uncertain or incorrect;
- Reasoning: to decide or to derive information;
- Usability of modelling formalisms;
- Efficient context provisioning.

Our research is mainly in the adaptive 3D interaction field. Yet, to achieve wider and better 3DI, a richer context with semantic information and/or intelligent agents is needed. Also reasoning needs will grow with the available information.

Examples	Representation	Reasoning	Semantic Approach	Uncertainty degree	Representation modification	Reasoning modification	Usability	Aims
SOCAM [13]	OWL (Web Ontology language)	FOL+Bayesian	Yes	Yes	High	High	Medium	Middleware for ubiquitous computing
GAIA [24]	FOL (First Order Logic)	FOL	Yes	Yes	High	High	Medium	Ubiquitous computing services
VR-UCAM [18]	5W1H tuples (Who, What, When, Where, Why, How)	Condition Matching	No	No	Low	Medium	High	Extend ubiquitous computing services to VR
VR-DeMo [20]	MBUID (model based user interface design)	Event Condition Action	No	No	Medium	Medium	High	Automatic personalized 3D interaction
Our Engine	CG (Conceptual Graphs)	CG theory, FOL	Yes	Yes	High	High	High	Context-aware services for VR. Applications to adaptive 3D interaction.

Fig. 3. Approaches comparisons

So our approach is generally part of the Intelligent Virtual Environments. Adaptive 3DI can be implicit with adaptations embedded in the interaction techniques [20][3], or explicit by using external processes [16][7][4][18]. Some frameworks are generic enough (examples and their comparison on Fig. 3) but not able to describe any situations, to modify their reasoning or difficult to reuse/to expand (particularly when thought for another domain).

- which performs semantic reasoning through logical rules on an ontology;
- which communicates with application tools: sensors to retrieve the context, and actuators to manage visual, audio and haptic modalities as well as interaction modifications;
- which is generic: pluggable to existing non-semantic virtual environment if tools are available.

Users will benefit from an automatic 3D interaction assistance that can supply support through modalities, interaction technique choice or application-specific help depending on the current situation. Besides, designers could reuse, rearrange and modify this 3DI adaptivity to share reasoning between applications or to create application-specificity. A good adaptive 3DI can also help to release the designers from the prediction of every situations, thus it should be able to deal with degree of unpredictability. Next, we discuss our choices for modelling context and reasoning to achieve these goals.

2   Knowledge Representation and Reasoning

We need to manage context and to decide how to react, which is a form of Knowledge Representation and Reasoning. More precisely, our system needs first to retrieve and represent items of information, possibly specific to an application, then to handle this context and to define its effects on 3DI (discussed by [11] for virtual reality). Several criteria led our choice for the engine core: semantic degrees, expressiveness (vs efficiency) and usability. We choose to base our representation on Conceptuals Graphs (CGs). They have a strong semantic founding and are built on an ontology. They provide a good expressiveness (a universal knowledge representation [21][8]) equivalent to First Order Logic (FOL) but with a better usability since they are also human readable. FOL is usually the most expressive choice made for context-awareness. Meantime, semantic reasoning with an ontology is the most used approach in context-awareness as it provides interoperability and a non-abstract representation. Moreover coupled with the CGs usability, the model may allow at some point a welcomed direct users involvement [6]. Semantic virtual worlds as a new paradigm is a discussed issue [15]. Several approaches offer to build full semantic worlds [14], often with semantic networks [19][17][2] which reinforce our conviction for CGs. However we will not try to build a full semantic world but to gather semantic information to help the 3DI. We aim at context-awareness in classic applications with an external representation and reasoning engine.

3 Overview of the Engine

The engine uses rules to take decisions regarding a stored context (knowledge, events etc.). Context and decisions concern the user, the interaction and the environment, which communicates with the engine through different tools (Fig. 4). Tools must have a semantic description of their uses in order to be triggered by the engine. They can be actuators with perceivable effects or sensors that retrieve information. Those tools can embed other forms of reasoning than the engine core (e.g Hidden Markov Models) to provide information.

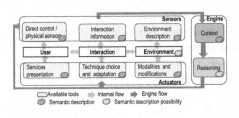

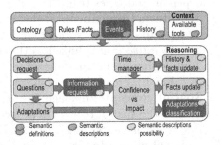

Fig. 4. An external engine - communication through semantic tools

Fig. 5. The engine - forms of context and reasoning

Context have various forms managed by the decision process(Fig. 5). First, the ontology lists concepts and relations with underlying semantic, which are used by CGs in order to describe rules and facts. Available tools and the past events in history are special facts. Events are newly integrated information and trigger a decision request in an automatic mode. The time manager checks the validity of the needed facts. When a decision with an associated tool is true, the engine aggregates its confidence and impact from facts, events' timing and rules. An acceptable total impact induces a knapsack problem as a last classification.

We use Virtools as our scene graph manager and the Amine platform [13] (a Java open-source multi-layer platform for intelligent systems) for the engine. This platform offers an ontology manager and a FOL backward chaining engine that handles CGs: Prolog+CG (PCG). Open Sound Control protocol (OSC) is used for communication between the scene and the engine.

4   Concepts and Conceptual Graphs in the Engine

The focus of the engine is to be easily modifiable, reusable, and expanded by designers and users. Therewith, we want to reason with ideas and situations rather than formulas. This is where the ontology is important as it defines our semantic vocabulary (written in italic afterwards). Situations can now be described using CGs built with these concepts and classified using CGs theory. In a final form, every logical combinations in a CG (that a user could enter) should be handled. And as the engine is used, the ontology is refined. This in order to allow simpler rules, easier to reuse reasoning as long as a better concepts classification. Next is a rough taxonomy of currently used concepts. We need to be able to express:

- **Reasoning concepts:** state what is true (*fact*) and what is just a matter of discussion (*proposition*); *rules* (*effects* depending on *causes*); degree of *confidence* in those concepts (e.g. Fig. 6 and Fig. 7). Also what decisions can actually be made (*reactions* like *adaptations* or *questions*, e.g. Fig. 8), etc.;
- **Reification concepts:** Manage *tools*, like *sensors* or *actuators*. Descriptions include *commands* to be sent for specific *uses* and their *impacts* (e.g. Fig. 9) depending on *cases* (e.g. Fig. 10);
- **3D interaction concepts:** the main focus of the overall generic engine. So we need to describes various *modalities*, *tasks* etc. For example, part of the user *cognitive load* is linked to the total amount of *impact* used;
- **Time concepts:** manage new *facts*, events (*fact* with a *date* and a *duration*) (e.g. Fig. 6), etc. *History* manage previous event, *reactions*, etc. ;
- **Spatial concepts:** manage *position*, *direction* etc. In virtual environment, a lot of the spatial issues are in fact handled by the scene graphs manager. But *zones* like *auras* or *focuses* are useful to understand the current activity.
- **General concepts:** base vocabulary to describe situations. For example to manipulate *attributes* like *identity* or express *active* states.
- **Application specific concepts:** applications can expand the knowledge base with their own concepts. For example *gestures* that can be named ('Z'), and/or classed (*right* and *up* are also *rectilinear* gestures).

5   Reactions Process

PCG is a backward chaining engine. Thus it can answer if specific facts can be inferred or not. A meta-interpreter has to be written to do forward-chaining, i.e to list what can be deducted given the available facts. Our meta-interpreter do both to manage forms of truth (as a PCG element, as a *fact* description,

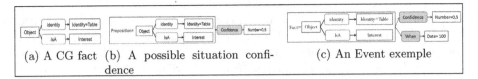

(a) A CG fact (b) A possible situation confi-   (c) An Event exemple
                        dence

Fig. 6. Facts examples: about interest, confidence and event

Fig. 7. Rule example: the enhancement will of an interest

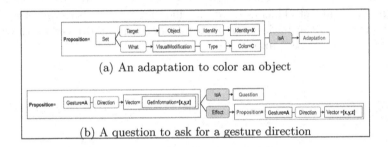

(a) An adaptation to color an object

(b) A question to ask for a gesture direction

Fig. 8. Reaction possibilities examples

as a CG *rules effect* etc.), degree of truth (*confidence*) and times (*duration validity, history* etc.). At any time, the engine store context elements (*facts, events,* etc.). When an application need a fitting *reaction* (after a new *event*, when ordered by the user, etc.), it send a decision request. The engine then use the meta-interpreter to seek eligible *reactions*. Those are *true adaptations* and *questions* (e.g Fig. 8) with an available associated *tool* (e.g. Fig 9). Then the engine aggregates decisions' *confidence*. A list of *confidence* is obtained by considering all paths leading to the *reactions*. Each path can combined different *confidence* expressions:

– A direct PCG fact (e.g. Fig 6a) has the maximum confidence: 1;
– A *fact* confidence or a generic knowledge confidence (e.g. Fig. 6b);
– Event confidence (e.g. Fig. 6c). A *fact* confidence, but time dependant as the initial supplied confidence is multiplied by the ratio of remaining validity.
– CGs rules induced confidence (e.g. Fig. 7). If true, the effects confidences are the average causes confidences times the rule confidence (0 instead). It is an iterative process.

We use a fusion function to convert this list into a single scalar. We consider that the more facts and rules led to a reaction, the more the confidence in it should increase, while kept bounded between 0 and 1. So for n confidences with $Mean$ as average value: $Globalconfidence = (1 - Mean) \times (1 - \frac{1}{n}) \times Mean + Mean$. The global confidence remain 0 (respectively 1) in case of absolute false when $Mean = 0$ (respectively absolute true, $Mean = 1$). Singleton is not modified.

Next, the engine aggregates the decisions impact. Each tool has an initial impact which is modified by specific cases. E.g Fig. 10, the impact of a decision already in the history increases (to reduce activation/deactivation cycles). Initial impact equals to 0 (without any impacts) or 1 (the most impacting) are unmodified. Otherwise, at each n applicable case, the impact is altered with a weight (W, 25% if not supplied) while kept bounded: $impact(n) = impact(n-1) + W \times (1 - impact(n-1))$ for $greater$ impacts or $impact(n) = impact(n-1) - W \times impact(n-1)$ for $lower$ impacts. Thus smaller steps are made for already extreme values (e.g. keeping impacting situations reachable).

Finally, decisions with a confidence on impact ratio greater than a threshold (1 by default) are eligible. Then, eligible decisions are selected to fill the available admissible impact. Thus this last classification is a knapsack problem. The available impact is the initial user impact (a first step into profiling the user) minus the active decisions impact.

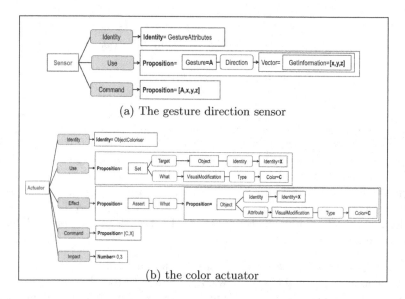

(a) The gesture direction sensor

(b) the color actuator

Fig. 9. Tools examples

Fig. 10. Impact increase case example: to avoid activation/reactivation cycle

6   Scenario and Case Study Examples

We test the engine with a case study: to try to automatically acquire some user's interests and enhance them. The interests are here linked to the user's hand. The application tools are:

- a Zones Of Interest (ZOI) sensor to add and report the content of 3D zones;
- a gestures recognition and a gestures attributes sensors (Fig. 9a).
- a sensor of hand movement speed and scope. Movement speed is qualified as high or low and movement scope as local or global;
- an actuator to change the color of an object (Fig. 9b);
- an actuator to add a haptic or a visual force to an object;

The engine uses general rules like:

- Define what is an interest (e.g is in a ZOI or is a previous interest);
- Try to enhance an interest (Fig. 7);
- Define possible enhancements: e.g object visual modifications through color change or interaction modifications through force (visual or haptic);
- General and adaptations states management:
  - remove visual modification for past interests;
  - remove a currently applied force if the movement is abnormal (e.g local+high=the user is "stuck").
- increase decision impact for some concepts (e.g haptic impact> visual impact and interaction modification impact > visual modification impact);
- increase decision's impact if present in history (Fig. 10);
- decrease interaction modification's impact for local movement.

Finally, the application specific rules are:

- Monitor the hand movement;
- Ask for the gesture attributes if a gesture is detected;
- Activate or deactivate a ZOI around the hand if a circular gesture occurred;
- Activate a ZOI in the direction of the gesture if a rectilinear gesture occurred;
- Deactivate this direction ZOI after 3s.
- Deactivate every adaptations if the "Z" gesture is detected.

As a result, the rules combine themselves as expected (adaptations examples Fig. 11), but with supplementary outcomes which were not fully planned. In fact, there are several interests: explicit, by creating voluntarily a ZOI, or implicit, either by moving rectilinearly toward an object (thus creating a ZOI) or with previous interest. With a ZOI around the hand activated, passing by an object colors it red, while standing next to it makes it also attractive (as movement is then local, diminishing the attraction impact). Colors are reset when the user moves far away. Depending on the color actuator impact and the history, the coloration time can vary, and can even flash for a while (not intended at first). When pointing an object or when moving toward an object during a global movement,

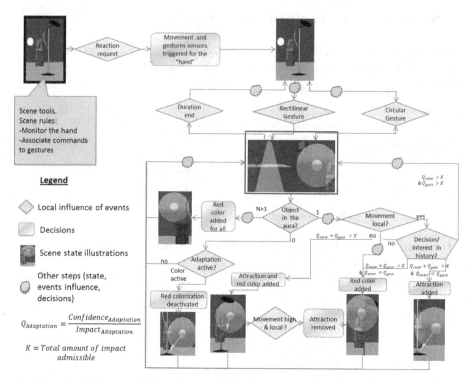

Fig. 11. The engine automatically apply adaptations depending on the context

the object is colored red. When pointing an object from a rest position or starting a new movement directly toward an object, it makes it also attractive (not
intended at first, this primary intention can be highlighted due to the latency
of the movement scope sensors, which still point the movement as local). Colors
are reset after this ZOI deactivation. In both cases, when pointed several times
as an interest (thus present as several current facts or history facts) attraction
can be activated regardless of the movement scope (global or local). Attraction
is removed when the user tries to resist it. When it has been deactivated, gain
usually cannot be reactivated for a time corresponding to history memory. Some
reactivations occur for coloring as the decision has initially less impact. More
complex situations occur when several objects are close to the hand: e.g only the
less impacting adaptation (coloring) is applied to a maximum of objects (even if
for now there is no specific treatment for groups, the most fitting adaptations is
applied until there is no more cognitive load thus a group logic emerged). Those
results depend on the initial impact, confidence and cognitive load values.

7   Conclusion

The engine aims to allow a semantic reasoning and the reuse of tools in a non-
semantic environment to help the 3DI. We propose an engine core with a semantic

base to achieve adaptation, which could be directly addressed by designers or users. Context-awareness properties (page 2) are almost all tackled but need deepening. The engine response delay is not well suited for a full automatic mode yet, but rather for punctual helps. This drawback can be lessen but is an inherent part of our approach. By adding a planning block later, we could refine the adaptations and allow more tools combinations. Indeed active decisions could be replaced by better ones in a new context. This currently can be done by freeing cognitive load and rethink all adaptations at each decision process. However, it is a particular case of a more complex resources and world states planning. Besides, we have started adding direct control of the engine. This part emphasizes the engine tailorability since changing the control from a gesture to another, or to any events, can easily be done directly into the engine (rather that remodelling application parts). And as a 3DI rules set can be reused, any applications can add their own rules set and controls possibilities. Also, the gestures recognition can be used to monitor the user activity and to deduce hints of intention. A possibility is to use our HMM recognition module on different data to learn and classify interesting situations. Our next step is to continue to explore context (especially user intention hints) and adaptations for virtual reality with their implementation using tools and the engine. This work is supported by the AP7 DigitalOcean project.

References

1. Bettini, C., Brdiczka, O., Henricksen, K., Indulska, J., Nicklas, D., Ranganathan, A., Riboni, D.: A survey of context modelling and reasoning techniques. Pervasive and Mobile Computing 6(2), 161–180 (2010)
2. Bonis, B., Stamos, J., Vosinakis, S., Andreou, I., Panayiotopoulos, T.: A platform for virtual museums with personalized content. Multimedia Tools and Applications 42(2), 139–159 (2008)
3. Boudoin, P., Otmane, S., Mallem, M.: Fly Over, a 3D Interaction Technique for Navigation in Virtual Environments Independent from Tracking Devices. In: Virtual Reality International Conference, Vric (2008)
4. Bouyer, G., Bourdot, P., Ammi, M.: Supervision of Task-Oriented Multimodal Rendering for VR Applications. In: Eurographics Symposium on Virtual Environments (2007)
5. Bowman, D.A., Chen, J., Wingrave, C.A., Lucas, J.F., Ray, A., Polys, N.F., Li, Q., Haciahmetoglu, Y., Sun Kim, J., Kim, S., Boehringer, R., Ni, T.: New Directions in 3D User Interfaces. International Journal of Virtual Reality 5, 3–14 (2006)
6. Brézillon, P.: From expert systems to context-based intelligent assistant systems: a testimony. The Knowledge Engineering Review 26(1), 19–24 (2011)
7. Celentano, A., Nodari, M.: Adaptive interaction in Web3D virtual worlds. In: Proceedings of the Ninth International Conference on 3D Web Technology, Web3D 2004, vol. 1(212), p. 41 (2004)
8. Chein, M., Mugnier, M.: Graph-bases Knowledge Representation: Computational Foundations of Conceptual Graphs. Springer (2009)
9. Coppola, P., Mea, V.D., Gaspero, L.D., Lomuscio, R., Mischis, D., Mizzaro, S., Nazzi, E., Scagnetto, I., Vassena, L.: AI Techniques in a Context-Aware Ubiquitous Environment, pp. 150–180 (2009)

10. Dey, A., Abowd, G.: Towards a better understanding of context and context-awareness. In: CHI 2000 Workshop on the What, Who, Where, When, and How of Context-awareness, vol. 4 (2000)
11. Frees, S.: Context-driven interaction in immersive virtual environments. Virtual Reality 14(4), 277–290 (2010)
12. Irawati, S., Calderón, D., Ko, H.: Semantic 3D object manipulation using object ontology in multimodal interaction framework. In: Proceedings of the 2005 International Conference on Augmented Tele-Existence, pp. 35–39. ACM (2005)
13. Kabbaj, A.: Development of Intelligent Systems and Multi-Agents Systems with Amine Platform. In: Schärfe, H., Hitzler, P., Øhrstrøm, P. (eds.) ICCS 2006. LNCS (LNAI), vol. 4068, pp. 286–299. Springer, Heidelberg (2006)
14. Latoschik, M.E., Biermann, P., Wachsmuth, I.: Knowledge in the Loop: Semantics Representation for Multimodal Simulative Environments, pp. 25–39 (2005)
15. Latoschik, M.E., Blach, R., Iao, F.: Semantic Modelling for Virtual Worlds A Novel Paradigm for Realtime Interactive Systems? In: ACM Symposium on Virtual Reality Software and Technology (2008)
16. Lee, S., Lee, Y., Jang, S., Woo, W.: vr-UCAM: Unified context-aware application module for virtual reality. In: Conference on Artificial Reality (2004)
17. Lugrin, J.-l., Cavazza, M.: Making Sense of Virtual Environments: Action Representation, Grounding and Common Sense. In: 12th International Conference on Intelligent user Interfaces (2007)
18. Octavia, J.R., Coninx, K., Raymaekers, C.: Enhancing User Interaction in Virtual Environments through Adaptive Personalized 3D Interaction Techniques. In: De Bra, P., Kobsa, A., Chin, D. (eds.) UMAP 2010. LNCS, vol. 6075, pp. 423–426. Springer, Heidelberg (2010)
19. Peters, S., Shrobe, H.E.: Using Semantic Networks for Knowledge Representation in an Intelligent Environment. In: 1st International Conference on Pervasive Computing and Communications (2003)
20. Poupyrev, I., Billinghurst, M., Weghorst, S., Ichikawa, T.: The go-go interaction technique: non-linear mapping for direct manipulation in VR. In: Proceedings of the 9th Annual ACM Symposium on User Interface Software and Technology, pp. 79–80. ACM (1996)
21. Sowa, J.F.: Chapter 5 conceptual graphs. In: Frank van Harmelen, V.L., Porter, B. (eds.) Handbook of Knowledge Representation. Foundations of Artificial Intelligence, vol. 3, pp. 213–237. Elsevier (2008)
22. Wingrave, C.A., Bowman, D.A., Ramakrishnan, N.: Towards preferences in virtual environment interfaces. In: Proceedings of the Workshop on Virtual Environments, EGVE 2002, pp. 63–72. Eurographics Association, Aire-la-Ville (2002)

Frog Sound Identification System
for Frog Species Recognition

Clifford Loh Ting Yuan and Dzati Athiar Ramli

Intelligent Biometric Research Group (IBG), School of Electrical
and Electronic Engineering, USM Engineering Campus, Universiti Sains Malaysia,
14300, Nibong Tebal, Pulau Pinang, Malaysia
claypod016@gmail.com, dzati@eng.usm.my

Abstract. Physiological research reported that certain frog species contain antimicrobial substances which is potentially and beneficial in overcoming certain health problem. As a result, there is an imperative need for an automated frog species identification to assist people in physiological research in detecting and localizing certain frog species. This project aims to develop a frog sound identification system which is expected to recognize frog species according to the recorded bio acoustic signals. The Mel Frequency Cepstrum Coefficient (MFCC) and Linear Predictive Coding (LPC) are used as the feature extraction techniques for the system while the classifier employed is k-Nearest Neighbor (K-NN). Database from AmphibiaWeb has been used to evaluate the system performances. Experimental results showed that system performances of 98.1% and 93.1% have been achieved for MFCC and LPC techniques, respectively.

Keywords: Frog Sound, Identification, Mel Frequency.

1 Introduction

Other than applications related to human identity recognition [1], biometric technology has been used on the identification of biological acoustic sounds which is imperative for biological research and environmental monitoring. This is particularly true for detecting and locating animals due to we often hear the animal sound rather than visually detect the animal [2]. In animals, the initiation of sound could be as a means of information transmission or as a by-product of their living activities such as moving, eating or flying. In general, animals make sounds to communicate with members of same species and thus their vocalizations have evolved to be species-specific. Therefore, identifying animal species from their vocalizations is meaningful to ecological research.

Interest towards automatic recognition of animal species based on their vocalization has increased and many researches based on these studies have been published. [3] investigated different types of animals includes birds, cats, cows and dogs according to the animal calls. In another research, 16 different classes of animal calls were successfully classified as reported in [4].

Apart of recognizing types of animals, recognizing of species of the same animals is also found especially for bird species identification as reported in [5], [6] and [7]. [5] proposed the segmentation sounds of bird syllable using spectrum over time

P.C. Vinh et al. (Eds.): ICCASA 2012, LNICST 109, pp. 41–50, 2013.

method and template matching was employed as classifier. Different representations of bird syllables have been studied in [6] while [7] executed the frequency information for syllables segmentation of bird species sounds.

However, studies on the frog species recognition is still in infancy. An automated frog call identification system for public online consultation has been developed by [8]. Three features i.e. spectral centroid, signal bandwidth and threshold crossing rate are extracted for the purpose of this study. This study revealed that, certain frog species can easily be recognized by proposed methods but some species such as Microhyla butleri Microhyla ornate needs further investigation. In another case, Dayou et al. [9] introduced three different types of entropy i.e Shannon entropy, Renyi entropy and Tsallis entropy as the features. This study is based on nine species of frog sound from Microhylidae family. The k-Nearest Neighbor, kNN was then used as classifier resulting identification accuracy more than 80%. Subsequently, Han et al. [10] used Fourier spectral centroid instead Tsallis entropy as feature extraction and the result has improved with an average accuracy more than 90%.

The interest of this project is to build a system which is able to identify the species of frog based on their sound. The acoustic signal of frog vocalizations can be represented as a sequence of syllables. Thus, syllable can be used as the acoustic component to identify the frog species. A syllable is basically a sound that a frog produces with a single blow of air from the lungs. Once the syllables have been properly segmented, a set of features will be calculated to represent each syllable. These features will later be used for training or identification purpose.

In this work, a frog call identification system is constructed based on audio signal sampled from recordings of frog call. This system can be divided into four modules, including digital frog call collection, feature extraction, matching module and decision module. This process can be illustrated as in Fig. 1.

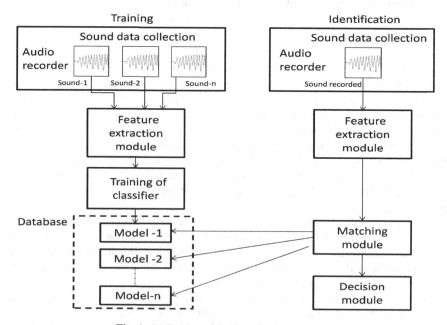

Fig. 1. Audio biometric identification system

2   Methodology

2.1   Data Acquisition

In this project, the digital frog call samples are obtained from AmphibiaWeb [11]. AmphibiaWeb is an online system enabling anyone with a Web browser to search and retrieve information relating to amphibian biology and conservation. AmphibiaWeb offers ready access to taxonomic information for every recognized species of amphibian in the world. Species accounts are being added regularly by specialist and volunteers and it also contains species descriptions, life history information, conservation status, audio signal, literature reference for many species [11].

The sampling rate and quantization bit of audio signals in AmphibiaWeb database are different due to the audio signals are offered by various contributors. Hence, the audio signals downloaded from AmphibiaWeb is converted and saved as 16-bit mono wav format. Table 1 lists the eight frog's audio signals that have been used in the project:

Table 1. List of frog call samples obtained from AmphibiaWeb

Types of Frog species
Adenomera_marmorata
Aglyptodactylus_madagascariensis
Ameerega_flavopicta
Anodonthyla_boulengerii
Aplastodiscus_leucopygius
Blommersia_wittei
Boophis_luteus
Boophis_miniatus

Each audio signal is then properly segmented as a syllable and a set of features can be calculated to represent each syllable as shown in Fig. 2.

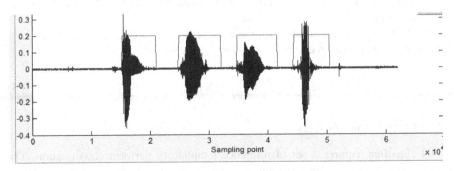

Fig. 2. Syllable segmentation

2.2   Feature Extraction

Mel-frequency cepstral coefficients (MFCC) which are commonly used as feature extraction for speech recognition and speaker recognition have been tested for frog sound recognition in this study. The computation of MFCC is based on short-term analysis [12]. The steps to implement MFCC are as follow:

1. Compute the Discrete Fourier Transform (DFT) of all frames of the signal. The DFT of all frames of the signal is

$$x_t(k) = X_t(e^{j\frac{2\pi k}{N}}), k = 0, 1, \ldots, N-1 \tag{1}$$

Equation (1) is also known as signal spectrum.

2. The signal spectrum is then processed by filter bank processing. Filter bank is a set of 24 band-pass filters which emphasize on processing spectrum which is below 1kHz. Filter bank is generally used to simulate the human ear processing. The m-th filter bank output is $Y_t(m)$, $1 \leq m \leq M$ and M is number of band-pass filters.

3. Compute the energy of the logarithm of the square magnitude filter bank outputs, $Y_t(m)$. This can reduce the complexity of computing the logarithm of the magnitude of the coefficients.

4. Perform the inverse DFT on the logarithm of the magnitude of the filter bank output

$$y_t^{(m)}(k) = \sum_{m=1}^{m} \log\{|Y_t(m)|\} \cdot \cos\left(k\left(m - \frac{1}{2}\right)\frac{\pi}{M}\right), k = 0, \ldots, L \tag{2}$$

k is number of cepstral coefficients excluding 0'th coefficient. In this project, k = 12. Each feature set consists of 12 mel cepstrum coefficients, one log energy coefficient.

By using Linear Predictive Coding processing, the speech wave and spectrum characteristic can be precisely represented by a very few number of parameters. The LPC implementation is as follows:

1. Compute the Discrete Fourier Transform (DFT) of all frames of the signal. The DFT of all frames of the signal is shown in equation (3.11). This also defined as signal spectrum.

2. Compute the autocorrelation coefficient at equation (2.37) by using the following short-time autocorrelation function. That is

3. Use Durbin's recursive solution for the autocorrelation equation.

4. Convert autocorrelation coefficient to complex cepstrum.

$$\dot{h}(n) = a_n + \sum_{k=1}^{n-1}\left(\frac{k}{n}\right)\dot{h}(k)a_{n-k} \quad 1 \leq n \tag{3}$$

2.3   Identification Process

K-NN classifier requires a set of reference template to perform classification. The steps to assemble the reference template based on training data and identification process are listed as follows:

1. Training data is first sampled and continue with feature extraction. The extracted feature is then resized to 4096 feature points.

2. Assemble a vector whose distinct values define the grouping of the rows in training data based on their species.

3. Testing data is first sampled and continue with feature extraction. The extracted feature is then resized to 4096 feature points.

4. Perform classification based on the input testing data, training data, assembled vector, k value, distance metric, and the rule that used to classify sample. In this project, 1-nn with Euclidean distance and "nearest" rule are set.

3 Result and Discussion

To evaluate the system, eight species with 24 frog call syllable segmentation are divided into two sets of data i.e. training data and testing data. For each species, four syllables are randomly selected as training data while the rest as testing data. The accuracy of the classifiers is defined as follows:

Table 2. True positive and false positive of MFCC-KNN and LPC-KNN on frog calls obtained from AmphibiaWeb

MFCC-KNN		Predicted class								Recognition Accuracy (%)
		Ad	Ag	Am	An	Ap	Bl	Lu	Mi	
Actual class (4 training data)	Ad	20	0	0	0	0	0	0	0	100
	Ag	0	20	0	0	0	0	0	0	100
	Am	0	0	19	1	0	0	0	0	95
	An	0	0	0	20	0	0	0	0	100
	Ap	0	1	0	0	18	0	0	1	90
	Bl	0	0	0	0	0	20	0	0	100
	Lu	0	0	0	0	0	0	20	0	100
	Mi	0	0	0	0	0	0	0	20	100
Mean Recognition Accuracy										98.1
LPC-KNN		Predicted class								Recognition Accuracy (%)
		Ad	Ag	Am	An	Ap	Bl	Lu	Mi	
Actual class (4 training data)	Ad	19	0	0	0	1	0	0	0	95
	Ag	0	18	0	0	0	0	2	0	90
	Am	0	2	18	0	0	0	0	0	90
	An	0	0	0	18	0	0	0	2	90
	Ap	0	0	0	0	18	0	2	0	90
	Bl	0	0	0	0	0	18	1	1	90
	Lu	0	0	0	0	0	0	20	0	100
	Mi	0	0	0	0	0	0	0	20	100
Mean Recognition Accuracy										93.1
Ad: Adenomera_marmorata				Ap: Aplastodiscus_leucopygius						
Ag: Aglyptodactylus_madagascariensi				Bl: Blommersia_wittei						
Am: Ameerega_flavopicta				Lu: Boophis_luteus						
An: Anodonthyla_boulengerii				Mi: Boophis_miniatus						

Table 3. Performances of MFCC-KNN and LPC-KNN at four, three, and two training data on frog calls obtained from AmphibiaWeb

| | K-NN | | | | | |
| | 4 training data | | 3 training data | | 2 training data | |
Species common name	MFCC	LPC	MFCC	LPC	MFCC	LPC
Adenomera_marmorata	20	19	20	19	20	19
Aglyptodactylus_madagascariensis	20	18	20	18	20	18
Ameerega_flavopicta	19	18	19	18	19	18
Anodonthyla_boulengerii	20	18	20	18	20	18
Aplastodiscus_leucopygius	18	18	18	18	18	18
Blommersia_wittei	20	18	20	18	19	18
Boophis_luteus	20	20	20	20	20	20
Boophis_miniatus	20	20	20	20	20	20
Matched syllable	157	149	157	149	156	149
total testing syllable	160	160	160	160	160	160
Accuracy (%)	98.125	93.125	98.125	93.125	97.5	93.125

Table 4. True positive and false positive of MFCC-KNN and LPC-KNN at different numbers of training data (a) 4 Training data, (b) 3 Training data, (c) 2 Training data

| | | MFCC-KNN | Predicted class | | | | | | | | Recognition Accuracy (%) |
			Ad	Ag	Am	An	Ap	Bl	Lu	Mi	
4 training data	Actual class	Ad	20	0	0	0	0	0	0	0	100
		Ag	0	20	0	0	0	0	0	0	100
		Am	0	0	19	1	0	0	0	0	95
		An	0	0	0	20	0	0	0	0	100
		Ap	0	1	0	0	18	0	0	1	90
		Bl	0	0	0	0	0	20	0	0	100
		Lu	0	0	0	0	0	0	20	0	100
		Mi	0	0	0	0	0	0	0	20	100
	Mean Recognition Accuracy										98.1

Table 4. (*continued*)

LPC-KNN		Predicted class								Recognition Accuracy (%)
		Ad	Ag	Am	An	Ap	Bl	Lu	Mi	
Actual class	Ad	19	0	0	0	1	0	0	0	95
	Ag	0	18	0	0	0	0	2	0	90
	Am	0	2	11	0	0	0	0	0	90
	An	0	0	0	18	0	0	0	2	90
	Ap	0	0	0	0	18	0	2	0	90
	Bl	0	0	0	0	0	18	1	1	90
	Lu	0	0	0	0	0	0	20	0	100
	Mi	0	0	0	0	0	0	0	20	100
Mean Recognition Accuracy										93.1

(a)

MFCC-KNN		Predicted class								Recognition Accuracy (%)
		Ad	Ag	Am	An	Ap	Bl	Lu	Mi	
Actual class	Ad	20	0	0	0	0	0	0	0	100
	Ag	0	20	0	0	0	0	0	0	100
	Am	0	0	19	1	0	0	0	0	95
	An	0	0	0	20	0	0	0	0	100
	Ap	0	1	0	0	18	0	0	1	90
	Bl	0	0	0	0	0	20	0	0	100
	Lu	0	0	0	0	0	0	20	0	100
	Mi	0	0	0	0	0	0	0	20	100
Mean Recognition Accuracy										98.1

LPC-KNN		Predicted class								Recognition Accuracy (%)
		Ad	Ag	Am	An	Ap	Bl	Lu	Mi	
Actual class	Ad	19	0	0	0	1	0	0	0	95
	Ag	0	18	0	0	0	0	2	0	90
	Am	0	2	18	0	0	0	0	0	90
	An	0	0	0	18	0	0	0	2	90
	Ap	0	0	0	0	18	0	2	0	90
	Bl	0	0	0	0	0	18	1	1	90
	Lu	0	0	0	0	0	0	20	0	100
	Mi	0	0	0	0	0	0	0	20	100
Mean Recognition Accuracy										93.1

3 training data

(b)

Table 4. (*continued*)

2 training data	Actual class	MFCC-KNN	Ad	Ag	Am	An	Ap	Bl	Lu	Mi	Recognition Accuracy (%)
		Predicted class									
		Ad	20	0	0	0	0	0	0	0	100
		Ag	0	20	0	0	0	0	0	0	100
		Am	0	0	19	1	0	0	0	0	95
		An	0	0	0	20	0	0	0	0	100
		Ap	0	1	0	1	18	0	0	0	90
		Bl	0	0	0	0	0	19	1	0	95
		Lu	0	0	0	0	0	0	20	0	100
		Mi	0	0	0	0	0	0	0	20	100
		Mean Recognition Accuracy									**97.5**
	Actual class	LPC-KNN	Ad	Ag	Am	An	Ap	Bl	Lu	Mi	Recognition Accuracy (%)
		Predicted class									
		Ad	19	0	0	0	1	0	0	0	95
		Ag	0	18	0	0	0	0	2	0	90
		Am	0	2	18	0	0	0	0	0	90
		An	0	0	0	18	0	0	0	2	90
		Ap	0	0	0	0	18	0	2	0	90
		Bl	0	0	0	0	0	18	2	0	90
		Lu	0	0	0	0	0	0	20	0	100
		Mi	0	0	0	0	0	0	0	20	100
		Mean Recognition Accuracy									**93.1**

Ad: Adenomera_marmorata
Ag: Aglyptodactylus_madagascariens
Am: Ameerega_flavopicta
An: Anodonthyla_boulengerii

Ap: Aplastodiscus_leucopygius
Bl: Blommersia_wittei
Lu: Boophis_luteus
Mi: Boophis_miniatus

(c)

$$\text{Accuracy (\%)} = \frac{N_c}{N_s} \times 100\% \tag{4}$$

Where N_c is the number of correctly recognized syllables, and N_s is the total number of test syllables. Besides, confusion matrix is also used to show the true positive and false positive of classifiers. True positive defined as the correct identification made by classifiers; false positive means the wrong identification made by classifiers [12].

In Table 2, the result shows that there are three false positives for MFCC-KNN based on frog calls obtained from AmphibiaWeb. This situation could be caused by the quality of recording. Higher quality of recording could increase the accuracy of K-NN classifier. In this case, K-NN classifier is able to identify all the species correctly since the numbers of false positive are much more fewer than number of true positive.

The accuracy of MFCC-KNN decreases with the decrement of the number of training data i.e. 98.1%, 98.1% to 97.5% as given in Table 3. On the other hands, the accuracy of LPC-KNN remains 93.1% when the numbers of training data change. However, as given in Table 4, the numbers of false positive and true positive maintain although the numbers of training data change. From the results, we can observe that the accuracy of LPC-KNN is not much affected by the numbers of training data.

4   Conclusion

In this study, a frog sound identification system which is expected to recognize frog species according to the recorded bio acoustic signals has been developed successfully. Experimental results revealed a very promising results and the developed identification system can be a viable approach in assisting people in physiological research in detecting and localizing certain frog species.

Acknowledgments. This project is supported by Short Term Grant USM, 304/PELECT/60311048.

References

1. Lip, C.C., Ramli, D.A.: Comparative Study on Feature, Score and Decision Level Fusion Schemes for Robust Multibiometric Systems. In: Sambath, S., Zhu, E. (eds.) Frontiers in Computer Education. AISC, vol. 133, pp. 941–948. Springer, Heidelberg (2012)
2. Lee, C.H., Chou, C.H., Han, C.C., Huang, Y.J.: Automatic recognition of Animal Vocalization using Averaged MFCC and Linear Discriminant Analysis. Pattern Recognition 27, 93–101 (2006)
3. Mitrovic, D., Zeppelzauer, M., Breiteneder, C.: Discrimination and Retrieval of Animal Sounds. In: 12th International on Multi-Media Modeling Conference Proceedings, p. 5 (2006)
4. Guodong, G., Li, S.Z.: Content-Based Audio Classification and Retrieval by Support Vector Machines. IEEE Transactions on Neural Network 14, 209–215 (2003)
5. Tyagi, H., Hegde, R.M., Murthy, H.A., Prabhakar, A.: Automatic Identification of Bird Calls using Spectral Ensemble Average Voiceprints. In: 13th European Signal Processing Conference Proceeding (2006)
6. Somervuo, P., Harma, A., Fagerlund, S.: Parametric Representations of Bird Sounds for Automatic Species Recognition. IEEE Transactions on Audio, Speech, and Language Processing 14, 2252–2263 (2006)
7. Harma, A.: Automatic Identification of Bird Species based on Sinusoidal Modeling of Syllables. In: International Conference on Acoustic Speech Signal Processing, vol. 5, pp. 545–548 (2003)

8. Huang, C.J., Yang, Y.J., Yang, D.X., Chen, Y.J.: Frog Classification using Machine Learning Techniques. Expert system with Application 36, 3737–3743 (2009)
9. Dayou, J., Han, N.C., Mun, H.C., Ahmad, A.H.: Classification and identification of frog sound based on entropy approach. In: International Conference on Life Science and Technology, vol. 3, pp. 184–187 (2011)
10. Han, N.C., Muniandy, S.V., Dayou, J.: Acoustic classification of Australian anurans based on hybrid spectral-entropy approach. Journal of Applied Acoustic 72, 639–645 (2011)
11. AMPHIBIAWEB: Information on amphibian biology and conservation. AmphibiaWeb, Berkeley, California, http://amphibiaweb.org/
12. Furui, S.: Comparison of Speaker Recognition Methods using Statistical Features and Dynamic Features. IEEE Transactions on Acoustics, Speech and Signal Processing 29, 342–350 (1981)

Contextually Aware Adaptive Systems for Enterprise Transformation

Gabrielle Peko, Ching-Shen Dong, and David Sundaram

Department of Information Systems and Operations Management, University of Auckland,
Auckland 1142, New Zealand
{g.peko,j.dong,d.sundaram}@auckland.ac.nz

Abstract. More than ever before, enterprises nowadays are faced with an environment characterised by asynchronicity, complexity, and uncertainty. We see three major shortcomings of many current approaches of enabling enterprises to adapt under these conditions: the proposed processes and systems often do not deal with the whole context surrounding the enterprise; enterprises still follow rather deliberate approaches when dealing with strategy and its execution; and decisions are limited in terms of their reach and range. Complex adaptive systems, and in particular autonomic systems, provide concepts and principles that could be leveraged to address these challenges. Furthermore, agent oriented implementation approaches could be harnessed to realise contextually aware and adaptive enterprise systems. In this paper we propose an adaptation lifecycle model, an agent oriented framework and architecture that enable enterprises to learn, adapt and be transformed.

Keywords: context, adaptive, agents, autonomic, enterprise transformation.

1 Introduction

Today's business environment is unpredictable, complex and uncertain. Enterprises that want to compete in this dynamic environment need to be able to respond rapidly and adapt to the ever-increasing rate of change. They have to overcome complexity, uncertainty, and rapid change at all levels of their internal and external environments [9]. Enterprises are wide ranging in terms of space and time. Enterprises need to be able to reach anyone, anywhere, anytime, and be able to conduct simple to sophisticated transactions in automated to semi-automated ways. Much of the current business environment change is driven by an insatiable customer demand for new, competitively priced, innovative products and services. These customers are less brand loyal and want greater choice resulting in the need for enterprises to constantly innovate. Yet, there is a global shortage of resources, such as business talent and investment funds, to fuel this innovation. Added to these factors is the relentless stream of mergers and acquisitions that change the enterprises operating environment. This volatility of the business environment creates uncertainty that necessitates change in terms of the way business is conducted [4]. This means there is a

P.C. Vinh et al. (Eds.): ICCASA 2012, LNICST 109, pp. 51–61, 2013.

corresponding change in business models along with the business processes (BP) and technology requirements that support those models [2]. Customers demand that their orders are fulfilled promptly so BP need to be created and executed quickly resulting in demand spikes for resources and sophisticated services. To address these problems, issues, and requirements we propose and discuss a contextually aware model, framework, and architecture that enable enterprises to learn, adapt and be transformed. This paper primarily consists of two parts. The first part explores the concept of an enterprise as a complex adaptive system (CAS) and the issues associated with enterprise adaptation. The second part proposes a conceptual model and framework that attempt to address these issues, especially in context of a contextually aware adaptive enterprise (CAAE). Finally, an agent-based system architecture to realise the proposed framework and support our model of enterprise adaptation is introduced.

2   Contextually Aware Adaptive Enterprise

Scheer [20] argues that for enterprises to be adaptive they need to balance flexibility with stability. He suggests that low levels of connectivity and high levels of control prevent flexibility and creative behaviours. The presence of rigid enterprise structures and rules and the lack of communication and interaction mean the work processes are set and people isolated. Scheer goes on to suggest that enterprises with traditional top down hierarchical management structures have high levels of intensity of control and low connectivity. In contrast, there are enterprises at the bleeding edge that are very reactive, connectivity between parties and the external environment is very high. They are constantly sensing the environment and trying to respond to change. However, these kinds of highly reactive volatile enterprises, such as many high tech start-up companies, have low levels of intensity of control [20]. Neither of these extreme positions is good [6], [20]. One is characterised by deliberation, control, and stability and the other position is characterised by chaos, flexibility, and possibly innovation and even anarchy. Scheer [20] suggests that the best place is to be on the edge of chaos where enterprise's balance flexibility and stability.

Based on the previous discussion we define the adaptive approach as a combination of deliberate approaches that support stable, evolutionary growth and emergent approaches that support more opportunistic, organic growth. A CAAE should interweave the deliberate and the emergent aspects of each subsystem of Scott-Morton's MIT90s framework [21] to form a cohesive adaptive whole. One way to conceptualise this notion of an adaptive enterprise as a CAAE is to interpret it as a Complex adaptive system (CAS). A number of authors have argued that an adaptive enterprise exhibits the generic constructs and operating mechanisms of a CAS [19], [10], [14]. In CAS, many agents, (may represent individuals, populations and enterprises) as part of a dynamic network, are constantly interacting and learning from those interactions to enable the enterprise to adapt [10]. A CAS can be described as a self-organizing system, consisting of multiple interacting components that emerges over time into a logical form and freely adapts without interference [14].

CAS theory has generated considerable interest within the management and organisational domains over the past decade. Topics such as enterprise transformation [17], strategy [13], innovation [6], and Information Systems [18], have been examined using a CAS theory lens. In these domains a CAS is viewed as an adaptive social system with a number of defining characteristics. At its core is a diverse population of agents (individuals) who are interdependent and linked together in causal relationships. These agents are also extremely context specific and their response to the same stimulus alters according to the current environment [14]. More recent concepts and models of an enterprise as CAS emphasise the characteristics of internal mechanisms of connectivity, self-organisation and emergence, as well as the interaction between the system and its environment, which results in the co-evolution of both [18] Given the aforementioned theories and models, the key characteristics of CAS used to define the concept in this research, are as follows, [19]. CAS are nested systems made up of various agents that can also be deemed as systems in themselves. Each system is part of a system hierarchy and can be either a sub-system or supra-system. CAS are unpredictable and dynamic, their control is decentralized and distributed throughout the CAS, which often leads to seemingly undirected chaotic system actions. Inherent in this seemingly lack of control is a feature of CAS known as emergence, namely the emergence of system's outcomes through the process of self-organisation rather than directed interference. The majority of changes in complex systems are considered to be emergent where patterns of actions are not deliberately designed. The interaction of the agents generates patterns of actions over time that regulates the action of the systems as a whole leading to further adaptation of the CAS. The key drivers of this adaption are: interactions between agents that can lead to positive or negative action outcomes, information flows, operative feedback loops, and time [14].

3   Managerial, Technological and Autonomic Approaches to Enterprise Adaptation

Many models for enterprise adaptation have been suggested but most of these models are either management oriented or technology oriented. In this section we first review the management and technology approaches to enterprise adaptation and then explore the autonomic approach. In particular, we explore the complementarity and potential enhancement of the management and technological approaches when interwoven with the autonomic approach.

Bhattacharya et al.'s [5] framework and Kumaran et al. [16] transformational approach are some of the few models for enterprise adaptation that interweave managerial concerns with technological responses in an integrated and holistic fashion. Bhattacharya et al.'s [5] framework differentiates four different models on different levels of abstraction. The strategy level model is at the highest level of abstraction, where business objectives are specified. These objectives drive the operational models. These models describe the structure of enterprise BP. In order to support enterprise BP with information technology, solution composition models are designed that combine necessary information technology functionality and the operational models. Solution composition models can be seen as an intermediate layer between business and information technology; rather than having to deal with implementation specifics, "solution architects" can operate on a more abstract level that simplifies the matching of business requirements to IT. This is sometimes referred to as "programming in the large" [11].

The Autonomic Systems (AS) computing paradigm is a key element of the autonomic approach for enterprise adaptation [8]. AS are able to self-manage, self-heal, and self-optimize. They are environmentally aware and operate intelligently and dynamically [22]. AS make autonomous decisions based on high level guidelines, the systems will constantly sense and optimise their status in order to dynamically adapt to the changing environment. In the AS paradigm the human element adopts a new role, rather than controlling the systems directly people define the guidelines and rules that support the self-management process. It can be argued that CAAE can leverage the automaticity and cost advantages offered by AS to augment and enhance their adaptive behaviours and ultimately transform the enterprise [15].

However, there are certain organisational processes that cannot be extensively automated such as the meta-decisional processes of strategy. The development of an enterprise's adaptive strategy is essentially a human activity that requires largely manual intervention. AS can support strategy development through the generation and migration of emergent patterns from the lower operational level of the enterprise. It is at this level emergent patterns are generated by the AS as they autonomously perform standardised BP. These patterns flow through the intermediate BP level to become the emergent input into the strategy development process. Conversely, once the strategy has been developed it is implemented at the intermediate and operational levels through the AS policy and rules, which guide the systems' autonomous decision making. A strategy that embraces the AS model significantly enhances an enterprise's ability to continually adapt to its environment through the generation, translation, and integration of emergent patterns into an adaptive strategy for sustainable competitive advantage.

Although strategy does not completely align with the AS model, other organisational level activities do lend themselves to automatic changes in the parameters. For instance, changes in the form of emergent patterns captured by the AS at the operational level of the enterprise can act as precursors to the creation of products and services that provide competitive differentiation. The creation of these products and services come about through the execution of higher level, cross-enterprise, innovative BP [3]. Essentially, AS enabled, standardized BP activities are used to compose AS enabled, composite BP. These composite BP, in turn, are orchestrated to become new, innovative BP for business growth.

4   Contextually Aware Enterprise Adaptation Lifecycle

A synthesis of the above concepts with respect to learning, context, adaptation, and strategy-driven processes and systems leads us to propose a model for enterprise adaptation (Fig. 1) that leverages the AS computing paradigm. This model explicitly considers the transformation of vision and strategy into appropriate enterprise BP. It considers the translation of these BP into potential solutions that compose and integrate activities to deliver effective and flexible implementations. Execution and monitoring of the implementation and contextual actions (internal and external CAS outcomes) enables us to pro-actively manage the performance of the enterprise through three distinct mechanisms; corrective (single-loop learning), optimising (double-loop learning), and aligning (double and triple-loop learning). These actions are captured and made available through information and communications technologies [8]. One such technology is (AS), they could be present within the enterprise capturing internal actions and presenting them to internal and/or external consumers. AS can potentially provide new and better options for enterprises to respond and adapt to their rapidly changing environments.

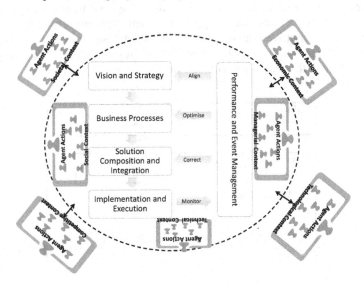

Fig. 1. Contextually aware enterprise adaptation lifecycle

5   Contextually Aware Adaptive Systems Framework

New paradigms of management for adaptation (and innovation) depend heavily upon technology. Open innovation (and adaptation) is difficult to implement without technological mechanism to access the knowledge of the various stakeholders. We suggest that technology should not be seen only as a means to achieve ends determined by a higher conceptual level but also as an integration, coordination, and collaboration mechanism to facilitate change. To illustrate this perspective of technology as an integrator, coordinator, and collaborator to drive change and to support our model of enterprise adaptation, we propose a contextually aware, adaptive, AS enabled, conceptual framework (Fig. 2). In this framework, technology is understood as a central mediator between the different kinds of context. Each context (internal and external) is a CAS in its own right, populated by agents and serves as an integral part of the environment in which it resides. The actions (behaviour) of agents are tightly tied to the actions of other agents through interactions that can lead to positive outcomes which cause the system to change through adaptation. The whole learning and changing process, or process of enterprise adaptation as described above, is mediated by technology some of which are AS. These technologies work as mediators between the context and the enterprise levels of strategy, BP and operational implementation. The mediation should, on the one hand, help to channel actions for the decision maker, which can be either AS at the lower organisational level or a human at the higher level. On the other hand, technology should help to transport the decision maker's decisions back to the context. For instance, if a change of strategy is decided upon this change must be reflected in the operational plans and communicated to decision makers (human or AS).

The proposed framework illustrates that actions (agent behaviours) originating from AS can be of different natures as they might originate from different contexts (Fig. 1). Real-time actions are a type of 'event' traditionally emphasised in discussions of event-driven architectures. These predominately allow capturing actions from the managerial and competitive context. Transactional actions are actions occurring in the predictable course of a BP.

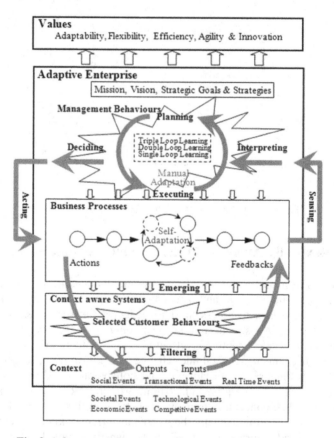

Fig. 2. A framework for contextually aware adaptive systems

Our framework emphasises the importance of capturing unpredictable competitive, social, managerial and technological actions through AS enabled technologies. We see these actions as primarily driving an enterprise's ability to learn and adapt to novel circumstances. This can be, for instance, the dissatisfaction of an employee (agent) with the way he has to conduct his work. There must be channels in which he can articulate his concerns and which directly influence decisional processes including the meta-decisional processes of strategy that influence enterprise reorientation. Capturing the actions of agents is an important aspect of managing emergent developments in formalised channels, as discussed above, and ultimately integrating the deliberate approach with the emergent approach.

The framework distinguishes three central learning processes informed by Argyris and Schön's notion of single loop learning and double loop learning [1]. Single loop learning occurs when BP are improved on an operational/implementation level. This learning process is driven by actions deriving from the external context and is technology-mediated. The actions arrive at the social, technical and managerial subsystems and filtered by technology. Based on these actions, the changes that the decision makers decide on are made a reality using technological means. Double loop learning occurs when the controlling subsystem reacts to actions, leading to a change of BP or enterprise structures or both. Triple loop learning occurs when the meta-level subsystem of the enterprise reacts to actions by changing the enterprises strategic direction. Besides single loop learning, which in some instances can be controlled by AS, the learning processes that enable the enterprise to evolve and adapt require a decision maker or a collective of decision makers to take a decision.

6   Contextually Aware Adaptive Systems Architecture

To meet customer demands in the rapid changing business environment, context aware BP and management systems are open dynamic systems. Incorporating adaptation to changes into BP makes them more complex than the traditional BP approach. Software agent based, oriented and coordinated BP help to address this problem [7]. Business activities in a BP are services provided by software agents. These services are proactive or reactive. The proactive services are aligned with business strategies and policies. The deliberative software agents have goals and plans to execute in order to achieve the goals under the facts that software agents believe the context existing in the current business environment. The reactive software agents respond to the situations with defined rules. Goal oriented BP can achieve full alignment to strategies set by top management. Each activity in BP is a service. The services used to support BP can be classified into three categories, routines, rule-oriented and goal-oriented. Routine business activities do not need changes. The rule-oriented business activities make decisions based on the setup business rules. These rules reflect business policies. Rules are determined by management and can be changed after initial setups. The changes or updates of rules are performed manually by employees or automatically by intelligent software agents. For goal-oriented services, each service has a goal and plans to achieve that goal. The plans can be activities or sub-activities. The BP can be configured and re-configured by business owners manually (e.g. by business rules) or by intelligent software agent automatically based on the existing business context [7].

In this section, we design a software agent-based contextually aware architecture (Fig. 3) to realise the proposed framework. In the architecture, software agent services consist of intelligent and mobile services. Software agent services can either be proactive or passive reacting to actions initiated in the contexts to provide agile changes required by the enterprise. Software agents can be stationary or mobile. Mobile agents can be sent to the business environment such as customer devices to collect context information. The different kinds of actions that drive learning in the framework require different kinds of software agents to act upon. Based on the internal and or external actions sensed and collected from various context systems, the goal seeking or deliberative intelligent agents select the plans to change the BP to adaptive to the changes detected from the environment. This is called self-adaptation.

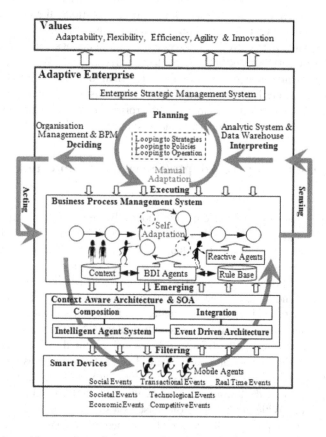

Fig. 3. An architecture for software agent-based contextually aware adaptive systems

Alternatively, the decision makers interpret the implications of the actions. Then they design responses using service integration, orchestration, choreograph and improvisation within the enterprise or across enterprise boundaries to achieve different levels of adaptability for enterprises. The changes can be made by changing the business rules for the BP. The reactive agents pick up the rules to implement them at the BP to reflect policy or strategy levels to support integration, coordination and collaboration within the enterprise and across organisational boundaries. This is called manual adaptation. The combination of self-adaptation and manual adaption makes the contextually aware action driven architecture provides enhanced flexibility, agility, and ultimately adaptability in comparison to more traditional system architectures.

Software agent-based contextually aware adaptive systems can be implemented for inter-organisational business integration (virtual enterprise for employees) and intra-organisational collaboration (virtual enterprise for networked business partners). Our argument is to use both approaches for innovative, adaptive enterprises. Transactional actions are traditionally handled well by ERP systems or service oriented architectures (SOA) whereas real-time actions can be processed using Event Driven Architecture (EDA) systems. Mobile agents can be sent to various business environments to collect social, technological, economic, and competitive action information. Other existing technologies can also be used to implement software agent based context aware systems for virtual organisations. At the context sensing layer, Web 2.0, EDA, CRM and social networking technologies can be applied to detect actions from various sources. While at the interpreting level, BPM, rules based systems, databases, and business intelligence technologies can be used to analyse the activities and contexts. Data mining and decision making technologies can be employed for strategic planning and selecting at the planning and deciding layer. At the acting level, ERP and BPM technologies can be utilised for performing and monitoring the operations responding to the actions detected. At the organisational structuring layer, grid, cluster, Web services, SOA, virtualisation, software agents, enterprise portal and middleware technologies can be exploited to integrate various enterprise information applications in a traditional system landscape.

7   Conclusion

It is a common thread in many streams of research, such as Enterprise Systems implementation, that information technology (IT) is not the remedy for enterprise inertia. Many factors besides the technology must be considered in order to achieve positive enterprise transformation. However, one common theme still persists in the literature; IT is often seen as a central enabler of enterprise change. In this paper we to argue for redefining the perspective on what adaptive IT can and cannot do and suggest the notion of IT as mediator of enterprise change rather than an enabler. This next generation of adaptive IT uses context as a driving force for technology-mediated enterprise change. Truly adaptive systems are not merely technological systems. They need to be strategy driven, learning oriented, process oriented, and service oriented to be truly adaptive. Consideration should also be given to the rapidly evolving managerial, technological, social, economic, and competitive contexts. In this paper we first investigate the notion of enterprises as multi-dimensional, complex, and context aware systems [12]. Given this, we reflect on the traditional perspectives of seeing technology as the central enabler of enterprise change. We contrast this with recent literature that emphasises the importance of linking the deliberate approach with the emergent approach in order to achieve an adaptive enterprise. Based on this discussion, we propose perceiving technology as a multi-dimensional mediator of context-driven change. To demonstrate this notion we propose an agent-based framework and architecture of a contextually aware adaptive system for enterprise adaptation. We posit this is one possible way for enterprises to adapt in a changing world of complexity and uncertainty.

References

1. Argyris, C., Schön, D.: Organizational Learning: A Theory of Action Perspective. Addison-Wesley (1978)
2. Axelrod, R., Cohen, M.D.: Harnessing complexity: Organizational implications of a scientific frontier. Simon and Schuster (2001)
3. Benbya, H., Passiante, G., Belbaly, N.: Corporate portal: a tool for knowledge management synchronization. International Journal of Information Management 24, 201–220 (2004)
4. Betts, B., Heinrich, C.: Adapt or Die: Transforming Your Supply Chain into an Adaptive Business Network. Wiley (2003)
5. Bhattacharya, K., Caswell, N., Kumaran, S., Nigam, A., Wu, F.: Artifact-centered operational modeling: lessons from customer engagements. IBM Syst. J. 46 (2007)
6. Brown, S., Eisenhardt, K.: Competing on the Edge: Strategy as Structured Chaos. Harvard Business School Press (1998)
7. Burmeister, B., Arnold, M., Copaciu, F., Rimassa, G.: BDI-agents for agile goal-oriented business processes. In: International Foundation for Autonomous Agents and Multiagent Systems (2008)
8. Chui, M., Löffler, M., Roberts, R.: The Internet of things. McKinsey Quarterly 2 (2010)
9. Dale, S.: Holistic BPM: From Theory to Reality. Keynote Presentation. 5th International Conference on Business Process Management, BPM 2007 (2007)
10. Dooley, K.J.: A complex adaptive systems model of organization change. Nonlinear Dynamics, Psychology, and Life Sciences 1(1), 69–97 (1997)
11. Emig, C., Langer, K., Krutz, K., Link, S., Momm, C., Abeck, S.: The SOA's Layers. Cooperation & Management, Universität Karlsruhe, Karlsruhe (2006)
12. Gharajedaghi, J.: Systems thinking: Managing chaos and complexity: A platform for designing business architecture. Morgan Kaufmann (2011)
13. Hammer, R., Edwards, J.S., Tapinos, E.: Examining the strategy development process through the lens of complex adaptive systems theory. Journal of the Operational Research Society (2011)
14. Holland, J.H.: Emergence: From chaos to order. Oxford University Press (2000)
15. Huebscher, M.C., McCann, J.A.: A survey of autonomic computing—degrees, models, and applications. ACM Comput. Surv. 40(3), 1–28 (2008)

16. Kumaran, S., Bishop, P., Chao, T., Dhoolia, P., Jain, P., Jaluka, R., Ludwig, H., Moyer, A., Nigam, A.: Using a model-driven transformational approach and service-oriented architecture for service delivery management. IBM Systems Journal 46, 513 (2007)
17. Lichtenstein, B.B., Plowman, D.A.: The leadership of emergence: A complex systems leadership theory of emergence at successive organizational levels. The Leadership Quarterly 20(4), 617–630 (2009)
18. Nan, N.: Capturing bottom-up information technology use processes: a complex adaptive systems model. MIS Quarterly 35(2), 505–532 (2011)
19. Rouse, W.B.: Health care as a complex adaptive system: Implications for design and management. Bridge-Washington-National Academy of Engineering 38(1), 17 (2008)
20. Scheer, A.W.: Jazz-Improvisation and Management. ARIS Expert Paper (2007)
21. Scott-Morton, M.: The Corporation of the 1990s: Information Technology and Organizational Transformation. Oxford University Press, USA (1991)
22. Soule, P.: Autonomics Development: A Domain-Specific Aspect Language Approach. Springer Basel AG (2010)

The Requirements to Enhance the Design of Context-Aware Mobile Patient Monitoring Systems Using Wireless Sensors

Mahmood Ghaleb Al-Bashayreh, Nor Laily Hashim, and Ola Taiseer Khorma

UUM College of Arts and Sciences, School of Computing,
06010 UUM Sintok, Kedah, Malaysia
mahmood.g.al-bashayreh@ieee.org, laily@uum.edu.my,
ola_khorma@hotmail.com

Abstract. Designing and developing Context-aware Mobile Patient Monitoring Systems (CMPMS) using wireless sensors are emerging in the biomedical informatics domain. However, previous studies related to this topic are fragmented. In fact, the literature has no standard types and sources of context information. These types and sources are required to design such systems. In addition, there is no standard context reasoning approach to facilitate the development of these systems. To address these absences, this paper is a survey of the CMPMS in the biomedical informatics to identify potential types and sources of context information as well as the context reasoning approaches that are required to be addressed in designing and developing such systems. The results are expected to help researchers to enhance the design and facilitate the development of CMPMS.

Keywords: context awareness computing, mobile patient monitoring systems, context information types, context information sources, context reasoning approach, requirements.

1   Introduction

The concept of context is broad and unclear, thus it must be defined. Literature revealed a large number of context definitions, each of which has different context information. Dey, Abowd, and Salber's [1] general definition of context is the most adopted and referenced definition in the literature. They defined a context as "any information that can be used to characterize the situation of entities (i.e., whether a person, place, or object) that are considered relevant to the interaction between a user and an application, including the user and the application themselves. Context is typically the location, identity, and state of people, groups, and computational and physical objects." [1] The term *situation* in this definition refers to "a description of the states of relevant entities" [2]. The term *context-aware computing* originally was coined by Schilit and Theimer [3], then it was elaborated on by Dey [2] to be more general to reflect the system capability to use "context to provide relevant information

P.C. Vinh et al. (Eds.): ICCASA 2012, LNICST 109, pp. 62–71, 2013.
© Institute for Computer Sciences, Social Informatics and Telecommunications Engineering 2013

and/or services to the user, where relevancy depends on the user's task" [2]. The main purpose of context-aware computing is to achieve application adaptability [4]. An application is considered context-aware, if it can adapt its behaviors to contextual changes without user interventions [2], [5], [6], [7], [8].

Wireless sensors and mobile technologies have played a primary role in the advancement of context-aware computing [9]. Wireless sensors have been represented as a primary source of context data [10], [8]. In fact, the more sensors are used, the more comprehensive information can be gained from combining the data from these sensors [6], [8]. Similarly, mobile devices such as smart phones and PDAs have been used widely in context-aware applications [11]. They are portable and have become part of users' lifestyles [12]. Additionally, they have the capability to obtain personalized context data from various sources [8], [13], [14], and process them locally [15], [16].

Some context-aware computing studies focus on defining context-awareness, while others focus on building context-aware applications [17]. These applications aim to make daily used appliances, devices, and objects context-aware [18]. Biomedical informatics is considered one of the richest domains for context-aware applications [19]. Context-aware mobile patient monitoring system using wireless sensors is among the application family of biomedical informatics [20]. Examples in this family include applications that monitor patients with chronic diseases, such as hypertension, diabetes, and epilepsy, in terms of vital signs, medication treatment, and disease symptoms.

However, developing Context-aware Mobile Patient Monitoring Systems (CMPMS) is very complex [5], [6], [21], [22]. The literature related to these emerging systems is fragmented. First, there are no standard types and sources of context information that are required to design CMPMS. Second, there is no standard context reasoning approach that is specific to facilitate the development of such systems. Therefore, the objective of this paper is to identify the potential types and sources of context information that are required to help researchers in enhancing the design of CMPMS. In addition, this paper identifies a potential context reasoning approach that is required to facilitate the development of such systems.

The remainder of this paper is structured as follows: Section 2 is a presentation of benefits of using CMPMS. The identified types and sources of context information in CMPMS are presented in Section 3 and Section 4 respectively. Next, context reasoning approach is identified and presented in Section 6. Finally, Section 7 contains conclusion and brief discussion of future work.

2   Context-Aware Mobile Patient Monitoring Systems

The need for personal lifetime health monitoring systems has inspired researchers to study the potential of adopting the technology of mobile devices (e.g. smart phones) and wireless sensors (e.g. wireless body sensor networks) to develop CMPMS [23], [24]. These systems play a key role in monitoring patient responses to any medication [25], managing and protecting them from chronic disease complications. Ideally, these systems continually perform repeatable tasks that are required for monitoring patients to help and complement the role of health care professionals outside the boundary of health care organizations [26].

Patient context can be defined as any information that can be used to characterize a patient medical situation such as high blood pressure (BP). This definition is based on Dey, Abowd, and Salber's [1] general definition of context. The context information in this definition can include patient's vital signs (e.g., body temperature), medical symptoms (e.g., dizziness), risk factors (e.g., cholesterol level), prescribed medications, physical activities (e.g., sleeping), and surrounding environments (e.g., room temperature). However, it was found that characterizing patients' medical situations, such as high BP, depends on patient context information such as vital signs (e.g., BP) and physical activities (e.g., running) [15]. For example, the normal BP during sleeping is less than during running [27], [28]. Therefore, identifying patient context based on context information enables effective characterization of the medical situation, hence, allowing CMPMS to adapt to the changes in a patient's medical situation. An example of such adaptation is to trigger an alarm or contact a health care professional once a critical medical situation is detected [28], [27], [15], [29].

3   Context Information Types in Patient Monitoring Systems

This study aims to combine multiple types of context information to support the design of context-aware patient monitoring systems using mobile device and wireless sensors. To achieve this goal, context information types have to be identified within the biomedical informatics, which are related to context-aware patient monitoring systems. Analyzing literature revealed that there is no consensus on the types of context information adopted in biomedical informatics studies. However, there are three most promising types of context information that are centralized on the patient and can contribute to the design of mobile patient monitoring systems. These types are classified as medical, physical activities, and environmental contexts. They are elaborated in the following subsections. These types of context information were identified using literature search method introduced in [30].

3.1   Medical Context

The medical context includes biomedical information that is required for monitoring patients. This type of context is classified into four subtypes of context information, which are described as follows:

Measurable Medical Context. This subtype of context information mainly represents patients' vital signs, which is widely adopted in the literature to provide continually measured medical personal information [31], [27], [15], [32], [11], [28], [33], [16], [14], [29]. In fact, vital signs represent the signs of life [34], defined in [35], as the "body's physiological status and provide information critical to evaluating homeostatic balance." However, there are five standard vital signs that must be measured and continually monitored. These are: body temperature, respiration rate, heart rate, blood pressure, and electrocardiogram (ECG) [36]. The interpretation of their signs, whether they are normal or not, depends on other types of medical context such as risk factors and prescribed medications context information, which are debated in the following subsections.

Non-measurable Medical Context. This subtype of context information describes medical symptoms that are difficult to be measured by wireless sensors (e.g., dizziness, vomiting, sleepiness, or headache). Thus, it is rarely adopted in biomedical informatics studies. It also provides dynamic medical personal information that is difficult to be measured by sensors [25]. However, it is able to complement the information obtained from the measurable medical context. For example, monitoring hypertension requires monitoring non-measurable medical contexts such as headache and constipation. These non-measurable medical symptoms complement measurable medical contexts such as BP and HR vital signs [25].

Risk Factors Context. This subtype of context information is also known as a health risk that is defined by the World Health Organization (WHO) [37] as "a factor that raises the probability of adverse health outcomes". These factors were adopted in a number of biomedical informatics studies to represent the personal health information that changes infrequently [33], [11], [31], [32]. In fact, risk factors are countless, and each disease has a number of associated risk factors. For instance, there are eight risk factors associated with hypertension, which are: alcohol consumption, tobacco consumption, BP, lack of physical activity, cholesterol level, blood glucose level, fruit and vegetable intake, and obesity. Obesity risk factor is calculated based on the body mass index (body mass index = weight in kilograms / (height in meters)^2) [38]. These eight risk factors are jointly responsible for more than 75% of deaths of hypertensive patients [37]. Furthermore, it was found that the risk factors affect the normal readings of vital signs [37], [15], [39]. For instance, the blood-pressure reading is affected negatively by either alcohol consumption or obesity. Similarly, the normal cholesterol level is affected by either smoking or fat intake [37].

Prescribed Medications Context. This subtype of context information presents the current prescribed medications for a patient [25], [15]. However, it is rarely adopted in biomedical informatics studies. In fact, these prescribed medications have effects on the patient's normal vital signs [25], [15], [39]. Therefore, health care professionals use this context information to assess the effects of the prescribed medications on patients to evaluate the patient's response to the treatment. For example, a health care professional can manage hypertension by prescribing a medication such as Amlodipine, a calcium channel blocker, with suitable frequency and dosage (such as 5 mg every morning). Then, the professional can monitor the effect of such medication on a patient's BP to assess the patient's response to the prescribed medication, and then take an appropriate follow-up decision or action [25].

3.2   Physical Activities Context

This type of context information represents the current patient's physical activities such as walking, running, eating, or sleeping, and it was adopted in several studies previously [13], [27], [15], [28]. In fact, patient's physical activities have direct effects on their vital signs. For example, the normal heart rate while running or climbing up stairs is higher than while walking or lying down [13], [39]. Similarly, normal BP during sitting or sleeping is less than during eating or doing physical exercise, such as running [28], [27], [39].

3.3   Environmental Context

This context type provides information about the surrounding environment that can affect a patient's medical state, such as temperature, light, humidity, and noise. It has been adopted widely in previous biomedical informatics studies [40], [27], [41], [29], [15], [31]. It also contributes to the monitoring of diseases. For instance, patients with Amyotrophic Lateral Sclerosis (ALS), which is "a disease of the nerve cells in the brain and spinal cord that control voluntary muscle movement" [42], can benefit from floor humidity to protect them from falling [27]. In addition, environmental context information also affects vital signs, e.g., room temperature affects the normal heartbeat and consequently, the change of heartbeat affects BP [27].

4   Context Information Sources in Patient Monitoring Systems

This study aims to obtain context information from four various context data sources, which include mobile patient profile, wireless body sensors, wireless environmental sensors, and mobile graphical user interface. These context data sources are adopted based on the literature analysis of studies related to context-aware patient monitoring systems within the biomedical informatics, by considering the identified context information in the previous section. To identify these sources of context information, the literature search method introduced in [30] was used. These context data sources are classified as mobile patient profile, wireless body sensors, wireless environmental sensors, and mobile graphical user interface, all of which are explained in the following.

4.1   Mobile Patient Profile Context Source

This context source is being widely adopted in the biomedical informatics studies as a main data source for obtaining the risk factors and the prescribed medications context [33], [16], [14], [32]. It contributes to the accuracy of context-aware mobile patient monitoring systems [43]. It also plays a primary role in personalizing the patient monitoring process [31], [32]. For example, this source can provide information about alcohol consumption. Alcohol consumption is one of the risk factors associated with hypertension, and negatively affects BP; thus, it has to be considered when monitoring a patient with hypertension [37]. However, if a patient does not consume alcohol, then the patient monitoring process has to be personalized by ignoring the effect of such a factor, thereby optimizing the patient monitoring process. Moreover, using a patient profile hosted on the patient's mobile device can contribute significantly to CMPMS. One advantage is that it supports the privacy protection of the patient's contextual data [44]. Furthermore, it is adequate to avoid continuous network communication costs required to transmit and receive data to and from the backend server [13], [45], [46]. Aside from this, it avoids the problems associated with wireless network interruptions. Moreover, a mobile patient profile can support context awareness and adaptation through direct detection of context changes [44]. Additionally, it supports real-time continuous patient monitoring [46], anywhere and anytime [14].

4.2 Wireless Body Sensors Context Source

This context source was used as a primary data source for measurable medical context information. In fact, it was used in most previous studies that have adopted this type of context information. Additionally, they were also used as a main data source for physical activities context in many previous studies [31], [27], [15], [32], [11], [28], [33], [16], [14], [29].

4.3 Wireless Environmental Sensors Context Source

This context source is also used as a primary data source for physical activities context in most studies that have adopted this type of context [13], [27], [15], [28]. Indeed, it was used as an essential data source for environmental context in most studies that adopted such type of context [40], [27], [41], [29], [15], [31]. They also play a primary role in supporting CMPMS by providing context information that can be measured continuously during the patient normal daily lives [47].

4.4 Mobile Graphical User Interface Context Source

This context source supports obtaining data directly from patients through manual answering of yes/no questions. However, it was rarely adopted in the literature [25]. It is considered as a main data source for obtaining a non-measurable medical context. Moreover, it plays a primary role in supporting context-aware patient monitoring systems that require dynamic context information that cannot be measured by wireless sensors or retrieved from the mobile patient profile [25].

5   Context Reasoning of Patient Monitoring Systems

Patient's context situations that are of interest for context-aware mobile patient monitoring systems using wireless sensors cannot be directly obtained. In fact, identifying this situation based on a single type of context information is not enough without incorporating other types of patient's context information, including: medical context, physical activities context, and environmental context as elaborated in Section 3. For example, various patients' context information types can be used to identify a change in patient situation, such as a change from normal BP to high BP. In other words, deciding that a patient has high BP situation can be inferred by integrating at least three types of context information. First, the medical context types, which include measurable context such as BP, non-measurable context such as headache [25], risk factors context such as overweight [37], and prescribed medications context such as Amlodipine; a calcium channel blocker [25]. Second, the physical activities context such as doing some physical exercises including running [28], [27], [39]. Third, the environmental context such as the room temperature [27].

The inference process used to identify a patient's context situation, as in the previous example, is the core of context-aware reasoning. The new derived context is called high-level context, which is also known as context situation. Meanwhile, all the other context information that is used to derive the high-level context is called low-level contexts, which are obtained directly from the context sources [22], [32].

Context reasoning aims to detect the change in high-level context information based on low-level context information [22], [32]. In the example above, high BP is called high-level patient context information or patient context situation. Meanwhile, the others are called low-level patient context information, which are context information used to derive the high-level context.

First-Order Logic (FOL) is one of the suitable solutions to represent context information and reasoning over the limited resources of mobile devices [44], [6], [32], [29], [31]. FOL is a language to represent knowledge. A potential model for FOL is described by a set of objects, relations among them, and functions that can be applied to them. Among the FOL reasoning algorithms is the resolution-based algorithm, which requires converting each FOL sentence into a Conjunctive Normal Form (CNF) sentence [48]. A CNF sentence is "a conjunction of clauses, where each clause is a disjunction of literals" [48].

In the context of this research, one or more context-aware monitoring queries that are required to detect change in the patient's medical situation (e.g., change from normal to high BP as high-level context information). Each query consists of one or more query elements that represent low-level context information (e.g., non-measurable context such as headache, risk factor context such as obesity, and physical activity context such as running). To facilitate processing such complex queries, they have to be normalized [49]. One of the practical approaches to normalize a query is CNF since it typically includes more AND [49]. To this end, each query is converted to CNF to represent a conjunction of query elements. For instance, while a high BP query is false, a patient's context situations in considered normal. However, once all the query elements in this query become true, then a change in the patient's context situation from normal to high BP can be detected. Using CNF in context-aware monitoring queries was introduced in [44].

6   Conclusion and Future Work

This paper is a discussion of ongoing research on designing and developing CMPMS. It begins by introducing the concept of context awareness and the benefits of using CMPMS. It also presents an overview of context information types, sources, and reasoning in previous studies that designed and developed CMPMS in the biomedical informatics domain. To this end, the results of this paper are twofold. Firstly, a set of context information types and sources were provided to enhance the existing design of CMPMS. Secondly, a recommended context reasoning approach was introduced to be used to facilitate the development of CMPMS. In the future, researchers can further enhance research in this domain by attempting to use the described context information types and sources, as well as the context reasoning approach to design and develop more accurate and more efficient real-life CMPMS.

References

1. Dey, A.K., Abowd, G.D., Salber, D.: A conceptual framework and a toolkit for supporting the rapid prototyping of context-aware applications. Hum. Comput. Interact. 16, 97–166 (2001)
2. Dey, A.K.: Understanding and Using Context. Personal Ubiquitous Computing 5, 4–7 (2001)
3. Schilit, B.N., Theimer, M.M.: Disseminating active map information to mobile hosts. IEEE Network 8, 22–32 (1994)
4. Hervás, R., Bravo, J., Fontecha, J.: A context model based on ontological languages, a proposal for information visualization. J. Univers. Comput. Sci. 16, 1539–1555 (2010)
5. Hoyos, J.R., García-Molina, J., Botía, J.A.: MLContext: A Context-Modeling Language for Context-Aware Systems. J. Electron. Commun. EASST 28, 1–14 (2010)
6. Esposito, A., Tarricone, L., Zappatore, M., Catarinucci, L., Colella, R.: A framework for context-aware home-health monitoring. Int. J. Autonom. Adapt. Comm. Syst. 3, 75–91 (2010)
7. Driver, C., Clarke, S.: An application framework for mobile, context-aware trails. Pervasive and Mobile Computing 4, 719–736 (2008)
8. Zhang, D., Adipat, B., Mowafi, Y.: User-Centered Context-Aware Mobile Applications–The Next Generation of Personal Mobile Computing. Comm. Assoc. Inform. Syst. 24, 27–46 (2009)
9. Preuveneers, D., Victor, K., Vanrompay, Y., Rigole, P., Pinheiro, M.K., Berbers, Y.: Context-Aware Adaptation in an Ecology of Applications. In: Stojanovic, D. (ed.) Context-Aware Mobile and Ubiquitous Computing for Enhanced Usability: Adaptive Technologies and Applications, pp. 1–25. Information Science Reference, Hershey (2009)
10. Paganelli, F., Giuli, D.: An Ontology-Based Context Model for Home Health Monitoring and Alerting in Chronic Patient Care Networks. In: 21st International Conference on Advanced Information Networking and Applications Workshops, pp. 838–845. IEEE Computer Society, Ontario (2007)
11. Kara, N., Dragoi, O.A.: Reasoning with Contextual Data in Telehealth Applications. In: 3rd IEEE International Conference on Wireless and Mobile Computing, Networking and Communications, p. 69. IEEE Computer Society, White Plains (2007)
12. van Sinderen, M.J., van Halteren, A.T., Wegdam, M., Meeuwissen, H.B., Eertink, E.H.: Supporting context-aware mobile applications: an infrastructure approach. IEEE Commun. Mag. 44, 96–104 (2006)
13. Mohomed, I., Misra, A., Ebling, M., Jerome, W.: Context-aware and personalized event filtering for low-overhead continuous remote health monitoring. In: 9th IEEE International Symposium on a World of Wireless, Mobile and Multimedia Networks, pp. 1–8. IEEE Computer Society, Newport Beach (2008)
14. Meneses, F., Moreira, A.: Technology Enablers for Context-Aware Healthcare Applications. In: Olla, P., Tan, J. (eds.) Mobile Health Solutions for Biomedical Applications, pp. 260–269. Information Science Reference, Hershey (2009)
15. Mohomed, I., Misra, A., Ebling, M., Jerome, W.: HARMONI: Context-aware Filtering of Sensor Data for Continuous Remote Health Monitoring. In: 6th Annual IEEE International Conference on Pervasive Computing and Communications, pp. 248–251. IEEE Computer Society, Hong Kong (2008)
16. Ashford, R., Moore, P., Hu, B., Jackson, M., Wan, J.: Translational Research and Context in Health Monitoring Systems. In: 4th International Conference on Complex, Intelligent and Software Intensive Systems, pp. 81–86. IEEE Computer Society, Kraków (2010)

17. Liu, C., Zhu, Q., Holroyd, K.A., Seng, E.K.: Status and trends of mobile-health applications for iOS devices: A developer's perspective. J. Syst. Software 84, 2022–2033 (2011)
18. Loke, S.W.: Context-aware artifacts: two development approaches. IEEE Pervasive Computing 5, 48–53 (2006)
19. Bricon-Souf, N., Newman, C.R.: Context awareness in health care: A review. Int. J. Med. Informat. 76, 2–12 (2006)
20. Mouttham, A., Peyton, L., Eze, B., Saddik, A.E.: Event-Driven Data Integration for Personal Health Monitoring. J. Emerg. Tech. Web. Intell. 1, 110–118 (2009)
21. Delicato, F.C., Santos, I.L.A., Pires, P.F., Oliveira, A.L.S., Batista, T., Pirmez, L.: Using aspects and dynamic composition to provide context-aware adaptation for mobile applications. In: ACM Symposium on Applied Computing, pp. 456–460. ACM, Honolulu (2009)
22. Bettini, C., Brdiczka, O., Henricksen, K., Indulska, J., Nicklas, D., Ranganathan, A., Riboni, D.: A survey of context modelling and reasoning techniques. Pervasive and Mobile Computing 6, 161–180 (2010)
23. Villarreal, V., Urzaiz, G., Hervas, R., Bravo, J.: Monitoring Architecture to collect measurement data and medical patient control through mobile devices. In: 5th International Symposium on Ubiquitous Computing and Ambient Intelligence, Riviera Maya, Mexico (2011)
24. Ren, Y., Pazzi, R.W.N., Boukerche, A.: Monitoring patients via a secure and mobile healthcare system. IEEE Wireless Comm. Mag. 17, 59–65 (2010)
25. Koutkias, V.G., Chouvarda, I., Triantafyllidis, A., Malousi, A., Giaglis, G.D., Maglaveras, N.: A Personalized Framework for Medication Treatment Management in Chronic Care. IEEE Trans. Inform. Tech. Biomed. 14, 464–472 (2010)
26. Sneha, S., Varshney, U.: Enabling ubiquitous patient monitoring: Model, decision protocols, opportunities and challenges. Decis. Support Syst. 46, 606–619 (2009)
27. Copetti, A., Loques, O., Leite, J.C.B., Barbosa, T.P.C., da Nobrega, A.C.L.: Intelligent context-aware monitoring of hypertensive patients. In: 3rd International Conference on Pervasive Computing Technologies for Healthcare, pp. 1–6. IEEE Computer Society, London (2009)
28. Roy, N., Pallapa, G., Das, S.K.: An ontology-driven ambiguous contexts mediation framework for smart healthcare applications. In: 1st International Conference on Pervasive Technologies Related to Assistive Environments, pp. 1–8. ACM, Athens (2008)
29. Paganelli, F., Giuli, D.: An Ontology-Based System for Context-Aware and Configurable Services to Support Home-Based Continuous Care. IEEE Trans. Inform. Tech. Biomed. 15, 324–333 (2011)
30. Brocke, J.V., Simons, A., Niehaves, B., Riemer, K., Plattfaut, R., Cleven, A.: Reconstructing the giant: on the importance of rigour in documenting the literature search process. In: 17th European Conference on Information Systems, Verona, Italy, pp. 2206–2217 (2009)
31. Zhang, D., Yu, Z., Chin, C.: Context-Aware Infrastructure for Personalized Healthcare. In: Nugent, C.D., McCullagh, P.J., McAdams, E.T., Lymberis, A. (eds.) Personalised Health Management Systems: The Integration of Innovative Sensing, Textile, Information and Communication Technologies, vol. 117, pp. 154–163. IOS Press, Washington (2005)
32. Ko, E.J., Lee, H.J., Lee, J.W.: Ontology-Based Context Modeling and Reasoning for U-HealthCare. IEICE Trans. Info. Syst. E90-D, 1262–1270 (2007)
33. Roy, N., Gu, T., Das, S.K.: Supporting pervasive computing applications with active context fusion and semantic context delivery. Pervasive and Mobile Computing 6, 21–42 (2010)

34. LeBlond, R.F., DeGowin, R.L., Brown, D.D.: DeGowin's diagnostic examination. McGraw-Hill Medical, New York (2009)
35. Smith, S.F., Duell, D.: Clinical nursing skills: nursing process model, basic to advanced skills. Appleton & Lange, Englwood (1992)
36. Gardner, R.M., Shabot, M.M.: Patient-Monitoring Systems. In: Shortliffe, E.H., Cimino, J.J. (eds.) Biomedical Informatics: Computer Applications in Health Care and Biomedicine, pp. 585–625. Springer, New York (2006)
37. World Health Organization (WHO): Global health risks: mortality and burden of disease attributable to selected major risks. World Health Organization, Geneva, Switzerland (2009)
38. Assess Your High Blood Pressure Related Risks, http://www.heart.org/heartorg/conditions/highbloodpressure/whybloodpressurematters/assess-your-high-blood-pressure-related-risks_ucm_301829_article.jsp#.tv7r63pssyk
39. Ellestad, M.H.: Stress Testing: Principles and Practice. Oxford University Press, New York (2003)
40. Paganelli, F., Spinicci, E., Giuli, D.: ERMHAN: A Context-Aware Service Platform to Support Continuous Care Networks for Home-Based Assistance. Int. J. Telemed Appl. 2008, 13 (2008)
41. Haghighi, P.D., Gillick, B., Krishnaswamy, S., Gaber, M.M., Zaslavsky, A.: Mobile Visualization for Sensory Data Stream Mining. In: Second International Workshop on Knowledge Discovery from Sensor Data, Las Vegas, NV (2008)
42. Bloom, R.L.: A Case-Based Approach to Teaching Evidence-Based Practice and Motor Speech Disorders. Contemporary Issues in Communication Science Disorders 37, 123–130 (2010)
43. Villarreal, V., Laguna, J., López, S., Fontecha, J., Fuentes, C., Hervás, R., de Ipiña, D.L., Bravo, J.: A Proposal for Mobile Diabetes Self-control: Towards a Patient Monitoring Framework. In: Omatu, S., Rocha, M.P., Bravo, J., Fernández, F., Corchado, E., Bustillo, A., Corchado, J.M. (eds.) IWANN 2009, Part I. LNCS, vol. 5518, pp. 870–877. Springer, Heidelberg (2009)
44. Kang, S., Lee, J., Jang, H., Lee, Y., Park, S., Song, J.: A Scalable and Energy-Efficient Context Monitoring Framework for Mobile Personal Sensor Networks. IEEE Trans. Mobile Comput. 9, 686–702 (2010)
45. Lewandowski, J., Arochena, H.E., Naguib, R.N.G., Chao, K.: A Portable Framework Design to Support User Context Aware Augmented Reality Applications. In: 3rd International Conference on Games and Virtual Worlds for Serious Applications, pp. 144–147. IEEE Computer Society, Athens (2011)
46. Mitchell, M.J., Meyers, C., Wang, A.A., Tyson, G.: ContextProvider: Context awareness for medical monitoring applications. In: 33rd Annual International Conference of the IEEE Engineering in Medicine and Biology Society, pp. 5244–5247. IEEE Engineering in Medicine and Biology, Boston (2011)
47. Aziz, O., Lo, B., Darzi, A., Yang, G.: Introduction to Body sensor networks. In: Yang, G. (ed.) Body Sensor Networks, pp. 1–39. Springer, New York (2006)
48. Russell, S., Norvig, P.: Artificial Intelligence: A Modern Approach. Prentice Hall, Upper Saddle River (2010)
49. Özsu, M.T., Valduriez, P.: Principles of Distributed Database Systems. Springer, New York (2011)

An Energy-Efficient Ring Search Routing Protocol Using Energy Parameters in Path Selection

Trung Dung Nguyen[1], Van Duc Nguyen[1], Thanh Tung Nguyen[2], Van Tien Pham[1],
Trong Hieu Pham[1], and Wakasugi Koichiro[3]

[1] Faculty of Electronic and Telecommunication
Ha Noi University of Technology, Ha Noi, Viet Nam
{dungnt,ducnv-fet,tienpv-fet}@mail.hut.edu.vn,
hieucot1289@gmail.com
[2] Faculty of Information Technology
Nguyen Tat Thanh University, Ho Chi Minh City, Viet Nam
nttung@ntt.edu.vn
[3] Kyoto Institute of Technology, Japan
Wakasugi@ac.jp

Abstract. Routing protocol is very important in Ad hoc network. From the EERS [3] protocol, we have improved AODV protocol to consume energy more efficiently. However, this method depends only on hop count number, but not energy. This leads to central nodes' exhaustion of energy and influences the entire network lifetime. In this paper, we propose two new protocols from EERS, called Avoid Bad Route (ABR) and Routing Dual Criterion (RDC). In both protocols, we base on energy criteria. Therefore, the lifetime as well as the throughput of the whole network are improved.

Keywords: Ad hoc, Sensor, Routing, AODV, ERS, EERS, RDC, ABR.

1 Introduction

Mobile Ad hoc Networks (MANETs) have become popular in the last couple of years. Routing protocols have been proposed for MANETs. Surprisingly, only a few studies have been made on routing protocols that consider energy consumption. Energy consumption is a major issue when the number of connections between nodes on MANETs increases. Nodes on MANETs and sensor networks are often equipped with small energy sources. The developments of applications on MANETs need to address the energy consumption issues.

There are not many works in the literature addressing the energy consumption in MANETs. In [1] authors proposed a cross layer solution in which route request (RREQ) messages are broadcast at the minimum power required to maintain network connectivity. The proposal leads to longer end-to-end paths but less distance per hop. Doshi et al [2] proposed an on-demand minimum energy routing protocol for ad hoc networks in which they modified the dynamic source routing (DSR) protocol to be an energy based routing protocol. In this protocol, a source node learns many possible

P.C. Vinh et al. (Eds.): ICCASA 2012, LNICST 109, pp. 72–85, 2013.
© Institute for Computer Sciences, Social Informatics and Telecommunications Engineering 2013

routes and selects the minimum energy route. The energy cost used is the energy required for transmission of a data-packet over the link.

There are drawbacks with [1] and [2]. First, they assume that the amplifier has the power transmission control capability that depends on the distance to the receiver. In practice, many amplifiers have a fixed power transmission and the hardware for adjusting the power transmission based on distance is very complicated. Also, unequal power transmissions result in unidirectional links which disconnect the network since the route discovery process cannot operate properly. Furthermore, the transmission power levels presented in [2] are small (from I mW to I00mW) compared with the power consumption in electronic circuits and amplifiers. Therefore, the transmission powers cannot become link cost metrics to make routing decisions since we need to consider the total power consumption of these devices.

In this paper, we will modify and add energy information to control packets. This modification will change the routing paths on the network. The purpose is to balance the energy consumption across nodes and to maximize the network life time.

The article is divided into 6 parts. Part I introduces Ad hoc network and proposed algorithm. The second discusses EERS algorithm in general. The third presents the proposed algorithm ABR. Part 4 presents the proposed algorithm RDC. After that, simulation results are presented. Finally, conclusion and future works are discussed.

2   Overview of AODV, ERS and EERS Algorithms

In our previous research, AODV-EERS (Efficient Expanding Ring Search) was presented to improve the shortcomings of AODV and ERS. Besides, the other parameters like hop count, throughput are also optimized more compared to ERS [3],[7],[8].

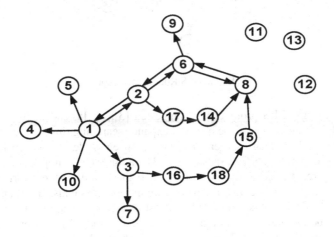

Fig. 1. AODV Routing protocol

Because in our proposal, AODV is a basic protocol that maintains connections on a network, it is helpful to summarize the AODV protocol. AODV is a reactive protocol. In reactive protocols, a route is created at the request of a source node when the node needs a route to a particular destination. In the AODV protocol, a source initiates a route discovery by flooding a Route Request (RREQ) packet when it needs to transmit data to a destination. Every node receiving the RREQ stores the route to the Originator of the RREQ before it forwards the RREQ to other nodes. The destination node or an intermediate node with recent information about the path replies by unicasting a Route Reply (RREP) along the reverse path to the Originator. As the RREP travels back to the Originator, any node receiving the RREP will add or update its route to the destination generating the RREP.

In Figure 1, when Node 1 wants to find path to Node 8, it will broadcast control message to all over the network. In this example, Node 8 replies with information about the path. As can be seen from the figure, Node 15 also participate in the selection process, thus a large amount of energy is consumed.

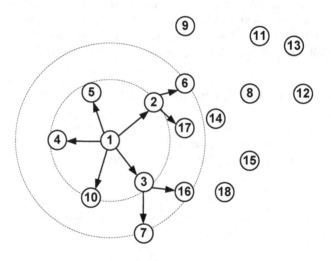

Fig. 2. ERS Routing protocol

To save energy, ERS protocol was suggested [3],[8]. Instead of broadcasting the message all over the network, the protocol expands searching ring with gradually until a path is selected. As can be seen in Figure 2, when Node 1 wants to find path to Node 8, it broadcasts the first message at the radius of one hop. At this time, the message only reaches Node 2, 3, 4, 5 and 10. If these nodes have information about Node 8, they will response, and the path searching process ends. If not any node has information, Node 1 will continue to broadcast the second message at the radius of 2 hops. This time the message will reach node 2, 3, 4, 5 and 10 which process and then forward it to nearby nodes, which are Node 6,7,16 and 17. These nodes receive and process the message. If they have information, they will reply to Node 1, and the process finishes. If not, Node 1 continues to increase the radius more. In the worst case, after several times of expanding ring without finding any path, ERS will come back to work as AODV, which is broadcasting message to the whole network. However, in general, previous researches show that energy is consumed more efficiently in most of the cases.

As can be seen in ERS algorithm, it is unnecessary for Nodes 4,5,7,9,10,11,12 and 13 to forward the message in expanding ring. Therefore, in the previous research [3], we proposed EERS protocol to set up an idle state, not forward message, of these nodes in the next expanding ring in order to save network's energy.

In EERS protocol, we assign one more variable to define whether a node state is forwarding or idle. In idle state, the node will not participate in routing in the following expanded rings any more. This can be explained as the following:

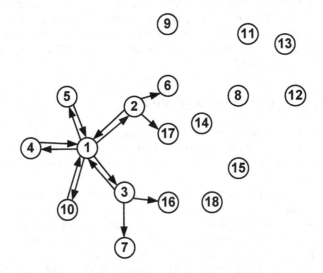

Fig. 3. EERS – operation 1

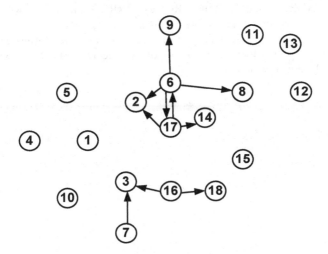

Fig. 4. EERS – operation 2

Initially, all nodes are forwarding. Node 1 broadcasts control searching message to Node 8. Node 1 sends this message to surrounding nodes, which are Node 2,3,4,5 and 10. After that, these nodes will forward it to their nearby nodes: Node 1, 6, 7, 16 and 17. This is shown in   Figure 3. In nature, forwarded message is in broadcast form so node 1 will receive response message from its nearby nodes. This is shown in Figure 3. For Nodes 2, 3, after forwarding message, their nearly nodes forward message and then receive their own message. Consequently, it remains in forwarding state. This is shown in Figure 4. The case is different for Node 4, 5 and 10. After forwarding message, without any node behind, they cannot receive any reply that is forwarded reversely. Thus, their state is in idle. They do not participate in the next expanding ring process. Repeatedly, after several times of expanding rings, Nodes 4, 5, 10, 7, 9, 11, 12, 13 will be in idle state because not any nearby nodes are behind. They are not involved in searching process any more. As the results, this process saves quite a large amount of energy in searching path. The details of EERS algorithm has already been specified in the paper [3].

3   Avoid Bad Route (ABR) Protocol

In Ad hoc network, node's energy will decrease over time due to sending and receiving message. The energy loss depends on the amount of data in the network. Obviously, nodes used more often will lose more energy than others. These nodes are often center nodes.

The remaining energy in each node at the same time is different. This makes nodes which have low energy will be run out of energy soon and decrease the network's life time. A load balancing process based on energy will reduce the work load on low energy node and increase network's life time. To implement this we add energy parameters in EERS's routing process.

We propose Avoid Bad Route (ABR) routing protocol which is an expansion of EERS routing protocol. It uses hop count and energy parameters in the route selection process. In ABR protocol, Route Request (RREQ) message will be added rq_min_energy field and Route Reply message will be added rp_energy field. The rq_min_energy field will store energy of the node which has the lowest energy on the path. The rp_energy field will store energy of the selected route and it will be added to routing table at source node.

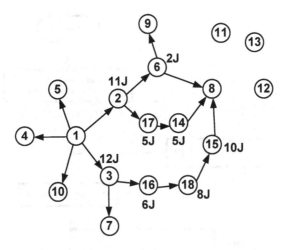

Fig. 5. ABR example

For example in Figure 5, we need to find route from Node 1 to Node 8. In the Figure, when Node 1 sends RREQ, Node 8 will receive three RREQ messages from three different routes that have different hop count number. In the old protocol, node 8 will reply three RREP messages and node 1 will choose the route which has the lowest hop count number. In this case, the chosen route will be 1-2-6-8. But in this route, Node 6 has lower energy. It has energy value of 2J. If this route is chosen, after few times, Node 6 will lose all energy and it will affect to network's life time, throughput and network stability. In ABR, we add energy threshold at Node 8 to ensure the chosen route will meet the energy standard and the node which has lower energy will be avoided. In this example, if we choose energy threshold is 3J, we have two routes that satisfy the energy condition: 1-2-17-14-8 and 1-3-16-18-15-8. In the two routes, we will choose the route which has lower hop count number. And the result is 1-2-17-14-8. If there are not any routes that satisfy the energy threshold, the energy threshold level will decrease. In Figure 5, if we set threshold at Node 8 equal 10J, the above three routes will not satisfy the energy condition. Route 1-2-6-8 has min energy value of 2J. Route 1-2-17-14-8 has min energy value of 5J. Route 1-3-16-18-15-8 has min energy value 6J. All of routes' min energy value is less than 10J. So energy threshold will decrease and its value is the different of max (2J, 5J, 6J) and 3J (3J is the estimated energy based on idle, sending and receiving energy of node in time between source that sends RREQ). So the new energy threshold is 3J. After Node 1 does not receive RREP message from Node 8 for sometimes, it sends RREQ message again. Node 8 receives the second RREQ message. At that time, the energy threshold of node 8 is 3J, so route 1-2-17-14-8 will be chosen because it has higher energy value than the energy threshold and the lowest hop count number. The detail algorithm will be described below:

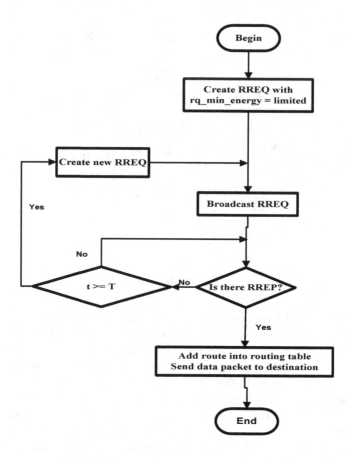

Fig. 6. Source node operation algorithm

Figure 6 describes the operation of source nodes. When a source node wants to find route to the destination, it will send Route Request message (RREQ) with *rq_min_energy* field added. Initially, this field is infinite. Next, the RREQ message is sent to all source's neighbors. The source node starts timer value T (time out value). If the real time reaches to T value and the source node still does not receive any RREP messages, it will resend RREQ message. This process repeats until it finds out the route to the destination.

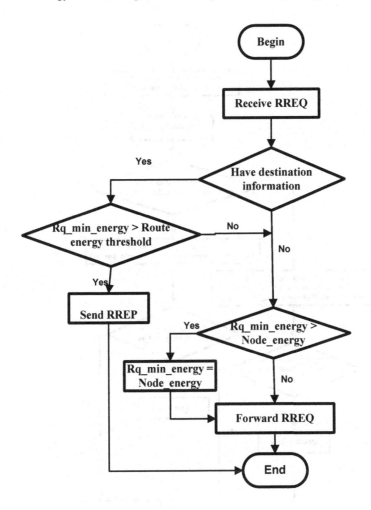

Fig. 7. Intermediate node operation algorithm

Figure 7 describes the operation of intermediate nodes. When a intermediate node receives RREQ message, it will check its routing table to find out information of the destination. If it has the information of the destination, it will compare *rq_min_energy* value in RREQ message with its energy value. If the *rq_min_energy* value is lower than its energy value, it will forward RREQ message to the next node. Otherwise, it will assign *rq_min_energy* value with its energy value. If this intermediate node has the information of the destination and *rq_min_energy* value is higher than route's threshold value from routing table, the intermediate node sends RREP message to the source node. The routing process finishes. And if the intermediate node has information of the destination node but does not satisfy the energy condition, it will be considered as no information about the destination.

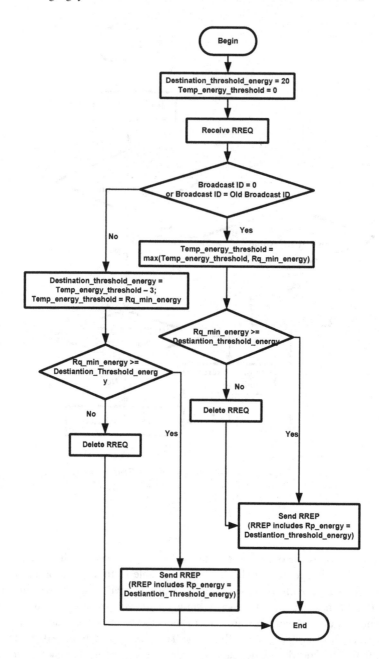

Fig. 8. Destination node operation algorithm

Figure 8 describes the operation of destination node. The destination node has the energy threshold value to determine which route will satisfy. This value is in *destination_threshold_energy* variance. In this example, it is set to 20J. This value depends on network topology and the energy of each node. The higher value is set, the more delay network is. We also add a variable *temp_energy_threshold*, and it starts with 0. This variable is used to store the highest *rq_min_energy* value from received RREQ messages in route finding process. In Figure 8, when the destination node receives RREQ message, it will check if this is the first time it receives the RREQ message by using broadcast ID value in the message. If this is the first time, the node will compare *rq_min_energy* field value in RREQ message with *temp_energy_threshold* value. If the *rq_min_energy* value is higher than the *temp_energy_threshold* value, the *temp_energy_threshold* value will be set to the *rq_min_energy* value. After that, the destination node will compare the *rq_min_energy* value and the *destination_threshold_energy* value. If the *rq_min_energy* value is higher than *destination_threshold_energy value*, the route satisfies the energy condition, the destination node will send RREP message to the source node. If the route does not satisfy the energy condition, it will drop the RREQ message and wait for the next RREQ messages.

In the above process, the selected route has enough energy to operate in long time. So the network's life time will be increased, and the connection lost problem will be minimized.

4   Routing Dual Criterion (RDC) Protocol

Routing dual criterion protocol is another improvement from EERS. This routing protocol is created simply by adding energy parameter in selecting route process. The route selection process using RREQ and RREP is similar to the standard EERS protocol [4],[9],[10],[11]. There are only a few small changes made in RDC.

In the RREQ message and the RREP message, we add *min_energy* field to discover energy value of nodes that these messages go through. In the old protocol, the source node will choose the route which has the lowest hop count number, so it has the energy problems described in the previous sections. In RDC, we select route based on *min_energy* parameter. The route has the lowest ratio between the hop count and the *min_energy* value will be chosen. As a result, the route with low energy is not often chosen, so the energy in network is balances. The simulation results of this algorithm will be described in the next section.

5   Simulation and Results

We use NS2 to develop our simulation because it is a popular tool. Many simulation models have been developed in NS2 and tested by many users. The AODV model used has been published on the NS2 community website and has been verified by many users. In our simulation, network lifetime, packet delivery ratio and throughput of new routing protocols RDC and ABR are compared with the original routing protocol EERS.

In the first simulation, we create five topologies with 50 nodes in an area of 500m x 500 m. The detail parameters are described as below:

Simulation time : 200 second
Transmit power : 0.2818 w
Initial energy : randomly from 80 to 120 joules
Idle power consumption : 1 w
Transmission power : 3w
Receive power : 1 w
Packet size : 512 bytes
Packet rate : 4 packets per second

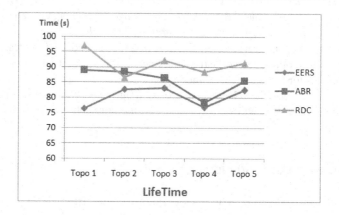

Fig. 9. Network lifetime

Let us define lifetime as the amount of time the network operate until the first node run out of energy. Figure 9 shows the lifetime of the network when using EERS, ABR and RDC routing protocols. The figure shows that the life time when using the ABR and RDC is higher than that when using EERS. In some topologies, it is 27% increase for RDC and 16.5% increase for ABR.

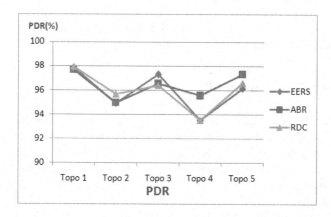

Fig. 10. Packet Delivery Ratio

Let us define the Packet Delivery Ratio (PDR) be the ratio between total messages received at the destination and the total messages sent at the source. Figure 10 shows the packet delivery ratio of network when using EERS, ABR and RDC. The diagram shows that the PDR is not much different between the three algorithms.

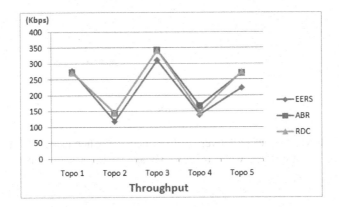

Fig. 11. Throughput

Let us define the Throughput be the total data transmission in a second. It likes bandwidth link. Figure 11 shows the throughput of network when using EERS, ABR and RDC. From this diagram we see that throughput in ABR and RDC is almost higher than in EERS. In some case throughput has increased up to 28.7% and 22.7% for ABR and RDC respectively.

In the second simulation, we create three topologies with 50 nodes, 75 nodes and 100 nodes in an area of 500m x 500m and different number of connections. The specific parameters are the same in the first simulation.

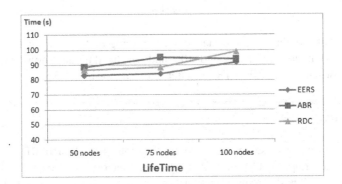

Fig. 12. Lifetime

Figure 12 shows the lifetime of network when using EERS, ABR and RC with different number of node in network. The diagram shows that the life time in ABR and RDC is still higher than in EERS.

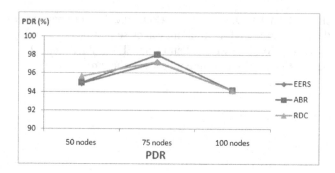

Fig. 13.

Figure 13 shows the packet delivery ratio of network when using EERS, ABR and RDC. We see that the PDR when using ABR and RDC is better than when using EERS for three topologies.

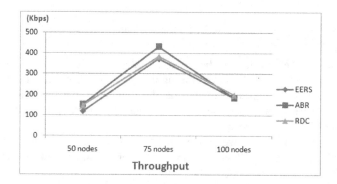

Fig. 14.

Figure 14 shows throughput of network when using EERS, RDC and ABR in three topologies 50 nodes, 75 nodes and 100 nodes. The diagram shows that network throughput when using ABR, RDC is better than when using EERS.

6   Conclusion

In this paper we propose two new routing protocols ABR and RDC. These two algorithms are improved from EERS by using energy parameter in the routing process. It modifies the route selection process selected and improves the network lifetime by avoiding the route with low remaining energy. The energy balance will prolong the lifetime of network and improve the quality of connections.

The result of simulation shows that network lifetime and throughput when using ABR, RDC is better than when using EERS. PDR is almost the same in all three routing protocols.

References

1. Bhuvaneshwar, V., Krunz, M., Muqattash, A.: CONSET: a cross-layer power aware protocol for mobile ad hoc networks. In: 2004 IEEE International Conference on Commnunications, vol. 7, pp. 4067–4071 (2004)
2. Doshi, S., Bhandare, S., Brown, T.X.: An on-demand minimum energy routing protocol for a wireless ad hoc network. ACM SIGMOBILE Mobile Computing and Communications 6, 50–66 (2002)
3. Pham, D.N., Van Nguyen, D., Van Pham, T., Nguyen, N.T., Do, X.B., Nguyen, T.D., Kuperschmidt, C., Kaiser, T.: An Expending Ring Search AlgorithmFor Mobile Adhoc Networks. In: 2010 ATC International Conference, pp. 39–44 (2010)
4. Tung, N.T., Egan, G.K., Lloyd-Smith, B., Pentland, B.: Energy based routing techniques in Mobile Ad hoc and Sensor Networks. In: 2005 13th IEEE International Conference on Communications, vol. 2 (2005)
5. Jung, S., Hundewale, N., Zelikovsky, A.: Energy Efficiency of Load Balancing in MANET Routing Protocols. In: Sixth International Conference 2005 and First ACIS International Workshop on Self-Assembling Wireless Networks, SNPD/SAWN 2005, pp. 476–483 (2005)
6. Mirza, D., Schurgers, C., Owrang, M.: Energy-efficient Wakeup Scheduling for Maximizing Lifetime of Networks, IEEE 802.15.4. In: Kang, I., Poovendran, R. (eds.) IEEE International Conference on Maximizing Static Network Lifetime of Wireless Broadcast Adhoc Networks, Communications, ICC 2003, vol. 3, pp. 2256–2261 (2003)
7. Perkins, C., Belding-Royer, E., Das, S.: Ad hoc On-Demand Distance Vector (AODV) Routing. RFC 3561 (Ex-perimental) (July 2003)
8. Song, J.-H.: Efficient On-Demand Routing for Mobile Ad Hoc Wireless Access Networks. IEEE Journal 22, 1374–1383 (2004)
9. Tung, N.T., Vinh, P.C.: The Energy-Aware Operational Time of Wireless Ad-hoc Sensor Networks. ACM/Springer Mobile Networks and Applications (MONET) Journal 17 (August 2012), doi:10.1007/s11036-012-0403-1
10. Tung, N.T.: The power-save protocol of wireless ad-hoc sensor networks. Mediterranean Journal of Computers and Networks 4 (October 2012) ISSN: 1744-2397
11. Tung, N.T.: Heuristic Energy-Efficient Routing Solutions to Extend the Lifetime of Wireless Ad-Hoc Sensor Networks. In: Pan, J.-S., Chen, S.-M., Nguyen, N.T. (eds.) ACIIDS 2012, Part II. LNCS, vol. 7197, pp. 487–497. Springer, Heidelberg (2012)

A Formal Approach to Modelling and Verifying Resource-Bounded Context-Aware Agents

Abdur Rakib[1] and Rokan Uddin Faruqui[2]

[1] School of Computer Science
University of Nottingham, Malaysia Campus
Abdur.Rakib@nottingham.edu.my
[2] Department of Computer Science and Engineering
University of Chittagong, Bangladesh
rufaruqui@cu.ac.bd

Abstract. There has been a move of context-aware systems into safety-critical domains including healthcare, emergency scenarios, and disaster recovery. These systems are often distributed and deployed on resource-bounded devices. Therefore, developing formal techniques for modelling and designing context-aware systems, verifying requirements and ensuring functional correctness are major challenges. We present a framework for the formal representation and verification of resource-bounded context-aware systems. We give ontological representation of contexts, translate ontologies to a set of Horn clause rules, based on these rules we build multi-agent context-aware systems and encode them into Maude specification, we then verify interesting properties of such systems using the Maude LTL model checker.

Keywords: Pervasive computing, Context-awareness, Multi-agent systems, Ontology, Model checking.

1 Introduction

It is widely acknowledged that computer systems are becoming increasingly nomadic and pervasive. The vision of this next generation technology intends to provide invisible computing environments so that a user can utilize services at any time and everywhere [1]. In these systems information can be collected by using tiny resource-bounded devices, such as, e.g., PDAs, smart phones, and wireless sensor nodes. In recent years much research in pervasive computing has been focused on incorporation of context-awareness features into pervasive applications. There is an extensive body of work in adapting the Semantic Web technologies to model context-aware systems (see e.g.,[2,3,4,5]). In the pursuit of making context-aware system much more useful we need to make its various devises communicate with each other and with the surrounding environment in a cooperative manner. In achieving this goal, agent-based techniques can be seen as a promising approach for developing context-aware applications in complex domains. The concept of agents, in the setting of this paper is used to refer to autonomous reasoning agents, where agents are capable of reasoning about their behaviour (using a knowledge base and inference rules) and interactions (capable of communicating with each other). In agent-based techniques agents (devices or

P.C. Vinh et al. (Eds.): ICCASA 2012, LNICST 109, pp. 86–96, 2013.

environment) are allowed to make intelligent decisions and perform appropriate actions. E.g., communication between battery-powered sensor nodes consumes most of the available power. In order to increase the life time of sensor nodes, the amount of information broadcast to other sensor nodes should be minimised. Each sensor node (assuming modelled as an agent) should make local decisions in order to determine what information should be communicated, and to whom. E.g., instead of broadcasting all the *WindSpeed* readings, a sensor node may only send the average or the maximum or minimum of *WindSpeed* readings taken over a specified amount of time.

The main emphasis of the existing research on context-aware computing including those presented in [2,3,4,5] is how can ontologies be utilised for context-modelling, knowledge sharing and reasoning about context for pervasive computing systems. However, that is not sufficient to make context-aware systems a key feature technology that has been moving into safety-critical domains including healthcare, emergency scenarios, and disaster recovery. Moreover, in real-world context-aware agents are often resource-bounded. In this trend, to develop smarter and reliable application of context-aware systems, we need a rigorous study not only on formal representation of such systems but also their formal specification and verification. In this paper, we consider these two problems jointly. In addition to the formal representation of context-aware systems, we consider distributed problem-solving in systems of communicating context-aware rule-based agents, and ask how much time (measured as the number of rule firings) and how many message exchanges it takes the system to derive a goal. We use the Maude LTL model checker [6] to verify interesting properties of such systems.

The remainder of the paper is organized as follows. In section 2, we discuss how contexts are represented using OWL 2 RL and SWRL, and ontological context reasoning to infer higher level contexts. In section 3, we describe our model of communicating multi-agent context-aware systems. In section 4, we briefly describe specification of the multi-agent context-aware systems into Maude, and to illustrate the application of the framework in section 5 we present an example system and experimental results. We discuss related work in section 6 and conclude in section 7.

2   Ontology-Based Context Representation

In context-aware computing, the definition of context has been at the centre of different research efforts, however, a universally consented definition of context has been difficult to realise. We view context is any information that can be used to identify the status of an entity. An entity can be a person, a place, a physical or a computing object. This context is relevant to a user and application, and reflects the relationship among themselves [7].

A context can be formally defined as a *(subject,predicate,object)* triple that states a fact about the subject where — the subject is an entity in the environment, the object is a value or another entity, and the predicate is a relationship between the subject and object. E.g., we can represent a context "a disaster event has site Southern Florida" as *(DisasterEvent,hasSite,SouthernFlorida)*.

Context modelling is a well studied topic in pervasive computing and it is a process of identifying "a concrete subset of the context that is realistically attainable from sensors, applications and users and able to be exploited in the execution of the task. The context

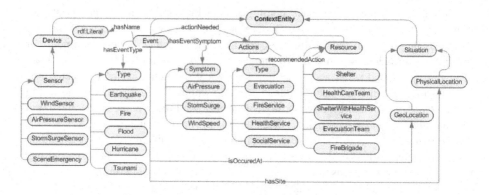

Fig. 1. A fragment of the disaster management ontology

model that is employed by a given context-aware application is usually explicitly specified by the application developer, but may evolve over time" [8]. In the literature various
context modelling approaches have been proposed, however, ontology-based approach
has been advocated as being the most promising one [9].

An ontology is a model of a domain that introduces vocabulary relevant to the domain and uses this vocabulary to specify the relationships among them [10]. That is, an
ontology can be used to represent knowledge of a domain which gives a clear and co-
herent view of that domain. This facilitates the development of formal context models
to share and reuse knowledge among the computational entities, such as, e.g., software
agents, and provides a foundation for interoperability among the agents in a multi-agent
system. Furthermore, ontology-based context modelling approach allows reasoning to
infer implicit knowledge from ontologies and to generate high-level implicit contexts
from the low-level explicit contexts.

The common trend in ontology-based
context modelling is to apply the hierarchical approach comprising of upper and
domain ontologies. The upper ontology
defines the high-level concepts that are
common among different context-aware
entities, and the domain ontology is an
extension of upper ontology, defining the
details of general concepts and their properties for a particular domain. For context
modelling we use OWL 2 RL, a profile
of the new standardization OWL 2, and
based on pD^* and the description logic
program (DLP) [11]. We choose OWL

Fig. 2. Individualised HurricaneEvent ontology

2 RL because it is more expressive than the RDFS and it is suitable for the design and development of rule-based systems. To illustrate our ontology-based modelling approach for context-aware systems, we use a disaster management scenario
adapted from [12]. Here we focus on the emergency response of the situation that

includes the activities designed to minimize loss of life and property. The upper on-tology contains the top-level concepts for a context-aware system proposed in [13]. We use *Device, Event, Actions, Resource*, and *Situation* as top-level concepts to rep-resent the context about devices (e.g., wind speed measurement sensor), events (e.g., hurricane event), rescue actions (e.g., evacuation), resources (e.g., health care team) and situation (e.g., physical location). The domain ontology can be an extension of the upper ontology for several disaster events such as earth quake, flood, tsunami, fire break, and hurricane. The domain ontology provides context about the event it-self, its causes, its symptoms (e.g., wind speed, air pressure, storm surge etc.), and resources (e.g., health care team, fire brigade etc.) available to respond. Fig. 1 de-picts a fragment of the disaster management ontology. An instance of the domain ontology can be, e.g., "disaster event" which is depicted in Fig 2. In this figure, we as-sert some low-level contexts for a disaster event namely, *hasSite(DisasterEvent, South-ernFlorida), hasStormSurge(DisasterEvent,15), hasWindSpeed(DisasterEvent,93), ha-sAirPressure(DisasterEvent,93)*, and *hasName(DisasterEvent,HurricaneEvent)*. It also includes some inferred contexts derived from context-reasoning using the DL reasoner Pellet. The context reasoner classifies the disaster event as a very strong hurricane by determining high-level contexts: wind speed level, air pressure level, and storm surge level. In addition to the Pellet, we use rule-base reasoning which is discussed in the next section onwards.

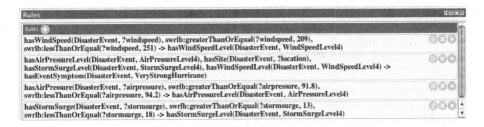

Fig. 3. Example SWRL rules

The combination of upper and domain ontologies described above, however only capture the static behaviour of a context-aware system. The context-aware systems modelled in our approach define their dynamic behaviour using Semantic Web Rule Language (SWRL). SWRL allows user to write rules using OWL concepts and its com-bination with OWL 2 RL provide more expressive language having greater deductive reasoning capabilities than OWL 2 RL alone. We can express more complex rule-based concepts using SWRL that cannot be modelled using OWL 2 RL, as shown in Fig. 3. Thus our approach of ontological representation of context-aware systems gives a clean ontology design based on the distinction between the static information represented us-ing OWL 2 RL and the dynamic aspects of the systems go into the SWRL rules. We build ontologies using Protégé version 4.1 [14].

3   Multi-agent Context-Aware Systems

Pervasive computing systems which include multiple interacting devices and human users can often be usefully modelled as multi-agent systems. Non-human agents in such a system may be running a very simple program, however they are increasingly designed to exhibit flexible, adaptable and intelligent behaviour. A common methodology for implementing the latter type of agents is implementing them as rule-based reasoners. We extract Horn clause rules from ontologies to design our rule-based agents. We developed a translator that takes as input an OWL 2 RL ontology in the OWL/XML format (output file of Protégé) and translates it to a set of plain text Horn clause rules. We use the OWL API to parse the ontology and extract the set of axioms and facts. In [11] a Description Logic Mapping (DLP) mapping is given to translate an OWL 1 ontology to a set of Horn clause rules. We extended the DLP mapping to accommodate new features of OWL 2 RL. The translation of SWRL rules is straightforward because they are already in the Horn clause rule format. The translation of OWL 2 RL + SWRL to Horn clause rules is automatic and is a part of TOVRBA[15].

We adopt the model of multi-agent systems presented in [16]. A multi-agent system consists of n_{Ag} (≥ 1) individual *agents* $\mathcal{A} = \{1, 2, \ldots, n_{Ag}\}$. Each agent $i \in \mathcal{A}$ has a program, consisting of Horn clause rules of the form $C_1 \wedge C_2 \wedge \ldots \wedge C_n \rightarrow C$ (derived from OWL 2 RL and SWRL), and a working memory, which contains ground atomic contexts taken from ABox representing the initial state of the system. In our model, agents share a common ontology and communication mechanism. To model communication between agents, we assume that agents have two special communication primitives $Ask(i, j, C)$ and $Tell(i, j, C)$ in their language, where i and j are agents and C is an atomic context not containing an Ask or a $Tell$. $Ask(i, j, C)$ means 'i asks j whether the context C is the case' and $Tell(i, j, C)$ means 'i tells j that context C' ($i \neq j$). The positions in which the Ask and $Tell$ primitives may appear in a rule depends on which agent's program the rule belongs to. Agent i may have an Ask or a $Tell$ with arguments (i, j, C) in the consequent of a rule; e.g., $C_1 \wedge C_2 \wedge \ldots \wedge C_n \rightarrow Ask(i, j, C)$ whereas agent j may have an Ask or a $Tell$ with arguments (i, j, C) in the antecedent of the rule; e.g., $Tell(i, j, C) \rightarrow C$ is a well-formed rule (we call it trust rule) for agent j that causes it to believe i when i informs it that context C is the case. No other occurrences of Ask or $Tell$ are allowed. Note that OWL 2 is limited to unary and binary predicates and it is function-free. Therefore, in the Protégé editor all the arguments of Ask and $Tell$ are represented using constant symbols and these annotated symbols are translated appropriately when designing the target system using the Maude specification.

Firing a communication rule instance with the consequent $Ask(i, j, C)$ adds the context $Ask(i, j, C)$ both to the working memory of i and of j. Intuitively, i has a record that it asked j whether context C is the case, and j has a record of being asked by i whether context C is the case. Similarly, if the consequent of a communication rule instance is of the form $Tell(i, j, C)$, then the corresponding context $Tell(i, j, C)$ is added to the working memories of both the agents i and j. The agents in the system execute synchronously. We assume that each agent executes in a separate process and that agents communicate via message passing. We also assume that there is a bound on communication for each agent i which limits agent i to at most $m_i (\geq 0)$ messages. Each agent has a communication counter, msg_i, which starts at 0 and is not allowed to exceed the value m_i. We further assume that each agent can communicate with multiple agents in the system at the same time. At each step in the evolution of the system, each agent chooses from a set of possible actions: Rule firing a rule, Communication agents can exchange messages regarding their facts using Ask and $Tell$, and Idle which leaves its state unchanged. The actions selected by the agents are then performed in parallel and the system advances to the next state.

4   Specifying Systems in Maude

We use extended version of the TOVRBA tool [15] to translate OWL/XML rules produced by Protégé into plain text Horn clause rules of the form: $\langle n : C_1 \wedge C_2 \wedge \ldots \wedge C_n \rightarrow C \rangle$, where n is the user annotated priority of the rule. In this step the system designer identifies which agents (s)he needs to design using which rules. The designer also determines the number of agents (s)he needs to model and their possible interactions. An agent can interact with one or more agents in the system, but not necessarily every agent interacts with every other agent in the system. When the rules are classified for the agents, the multi-agent system can be implemented in Maude. The internal configuration of the rules in Maude specification has the following form: $\langle n : [t_1 : C_1] \wedge [t_2 : C_2] \wedge \ldots \wedge [t_n : C_n] \rightarrow [t : C] \rangle$, where the t_i's and t represent time stamps of contexts automatically inserted by TOVRBA. When a rule instance of the above rule is fired, the newly generated context C will be added to the working memory with time stamp $t = t' + 1$, i.e., t will be replaced by $t' + 1$, where t' is the current cycle time of the system. The associated time stamp reflects when a particular context has been generated. Initially all the working memory contexts have time stamp 0 and the system moves and generates new contexts at different time points.

A multi-agent rule-based system has three components: the knowledge base (KB) which contains rules, the working memory (WM) which contains facts, and the inference engine which reasons over rules when the application is executed. In our framework, the inference engine have some reasoning strategies often used in rule-based systems [17] including rule ordering, depth, breadth, simplicity, and complexity.

In Maude specification each agent in the system has a local configuration and the (parallel) composition of all these local configurations make the global configuration of the multi-agent system. To implement the local configuration of an agent (working memory, program, agenda, reasoning strategies, message counters, time stamps etc.) we declared a number of sorts, including Context, Term, WM, TimeC, TimeWM, Rule, and Agenda, and define their relationships, e.g., TimeC is a subsort of TimeWM, Rule is a subsort of Agenda and so on. In addition, we use a number of Maude library modules such as NAT, BOOL, and QID. The local configuration of an agent i is represented as a tuple [A | RL | TM | M | t | msg | syn], where the variables A and RL are of sort Agenda, TM is of sort TimeWM, M is of sort WM, and t, msg, syn are of sort Nat. The variables t, msg, and syn have been used to represent respectively the time step, message counter, and a flag for synchronisation.

In this paper we don't discuss complexity issues, however, the translation of the ontology-driven rules in Maude takes polynomial space. The rules of an agent i are defined using an operator which takes arguments as a set of contexts known as antecedents (of sort `TimeWM`) and a single context known as consequent (of sort `TimeC`) and it returns an element of sort `Rule`. Therefore, each rule of an agent i is an element of sort `Rule`. These rules are represented using Maude equations, one equation for each rule. As an example, the rule $\langle 1 : \ C1 \rightarrow C2 \rangle$ can be represented as follows:

```
ceq ruleIns(A,[t1:C1] TM, M ) = <1:[t1:C1]-> [0:C2]> ruleIns(<1:
[t1:C1]-> [0:C2] A, [t1:C1] TM, M ) if (not inAgenda(<1:[t1:C1]
->[0:C2]>, A) /\ (not inWM(C2, M)) .

eq ruleIns(A, TM , M) = void-rule [owise] .
```

The inference engine is implemented using a set of Maude rules: `Generate`, `Choice`, `Apply`, `Idle`, and `Communication`. The `Generate` rule causes each agent to generate its conflict set by calling recursively rule equations like defined above. Each equation may give rise to more than one rule instance depending on the elements in working memory. To prevent the regeneration of the same rule instance, the conditional equation checks whether the rule instance and its consequent are already present in the agenda and working memory. The `Choice` rule causes each agent to apply its reasoning strategy, the `Apply` rule causes each agent to execute the rule instances selected for execution, the `Idle` rule executes only when there are no rule instances to be executed (the application of the `Idle` rule advances the cycle time of the agent i, leaving everything else unchanged), and communication among agents is achieved using the `Communication` rule. When agents communicate with each other, one agent copies the communicated fact from another agent's working memory. Copying is only allowed if the fact to be copied is not already in the working memory of the agent intending to copy.

5   Verifying Time and Communication Costs

This section shows how a context-aware multi-agent system specified in Maude can be formally verified using the Maude LTL model checker. Model checking in Maude involves a Maude specification of a system (as described in the previous section) together with a property of interest. A property is a Linear Temporal Logic (LTL) formula interpreted as a property of computations of the system (linear sequences of states generated by application of rewrite rules).

We build a multi-agent rule-based system whose rules are derived from the ontology of the disaster event scenario mentioned in Section 2. The system consists of eleven agents, Fig. 4 depicts disaster management agents and their possible interactions. The sensor agents 1, 2, and 3 are able to infer high-level contexts from sensed low-level contexts using Horn clause

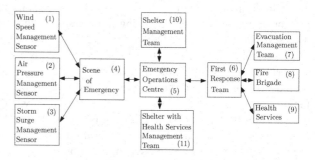

Fig. 4. Agents and their possible interactions

rules in their KB. They can classify wind, air, and storm into different levels based on wind speed, air pressure, and storm surge. E.g., agent 1's KB contains rules including the following:

⟨1   :   *hasWindSpeed(DisasterEvent,?windspeed)&   greaterThanOrEqual(?windspeed,209)&   lessThanOrEqual(?windspeed,251)   →hasWindSpeedLevel(DisasterEvent,WindSpeedLevel4)* ⟩;

and

⟨2 : *hasWindSpeedLevel(DisasterEvent,WindSpeedLevel4)→ Tell(1,4,hasWindSpeedLevel(DisasterEvent,WindSpeedLevel4))* ⟩.

The first rule classifies that the disaster event has *WindSpedLevel4* if wind speed is greater than or equal to 209km/h and less than or equal to 251km/h. That is agent 1 may infer high-level context *hasWindSpeedLevel(DisasterEvent, WindSpeedLevel4)* from the low-level contexts, e.g., *hasWindSpeed(DisasterEvent, 220), greaterThanOrEqual(220, 209)*, and *lessThanOrEqual(220, 251)*. In our model we classify five different levels of wind speed, air pressure, and storm surge based on NOAA/National Hurricane Center's information.[1] The second rule is a communication rule of agent 1 through which it interacts with agent 4 and sends context *hasWindSpeedLevel(DisasterEvent, WindSpeedLevel4)* when it believes that current wind speed has *WindSpeedLevel4*. Similar to the above, agent 1 has eight other rules for the other four different wind speed levels. In a similar fashion, agent 2 may infer context *hasAirPressureLevel(DisasterEvent, AirPressureLevel4)* if current air pressure is greater than or equal to 91.7kPa and less than or equal to 94.2kPa, and agent 3 may infer *hasStromSurgeLevel(DisasterEvent, StormSurgeLevel4)* if current storm surge is greater than or equal to 13ft and less than or equal to 18ft, and so on. Once these agents infer high level contexts they can interact with agent 4 and send those information. Agent 4's KB contains rules including:

⟨1 : *Tell(1,4,hasWindSpeedLevel(DisasterEvent,WindSpeedLevel4))→hasWindSpeedLevel(DisasterEvent, WindSpeedLevel4)*⟩;

⟨2 :*hasWindSpeedLevel(DisasterEvent,WindSpeedLevel4)& hasAirPressureLevel(DisasterEvent, AirPressureLevel4)& hasStormSurgeLevel(DisasterEvent,StormSurgeLevel4)& hasSite(Disaster Event,?location)→hasEventSymptom(DisasterEvent, VeryStrongHurricane)* ⟩; and

⟨3 :*hasEventSymptom(DisasterEvent,VeryStrongHurricane)& hasSite(DisasterEvent,?location) → Tell(4,5,hasOccurredAt(VeryStrongHurricane,?location))*⟩.

The first rule is a trust rule for agent 4 that causes it to believe agent 1 when agent 1 informs it that context *hasWindSpeedLevel(DisasterEvent, WindSpeedLevel4)*. Upon receiving context information from three different measurement sensor agents, using the second rule, agent 2 infers, e.g., the context *hasEventSymptom(DisasterEvent, VeryStrongHurricane)*. Using the third rule agent 4 interacts with agent 5 and informs that very strong hurricane took place at Southern Florida if it already believes context *hasSite(DisasterEvent, SouthernFlorida)* i.e., tells the context *hasOccurredAt(VeryStrongHurricane, SouthernFlorida)*. Due to space limitations, we are unable to represent example rules of other agents in the system. However, agent 5 then interacts with agent 6 and informs that an action is required against very strong hurricane that has taken place at Southern Florida. Depending on the hurricane category, agent 6 interacts with various services including agents 7, 8, and 9. Agent 7 then reply back to

---

[1] http://www.nhc.noaa.gov/aboutsshws.php
http://hypertextbook.com/facts/StephanieStern.shtml

agent 6 that immediately n number simple shelters and m number shelter with health services are needed. Agent 6 relays these information to agent 5. Agent 5 then enquires to agents 10 and 11 whether required number shelters are available, and receives shelter availability replies. Similarly, depending on the hurricane category agent 8 and agent 9 might take different actions including Land Fire Brigade, Air Tanker, Boat Ambulance and Air Ambulance Services. In order to model this scenario we have used 122 Horn clause rules distributed to the agents. E.g., the KB of each of the measurement sensor agents contains 10 rules, agent 4 is modelled using 25 rules, agent 5 is modelled using 16 rules, and so on. We verified a number of interesting resource-bounded properties of the system including the following:

$G(B_4\ hasSite(DisasterEvent, SouthernFlorida))$
$\wedge\ B_4\ Tell(1, 4, hasWindSpeedLevel(DisasterEvent, WindSpeedLevel4))$
$\wedge\ B_4\ Tell(2, 4, hasAirPressureLevel(DisasterEvent, airPressureLevel4))$
$\wedge\ B_4\ Tell(3, 4, hasStormSurgeLevel(DisasterEvent, stormSurgeLevel4))$
$\rightarrow X^n\ B_4\ Tell(4, 5, hasOccurredAt(VeryStrongHurricane, SouthernFlorida)))$

the above property specifies that whenever agents 1, 2, and 3 tell agent 4 that the wind speed, air pressure, and storm surge have reached fourth level at the disaster event site Southern Florida, within n time steps agent 4 informs agent 5 that very strong hurricane has occurred at Southern Florida (where B_i for each agent i is a syntactic doxastic operator used to specify agent i's 'beliefs' or the contents of its working memory, and X^n is the concatenation of n LTL next operators X) and

$G(B_5\ Tell(4, 5, hasOccurredAt(VeryStrongHurricane, SouthernFlorida))$
$\rightarrow X^n\ B_5\ Ask(5, 10, hasAvailableShelter(SouthernFlorida, 10000)) \wedge msg_5{}^{=m})$

which specifies that whenever agent 5 receives information from agent 4 that very strong hurricane has occurred at Southern Florida, within n time steps agent 5 asks agent 10 if shelter is available for 10000 homeless people at Southern Florida while exchanging m messages ($msg_5{}^{=m}$ states that the value of agent 5's communication counter is m).

The above properties are verified as true when the value of n is 5 in the first property, and the values of n and m are 18 and 5 in the second property; and the model checker uses 1 seconds for each property. However, the properties are verified as false and the model checker returns counterexamples when we assign a value to n which is less than 5 in the first property, and values to n and m which are less than 18 and 5 in the second property. This also demonstrates the correctness of the encoding in that the model checker does not return true for arbitrary values of n and m.

6   Related Work

We present a brief existing research on context-aware systems concentrating on the ontology-based approaches which have influenced the work presented in this paper. In [2], Wang et al. proposed OWL encoded context ontology (CONON) for modelling and reasoning in pervasive systems. In addition to the ontological reasoning they use a set of user-defined FOL rules to reason over data, i.e., LP reasoning combined with DL reasoning in separate tasks. In contrast, OWL 2 RL and SWRL have been used in our work which give an expressive ontology language to capture the knowledge of complex context-aware systems. In [4], Keßler et al. has shown the usefulness of SWRL rules in modelling context-aware scenarios, and how those rules can be used for personalised mappings between the numeric sensor world and information stored in ontologies. The main focus of their work is context-aware instantiation based on SWRL rules and built-ins. In [5], OWL ontologies are used to model context-aware systems, the authors exploited classes and properties from ontologies to write rules in Jess to derive multi-agent rules based system. Thus their modelling part of the system only reflects the static behaviour. In contrast, our ontology-based modelling captures both static and dynamic behaviour of the system using OWL 2 RL and SWRL. A prototype of context management model is presented in [3] that supports collaborative reasoning in a multi-domain pervasive context-aware application. The model facilitates the context reasoning by providing structure for contexts, rules and their semantics. However, none of the existing approaches discussed above considers formal specification and verification of context-aware systems.

7 Conclusions and Future Work

In this paper, we proposed a formal approach to modelling and verifying context-aware systems. We gave ontological representation of contexts and shown how we build context-aware systems as multi-agent systems, specify them in Maude and ultimately verify their interesting properties using model checking. Our approach gives a clean ontology design based on the distinction between the static information represented using OWL 2 RL and the dynamic aspects of the systems go into the SWRL rules. In future work, we would like to present a formal logical model for context-aware systems based on temporal epistemic description logics. In addition to the time and communication resources, we will also consider space requirement for reasoning.

References

1. Weiser, M.: The computer for the 21st century. ACM SIGMOBILE Mobile Computing and Communications Review - Special Issue Dedicated to Mark Weiser 3(3), 3–11 (1999)
2. Wang, X.H., Zhang, D.Q., Gu, T., Pung, H.K.: Ontology based context modeling and reasoning using owl. In: PerCom Workshops 2004, pp. 18–22 (2004)
3. Ejigu, D., Scuturici, M., Brunie, L.: An ontology-based approach to context modeling and reasoning in pervasive computing. In: PerCom Workshops 2007, pp. 14–19 (2007)
4. Keßler, C., Raubal, M., Wosniok, C.: Semantic Rules for Context-Aware Geographical Information Retrieval. In: Barnaghi, P., Moessner, K., Presser, M., Meissner, S. (eds.) EuroSSC 2009. LNCS, vol. 5741, pp. 77–92. Springer, Heidelberg (2009)
5. Esposito, A., Tarricone, L., Zappatore, M., Catarinucci, L., Colella, R., DiBari, A.: A Framework for Context-Aware Home-Health Monitoring. In: Sandnes, F.E., Zhang, Y., Rong, C., Yang, L.T., Ma, J. (eds.) UIC 2008. LNCS, vol. 5061, pp. 119–130. Springer, Heidelberg (2008)
6. Eker, S., Meseguer, J., Sridharanarayanan, A.: The Maude LTL Model Checker and Its Implementation. In: Ball, T., Rajamani, S.K. (eds.) SPIN 2003. LNCS, vol. 2648, pp. 230–234. Springer, Heidelberg (2003)
7. Dey, A.K.: Understanding and using context. Personal Ubiquitous Comput. 5(1), 4–7 (2001)
8. Henricksen, K.: A Framework for Context-Aware Pervasive Computing Applications. PhD thesis, The University of Queensland (2003)

9. Baldauf, M., Dustdar, S., Rosenberg, F.: A survey on context-aware systems. International Journal of Ad Hoc and Ubiquitous Computing 2(4), 263–277 (2007)
10. Gruber, T.: A translation approach to portable ontology specifications. Knowledge Acquisition - Special issue: Current issues in knowledge modeling 5(2), 199–220 (1993)
11. Grosof, B.N., Horrocks, I., Volz, R., Decker, S.: Description logic programs: Combining logic programs with description logic. In: WWW 2003, pp. 48–57. ACM Press (2003)
12. Rinner, C.: Multi-criteria evaluation in support of emergency response decision-making. In: Joint CIG/ISPRS Conference on Geomatics for Disaster and Risk Management (2007)
13. Baumgartner, N., Retschitzegger, W.: A survey of upper ontologies for situation awareness. In: Proceedings of the 4th IASTED International Conference on Knowledge Sharing and Collaborative Engineering, pp. 1–9 (2006)
14. Protégé: The Protégé ontology editor and knowledge-base framework (Version 4.1) (July 2011), http://protege.stanford.edu/
15. Rakib, A., Faruqui, R.U., MacCaull, W.: Verifying Resource Requirements for Ontology-Driven Rule-Based Agents. In: Lukasiewicz, T., Sali, A. (eds.) FoIKS 2012. LNCS, vol. 7153, pp. 312–331. Springer, Heidelberg (2012)
16. Alechina, N., Logan, B., Nga, N.H., Rakib, A.: Verifying Time and Communication Costs of Rule-Based Reasoners. In: Peled, D.A., Wooldridge, M.J. (eds.) MoChArt 2008. LNCS, vol. 5348, pp. 1–14. Springer, Heidelberg (2009)
17. Culbert, C.: CLIPS reference manual. NASA (2007)

Context-Aware Design of Semantic Web Services to Improve the Precision of Compositions

Angelo Furno and Eugenio Zimeo

University of Sannio, Department of Engineering, Benevento 82100 Italy
{angelo.furno,eugenio.zimeo}@unisannio.it

Abstract. Service-based systems are usually conceived and executed in highly dynamic environments. To support their automatic adaptation to this variability, execution context should be considered as a first-class concept during their design.

This paper proposes a design approach that exploits semantics for modeling contexts and related systems' behaviors. The context model extends the OWL-S ontology to enrich the expressiveness of each section of an OWL-annotated service, by means of conditions and adaptation rules. These additional descriptions can be exploited by a discovery/-composition tool to automatically find the services better-tuned to the requestor's behaviors and the particular situations of the environment.

Keywords: Context-aware Computing, Context Modeling, Semantic Web Services, Service Design, Service Discovery, Service Composition.

1 Introduction

A characterizing feature of service-based systems is their dynamicity in selecting the functions satisfying user requirements. Service composition plays a fundamental role in this kind of software systems. So far, many researchers have investigated techniques to support automatic generation of service compositions from a set of published services (*domain*), given a goal to reach (*problem*). In many cases, composition techniques and related tools exploit IOPE (*Input, Output, Preconditions* and *Effects*) predicates that characterize structural (WSDL [5]) and semantic (e.g. OWL-S [1]) service descriptions to generate the compositions.

However, the potential of SOA (Service Oriented Architecture) could be better exploited if such ability of building an application by composing (even on the fly) existing functions were augmented with the awareness of the surrounding context where composition takes place. This way, services and related compositions could be forged to adapt their malleable aspects to the specificity of the environment. This impacts the design phase of the services, but also the definition of the problem and the goal used to drive a specific composition.

Designing services with this new approach means to extend their semantic descriptions with new attributes and rules that are able to slightly change the structure and behavior of the services according to the needs emerging in the specific context where they will be used. This is a desirable property in SOA, where

P.C. Vinh et al. (Eds.): ICCASA 2012, LNICST 109, pp. 97–107, 2013.

services, differently from components, should be implemented to be exploited in contexts that could change even during the same execution.

This paper proposes an approach to design context-aware services by extending the OWL-S ontology with the context dimension. Services designed according to the proposed model can be discovered and composed by dynamically tailoring a service search space to the specific user needs or preferences and the current situation of the environment where the services have to be executed. In particular, the paper presents a model for context representation and its implementation in OWL [2] and an extension of OWL-S for allowing context-awareness in semantic service descriptions and their adoption during composition.

The rest of the paper is organized as follows. In Section 2, an application scenario is introduced to highlight the importance of context-awareness in Web Service composition. Section 3 reports on related work about context-awareness. In Section 4, the conceptual model for context representation is described, while in Section 5, the OWL-Ctx ontology based on that model is detailed, together with the extension of the OWL-S ontology for service description. Section 6 describes our context-aware service composition system and discusses it by using an example. Section 7 concludes the paper.

2   Motivating Scenario

Bob likes TV-Shows. He wants his home media server to automatically check the availability of new episodes every day, by connecting to the websites of the major broadcast companies or authorized external media providers. When download is not possible, since the provider only allows for streaming, or disk space is limited, only minimal information about the show (e.g. title, air date, stream URI, etc.) is available for selection, while playing has to be performed by connecting to the stream when required. For each retrieved TV show, if the language is different from Bob's native one, subtitles for that episode should be retrieved. Bob wants his media-player to prompt the list of available new TV-Show episodes, allowing him to choose the one to play. He prefers subtitles to be shown in a large font size. Also, blinds and artificial lights in Bob's TV room should be automatically adjusted to guarantee the best light conditions for watching TV.

A single service could not satisfy Bob's complex goals, but they may be achieved by composing some of the services available. Current context (e.g. time, location, profile information, etc.) and user preferences (subtitle language or font size, favorite TV-Shows, lighting levels, etc.) have to be taken into account to fully implement the scenario above.

3   Related Work

Context-awareness in information systems represents an enabling solution for handling adaptation [6,14] and it is crucial in service-based systems [13,18].

In [19], the authors propose a context modeling approach based on ontologies to dynamically handle context types and values. Ontologies enhance the meaning of user's context values and allow for automatically retrieving relations among them. However, context-aware service composition is not addressed in the paper.

The authors of [11] propose meta-models and an aspect-based pattern for context-awareness of services. A *Context* is a set of *Parameters* and *Entities* that can be structured in *SubContexts*. *ContextAwareServices* are services with associated *ContextViews*, containing adaptation rules and actions. Based on this model and the Aspect-Oriented Paradigm (AOP), context-aware adaptations can be dynamically performed by means of adaptation aspects dynamically woven into the core services. Despite some similarities with our model, their focus is on AOP in service modeling and implementation, instead of semantic composition.

AOP is also exploited in [12] to support context-aware semantic service composition, by weaving context aspects, defined by means of ontology concepts, within plain compositions. Weaving is performed statically, before starting the execution of the main service. However, automatic composition is not considered: plain compositions already exist and are modified by adding context services.

Exploiting context is also essential in pervasive environments [17, 20], where most service discovery or composition requests are implicitly driven by state changes. In [20], the authors introduce a design process and an architecture for building context-aware pervasive service compositions, while, in [17], an approach for personalized service discovery in pervasive environments, based on a multi-dimensional context space (*Hyperspace Analogue to Context*), is proposed. The approach is only limited to event-driven service discovery.

4   Context Model

By the term *application state* we mean the set of variables and corresponding values the application is able to access or modify. We distinguish between *internal* and *external application state*.

The *internal state* is the set of variables only visible to the application itself. They are created, used and eventually destroyed by the application and are not accessible outside it. Besides *input* and *output* parameters, the application may have predicates to be satisfied in order to execute it (*pre-conditions*) and predicates that are satisfied after the application is executed (*post-conditions*).

The *external state* is the set of variables accessible also outside the application. They can be read or modified by users, devices or applications other than the one the state is referred to. This set of variables represents the **context** in our model: it includes every attribute that characterizes a user and/or the (smart) environment a distributed application interacts with.

Context-Aware Applications may exhibit dependencies from the context. They may interest both application pre- and post- conditions. When the properties above apply to Web Services, we call them *Context-Aware Web Services* (CAWS).

5   Context-Aware Semantic Service Design

To support design and composition of context-aware services we propose: an OWL ontology (OWL-Ctx), supporting the description of sets of contexts in specific domains (sub-section 5.1) and an extension of the OWL-S ontology for services (OWL-SC, sub-section 5.2), allowing for the specification of OWL-Ctx-based context adaptation rules.

Context-aware descriptions can be exploited during service composition to automatically generate compositions better-tuned to the requestor's behaviors and preferences and to the particular situations of the surrounding environment.

5.1   OWL-Ctx: An OWL Ontology for Modeling Context

Fig. 1 shows OWL-Ctx, an extensible OWL ontology for describing contexts according to our model (Section 4).

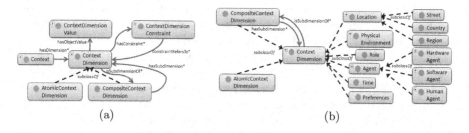

(a)   (b)

Fig. 1. OWL-Ctx: ontology language (a) and (partial) middle ontology (b)

The *Context* related to a software system is composed of a set of *ContextDimensions*, each describing one relevant aspect, or dimension, of the environment enclosing the particular software system. Each dimension can be modeled at different level of abstractions, according to the specific requirements in the considered application domain. In this sense, we distinguish between composite or atomic *ContextDimensions*.

Differently from an *AtomicContextDimension*, a *CompositeContextDimension* can be further decomposed in one or more sub-dimensions (*hasSubdimension* property), helpful for a better characterization of the associated context aspect. A *ContextDimensionValue* can be defined for each *ContextDimension* to describe complex values. Otherwise, if a concrete XML-Schema built-in datatype (e.g. *string*, *int*) is sufficient for representing the context dimension values, the *hasValue* datatype property (not shown in the figure) can be used, by introducing a sub-property having the required xsd type as range. *ContextDimensionConstraints* allow for specifying constraints applying to *ContextDimensions*.

In the partial middle ontology of Fig. 1(b), *Time, Agent, Location, Preferences, Role* and *PhysicalEnvironment* describe generic context dimensions, typically relevant in many application domains.

Considering the scenario illustrated in Section 2, a designer could specify the properties of possible contexts in a Media ontology as follows:

```
1  <owl:Class rdf:about="&Media;MediaContext">
2    <rdfs:subClassOf rdf:resource="&OWL-Ctx;Context"/> ...
3    <owl:equivalentClass><owl:Class><owl:intersectionOf rdf:parseType="Collection">
4      <rdf:Description rdf:about="&OWL-Ctx;Context"/>
5      <owl:Restriction><owl:onProperty rdf:resource="&OWL-Ctx;hasDimension"/>
6      <owl:someValuesFrom><owl:Class><owl:unionOf rdf:parseType="Collection">
7        <rdf:Description rdf:about="&OWL-Ctx;Agent"/>
8        <rdf:Description rdf:about="&Media;MediaContent"/>
9        <rdf:Description rdf:about="&OWL-Ctx;PhysicalEnvironment"/> ...
```

MediaContext is a specialization of *OWL-Ctx:Context*, with a restriction over the range of the *hasDimension* property to *Agent*, *PhysicalEnvironment* and *MediaContent* (a concept from the Media ontology), since the user (Bob), the devices (Bob's TV, Bob's PC), the media content (TV-Shows) and the location (TV-Room) represent the relevant context dimensions.

5.2   OWL-SC: An OWL-S Extension for Context-Aware Service

The OWL-Ctx ontology is exploited by the OWL-SC ontology, our extension of the OWL-S service ontology for describing context-aware semantic services. The most relevant elements extending OWL-S are reported in Fig. 2(a).

Each of the three OWL-S core concepts for describing a *Service* (i.e. *Profile*, *Process* and *Grounding*) can be associated (Fig. 2(b)) to a context adaptation rule (*CtxAdaptationRule*), by means of the proper *has*AdaptationRule* object property.

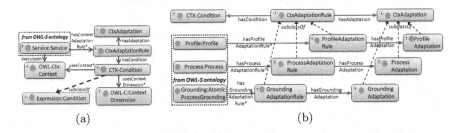

(a)   (b)

Fig. 2. OWL-SC: ontology language (a) and (partial) middle ontology (b)

A service designer may be aware of a set of contexts or context dimension values, which can be used to specify at design-time conditions for the service to change its basic features (i.e. profile, process or grounding properties). A reference to the current context may be used to relate context conditions to the situation at the moment the extended service description will be analyzed (relationship *executesIn* between *Service* and *Context*) for discovery or composition.

A *CtxAdaptationRule* (and its sub-concepts) is defined by means of a context condition (*CTX-Condition*) and a context adaptation action (*CtxAdaptation*). It prescribes the context-dependent condition to be satisfied in order to apply the associated adaptation to the specific section of the OWL-S description. If at least one *ProfileAdaptationRule*, *ProcessAdaptationRule* or *GroundingAdaptationRule* is specified in the description, the service is a CAWS.

The main context adaptations over OWL-S sections currently supported are:

- Defaulting an input/output parameter;
- Nulling a parameter, not applicable for a specific context condition;
- Changing the owls $<process{:}parameterType>$ of an input/output parameter to a different ontology concept;
- Replacing pre-conditions or effects of the basic OWL-S service description;
- Changing the $WsdlAtomicProcessGrounding$ input/output section of an atomic Process with a new Wsdl MessageMap;
- Changing the $WsdlAtomicProcessGrounding$ section of an atomic Process with a new WSDL operation and/or WSDL portType.

Context conditions, supported by our OWL-SC ontology, include:

- `current_ctx matches ref_ctx`
- `current_ctx includes "concept hasValue individual"`
- `current_ctx includes "concept.datatype_property = value"`
- `current_ctx includes "concept.object_property hasValue individual"`

where `current_ctx` is the context reference for the context at the moment in which the composition domain is explored for finding a solution to the submitted problem. Both `current_ctx` and `ref_ctx` specifications can be verified according to an approach like the one used in [9].

Currently, we are using the Semantic Web Rule Language [3] (SWRL) to express the last three kinds of condition. An example of SWRL context condition, related to the *Media* context specialization previously defined, is given:

$$OWL\text{-}Ctx{:}hasDimension(\texttt{current\_ctx}, \text{?hwAgent}) \land \texttt{Media: HWAgent(?hwAgent)} \land$$
$$OWL\text{-}Ctx{:}hasSubdimension(\text{?hwAgent}, \text{?role}) \land OWL\text{-}Ctx{:}Role(\text{?role}) \land sameAs(\text{?role},$$
$$\texttt{Media:DownloadServer}) \land OWL\text{-}Ctx{:}hasSubdimension(\text{?hwAgent}, \text{?disk}) \land \texttt{Media:Disk(?disk)} \land$$
$$\texttt{Media:diskMBSpace(?disk}, \text{?avSpace}) \land swrlb{:}lowerThanOrEqual(\text{?avSpace}, 500)$$

The condition verifies whether the disk of a media server has not enough space ($\leq 500\text{MB}$) to download some file.

6   Context-Aware Service Composition

Context-aware compositions are supported by a semi-automatic tool, the composer (Fig. 3), presented in [7] and extended in order to support context-aware semantic descriptions of services and problems. Part of a more complex system, namely Semantic Autonomic Workflow Engine (SAWE) [16], the composer can be used either for the initial definition (plan) of a service composition or for re-planning an already defined composition, to be changed completely or in part in order to react to external events.

A traditional composition process consists of exploring a set of candidate Web Services (the service domain) in order to find a flow of activities (a plan) that, starting from the provided description of the initial state (i.e. predicates true before the task beginning), is able to reach the goal state (i.e. predicates to be true at the end of the service chain).

When performing context-aware composition, the set of semantically described candidate services may include CAWSs (the OWL-SC domain) and is provided as

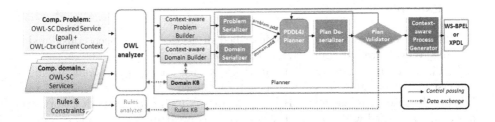

Fig. 3. Composer Architecture

an input to the system (manually or automatically via a matchmaking process), together with the semantic description of the initial state of the environment and the goal. OWL input files are analyzed and used by the *OWL Analyzer* to build the internal representation of the composition problem. Then, context is exploited for preparing the planning phase. The *Context-aware Domain Builder* evaluates the context dependencies in pre-conditions, effects and adaptation rules of service descriptions with respect to the current context and generates a contextualized instance of the domain, suited to be converted into the planner language (PDDL [10]). Similarly, the *Context-aware Problem Builder* augments the problem representation given by the user, by injecting relevant context information derived from our SAWE monitoring support.

The *Planner* is the component deputed to the processing of contextualized domain and problem for producing an action plan satisfying the problem. The current implementation of the tool uses PDDL4J [15], based on the Graphplan algorithm [8]. The *Context-aware Process Generator* generates a concrete (WS-BPEL [4]) representation of the plan (binding phase), executable on a process engine, by exploiting the available contextualized grounding information.

It is worth to note that, in general, the context can be extremely dynamic, evolving so rapidly that it could be not possible to complete the composition process without taking into account the mutated environmental conditions. However, in the present work, we assume context variations to be reasonably slower than the time required for a typical composition problem to complete. By this assumption, composition may be completed in relation to the contextualized domain and problem, being the final composition still meaningful. Also, in the current SAWE implementation, context changes, following the composition process, may be addressed by re-planning, according to a reactive approach to adaptation. Alternatively, a proactive strategy, based on probabilistic techniques (e.g. Bayesian networks, Markov processes), might be used for learning context transition probabilities from past experience. This way, alternative compositions could be computed in advance for highly probable context transitions, minimizing (with respect to reactive strategies) the time the running system is unavailable when context actually changes.

6.1   Example

A synthetic version of the scenario described in Section 2 has been considered
in order to evaluate our context-aware composer.

In Fig. 4(a), a user requests an abstract service for retrieving and playing
the last episode related to some specified TV-Show; subtitles are requested to
be superimposed to the video. Besides the desired service IOPE description,
our composer is fed with the OWL-Ctx current context representation as input,
which can be automatically acquired and updated by our SAWE system. In Fig.
4(b), a subset of the OWL-SC service domain is shown together with the relevant
dependencies on the context, used in the adaptation rules.

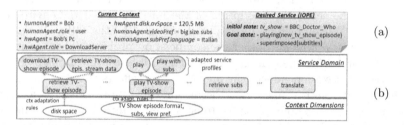

Fig. 4. Problem description: current context, goal IOPE (a) and domain (b)

The OWL-SC service for retrieving a TV-Show episode provides the effect
newEpisodeAvailable(TV-ShowEpisode) and, in the basic case, the download of
the last *TV-Show* episode file (effect *downloaded(TV-ShowEpisode)*).

The profile and its service atomic process have been extended with a context
adaptation rule, changing the process result in case the download server has not
enough space to store the episode file. The context condition used to control this
profile/process adaptation in the OWL-SC description is the SWRL condition
reported at the end of Section 5.2. The adaptation replaces the downloaded result
with the effect *streamDataAcquired(TV-ShowEpisode)*. The same condition also
controls a grounding adaptation rule, changing the concrete service from the one
used to download the file to the one for retrieving the stream information.

Since the disk space amounts to 120.5 MB in the current context of Fig. 4(a),
the rule is activated and the adaptation applied by the *Context-aware Domain
Builder*. The stream retrieval service (i.e. *RetrieveTV-ShowEpisodeStreamData*
in Fig. 4(b)) is included within the contextualized domain, while the download
one is not. When converting to PDDL, the stream retrieval service is the only to
appear as a PDDL domain action, thus reducing the actual size of the domain,
with benefits over composition performances.

The *PlayTV-ShowEpisode* service contains pre-condition *newEpisodeAvail-
able(TV-ShowEpisode)* and parameter *TV-ShowEpisode* as an input. The effect
playing(TV-ShowEpisode) is provided. A context-dependent adaptation is included in the OWL-SC description for the grounding section: depending on the
streamDataAcquired(TV-ShowEpisode) or *downloaded(TV-ShowEpisode)* condition a different concrete service will be grounded to the service process. The

grounding adaptation rule does not generate different services in the domain. Instead, two groundings are stored for being later used by the Process Generator when the final WS-BPEL process has to be created. The profile and atomic process sections of the *PlayTV-ShowEpisode* service contains an adaptation rule for subtitle rendering. Depending on the availability of subtitles, they have to be considered as an additional input and their superimposition as an additional effect. Since at the moment of domain building it is not known whether the subtitles are going to be available or not, the Context-aware Domain Builder includes both the two services to the domain (the one including subtitles as input and the one not including them). Also, since view preferences are another input of the service and part of the context, the Context-aware Problem Builder expands the set of known inputs for problem solution with them.

The *RetrieveSubtitles* service only downloads English subtitles and a *Translate* service to the user's language (i.e. Italian) is also available in the domain.

After contextualized domain and problem conversion to PDDL, the Graphplan planner generates an abstract PDDL plan, containing the sequence of *RetrieveSubtitles* and *Translate* in parallel with *RetrieveTV-ShowEpisodeStreamData*. The parallel is in sequence with the *PlayWithSubs* service. The translate service appears because the user's preference about subtitle language (Italian) has been added to the goal of the problem by exploiting available context knowledge. Without context-awareness, the composer would have not been able to find such a suitable composition, according to the assumption that *RetrieveSubtitles* only retrieves English subtitles and the user has not explicitly indicated the Italian language preference in his/her goals.

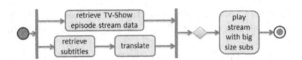

Fig. 5. Resulting concrete service composition

The WS-BPEL generator produces the resulting concrete process of Fig. 5 from the abstract plan, using the available grounding and context knowledge.

7   Conclusion

The paper has presented a model to design context-aware services that can be exploited as a flexible domain to automatically generate context-aware compositions by means of a specific tool. Besides extending the services, the tool exploits an extension of the problem definition that includes also the context representation (defined by designers or implicitly inferred by the system).

The analysis conducted during the definition of the model has highlighted a further problem to address: by exploiting context for problem expansion and evaluation of adaptation rules before planning, valid composite solutions might be indirectly excluded during domain construction if, for an abstract service, more than one post-condition may fit the context, but only one of them satisfies the pre-conditions of the next services (e.g. there is disk space for retrieving a HD file but the player is not able to play it). This requires the contextualized expansion of services to be performed during planning to take into account the state dependencies when context rules are applied.

References

1. OWL-S: Semantic Markup for Web Services, http://www.w3.org/Submission/OWL-S/
2. OWL: Web Ontology Language Overview, http://www.w3.org/TR/owl-features/
3. SWRL: A Semantic Web Rule Language Combining OWL and RuleML, http://www.w3.org/Submission/SWRL
4. Web Services Business Process Execution Language Version (WS-BPEL) 2.0., http://docs.oasis-open.org/wsbpel/2.0/wsbpel-v2.0.html
5. Web Services Description Language (WSDL) 1.1., http://www.w3.org/TR/wsdl
6. Abowd, G.D., Dey, A.K., Brown, P.J., Davies, N., Smith, M., Steggles, P.: Towards a Better Understanding of Context and Context-Awareness. In: Gellersen, H.-W. (ed.) HUC 1999. LNCS, vol. 1707, pp. 304–307. Springer, Heidelberg (1999)
7. Bevilacqua, L., Furno, A., di Carlo, V., Zimeo, E.: A tool for automatic generation of ws-bpel compositions from owl-s described services. In: 2011 5th International Conference on Software, Knowledge Information, Industrial Management and Applications (SKIMA), pp. 1–8 (September 2011)
8. Blum, A.L., Furst, M.L.: Fast planning through planning graph analysis. Artificial Intelligence 90(1), 1636–1642 (1995)
9. Bolchini, C., Curino, C.A., Orsi, G., Quintarelli, E., Rossato, R., Schreiber, F.A., Tanca, L.: And what can context do for data? Commun. ACM 52(11), 136–140 (2009)
10. Ghallab, M., Isi, C.K., Penberthy, S., Smith, D.E., Sun, Y., Weld, D.: PDDL - the planning domain definition language. Tech. rep., CVC TR-98-003/DCS TR-1165, Yale Center for Computational Vision and Control (1998)
11. Hafiddi, H., Baidouri, H., Nassar, M., Kriouile, A.: An aspect based pattern for context-awareness of services. International Journal of Computer Science and Network Security 12(1), 71–78 (2012)
12. Li, L., Liu, D., Bouguettaya, A.: Semantic based aspect-oriented programming for context-aware web service composition. Information Systems 36(3), 551–564 (2011)
13. Maamar, Z., Benslimane, D., Narendra, N.C.: What can context do for web services? Commun. ACM 49(12), 98–103 (2006)
14. Pascoe, J.: Adding generic contextual capabilities to wearable computers. In: Second International Symposium on Wearable Computers, Digest of Papers, pp. 92–99 (October 1998)
15. Pellier, D.: PDDL4J (2011), http://sourceforge.net/projects/pdd4j/
16. Polese, M., Tretola, G., Zimeo, E.: Self-adaptive management of web processes. In: 2010 12th IEEE International Symposium on Web Systems Evolution (WSE), pp. 33–42 (September 2010)

17. Rasch, K., Li, F., Sehic, S., Ayani, R., Dustdar, S.: Context-driven personalized service discovery in pervasive environments. World Wide Web 14, 295–319 (2011)
18. Truong, H.L., Dustdar, S.: A survey on context-aware web service systems. International Journal of Web Information Systems 5(1), 5–31 (2009)
19. Xiao, H., Zou, Y., Ng, J., Nigul, L.: An approach for context-aware service discovery and recommendation. In: 2010 IEEE International Conference on Web Services (ICWS), pp. 163–170 (July 2010)
20. Zhou, J., Gilman, E., Palola, J., Riekki, J., Ylianttila, M., Sun, J.: Context-aware pervasive service composition and its implementation. Personal Ubiquitous Comput. 15(3), 291–303 (2011)

Context-Awareness for Self-adaptive Applications in Ubiquitous Computing Environments

Kurt Geihs and Michael Wagner

EECS Department, University of Kassel
Wilhelmshöher Allee 73, 34121 Kassel, Germany
{geihs,wagner}@vs.uni-kassel.de

Abstract. Context-awareness is a prerequisite for self-adaptive applications that are able to react and adapt to their runtime context. We have built and evaluated a comprehensive development framework for context-aware, self-adaptive applications in dynamic ubiquitous computing scenarios. The framework consists of a middleware and an associated model-driven development methodology. In this paper we focus on the context-awareness part of the framework. We discuss design objectives, design decisions, and lessons learnt. The main contributions of this paper are generally applicable insights into the design and seamless integration of context-awareness, dynamic service landscapes, and application adaptation management for applications in highly dynamic execution environments. These insights not only relate to the functional requirements and constraints, but also to non-functional aspects that have a strong influence on the user acceptance of such applications.

Keywords: context-awareness, self-adaptation, middleware, socio-technical requirements.

1 Introduction

Context-awareness is an exciting feature that enables new kinds of self-adaptive applications. Our notion of context agrees with the authors of [17] who stated that *"There is more to context than location"*. Thus, we adopt the more general and widely-accepted definition: *"[Context is] any information that can be used to characterize the situation of an entity"* [1]. Self-adaptive applications monitor and reason about external context conditions and react to changes by automatically adapting their application behavior in order to provide adequate service under changing conditions. Particularly in mobile and ubiquitous computing environments, where dynamic change is a characteristic, often unavoidable feature, self-adaptation is an attractive option, if not a requirement.

Basic hardware and software support for context-aware applications is available today in mobile computing devices such as smartphones and pad/tablet computers that contain sensors for location, acceleration, sound, light, orientation, and more. Needless to say, these mobile computing devices have the computing and memory capacity to execute sophisticated applications and systems software.

Building context-aware and self-adaptive applications is an inherently complex task. Not only need the developers be concerned about the main functionality of the

P.C. Vinh et al. (Eds.): ICCASA 2012, LNICST 109, pp. 108–120, 2013.
© Institute for Computer Sciences, Social Informatics and Telecommunications Engineering 2013

application, but also they have to understand which context parameters influence the application functionality, how application variants depend on these parameters, and which variant should be activated under which context conditions. Thus, building such applications requires specific software development and run-time support.

Project MUSIC (Self-Adapting Applications for Mobile Users in Ubiquitous Computing Environments) was a European research project in the 6th Framework Program that particularly tackled this challenge. It provided a model-driven development methodology for context-aware, self-adaptive applications, including supporting tools, as well as an adaptation middleware that features sophisticated context management, adaptation reasoning, and application reconfiguration. The results of MUSIC were evaluated through the development of a number of realistic applications and their demonstration in live settings, e.g. in the Paris Métro.

In this paper we focus on the evolution of the context-awareness support in the MUSIC framework, and in particular we focus on insights and lessons learnt that reach beyond MUSIC. These insights were derived as part of the MUSIC activities but also in follow-on projects where the MUSIC technology was employed and evolved. The details of the overall MUSIC approach and technology have been presented already in several publications, e.g. [4, 16]. Consequently, we explain design and implementation details only as far as necessary and refer to more technically focussed papers for further explanations.

The context management middleware of MUSIC was built as a self-contained, separately reusable component. As such it can be used without the adaptation management of MUSIC in order to enable context-awareness features in other application scenarios that do not require adaptation and reconfiguration. Hence, the contributions of this paper are not only relevant within the scope of the MUSIC project, but provide general advice for designers of context-aware systems in highly dynamic application environments.

The rest of this paper is structured as follows: Section 2 covers objectives and requirements for the design of context-aware, user-centric applications in open and dynamic execution environments. In Section 3 we present a very short overview of the MUSIC middleware architecture which is needed for the subsequent discussions. Section 4 discusses the design decisions for our specific context-awareness features that follow from the stated requirements and objectives for dynamic ubiquitous computing scenarios. In Section 5 we present an assessment of these features combined with a comparison to related work. Section 6 concludes the paper and gives an outlook to future work.

2   Objectives and Requirements

Our main goal is to provide context-awareness for self-adaptive applications in mobile and ubiquitous computing environments. Such environments are characterized by continuous change of conditions and by a variable, open service landscape where services may appear and disappear at any time and are provided by independent service providers.

We assume that applications are component-based. Adaptation can be achieved by several adaptation mechanisms, such as compositional (also known as architectural), parametric, distributed deployment, and service-based adaptation. Among these adaptation techniques we have specifically aimed at support for compositional and service-based adaptation: Compositional adaptation allows the modification of the application architecture, i.e. components may be added, removed, or replaced, in order to change the application behavior. Service-based adaptation allows the replacement of an application component by a dynamically discovered and bound external service, if the resulting configuration provides a better utility. The middleware takes care of service discovery, utility evaluation, adaptation planning, and service binding.

Context-awareness is key for all self-adapting systems. As stated above, our notion of context encompasses *"any information that can be used to characterize the situation of an entity"* [1] – as long as there are sensors (i.e. information sources) available for it, one might want to add. Thus, context information includes information on the state of the execution environment (e.g. location, speed, light, sound etc.), the state of the computing device (e.g. computing and memory capacity, battery status etc.) as well as user preferences (e.g. priorities for certain operation modes). In addition to these classical context parameters, the availability of accessible services is considered a special kind of context information. We will come back to this later.

The stated application and context assumptions lead to a number of requirements and challenges for the context management middleware (CMM). First of all, a general software engineering principle needs to be achieved, i.e. *separation of concerns*. This is important in order to clearly separate collecting, storing, providing, and managing context data from the functionality that consumes it. This kind of separation also facilitates the sharing of the context middleware between several applications, i.e. one instance of the middleware can serve several applications concurrently.

Since the CMM is meant to operate in an open dynamic environment sensor availability and sensor heterogeneity are major concerns. If we assume that applications will not only use context sensors that are built into the computing device, but also external sensors, for example an indoor positioning system or an external speedometer, we need a CMM architecture that supports a *flexible configuration* of sensor components and a loose coupling between sensor provider and sensor consumer. Basically, it leads to a "context as a service" model [20] where a sensor is viewed as a dynamically discoverable service providing information on certain attributes of the environment. Thus, language and middleware support is required for offering and requesting context sensors.

Going further along this avenue, the need for mastering the *heterogeneity* of sensor information arises – syntactically as well as semantically. This may involve operations ranging from simple data type conversions (e.g. short to long integer) over translating different metrics (e.g. Fahrenheit to Celsius) to more sophisticated semantic mappings (e.g. street address to GPS coordinates). However, where does the required meta-level information come from? Clearly, some form of semantical representation is required to capture the relationships and potential mappings between data types, parameter metrics, and other kind of context information. A context ontology would be appropriate to store this information. The ontology should also support reasoning about possible transformation chains that convert data items in multiple steps by a set of consecutive intermediate conversions if no direct one-step conversion is available.

Developing context-aware applications requires a well-defined context query interface in order to provide applications with powerful, distribution and device transparent access to different kinds of sensor information. Ideally, the *query language* should support typical sensor related functions such as selecting, filtering, aggregating, and accessing sensor data. While this requirement has been addressed already in several projects that have provided database-like query languages for context management (e.g. [7, 10]), here we emphasize the specific aspects of dynamic and heterogeneous sensor landscapes where designers have to cope with different sensor data types, representations, and semantics.

A key challenge in the envisaged application scenarios is the dynamic appearance and disappearance of services which applications would like to exploit in order to improve their performance. This requires appropriate middleware functionality for discovering services, negotiating service usage agreements, generating service proxies on-the-fly, and binding to services. In addition, in order to integrate the services and their properties into the context-dependent adaptation planning we need to *align the service model with the context model* and relate service properties and context properties. From the perspective of adaptive applications, both kinds of events, i.e. context changes and service appearance / disappearance, may open up opportunities for improving the application utility. Computing the utility of potential application variants generally requires input on the state of the context and the properties of the offered services. Thus, we need an integrated model for an application's context and service dependencies.

Another concern with context-aware applications on mobile computing devices is the *battery capacity*. Generally, smartphone sensors tend to be very resource consuming components. For example, it is well known that continuous GPS tracker applications on smartphones put an enormous stress on the battery. Therefore, from a practical viewpoint we demand that unused context sensors should not consume resources and should be switched off automatically. Likewise, if several applications request the same kind of context data, there should be shared access to the sensor data instead of separate access.

Last but not least there arise non-functional, socio-technical concerns when dealing with context-awareness in user-centric applications. By the term user-centric here we refer to applications that exploit sensitive user data as part of the context-aware behavior. Obviously, tracking, storing, and transmitting data about the activities of a user or even monitoring and processing vital data of a user raises a whole bunch of questions related to security, privacy, legal constraints, trust in the technology, and more. Questions on the legal constraints might be: How can we include legal considerations into the design process such that the processing, storing and sending of user-oriented context-awareness data do not violate existing law? What kind of service contracts do we use (implicitly or explicitly) if third party service providers are involved? Likewise, trust related questions are: How can the user build up trust in a system which monitors the user's context and adapts automatically? Does the system really behave as the user wants it to behave? What kind of technical mechanisms support trust-building of users? How and where are trust-supporting components integrated into UC systems?

The developer of such user-centric context-aware applications necessarily needs to pay attention to these aspects that add further complexity to the development process. Likewise questions related to the usability of the application, i.e. the design of the human-computer-interface, pop up with innovative context-aware and self-adaptive applications: How do we make sure that a user is not overwhelmed by complex context-awareness and self-adaptation features? How can we make sure that the user can handle and interact with a system where many components are hidden in the environment and where many activities happen automatically? What is a good compromise between usage simplicity and attractive functionality? Should we equip these applications with different usage levels for the more or less experienced and skilled user?

Typically, a software engineer will be unable to cope with such non-functional requirements and concerns, and hence interdisciplinary domain experts need to be involved during the requirements, design and evaluation phases. Unfortunately, except for security and privacy concerns, which mostly are viewed as part of the functional requirements, there is little systematic development support available today to ensure that the socio-technical aspects are integral ingredients in the software development process. One of our main research goals is to develop such an interdisciplinary development methodology.

3   Architecture Overview

Before continuing with the discussion of context-awareness and self-adaptation we need to define at least a coarse architectural frame that clarifies our view of the position and role of the context management and adaptation management middleware. Figure 1 illustrates the architecture of the MUSIC middleware which is used as reference architecture for the following discussions. For further details the reader is referred to [16].

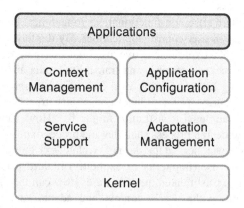

Fig. 1. Basic building blocks of the MUSIC middleware

The middleware implements a control loop which complies with the well-known MAPE (Monitor, Analyse, Plan, Execute) loop in autonomic computing [9]. It monitors the relevant context sensors, and when significant changes are detected, it triggers a planning process to decide if adaptation is necessary. When this is the case, the planning process finds a new configuration that fits the current context better than the one that is currently running, and triggers the adaptation of the running application. To do this the middleware relies on an annotated quality of service-aware architecture model of the application available at runtime, which specifies its adaptation capabilities and its dependencies on context information. This model corresponds to the "Knowledge" component of the autonomic manager in the autonomic computing blueprint. The planning process evaluates the utility of alternative configurations, selects the most suitable one for the current context (i.e. the one with the highest utility for the current context which does not violate any resource constraints) and adapts the application accordingly.

Context information is provided by context sensors and context reasoners in the Context Management middleware which is designed as a separately reusable stand-alone component in the MUSIC middleware. Applications may directly access the context information. The Context Management performs basic reasoning about the type of context changes and their significance for the application. The application designer needs to specify at design time when a context change is considered significant. Furthermore, the application designer needs to provide an adaptation model for the application. The adaptation model specifies all possible application variants and how these variants are related to context parameters. A runtime representation of this adaptation model is stored in the Adaptation Management part of the middleware.

Adaptation planning is triggered by notifications from the Context Management about significant context changes. The Adaptation Management evaluates the utility function for all application variants given the particular context situation, and selects the application variant with the highest utility for the given situation. As a result, the Application Configuration is triggered by the adaptation manager if an application needs to be reconfigured.

A unique feature of the MUSIC framework is the seamless support for discovering and binding external services as part of the context-awareness and self-adaptation. A local software component (e.g. a data storage component) can be replaced by an external service (e.g. a database on a server) if this is a specified application variant and if this configuration leads to a higher application utility. Thus, Service Support in Figure 1 comprises protocols and functions for service discovery, negotiation and monitoring of service level agreements, QoS management, service binding, and more. The Adaptation Management evaluates the available service offerings in terms of their service properties and quality of service guarantees and compares all possible application configuration alternatives when planning an adaptation. Thus, service-based adaptation planning must pay attention to the service availability and depends on the quality of service guarantees that – from the viewpoint of adaptation planning – become a special kind of context parameters.

The Kernel of the middleware provides basic services for communication, storage of metadata, and more.

4   Specific Context-Awareness Features

In this section we return to the requirements of Section 2 and discuss their technical implications and our resulting design decisions.

Separation of Concerns. The MUSIC middleware is built as a collection of clearly separated components that can be evolved and replaced independently. Context Management is decoupled from Adaptation Management, and can be reused without the other middleware components. Context Management is realized as a plug-in architecture where context sensors and context reasoners are plug-ins that can be replaced easily according to the specific application scenarios and requirements. It supports the on-the-fly integration of newly discovered sensors, following a new "sensor as a service" design principle. The activation of the plug-ins is implemented using an automated mechanism which monitors the varying context needs of the applications and starts and/or stops the plug-ins accordingly, thus achieving significant resource savings [11]. While some context plug-ins are readily available in repositories, developers often want to develop their own, tailored to the specific needs of the application and runtime environment. Another benefit of the plug-in concept is that code reuse is greatly facilitated via plug-in repositories, which allow posting, searching and accessing generic as well as specific context plug-ins.

Context Management and Adaptation Management together share the abstract, platform-independent adaptation model that specifies how applications are linked to context parameters and how the values of these parameters affect the utility of the application variants.

Heterogeneity. The targeted application scenarios in mobile and ubiquitous computing environments are inherently open and dynamic. Thus, heterogeneity in many forms is an unavoidable consequence. The foundation for coping with heterogeneous sensor information in the MUSIC framework is a domain ontology that captures the necessary knowledge about mappings between heterogeneous sensor types and data representations [14, 15]. The ontology supports simple data type mappings as well as more elaborate reasonings about the relationship and mapping between different sensor information.

Dynamic Sensor Configurations. As stated above, mobile and ubiquitous computing environments are inherently open and dynamic. This implies not only questions of sensor heterogeneity but also questions of sensor availability, in particular since we must assume that applications may want to access device-external sensors, e.g. for more accurate information. Thus, we have extended the context management middleware of MUSIC towards a loosely coupled "context as a service" model. A sensor is viewed as a dynamically discoverable resource, and language support is provided for offering and requesting context sensors, very similar to general service offer and request languages [20].

Context Query Language. While the Context Management of MUSIC offers a straightforward programmatic API which allows both synchronous context queries (i.e., asking for sensor readings) and asynchronous context queries (i.e., subscribing to context changes by providing a context listener), this simple API has been complemented by a more powerful interface based on a new Context Query Langauge (CQL) in order to support filtering and aggregating context information at a higher level of abstraction in a convenient and transparent way.

For instance, if an application needs the maximum value of some sensor over the last hour, there is no need for the application developer to explicitly access all sensor readings available for the defined time period and infer the desired data from that. MUSIC provides the Context Query Language (CQL) for selecting, filtering and accessing context information [3, 13]. Having such an interface offers two main benefits: First, the developer can work at a higher level of abstraction thus reducing the amount of code and the risk of bugs. Second, the runtime performance is improved because the sensor data is processed while still in the context repository, thus avoiding unnecessary data movement.

CQL is XML-based and allows applications to submit complex queries about an entity or a set of entities of the same type, providing advanced features such as:

- access to current and past context elements - raw or derived from other context data - using a single query;
- filters and constraints to select context data and to subscribe to asynchronous context change events, on both context data and metadata;
- logical operators to combine elementary conditions into more complex ones.

Let's take the user's location as an example. An application can subscribe to periodic notifications (e.g., the position is periodically sent every 10 seconds regardless its specific value), for location changes (e.g. depending on the query, notifications are sent if the geographical coordinates or the civil address change), or for specific location values expressed using query constraints (e.g., notifications are sent only if the user is located in the kitchen). Moreover, the language enables the composition of queries that incorporate semantic references and aggregation (e.g.,"the average passenger age is below 40"). CQL syntax also supports the definition of relations between entities, allowing more abstract queries, such as subscribing to the event "user Mary is at home". More details on the CQL can be found in [3].

Service Discovery as Part of the Context. In order to exploit fully the potential of dynamic ubiquitous computing environments we support the integration of external dynamically discovered services as replacements for local application components if that improves the utility of the application. Thus, the appearance of a new service instance is a context event that may trigger a new round of adaptation planning. If an application component potentially can be replaced by an external service, semantic service discovery and matching are supported by annotating the corresponding component type in the UML-based adaptation model by a specification of the required port types, interfaces, and semantic constraints. Such annotations are attached only to component types that may be the target of dynamic service discovery and binding. Clearly, core components that are crucial for the general functionality of the application will most likely not be candidates for dynamic substitution by externally provided services.

Adaptation reasoning with services depends on the actual service properties, i.e. QoS properties. From the perspective of adaptation reasoning these properties correspond to the context parameters provided by context sensors and reasoners. In order to enable such QoS-driven adaptation reasoning, discoverable services are expected to provide information about their offered QoS properties. In general, QoS guarantees of services are defined in SLAs and established by a negotiation process. Typically, a service can provide different levels of guarantees. Therefore, we have integrated a plug-in negotiation component into the middleware that handles the negotiation of service level agreements. Several standards are available for service level negotiation. The plug-in mechanism of the middleware facilitates the integration of different protocols.

By aligning context model and service model, dynamically discoverable services are made part of the application context that controls the application adaptation.

Distributed Context. An important feature of the MUSIC context management middleware is its support for context distribution, i.e. context information gathered by a node can be shared with other nodes within a defined domain. Distributed context can be used to trigger adaptation on a remote device. For instance, an error occurring on one node may lead to adaptation on other nodes. Context distribution is completely transparent to both the plug-in and application developers. The context middleware keeps track of which devices are available, together with their offered context information types and privacy policies. When a context entity is queried (or subscribed to) the context middleware will know how to fetch the requested data.

Energy Efficiency. In order to save battery power mobile devices cannot afford to run energy hungry resources even if they are not needed currently. Therefore, a local sensor plug-in can be disabled if none of the applications accesses the sensor.

Socio-technical Concerns. Widespread adoption of a new technology, in particular if it is a user-centric technology such as context-aware and adaptive ubiquitous computing, not only depends on the technical progress, but also on "soft factors" that determine the user acceptance. Our goal is to support the development of context-aware applications that are *socially compatible* by design. We intend to avoid the often encountered situation that a new software product is rejected in the end because it has non-technical flaws and risks.

In our research we have asked ourselves what non-functional requirements are crucial to the acceptance, i.e. social embedding, of user-centered context-aware UC applications, and we decided to concentrate first on three key concerns: trust, usability, and legal conformance. Clearly, there are more than these three areas of socio-technical concerns in the development of user-centered context-aware applications. This is future work. Note that indeed we view security and privacy of user data as very important concerns in ubiquitous computing applications. From our perspective these elementary concerns are part of the technical requirements. Therefore, we explicitly include security and privacy provisions in the technical requirements of an application and not in the socio-technical requirements.

Socio-technical requirements are difficult to assess and to translate into technical artefacts in the middleware or application. For example, there is no prefabricated component that encapsulates the handling of trust issues inside a modular component. In our solution the socio-technical concerns trust, usability, and legal conformance are taken into account in the design process of a context-aware application, particularly in the requirements analysis and conceptual design phases.

5   Assessment and Related Work

The MUSIC framework including its context management middleware was evaluated by building and experimenting with a range of prototype applications in real application environments, such as live experiments in Metro stations in Paris. A detailed discussion of evaluations and measurement results can be found in [2]. Here we focus particularly on the discussion of the design of context-awareness features.

The main trade-off we faced during the design of the overall context management system, and particularly the context modelling, was that of sophistication versus simplicity. On the one hand, we aimed at a context management approach that included state-of-the-art practices for context gathering, modelling, and management. But at the same time we also aimed at a flexible and extensible infrastructure that would allow us to replace functionality as needed by different application scenarios and thus to facilitate the experimental evaluations, e.g., replacing the inter-representation transformations or the context repository.

The design of the overall context management approach, the context model, and the corresponding context query language [13, 14] was heavily influenced by previous work on context-aware systems [6, 7, 8, 18]. However, none of the existing solutions provided all the features that we needed for ubiquitous, self-adaptive computing applications in open and dynamic environments. So we had to select and integrate features from several best-of-breed state of the art solutions. For example, our basic information model for context sources is based on [18]: Every context entity is associated with a scope and a representation. Mapping of different scopes and representations in a heterogeneous environment can be performed if the context ontology contains the required semantic relationships. Another example for how the MUSIC context management reuses and extends existing solutions is our two-level domain ontology that stands behind the context model. It is similar to the one of SOCAM [5]. However, we distinguish between a top-level ontology capturing general concepts and global knowledge and domain-specific lower level extensions for application specific details. In particular, we extend the SOCAM approach by provisions for the service-based adaptation, described in the previous section.

A strong and unique feature of our context model is the ability to model nearly any type of context information via an extensible ontology, including service interfaces and service properties. Furthermore, the context query language excels at raising the abstraction level of the way developers specify context information and context filtering conditions, while the context middleware automatically handles the representation heterogeneity and transformations, and thus takes this burden from the developers. Context model, context query language, and context ontology go hand in hand in a synergetic manner.

This level of abstraction and transparency comes at a price. Design, implementation, and configuration of the context management system have been rather complex undertakings, which is mainly due to the richness of features and capabilities. On the other hand, extensive experience with building context-aware applications on top of the MUSIC context management middleware has revealed that some of the features are rarely used. As mentioned above, the context management approach is built on top of a context ontology that enables sophisticated functionality including automatic transformation of context data between different representations, inference of context information based on the relationship of the corresponding entities, as well as semantic disambiguation. This rich functionality is blamed by application developers as a source of relatively high cost in terms of learning and application development effort. Application developers have particularly pointed to the steep learning curve of understanding and using the context model [12]. There is room for improvement and fine-tuning in future versions.

6   Conclusions

The overall goal of the MUSIC project was to facilitate the engineering of self-adaptive applications in ubiquitous computing environments, which are characterized by inherent openness, dynamism, and heterogeneity. The project has delivered a comprehensive development methodology and middleware framework for self-adaptive applications. The technical results were tested and evaluated by building a range of application demonstrators. The experiments proved the viability and effectiveness of the MUSIC achievements.

In this paper we have focused on the context management middleware of MUSIC. We have highlighted the unique requirements and resulting features of context management in dynamic and open ubiquitous computing application scenarios where dynamically discoverable services are considered part of the application context. In particular, our intention was to convey experience with context-awareness that have not been documented elsewhere. Thus, the main contributions of this paper are advice and guidelines for developers of context-aware systems.

Overall MUSIC has opened up several new avenues for further research that are being tackled in follow-on projects. For example, the interdisciplinary VENUS project [19] at the University of Kassel aims at an enhanced development methodology for self-adaptive ubiquitous computing applications that explicitly includes extra-functional concerns, such as usability of adaptive software, trust in context-awareness features, as well as legal constraints on the gathering, storing, and processing of personal context information. We believe that convincing answers to such questions are crucial for the acceptance of new technologies, in particular if they involve user-related context information.

Acknowledgments. The contributions of the MUSIC and VENUS project teams are gratefully acknowledged.

References

1. Dey, A.K.: Providing architectural support for building context-aware applications. PhD thesis, College of Computing, Georgia Institute of Technology (2000)
2. Floch, J., Frà, C., Fricke, R., Geihs, K., Wagner, M., Lorenzo, J., Soladana, E., Mehlhase, S., Paspallis, N., Rahnama, H., Ruiz, P.A., Scholz, U.: Playing MUSIC — building context-aware and self-adaptive mobile applications, Software: Practice and Experience. John Wiley & Sons, Ltd. (2012), doi:10.1002/spe.2116
3. Frà, C., Valla, M., Paspallis, N.: High level context query processing: an experience report. In: Proceedings of the 8th IEEE Workshop on Context Modeling and Reasoning (CoMoRea 2011) in Conjunction with the 9th IEEE International Conference on Pervasive Computing and Communication (PerCom), pp. 421–426. IEEE Computer Society (2011)
4. Geihs, K., Reichle, R., Wagner, M., Khan, M.U.: Modeling of Context-Aware Self-Adaptive Applications in Ubiquitous and Service-Oriented Environments. In: Cheng, B.H.C., de Lemos, R., Giese, H., Inverardi, P., Magee, J. (eds.) Self-Adaptive Systems. LNCS, vol. 5525, pp. 146–163. Springer, Heidelberg (2009)
5. Gu, T., Wang, X.H., Pung, H.K., Zhang, D.Q.: An Ontology-based Context Model in Intelligent Environments. In: Proc. of Communication Networks and Distributed Systems Modeling and Simulation Conference, pp. 270–275 (2004)
6. Henricksen, K., Indulska, J.: A Software Engineering Framework for Context-Aware Pervasive Computing. In: IEEE Int. Conf. on Pervasive Computing and Communications, pp. 77–86 (2004)
7. Henricksen, K., Indulska, J.: Developing context-aware pervasive computing applications: Models and approach. J. of Pervasive and Mobile Computing 2(1), 37–64 (2006)
8. Hönle, N., Käppeler, U., Nicklas, D., Schwarz, T.: Benefits Of Integrating Meta Data Into A Context Model. In: Proc. of IEEE PerCom Workshop on Context Modeling and Reasoning, pp. 25–29 (2005)
9. Kephart, J.O., Chess, D.M.: The vision of autonomic computing. IEEE Computer 36(1), 41–50 (2003)
10. Korpipää, P., Mäntyjärvi, J., Kela, J., Keränen, H., Malm, E.J.: Managing context information in mobile devices. IEEE Pervasive Computing 2.3, 42–51 (2003)
11. Paspallis, N., Rouvoy, R., Barone, P., Papadopoulos, G.A., Eliassen, F., Mamelli, A.: A Pluggable and Reconfigurable Architecture for a Context-Aware Enabling Middleware System. In: Meersman, R., Tari, Z. (eds.) OTM 2008, Part I. LNCS, vol. 5331, pp. 553–570. Springer, Heidelberg (2008)
12. Paspallis, N.: Middleware-based development of context-aware applications with reusable components, PhD thesis, University of Cyprus, Nicosia, Cyprus (2009)
13. Reichle, R., Wagner, M., Khan, M., Geihs, K., Valla, M., Fra, C., Paspallis, N., Papadopoulos, G.A.: A Context Query Language for Pervasive Computing Environments. In: IEEE Int. Conf. on Pervasive Computing and Communication, pp. 434–440 (2008)
14. Reichle, R., Wagner, M., Khan, M.U., Geihs, K., Lorenzo, J., Valla, M., Fra, C., Paspallis, N., Papadopoulos, G.A.: A Comprehensive Context Modeling Framework for Pervasive Computing Systems. In: Meier, R., Terzis, S. (eds.) DAIS 2008. LNCS, vol. 5053, pp. 281–295. Springer, Heidelberg (2008)
15. Reichle, R.: Information Exchange and Fusion in Dynamic and Heterogeneous Distributed Environments, PhD thesis, University of Kassel, Kassel, Germany (2010)

16. Rouvoy, R., Barone, P., Ding, Y., Eliassen, F., Hallsteinsen, S., Lorenzo, J., Mamelli, A., Scholz, U.: MUSIC: Middleware Support for Self-Adaptation in Ubiquitous and Service-Oriented Environments. In: Cheng, B.H.C., de Lemos, R., Giese, H., Inverardi, P., Magee, J. (eds.) Self-Adaptive Systems. LNCS, vol. 5525, pp. 164–182. Springer, Heidelberg (2009)

17. Schmidt, A., Beigl, M., Gellersen, H.-W.: There is more to Context than Location. Computers & Graphics Journal 23(6), 893–901 (1999)

18. Strang, T., Linnhoff-Popien, C., Frank, K.: CoOL: A Context Ontology Language to Enable Contextual Interoperability. In: Stefani, J.-B., Demeure, I., Zhang, J. (eds.) DAIS 2003. LNCS, vol. 2893, pp. 236–247. Springer, Heidelberg (2003)

19. VENUS Project, http://www.iteg.uni-kassel.de/venus/

20. Wagner, M., Reichle, R., Geihs, K.: Context as a service - Requirements, design and middleware support. In: Proceedings of the 9th Annual IEEE International Conference on Pervasive Computing and Communications, PerCom 2011, Seattle, WA, USA, March 21-25, pp. 220–225. IEEE (2011)

Towards Context-Aware Recommendation for Personalized Mobile Travel Planning

Chien-Chih Yu and Hsiao-ping Chang

Dept. of MIS, National ChengChi University
NO. 64, Sec. 2, ZhiNan Rd., Wenshan District, Taipei City 11605, Taiwan
ccyu@nccu.edu.tw, ping623.chang@msa.hinet.net

Abstract. The system design and development of context-aware recommendation for personalized mobile travel planning is an important issue for both research and practices. The goal of this paper is to propose a system development framework and processes for directing the design and implementation of a context-aware recommender system that provides personalized mobile travel planning services. Design science is chosen as the research methodology and technologies integrated for building the system include rule-based reasoning, model based computing, and context data modeling. A prototype system is also constructed and evaluated to validate the feasibility and effectiveness of the proposed system development approach.

Keywords: Recommendation services, mobile travel planning, context awareness, personalization, system development.

1   Introduction

Personalized recommender systems are systems capable of providing the most suitable solutions to users based on their needs and preferences. Personalized recommendation and enabling intelligent technologies have long been important yet complex research as well as practical issues. It has been noted that, without proper functional architecture and system support, the integrated processes of searching and filtering objects, comparing alternatives, as well as selecting and recommending appropriate solutions for user evaluation can be extremely complicated and hard to be carried out [4]. Furthermore, the complexities of the problem scope, solution processes, and system design and implementation methods expands drastically when taking into account the support of mobile users with a variety of mobile devices accessing personalized recommendations [1]. On the other hand, context-awareness which captures user's contextual information such as location and time, needs and interests, and/or social interactions, has become an increasingly desired mechanism for enhancing personalized mobile recommendations [2,3,5]. However, to date, existing works incorporating context awareness into personalized mobile recommendations are still very limited.

Travel planning, as a major functional service in tourism applications, is a process of searching, selecting, grouping and sequencing destination related attractions

P.C. Vinh et al. (Eds.): ICCASA 2012, LNICST 109, pp. 121–130, 2013.
© Institute for Computer Sciences, Social Informatics and Telecommunications Engineering 2013

including sightseeing spots, events, hotels and restaurants. Due to more availability of comprehensive data about travelers and destinations as well as more exchange of information among travelers, how to provide context-aware recommendation services for facilitating personalized travel planning inevitably becomes a critical research and practical issue in the mobile tourism domain [1,4,6]. Ideal context-aware personalized mobile travel planning recommendation services should be able to integrate and match information about tourists' location and time, needs and preferences, conditions and constraints with destination and attraction information, as well as to subsequently recommend personalized travel plans in which sightseeing spots, restaurants, and hotels are bundled to best fit the user context based on suitable recommendation models and rules. Although some specific technologies such as content and collaborative filtering had been applied for conducting personalized recommendations, there are very few previous research efforts undertaking the integrated issues of context-aware personalized travel plan recommendations for mobile tourists. The objective of this study aims at filling the gap by providing system architecture and development method for efficiently and effectively guiding the design and implementation of the demanded context-aware recommender system to support personalized mobile travel planning. In the following sections, a literature review, the proposed system framework and development process, a prototype system, and concluding remarks are presented in section 2 to section 4 respectively.

2   Literature Review

Among many research works regarding design and development of personalized recommendation services in the tourism domain, Garcia et al. (2011) put emphasis on a domain-independent taxonomy-driven recommender system and illustrate examples of individual and group tourism recommendation services based on the tastes of users, their demographic classification and the places they have visited in former trips [6]. As for mobile tourism applications, Kabassi (2010) provides a review of user modeling and personalization techniques as well as some development steps for a personalized mobile tourism recommender system [4]. Yu (2010) proposes a system architecture that integrates personalized and community services for supporting mobile travel planning [12]. Noguera et al. (2012) presents a mobile recommender system combining a hybrid recommendation engine and a mobile 3D GIS architecture to provide tourists with 3D map-based interface and real-time location-sensitive recommendations [8]. On the other hand, Tsai and Chung (2012) develops a route recommendation service to provide theme park visitors with proper route suggestions on facilities they should visit and in what order based on their personal preferences and intended visitation time, as well as tourists' behaviors (i.e., visiting sequences and corresponding timestamps) that are persistently collected using a Radio-Frequency Identification (RFID) system and stored in a route database [9]. Yang and Hwang (2012) develops a travel recommender system to provide tourists with on-tour attraction recommendation services that employs mobile peer-to-peer communications for exchanging ratings on visited attractions with other tourists of similar interests [1].

When context aware functionalities are taken into account, previous works that explore the integrated issues involving context awareness, personalization, mobility, and recommender systems for tourism applications are very rare. Aiming at offering a taxonomy for mobile guides, Emmanouilidis et al. (2012) discuss technical considerations in several aspects of mobile applications including context awareness, client architectures, mobile user interfaces, and service functions [5]. Yilmaz and Erdur (2012) address the issue of design and development of an intelligent context-aware system for recommending attraction points to mobile users according to their contexts, and propose rule-based context reasoning and multi-agent technologies for fulfilling the jobs [7].

As can be seen, research regarding the development and delivery of context-aware personalized mobile travel planning recommendation services is still in its initial stage and only partial solutions have been provided. To efficiently and effectively support context-aware recommendation of personalized travel plan for mobile users, the need of an integrated system framework and development method for guiding system design and implementation is obvious and strong. The goal of this study is to tackle the key problem and propose feasible solutions.

3   Context-Aware Recommendation for Mobile Travel Planning

Design science is adopted as the research methodology because the nature of this study is an information system research that deals with design and implementation issues for developing personalized recommender systems. Four research activities in the design science research on information technology proposed by March and Smith (1995) are to build, evaluate, theorize, and justify; while the research outputs include constructs, model, method, and instantiation [10]. Peffers et al. (2007), instead, propose six activities for the design science research methodology that include problem identification & motivation, objectives of a solution, design & development, demonstration, evaluation, and communication [11]. Based on the design science research methodology proposed by [11], this study presents a system development framework and processes for building context-aware personalized mobile travel planning recommendation services. Intelligent information technologies integrated in this research include rule-based reasoning, model based computing, and context data modeling. A prototype system for demonstrating personalized mobile travel planning recommendation is implemented and evaluated to show the feasibility and effectiveness of the proposed system development approach. The evaluation criteria for the prototype system include user interface & layout, functionality, ease of use, understandability, satisfaction, and intention for future use.

3.1   System Requirements and Processes

The contextual information requirements for supporting context-aware personalized mobile travel planning recommendation include (1) users' current location and time, (2) users' needs and preferences, (3) users' conditions and constraints, (4) users' self-specified evaluation criteria, and (5) destination related sightseeing, accommodations, and dinning information. Decision requirements include decision associated model, knowledge, and processes. Specified information for sightseeing attractions includes sightseeing theme, opening hours, ticket price, location with address and map, briefings and suggested visiting time, etc. Specified information for accommodations includes hotel name, hotel class (star rating), brief introduction, hotel location with address and map, distances to nearby attractions, check-in/checkout times, room types, facilities, price per room per night, website and photos, contact information, and customer ratings, etc. Specified restaurant information includes restaurant name, food type, location with address and map, opening hours, customer ratings, and recommended food lists, etc. Functional requirements specified for the system include user profile management, tourism information management, context-aware recommendation of attractions (e.g. sightseeing spots, restaurants, hotels) and travel plans, travel plan management, as well as map-based positioning and visualization. Additional functions required for the back end system include database, model base and knowledge base management, and possibly ontology and case base management.

Based on the information and functional requirements, a system framework for context-aware personalized mobile travel planning recommendation is shown in Fig. 1. The personalized mobile travel planning recommendation services are comprised of four types of recommendations including hotel, restaurant, and sightseeing recommendation, as well as the travel plan recommendation. These recommendation processes receive requests from mobile users, retrieve user and destination related contextual data, filter and obtain data of relevant destination and attraction objects, activate corresponding recommendation knowledge and models for object evaluation, select and recommend objects with higher ranks in matching users' needs and preferences, and then present recommended results with information and maps to users' mobile devices. Rule inference is used for knowledge processing tasks that generate match scores for all items of specified evaluation criteria. Evaluation models for specific recommendations are responsible for computing the final weighted scores for selected objects and placing ranks to these objects based on their match levels. There are three back-end supportive services: the tourism-related information services, location-based services, and Google map services. These supportive services allow tourists to access tourism information, tourist location information and location aware attraction information, as well as attraction related geographical information and maps. The contextual oriented user profiles and tourism related databases, model bases, and knowledge bases, etc. are built to form the back end system.

Fig. 1. A functional framework for personalized mobile travel planning recommendation

In the following, a complete recommendation process of context-aware personalized mobile travel planning for an example scenario is described and illustrated in Fig. 2. Assume that a tourist just steps out of the main station of a city and requests the recommendation of a one-day tour plan via his smart phone. He specifies the time periods for lunch and dinner time to be 11:00 am -14:00 pm and 18:00-21:00 pm respectively, the maximal number of visiting places to be 7, and the time for the end of the single day tour to be 21:00 pm. The search range of attractions is set to be 3 km from the current location. The needs, preferences, and evaluation criteria for selecting the sightseeing spots, restaurants, and hotels are specified online and/or obtained from the user profile. As the travel planning recommendation process started, the tourist's current location and time are identified and recorded. During the recommendation process, if the updated current time is around the lunch time or dinner time periods, and the tourist has not eat yet, then the restaurant recommendation service is launched to locate preferred restaurants of specified food type and within specified search range. If the current time is not in the lunch and diner time intervals and is no later than 21:00 pm, the number of visited sightseeing spots is less than 7, and there are suitable nearby unvisited sightseeing spots still open with sufficient time to visit, then the recommendation process continues to perform the sightseeing recommendation services. If the current time reaches the time constraint 21:00 pm or the number of visited sightseeing spots reaches 7, then the hotel recommendation service is processed. Finally, the complete tour plan consisting of sequentially arranged attractions including recommended sightseeing spots, restaurants, and hotel is sent with information and maps to the tourist's mobile device.

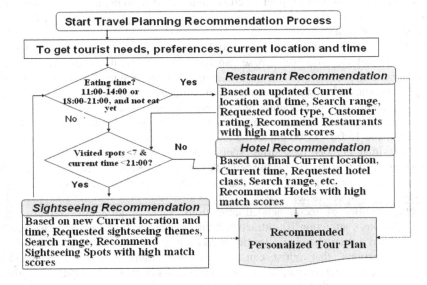

Fig. 2. An example recommendation process of context-aware mobile travel planning

3.2   System Design and Implementation

To facilitate the design and development of the contextual database, the object-oriented (OO) database design approach is applied to create the conceptual data model, and then the OO data model is translated into an entity-relationship (ER) model which is further transformed into the internal relational model for physical database implementation. In the OO data model, identified objects include Tourist, Tourism Information, Recommendation Process, and Tour Plan. The Tourist object composes of Needs and Preferences (N&P), Search and Evaluation Criteria, as well as Current Location and Time objects. The general N&P object is further classified into specific Sightseeing N&P, Restaurant N&P, and Hotel N&P objects. The Tourism Information object has three sub-class objects including Sightseeing Spots Information, Restaurant Information, and Hotel Information objects. The Recommendation Process object contains several component objects including Process Input, Recommendation Model, Recommendation Rule, and Process Output. The Tour Plan object consists of Sightseeing Spot Selection, Restaurant Selection, Hotel Selection, and Plan Schedule objects.

Table 1 describes partially the relational schema of the database. Relational tables created for the prototype system include the Tour plan table, Tour plan schedule table, Hotel table, Hotel room type description table, Hotel room status table, Restaurant table, Food type description table, Sightseeing spot table, Sightseeing theme description table, as well as tourist's location and time tables, and a set of needs, preferences, and criteria tables with respect to sightseeing spots, restaurants, and hotels. A field with underline represents the primary key of the table while the dotted underline indicates the foreign key. The mobile phone number is used as the identification of the tourist, and set as the primary key or part of the composite key for tourist related tables. Based on different types of recommended attractions, the attraction place ID in the tour plan schedule table is linked to the hotel ID in the hotel table, the restaurant ID in the restaurant table, or the sightseeing spot ID in the sightseeing spot table.

As for the design of model base and knowledge base, the process modeling, decision modeling, and rule base approaches are used. Examples of the recommendation process model as well as associated decision model and rules for the tour plan recommendation and restaurant evaluation are shown in Fig. 3-4. The inputs to travel planning recommendation process include tourist current location and time, search range (e.g. 3 km to the current location), constraints and criteria (e.g. 11:00 am - 14:00 pm and 18:00 - 21:00 pm as the lunch and dinner time periods respectively, 7 as the maximal number of visiting spots), as well as needs and preferences for sightseeing spots (e.g. specific sightseeing theme type), restaurants (e.g. specific food type), and hotels (e.g. specific hotel class, room type, room rate, and room facility). The resulting output elements of a recommended tour plan include tour plan ID, sequential number of recommended attractions, type of attractions (sightseeing, restaurant, hotel), attraction ID, attraction name, suggested time for visit, distance to attraction, and a map showing all ordered recommended attractions. By clicking on specific attractions, the tourist can access detail information of recommended sightseeing spots (e.g. name, location, address, distance to the updated current location, sightseeing theme, suggested visiting time, etc.), restaurants (e.g. name, location, address, distance to the updated current location, food type, suggested eating time, customer rating score, etc.), and hotel (e.g. name, location, address, distance to the updated current location, hotel class, room type, room rate, check-in/check-out times, facilities, distances to point-of-interest, distance to the updated current location, customer rating score, etc.).

Table 1. Relational Schema (partial)

Table	Field
Tour plan	TourPlanID, MobilePhoneNumber, travelDate
Tour plan schedule	TourPlanID, AttractionID, sequenceNo, attractionType, recommStartTime, recommEndTime, distanceToPrevLocation
Hotel	HotelID, hotelName, hotelClass, hotelPhoneNumber, hotelAddress, hotelCheckinTime, hotelCheckoutTime, hotelBriefing, hotelPhoto, hotelMap, hotelLongitude, hotelLatitude, hotelCustomerRating
Room type description	RoomTypeID, HotelID, roomTypeName, roomTypeDescription, roomRate, numberOfRoom
Room status	RoomID, HotelID, roomNo, RoomTypeID, facilityList, roomAvailability
Restaurant	RrestaurantID, restaurantName, restaurantPhoneNumber, restaurantAddress, restaurantOpenHours, restaurantBriefing, r-Map, r-Longitude, r-Latitude, r-CustomerRating
Food type description	FoodTypeID, RrestaurantID, foodTypeName, foodTypeMenu
Sightseeing spot	SightseeingID, sightseeingName, sightseeingPhoneNumber, sightseeingAddress, sightseeingOpenDays, sightseeingOpenHours, sightseeinBriefing, recommVisitingTime, ticketPrice, s-Map, s-Longitude, s-Latitude, s-CustomerRating
Sightseeing theme description	SightseeingThemeID, SightseeingID, sightseeingThemeName, sightseeingThemeDescription, featureList
Tourist needs	MobilePhoneNumber, searchRange, requestedHotelClass, requestedFoodType, requestedSightseeingThemes, requestedCustomerRating
Tourist location	MobilePhoneNumber, touristLongitude, touristLatitude

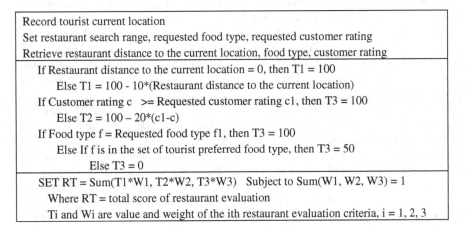

Record tourist current location
Set restaurant search range, requested food type, requested customer rating
Retrieve restaurant distance to the current location, food type, customer rating

If Restaurant distance to the current location = 0, then $T1 = 100$
    Else $T1 = 100 - 10*$(Restaurant distance to the current location)
If Customer rating $c \geq$ Requested customer rating $c1$, then $T3 = 100$
    Else $T2 = 100 - 20*(c1-c)$
If Food type f = Requested food type $f1$, then $T3 = 100$
    Else If f is in the set of tourist preferred food type, then $T3 = 50$
        Else $T3 = 0$

SET $RT = Sum(T1*W1, T2*W2, T3*W3)$ Subject to $Sum(W1, W2, W3) = 1$
    Where RT = total score of restaurant evaluation
    Ti and Wi are value and weight of the ith restaurant evaluation criteria, $i = 1, 2, 3$

Fig. 3. Restaurant evaluation model and rules

Record current location and current time
Set restaurant search range, requested lunch and dinner food type, restaurant rating
Set sightseeing search range, requested sightseeing theme, opening hours
Set hotel search range, requested hotel class, room type, room rate, facility, customer rating
Set temp_time=current time
Set temp_location=current location
While loop
If temp_time is between 11:00 am and 14:00 pm and lunch status=no
    or temp_time is between 18:00 pm and 21:00 pm and dinner status=no
        then Activate Restaurant Recommendation Service Model (temp_location, restaurant
        search range, requested food type, requested customer rating)
    temp_time = temp_time + suggested_eating time
    temp_location = location_of_recommended_place
If temp_time<21:00 pm and the number_visited_site< 7
        Then Activate Sightseeing Recommendation Service Model (temp_location,
        sightseeing search range, requested sightseeing theme, opening hours)
    temp_time = temp_time + suggested_visitng_time
    temp_location = location_of_recommended_place
End loop
Activate Hotel Recommendation Service Model (temp_location, hotel search range,
    requested hotel class, room type, room rate, facility, customer rating)
Output tour plan (selected sightseeing spots, restaurants and hotel with sequence numbers)

Fig. 4. The process model for context-aware travel planning recommendation

4   The Prototype System

A prototype system that enables the provision of the context-aware personalized mobile travel planning recommendation services is developed for demonstration and evaluation. In the system operating environment, system and application software used in the back-end server side include Windows XP, Microsoft IIS Web Server 5.1, Microsoft SQL Server 2008, Microsoft Visual Studio 2010, and Google Map API 3.0. The CHT Windows Mobile 5.0 Smart Phone Emulator is used as the client-side emulator. Besides, one HTC 3G PDA phone and one Apple iPhone 4S are used for system testing and evaluation.

Fig. 5 illustrates some example screenshots of the prototype system. The two left side screenshots indicated as (A) and (B) displays user interfaces for setting needs and search criteria by inserting values to listed items such as search range, sightseeing themes, lunch and dinner food types, hotel class, room rate, and facilities, as well as levels of attraction related customer ratings. The third screenshot (C) presents the overview of the recommended tour plan with photos and names of attractions, sequential numbers (in red balloon), distances to previous locations, suggested time frames for visit, and location maps. Clicking on these attractions will show enlarged pictures and detailed information of the corresponding recommended sightseeing spots, restaurants, and hotel. The right hand screenshot (D) is a Google Map display that visually spots all recommended places with sequential numbers.

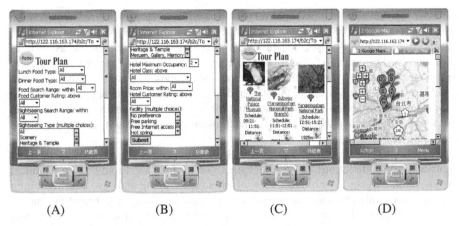

(A)   (B)   (C)   (D)

Fig. 5. Example screenshots of context-aware mobile travel planning recommendation services

The system evaluation of the prototype system is performed through laboratory experiment with actual mobile devices and 3G mobile Internet connections. In the experiment, the user location is configured to a pre-specified geographical region in Taipei, Taiwan. Compared with emulators in the notebooks, the actual mobile devices reflect the real usage for mobile users. The user location is pre-defined because as a testing mobile service, it is hard for this study to access the location of the mobile phone number from 3G operators for privacy issues. Survey questionnaire is employed as a data collection method for system evaluation. Participation is voluntary and anonymous. Testing candidates are randomly selected in a university cafeteria. After a brief orientation explaining the purpose and procedure of the study and experiment, those who agree to participate are presented with a quick review of the prototype system. Participants are encouraged to practice with the prototype system to get familiar with the menus and functions of the recommendation services for personalized mobile travel planning. Then, the participants are asked to perform some typical travel planning tasks using the prototype system and to complete the system evaluation questionnaire. Data of the prototype system evaluation is collected from a sample of thirty participants with 50% being female. Based on a 5-point Likert scale (1 as strongly disagree and 5 as strongly agree), the average scores of six performance criteria including user interface & layout, functionality, ease of use, understandability, satisfaction, and intention for future use are 3.93, 4.13, 4.14, 4.48, 3.80, and 3.87 respectively. The overall average score is 4.06. This result indicates positively the applicability and effectiveness of the proposed recommender system framework and development method for context-aware personalized mobile travel planning.

5   Concluding Remarks and Future Studies

Based on the design science research methodology, this paper proposes a system framework, process models, as well as design and development methods for building context-aware recommender system to support personalized mobile travel planning. This research integrates advanced mobile and recommendation technologies to direct and facilitate the development and delivery of powerful context-aware recommendation services for enabling pre-trip and/or during-the-trip personalized travel planning that take into account mobile tourists' location and time, needs and preferences, as well as constraints and criteria. The construction, testing, and evaluation of the prototype system reflect the feasibility and effectiveness of the proposed system framework and development processes. In short, the system design and development approach presented in this paper provides guidance and example for both the academia and professionals in the separate and integrated fields of context-aware recommendation and personalized mobile travel planning.

In order to fully realize the potential of the proposed system development approach, some directions for future works are as follows. Firstly, as a technical extension, intelligent technologies such as ontology mapping and case-base reasoning will be incorporated into the recommendation functions. Secondly, formal evaluation of the proposed methods and systems will be conducted using a set of real businesses cases with different levels of complexity and different types of mobile devices to capture the impact relationships between specific design practices and performance outcomes.

References

1. Yang, W.-S., Hwang, S.-Y.: iTravel: a recommender system in mobile peer-to-peer environment. Journal of Systems and Software (in press, 2012)
2. Mehra, P.: Context-aware computing: beyond search and location-based services. IEEE Internet Computing 16, 12–16 (2012)
3. Yndurain, E., Bernhardt, D., Campo, C.: Augmenting mobile search engines to leverage context awareness. IEEE Internet Computing 16, 17–25 (2012)
4. Kabassi, K.: Personalizing recommendations for tourists. Telematics and Informatics 27, 51–66 (2010)
5. Emmanouilidis, C., Koutsiamanis, R., Tasidou, A.: Mobile guides: taxonomy of architectures, context awareness, technologies and applications. Journal of Network and Computer Applications (in press, 2012)
6. Garcia, I., Sebastia, L., Onaindia, E.: On the design of individual and group recommender systems for tourism. Expert Systems with Applications 38, 7683–7693 (2011)
7. Yilmaz, O., Erdur, R.C.: iConAwa – an intelligent context-aware system. Expert Systems with Applications 39, 2907–2918 (2012)
8. Noguera, J.M., Barranco, M.J., Segura, R.J., Martinez, L.: A mobile 3D-GIS hybrid recommender system for tourism. Information Sciences 215, 37–52 (2012)
9. Tsai, C.-Y., Chung, S.-H.: A personalized route recommendation service for theme parks using RFID information and tourist behavior. Decision Support Systems 52, 514–527 (2012)
10. March, S.T., Smith, G.F.: Design and natural science research on information technology. Decision Support Systems 15, 251–266 (1995)
11. Peffers, K., Tuunanen, T., Rothenberger, M.A., Chatterjee, S.: A design science research methodology for information systems research. Journal of Management Information Systems 24, 45–77 (2007)
12. Yu, C.-C.: Integrating Personalized and Community Services for Mobile Travel Planning and Management. In: Papasratorn, B., Lavangnananda, K., Chutimaskul, W., Vanijja, V. (eds.) IAIT 2010. CCIS, vol. 114, pp. 202–213. Springer, Heidelberg (2010)

A Spatio-temporal Surveillance Approach for Business Activity Monitoring

Gabriel Pestana[1], Joachim Metter[2], and Pedro Reis[3]

[1] IST / INOV, Lisbon, Portugal
gabriel.pestana@inov.pt
[2] BIJO-DATA GmbH, Sesslach, Germany
jmetter@bijodata.de
[3] ANA-Aeroportos de Portugal, Lisbon, Portugal
pereis@ana.pt

Abstract. The SECAIR project provides an event-driven architecture for dealing with spatio-temporal requirements. It adopts a multi-sensor data fusion process to handle with event streams emitting continuously location based data regarding a vast number of different business objects. It is therefore well-suited for business activity monitoring, supporting managers at analysing and processing complex event streams in real-time. A prototype applied to the surveillance of situation awareness requirements for airport environments is presented, in particular to monitor ground movements in very congested areas for indoor and outdoor areas. Outputs are presented using an advanced Graphical-User Interface, addressing a collaborative environment for airport stakeholders to manage ground handling operational procedures more efficiently and in compliance with airport business rules.

Keywords: Situation and Context Awareness Services, Spatio-temporal data, spatial Data Warehouse, Spatial Dashboard.

1 Introduction

In today's highly competitive service-oriented business environment, it is essential to keep decision makers informed about which events are affecting business-critical operations. This requirement is even more relevant in much regulated environments, with a set of business rules which need to be continuously checked to minimize delays or reduce the likelihood of risky events [1]. This is the case of an airport, usually classified as a system of systems, which following the Advanced Surface Movement Guidance and Control Systems (A-SMGCS) recommendations need to encompass functionalities for unambiguous identification of all surface traffic (e.g., aircraft and vehicles) without reducing the number of operations or the level of safety [2].

The main concerns of levels I and II of the A-SMGCS concept rely on the improvements of safety, whereas the ground movement's efficiency is dealt with in levels III and IV. This means that the surveillance service is a pre-requisite for implementing all the other A-SMGCS services.

P.C. Vinh et al. (Eds.): ICCASA 2012, LNICST 109, pp. 131–140, 2013.

In the airport environment, surveillance must be able to respond to an increasingly complex range of threats. It also requires the integration of multiple technologies to continuous monitor and effectively manage the processing of aircraft, passengers and cargo data. To reach such level of data integration for decision-making, we need an informational cockpit capable to graphically impart large amounts of relevant information into the screen. A feature typically assigned to corporate dashboards.

Indeed, one way to keep tabs on every tiny piece of airport situation awareness and simultaneously get a big-picture mosaic of the airport is through spatial dashboards. When combined with map viewers and human understanding, spatial dashboards also provide business users with the ability to make balanced decisions when monitoring business activities.

In this paper an innovative event-driven approach for monitoring daily operations is presented based on the prototype that is being designed within the SECAIR project [3]. The project makes use of a spatial data warehouse (SDW) and deals with complex event streams using multiple localisation technologies as sensor devices. It is therefore well-suited for business activity monitoring, supporting the decision-making process of business users at analysing complex event streams in real-time.

The remainder of the paper is organized as follows. Section 2 provides a short analysis of related work, outlining technologies used to continuously collect data about airport surface movements. Section 3 and 4 presents the system overall description, emphasizing the main points which make the proposed solution different from usual tracking systems. Section 5 shortly describes the chosen technology for the development of the control services, outlining the most relevant ones. The paper ends with conclusions in section 6.

2   Related Work

Airport surveillance demands security requirements to protect passengers, staff and critical infrastructure from serious safety infringements that may compromise airport operations [4]. The range of location–based and sensing technologies required to provide the early detection and intervention in an airport environment typically include a mix of many different systems. For instance, surface movement radar (SMR) and secondary surveillance radar (SSR) systems are quite common in large airports. However these solutions are extremely expensive to purchase and operate, and are subject to masking and distortion in the vicinity of airport buildings, terrain or plants [5].

The extensive deployment of satellite system and air-to-ground data links results in the emergence of complementary means and techniques. Among these, ADS-B (Automatic Dependent Surveillance-Broadcast) and MLAT (Multilateration) techniques may be the most representative [6]. However, current radar based systems have many problems to track surface targets, especially in very dense traffic areas, such as the apron area or the taxiways. On the other hand, most of the aircrafts turn-off their transponders after landing, compromising their identification possibilities. This means that such systems will not detect non-cooperative vehicles or aircrafts that are not equipped with such a transponder. Therefore there is a strong demand for a new sensing technology, in particular for smaller/medium airports. Such sensors include near-range radar networks, Mode 3/A, S or VHF multilateration [5], CCTV systems with video analytics [7], magnetic flux sensors [8] or D-GPS installed in vehicles [9]. Although none of these sensors is individually able to meet all the user's requirements for airport surveillance, the fusion of the information they give can achieve an acceptable solution.

Most of existing systems operate independently from each other [4], limiting the opportunity for providing automated decision support [10]. The function of tracking, correlating and forecasting operationally relevant data from the information presented, is left as a task for the business users. In recent work [11], it is already possible to find algorithms addressing the very stringent integrity requirements to support aircraft surface movement.

In the literature it is possible to find research projects (e.g., 2004: Airnet at *www.airnet-project.com* and ISMAEL at *www.ismael-project.net*, 2006: EMMA at *www.dlr.de/emma*, 2008: AAS at *www.aas-project.eu* and LOCON at *www.locon-eu.com*), with different technologies that have been developed and successfully tested for ground movements detection, providing real time analysis and presenting actionable data with a high degree of certainty or as a cost-effective solution.

Within the SECAIR project, one of the technical requirements is that all location–based technologies are coherently integrated using advanced data-fusion techniques in order to reduce installation costs and to address multipath effects reduction. The project advanced fusion techniques operating with high-performance Global Navigation Satellite System (GNSS) and improved radio based tracking, combined with video based technology will enable the accomplishment of an automatic and reliable prediction of safety events. This broad-level integration extends the state-of-the-art for the surveillance of airport surface traffic, enabling unique automated decision support capabilities, with new context aware services, that have not thus far been available.

3   System Description and Operational Scenarios

The SECAIR system is being designed to monitor ground vehicle and aircraft movement at airports. Tests have shown that the system can be used for surveillance, either as a complementary system for existing and future A-SMGCS at large airports or as a cost-effective stand-alone solution that uses commercial available location-based technologies for monitoring critical areas at medium and small airports. For instance, to track handling operations at congested areas for indoor and outdoor environments (e.g., boarding gates at the passenger terminal and aircraft parking areas at the apron).

The SECAIR system was defined assuming that video cameras are installed for a complete video surveillance and homogeneous coverage of the target area for daylight/good visibility conditions and operational situations. It also assumes that site tests are performed without any wireless data communication problems and that some resources (i.e., vehicles, equipment, and staff) are equipped with at least one localisation technology. The positions of surveyed objects are continuously transmitted and are coherently integrated using advanced data-fusion techniques to address multipath effects reduction and improve quality of location (QoL). The Data-fusion algorithm operates with the following localization technologies:

- Vehicle, GSE or person positions
  - A standalone GNSS, collecting a new position each second;
  - An indoor-outdoor tracking system based on radio frequency localization (IOTS), collecting at least 1 position per second;
  - A video surveillance and tracking system (VSTS), capable at providing a new position each 0.5 seconds;
  - IEEE 802.15.4a Ultra Wide Band (UWB) standard for a low-rate wireless personal area network.
- Aircraft (A/C), the point feature representing the position of the A/C corresponds to the A/C central point with a clearance defined by the A/C classification (i.e., wingspan and length).

To perform this correlation, and to present the results to business users in an easy to understand way, the system performs a WGS84 coordinate transformation to all location-based data. Non-cooperative objects positions and identifier (e.g., Aircraft and Staff) are provided by the VSTS in a vector format. The demanded result of this correlation (fusion) step is an only track for each mobile. The surface conformance monitoring capability will provide a notification to all connected business users when there is an event. When an event is detected, a timely response is required to reduce the impact on safety or efficiency. For instance, whenever a vehicle protection area intersects with another moving object or infrastructure, a collision avoidance event is triggered informing the driver to move to a safety distance. This scenario requires the vehicle to be equipped with an onboard unit, which includes a touch screen display and a radiofrequency (RFID) reader for an automatic login procedure that uses the airport ID card of the driver to simultaneously validate if the diver is authorized to operate the identified vehicle.

In order to validate the SECAIR system and outline its benefits at accurately detecting the presence of objects (i.e., persons, vehicles, goods), inside or in the surrounding area of predefined locations, a system prototype for a pilot test is being installed at Airport of Faro (AFR), Portugal. The implementation comprises the system deployment, the interfaces to heterogeneous localization technologies and a set of client applications with a self-configuring graphical user interface (GUI).

For field tests, ANA-Aeroportos de Portugal (ANA) - the main Portuguese airport's management company, will provide airport vehicles together with a wireless network covering all airport operational areas. The system deployment also comprises interoperability with existing airport systems, for instance, to collect flight information and data about Staff. This interaction brings to the forefront information requirements relevant to assist operational managers in responding more efficiently and on time to events requiring their immediate intervention.

4   Event-Driven Architecture for Spatio-temporal Data Analysis

The SECAIR project constructs the whole system according to a centralized event-driven architecture [12]. Fig. 1 illustrates the system multi-layer architecture, covering requirements ranging from levels of the data communication layer to the presentation layer of user interaction.

The architecture consists on a set of interconnected components, on the deployment of IP-based wireless communication networks, on a middleware platform responsible to integrate positioning data into accurate location information, on a business logic that acts as a gateway between the business requirements and the client applications, for instance, to provide semantic meaning to events triggered by the server, on a client Graphical User Interface (GUI) that act as a control center for end-users to interact with the system as a whole.

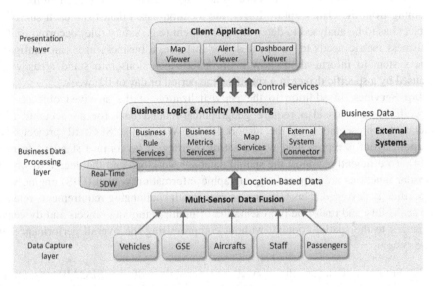

Fig. 1. Block diagram with a high level view of the SECAIR system

Since the system operates with heterogeneous sensors, prior to the data fusion process, it receives multiple positioning data from the Data Capture layer. But after the multi-sensor data fusion process, we obtain one computed position per object that is reliable. The Business Data Processing layer includes software modules such a role-classified multi-view of business rules, customized business metrics and the segmentation of the airport into multiple operational areas interacting with each other over a common stream of location-based data.

The Multi-Sensor Data Fusion module takes lessons learned from the LocON project [9] in relation to techniques for multi-target, multi-sensor tracking. The project advanced fusion techniques operate with improved radio based tracking and video based technology enabling the surveillance of non-cooperative resources (i.e., vehicle, GSE or personnel not equipped with a localisation device). At the server side, the system core functionalities are managed by the following software components:

- **Business Rule Services**, establishes the link between the definition and the execution of all business rules within the system [13], enabling organizational policies and the repeatable decisions associated with those policies, such as restricted areas incursions, to be defined, deployed, monitored and maintained centrally at the server side. When changes occur at the business level, this service also assists in finding the set of existing rules that are influenced by those changes. The Business Rule Services interacts with the SDW to store all incoming events with the right classification.

- **Business Metrics Services**, constructs a layered hierarchy of business indicators. It uses a decision dendrogram with its nodes weighted. Granular indicators are at the bottom (leaf) level and the derived indicators (usually more aggregated) are the nodes of the dendrogram. Updates to metric values have to be computed in almost real-time to enable a short reaction time. This means that for each inline data coming from the Data Capture Layer, the location-based data from each survived object has to be analysed to determine if an event (e.g., safety rule) occurred or if a business metric needs to be updated. For instance, a business user can configure the system to inform about how many safety incursions into stand areas were caused by a specific driver in a specific time period or day of the week.

- **Map Services**, in addition to the geovisualization of the survived objects, the specified scenarios also require geographical-related data for an accurate and detailed representation of the airport layout. Within the SECAIR project, the airport layout is represented with a set of overlapped layers in a standard format [14]. To efficiently support the spatial database workload and the degree to which spatial functions are required, a geographic information system (GIS) engine was specifically designed. This GIS engine copes with challenging requirements related to scalability and real-time representation of multiple moving objects and dynamic changes to the spatial context, without compromising the overall performance of the system.

At the Presentation layer, the surveillance capability of the SECAIR system is presented to business users in three different ways. The Map Viewer represents moving objects as colour coded point features with a timestamp and a set of descriptive data (see Fig. 2); this may include additional data (metadata) about aircrafts, vehicles, drivers, flight data, and descriptive data about the airport operational. The Alert Viewer presents a textual description of the alert messages, with indication of start and end time, plus a set of additional descriptive data related to each event. The Dashboard Viewer expresses in a graphical layout, the values of spatio-temporal business indicators enabling each Client Application to provide a clear picture of the airport status. In Fig. 2, the three vehicles visualized with a colour coded labelled outline different levels of alert messages presented at the Alert Viewer.

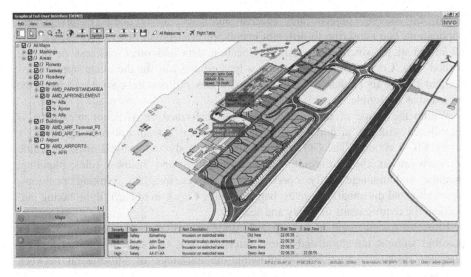

Fig. 2. Prototype version of the GUI layout

By default any client application connecting to the system automatically subscribes the Locations control service to start receiving the location of all ObjectIDs being surveyed. In parallel the location of each ObjectID is checked to validate if an alert message needs to be trigged to the presentation layer and consequently assign the proper semantic and risk level to each alert message. Infractions caused by each ObjectID need to be classified at the server side before passing the information to the presentation layer, otherwise the end-user will not understand what is being presented at the Map viewer. To provide this service, a database storing business rules, policies and additional relevant data for each map feature is required.

5   Data-Flow between Layers Managed by Control Services

Within the SECAIR project, Windows Communication Foundation (WCF) provides an explicit support for service-oriented development with a unified programming model for rapidly build service-oriented interfaces. Built on .NET Framework 4, WCF is implemented primarily as a set of classes on top of the .NET Framework's Common Language Runtime (CLR). WCF doesn't define a required host, allowing creating clients that access services running in different context environments.

The WCF cope with most of the communication requirements because the interface must be remotely accessible as the GUI can run on a different hardware/technology than one where the business logic or the external systems are. The interface is mainly event driven, with the business logic and the external systems continuously sending events to update the GUI after a successful login.

Control services are the building blocks to implement business logic, enabling business users to dynamically manage and interact with the target environment, changing the status of the business context as well as to obtain detailed information about the moving objects and receive automatic alerts about events. Client applications can subscribe to different events, receiving also in an event-driven way all information, which can consist of location data and other business or device related data. Control Services perform a background job for the client applications without adding more than a slight delay of a few milliseconds, so it can likely be regarded as negligible.

Within the scope of the field tests to be performed at ARF, an integration is established with the airport operational management system common to all ANA airports (GO system). The GO system enables the study and analysis of the schedule for each season, the configuration of infrastructures and business rules, planning, monitor and manage daily operations in subsystems like, parking positions, embarking and disembarking gates, baggage belts, Check-in to each flight, taking into account the requirements of safety and security.

Effective management and integrated complexity of the operation would not be possible without the input and output interfaces, the GO system states with very different systems / applications, allowing the exchange of information between stakeholders.

To conclude this section, Table 1 presents the multidimensional database structure of the Spatial Data Warehouse (SDW) that will hold the analytical processing capabilities of the SECAIR system. The matrix lists at the columns the dimensions used to describe business logic and at the lines the events (facts) related to the different domains of business activity monitoring. The intersection between lines and columns defines the star schema for each fact table. Any dimension (column) with more than one "X" implies that this dimension must be conformed across multiple fact tables (lines), forming a constellation.

Table 1. The SDW Matrix of the SECAIR Data Structure

Dimensions Granular Facts (ROLAP)	Airport Layout	Aircrafts	VehiclesGSE	Stakeholders	Flights	Staff	Tasks	Alerts	Time Hour	Time Day
Ground Movements	X	X	X	X	X	X	X	X	X	X
Safety Security Events	X	X	X	X		X		X		X
Vehicle Services	X		X	X	X	X	X		X	X

The Airport Layout dimension is a spatial dimension storing the thematic layers which characterize the airport layout in conformity with the ED119 std. [14]. It also stores metadata about each operational area. For instance, airport circulation constraints on areas related to ground traffic movements include speed limits for different types of moving objects (e.g., operational vehicles and A/C), constrains for specific vehicles categories (e.g., auto-stairs, high-loaders, passenger busses), data related to the airport operational status (e.g., normal or low visibility operations). The other dimensions are non-spatial in the sense that they only store business data obtained through interoperability with the GO system.

The three fact tables store specific events related to ground movements, therefore classified as spatial facts with a new coordinate position stored for each object being monitored. The Ground Movements is the most granular and detailed fact table, classifying each movement in relation to any business rule infringement. The Safety Security Events stores aggregated data related only to safety and security events. Finally the Vehicle Services fact table is particularly adjusted for fleet management.

The SDW is accessed by all software components from the Business Data Processing Layer. The External System Connector is configured to connect to the GO system to collect operational data in a format usable by SECAIR. At the Presentation Layer, the user profile determines the level of detail established to access the information stored in the SDW. The goal is to provide business users with the required information to remotely monitor/coordinate on-going operations or to analyse historic events.

6   Conclusions

The paper presents an event-driven architecture, with a multi-sensor fusion algorithm and GIS functionalities to support spatio-temporal data processing of numerous continuous event streams. The proposed event-driven architecture is a pragmatic and reliable way to ensure fast response times, meaning that any occurrences are shown immediately (within fractions of a second) and, as far as possible, dealt with automatically.

The system adopts a multi-layer approach with heterogeneous localization technologies and a multi-sensor data fusion process to handle with event streams emitting continuously location-based data for each surveyed object. It is therefore well-suited for business activity monitoring, supporting business users at analysing and processing complex event streams in real-time.

The proposed system is being designed to deal with spatio-temporal requirements, including scalability and security of data. A SDW was specified to hold a very high volume of fine-grained events, which must be processed and analyse individually before taking appropriate control actions. The innovative mix between geovisualization functionalities, the treemap approach for the spatial dashboard and the use of control services also introduce new challenges to the data fusion process contributing to improve situation awareness and situation management capabilities for coordinating apron operations and monitor, in real-time, the compliance of ground traffic operations with airport business rules.

Acknowledgements. The SECAIR (ref. E6030) is an R&D project, partially funded under the EUROSTARS program, which started in September 2011. The SECAIR consortium includes partners from 6 EC Member States, with a pilot at the Airport of Faro (AFR), Portugal.

References

[1] Kang, J., Han, K.: A Business Activity Monitoring System Supporting Real-Time Business Performance Management. In: Proc. of 3rd International Conference on Convergence and Hybrid Information Technology (2008)

[2] ICAO: Safety Management Manual (SMM), 2nd ed. Doc 9859 AN/474 (2009) ISBN 978-92-9231-295-4

[3] Metter, J.: Project coordinator. Security on airport and other critical large infrastructures (SECAIR). EUREKA-Eurostars project ref. E!6030 (2011-2014)

[4] Stocking, C., et al.: Integrating Airport Information Systems. ACRP Report 13, Research sponsored by the Federal Aviation Administration (2009)

[5] Hu, T.T.W., Wang, L., Maybank, S.: A survey on visual surveillance of object motion and behaviors. IEEE Transacions on Systems Man, and Cybernetics-part C: Applications and Reviews, 334–351 (2004)

[6] Soto, A., Merino, P., Valle, J.: ADS-B integration in the SESAR surface surveillance architecture. In: Proceedings of Enhanced Surveillance of Aircraft and Vehicles (ESAV), pp. 13–18 (2011)

[7] Besada, J.A., et al.: Image-based automatic surveillance for airport surface (2009), http://www.giaa.inf.uc3m.es

[8] Gao, H., et al.: Safe airport operation based on innovative magnetic detector system. Institution of Engineering and Technology, Transp. Syst. 3(2), 236–244 (2009)

[9] Pestana, G., Rebelo, I., Duarte, N., Couronné, S.: Addressing stakeholders coordination for airport efficiency and decision-support requirements. Journal of Aerospace Operations (JAO11) (2011)

[10] Mehta, V., et al.: Decision Support Tools for the Tower Flight Data Mananger System. In: Integrated Communications, Navigation and Surveillance Conference (ICNS), pp. I4-1 – I4-12(2011)

[11] Schuster, W., Bai, J., Feng, S., Ochieng, W.: Integrity monitoring algorithms for airport surface movement. SpringerLink 16(1), 65–75 (2012)

[12] Dunkel, J., Fernández, A., Ortiz, R., Ossowski, S.: Event-driven architecture for decision support in traffic management systems. Expert Systems with Applications 38, 6530–6539 (2011)

[13] Agaram, M., Liu, C.: An Engine-independent Framework for Business Rules Development. In: Proc. of 15th IEEE International Enterprise Distributed Object Computing Conference (2011)

[14] EUROCAE: ED-119B - Interchange Standards For Terrain, Obstacle, and Aerodrome Mapping Data (2011)

Smart Communication Adviser for Remote Users

Marek Penhaker[1], Ondrej Krejcar[2], Martin Cerny[1], Miroslav Behan[2],
and Pavlina Penhakerova[1]

[1] VSB – Technical University of Ostrava, FEECS, Department of Cybernetics and Biomedical Engineering, 17. listopadu 15, Ostrava – Poruba, 708 33, Czech Republic
{Marek.Penhaker,Martin.Cerny}@vsb.cz,
Pavlina.Penhakerova@seznam.cz
[2] University of Hradec Kralove, FIM, Department of Information Technologies, Rokitanskeho 62, Hradec Kralove, 500 03, Czech Republic
Ondrej.Krejcar@ASJournal.eu, Mirek.Behan@gmail.com

Abstract. In present days there are many innovations that improve communication for the remote user's application. There is necessary to adapt user interface in content of application and age experience of user. There is presented the concept for applicable and spatially smart established applications focused on utilization and emphasis of information implemented with fuzzy logic recognition.

Keywords: Smart, Mobile, Communication, Wifi, Service, Fuzzy logic.

1 Introduction

Enormous potential of ICT, which are nowadays developed massive thanks sub-miniaturization of implementation of implementation and increased computing power, together with increased data throughput of mobile networks has been a stimulus to create standalone applications connected with the environment and cloud storage, which could easily help users headlong current information that influence them. At the same time, the data stored in the cloud storage and reduce time and mental stress spent on communications controlling with a mobile device.

In the last few years there has been a huge expansion of new technologies and platforms that thanks to globalization existing technologies introduce significant competition. Hall is more used in mobile communication technology equipment, which of these systems is still a powerful tool to use in everyday reality in the semi on-line applications, conforming to the actual circumstances. Among the best-known player on the market in operating systems working on real-time processing Android, iOS, Windows Mobile penetrating and innovative systems based on Bada, MeeGo or SymbianOS.

Much of the users using mobile devices to remotely manage multiple communication channels simultaneously. Above all, however, are the applications that only minimally affect the activity and location of users even though users would it welcome..

P.C. Vinh et al. (Eds.): ICCASA 2012, LNICST 109, pp. 141–150, 2013.

The time of closed development is definitely over and the open development we acknowledge as a mainstream for mobile device evolution progress which comes out from creativity, social networked and intellectual power hided in great number of many individuals. Today most people using mobile devices primarily for daily communication. However by changing establishment of current mobile provider's profits to more close of customers usability with mobile devices, we see more and more only internet online connected devices combining all possibilities of smart device features, where one single mobile device would step up all personal needs.

Nowadays it is no longer the domain of only populated agglomerations, but also places in the countryside with good coverage, where users require quality results depending on the Internet service provider. Often it is practically limited by the user such as the quality of wireless application protocol and used applied reduce deployment for operations requiring complex data support machine vision, learning and recognition [1]. The advantage of short outreach applications, in addition to the high bitrate possibility of using a more precise localization of persons in both buildings and underground or where there is sufficient signal strength of the mobile operator, or PS transmitters. This mass-used by the WLAN network coverage using Wifi router, which increased rapidly in the last decade and the number of smart phones with WLAN capability has grown in recent years. At present, the increasing penetration of these quick short outreach networks and domestic environment both coverage and signal internet creating intranets within the household to household appliances.

2   Problem Definitions

There are basically still the same methods of communication in today's mobile networks and new trends are not currently anticipated. Therefore there is the need to use their own computing device options and cloud storage to enhance interactivity among users but also to the user in the form of smart graphics using fuzzy logic. Based on previous user behavior can improve and adjust approaches to display and interact with user. Within approaches are both text messages and voice conversations further and spoken communication where can trace both forms of communication and intonation, stress and mental condition. Lastly, it's multimedia and visualization between the mobile device and the user. This area is considered a major and beneficial. Although human visual perception in the total amount of information is the main source, but under certain circumstances anonymization environment where mimics and background scenes picture would lead to distortions in the communication process, we show non-visual and face-face communication as equivalent in terms quality of life and perception [3].

Also, there are different kinds of relationship communication, one by one, one row or many-to-many in a bi-direction relationship, and we would consider active (synchronized) or passive (asynchronous) interaction between actors. Others view is about networks and current options.

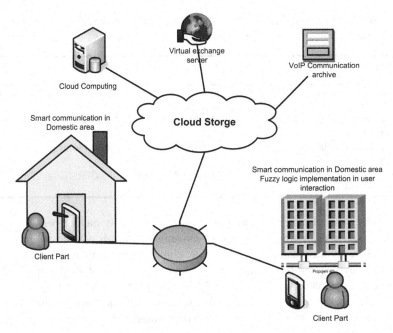

Fig. 1. Smart communication adviser with the fuzzy logic user interaction implementation

Networks for mobile devices are a major problem in the field of mobile communication and how mobile devices can access the network. One well-known standards used by mobile operators is a global system for mobile communications (GSM). Another standard we consider wireless local area networks (Wi-Fi). In the first case, we consider the quality of services in short the major ones are the second generation 2G (GPRS), 2.5G (EDGE), 3G (UTM) or 4G (LTE). Network coverage is analogous soil decreases with increasing generation level. In the second case, it is interesting to IEEE 802.11e standard, which supports services and duality Voice operational Program.

While we are very familiar technological aspects of behavior are influenced by communication protocols and standards. Short message system from the perspective of communication is well known standard for mobile devices, and as the current flow to announce short message service (SMS), where technical restrictions such as length of transmitted messages, and lack of user status confirmation. The maximum message length is defined as 160 characters encoded with 7bits, 140 NUMBER from 8bits or 16bits to 70 chars.

In principle it is possible to communicate via SMS level consider obsolete and this type can be used in case of insufficient data connectivity. The purpose of the smart behavior of users is important to realize that the social objectives based daily human needs, where the information is part of the social union are required as necessary. Social information on inter-personal circle the relationships are with its subjectivity and the importance of the message bridge other information that is based on global knowledge without non-interactivity relationship. For this reason, the natural increase of the applicability of social instant messaging and are aware of the report on the future supply.

Table 1. Request/Response local measurement with object persistence on server side tested with client Android mobile device ZTE Blade

Communication Method	Technology	Latency
AppServer/DB Engine/HTTP-POST	Appengine/ Objectify(JPA)	250ms-400ms (avg. 300ms)
AppServer/Remote Cloud DB/ HTTP-POST	Appengine/ MySQL	450ms-600ms (avg. 500ms)
AppServer/Local DB/ HTTP-POST	Tomcat7/ObjectDB	350ms-450ms (avg. 370ms)
JVM Server/DB Engine/ TCP/Socket-Object Serialization	Socket Server/ ObjectDB/	20ms-30ms (avg. 23ms)

The main type of communication is voice services. It means two-way voice communication with minimum latency of movement towards active speech type of process. There is technical aspect of voice communication in real-time needs of network latency. Therefore we take into account the concept of Real Time Protocol (RTP) to exchange data with low latency [2] in combination with the original session protocol (SIP) as the control flow of communication. All client-server-client cases to consider latency and network speed for proper recommendations regarding the quality of services available.

The table tested server / client technology, which uses the Android mobile device and said appropriate usability.

3   Methods

Outline of a possible solution is a diagrammatic view in higher abstraction introduced in this paper gradually. Context description for the basic representation of the current scenario as the most common cases is shown in Figure 2a we focus on the communication process of the system itself smart interactive user environment with fuzzy logic recognition neighborhood. (see Figure 2).

Home environment where network access is provided by home WLAN access point, a personal mobile device that is able to recognize the real environment of the user location to the specified credential wireless docking station or GPS location. Access to the environment recognition is defined by user input. In some cases, recognizing only the Wi-Fi connection should be sufficient for intelligent behaviour. [5]

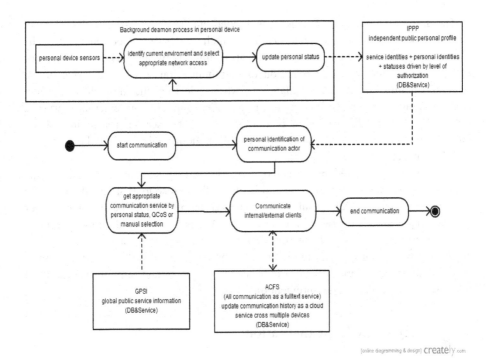

Fig. 2. Schema of communication process

The proposal was divided into three separate parts, which were mandatory for the success of intelligent communication behavior counseling. The first defines the independent public profiles personal services, which basically getting information from various sources, such as social networking, messaging servers, and other authorized external inputs. This service is to be personally responsible for the location and status of the connection based on the availability of services and the current environment.

A knowledge base for mobile applications is the second mandatory part of the concept of an independent information service where the cost and quality of the descriptions.. Is it possible to call this type of service as the cost and quality of the knowledge base, which will increase in accuracy over time [6].

Other compulsory part of the concept is an interface for mobile devices marked in the schema as cell tower that would be necessary as extensional bridge in terms of the concept of usability. And the last is a mandatory part of mobile applications consider the iPhone, Android and Windows Mobile platform-based client, which informs the user about the quality and price of services by location and environment. Supports part of the concept should be open Wi-Fi community where independent Wi-Fi providers could propose micro real low cost of Internet access. For better understanding, the following section describes the communication process (see Figure 1).

The draft communication process was divided into several parts. The first element was designed with personal identification, which is desired to communicate. The second element is to establish communication links between players in online or offline mode. That influence selection of communication services in terms of the required quality, price and availability. After selecting the defined or default configuration of communication itself provides internal or external services. Optionally, history of interaction is stored as a cluster service for future use on different devices accessible via the web client or mobile client. The whole process ends by any act or failure services [7].

The assessment, based on knowledge of the cost of services as a set of data obtained from a mobile operator in the price lists. These resources are available on the website providers, which would be processed automatically pages analyzer or manually by a human operator into the system. Another way would be by agreement with the provider of the information extraction than external data format such as XML. Knowledge of the quality of service is based on empirical data obtained from the mobile device applications, where it is, under certain circumstances, have influence on the accurate measurement of the network [8].

4   Fuzzy Logic Implementation

The expert systems are specialized computer programs for decision support. Diagnostic expert systems (Fig. 4.) are designed for a predetermined set of valuation of alternative solutions (diagnoses). Carry out an effective interpretation of the data to determine which of a predetermined set of the final best solution corresponds to the real data concerning a particular case. The system's knowledge base in which are stored in the form of procedural knowledge to solve the case. Knowledge is obtained from the expert. The specific data to the problem are stored in the user data base. Confrontation of specific data and general knowledge performs control mechanism that gradually evaluating each hypothesis generates the hierarchical list [9].

There is huge possibility to use fuzzy logic expert system in our task. The main task is to define relationship functions, to we can precisely define position and other thing defined in background daemon process in mobile device. The main parts of fuzzy model will be processing of data form mobile device sensors and actuators, which could produce bigger amount of information. It is based on fuzzy rule-based language model, in which the formalization of linguistic terms (linguistic values of input and output linguistic variables) using fuzzy sets to represent knowledge about how to troubleshoot the application of rules of type IF-THEN, for operation over knowledge and learning procedures are used fuzzy logic as defined below.

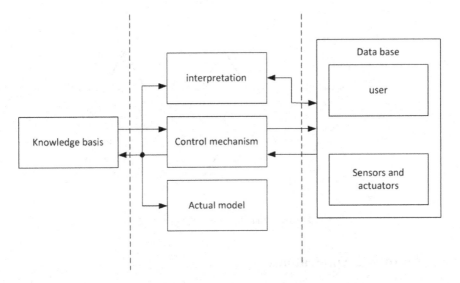

Fig. 3. Fuzzy model decision system structure

$$R_m^{(k)} : IF\left(X \; je \, LX^{(k)}\right) \; THEN \; \left(Y \; je \, LY^{(k)}\right) \quad k = 1, 2, ... n \tag{1}$$

There is presumption, all the rules are in the rule set connected by fuzzy logic operator or with interpretation as the normal disjunction (max). These rules set declares knowledge basis of basic fuzzy logic expert system. This kind of summation fuzzy model is the basis of our work. The final relation in our model we can describe as below:

$$R_m(x, y) = \bigcup_{k=1}^{n} R_m^{(k)}(x, y) \tag{1}$$

The final decision should be interpreted in graphical way too as displayed below. Basic variable definition could be described is described in standard way by using triangular relationship function as defined below. The each row is for each rule in rules set, each chart in row describes value of input value and the third chart in the row is output variable function with two values (M and V).

The relationship function is defined in normalized space; it means the values at x axis have the maximum value equal to one. The y axis has probability ratio as defined in [4]. Under the definition of input variables triangular function it is important to define model output variable. Information about wifi networks and RSSI values of Wifi networks should be done by this fuzzy logic system the first. The very important thing is to obtain in minimal three wifi networks with minimally 20% signal in the range. The next input value for our fuzzy logic system should be GPS sensor with for the satisfactory quality of service or A-GPS with internet connection. Elements of these approaches will be most important part of future work. [4]

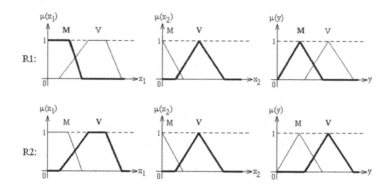

Fig. 4. Decision making in fuzzy expert system

5   Prototype Applications

The android mobile application is a part of our concept now. This application is not using described fuzzy logic solution, but it is fully prepared for that. This application is available through Google play market. This application gathers information about wifi networks in the range without any data pre-processing in smarter mathematical tools. The collected data are sent to remote community server (OWICO). GPS data are used as location information, which are collected from included GPS sensors and form A-GPS platform, using internet connection, which should be every time available, because the wifi connection is mostly used as internet provider service. Proposed system could be used without internet provider too, the standard wifi network is satisfactory too. Our system was tested in the same condition. It is important to thing about speed and latency criteria, which are marked for each location.

The packets of measured data are delivered to the server (OWICO). This is influenced by wifi network quality and location, what should be very restrictive for quality of implementation. Building global knowledge based system with more precise results it is important the independent user community would start up and is encouraged by free of charge access to internet by Wi-Fi networks at high frequent locations. We considered the environmental behaviour when mobile device stops moving it triggers background processes. They are searching the best QoS and reassign communication clients or change communication status. Only allowed viewers and run predefined tasks in recognized environment are allowed. This is a possible enhancement of our prototype.

6   Conclusions

This mind experiment produces technical concept of smart communication. It leans to design of independent required services. Very important part will be fuzzy logic implementation, which helps to solve the desired problem in the networks and Smart Communication Adviser for Remote Users. It encouraged development of real communication clients which supports concepts of smart environment services. The behaviour of users and devices should be hooked on global knowledge base, supported by fuzzy logic decision databases too. Reasoning of home, public and work environments as well as capabilities of network (up to 4G networks and wifi) is the challenge for next future works as an improvement of this mind experiments. Users behaviour will be influenced by QoS and technical requirements and of course the dramatically is the passive and active communication too. It is necessary to keep in mind the influences of social media. It would be catastrophic to commute user's behaviour from social media only, the underlying changes could be done in proposed system. The system should be tested by any reference system, which could be camera system of buildings, or street camera systems. The system could be implemented to smart workplaces management too. In this case it will be very useful to measure the other signals too. The biological signals like pulse frequencies – which show us possibly useful information about human effort. This could help us to make the system more precise. The next biological signal should be body movement too. There is very useful to used fuzzy logic decision system, because measured biosignal data could be declared as stochastically measured data.

The concept supposed to be a pattern for development cross-platform application which provide advisory in inter-personal communication and inspire of cohesion services possibilities.

Acknowledgment. The work and the contribution were partially supported by the project (1) "SMEW – Smart Environments at Workplaces", the Grant Agency of the Czech Republic, GACR P403/10/1310; (2) "Smart Solutions in Ambient Intelligent Environments", University of Hradec Kralove under the project SP/2012/6; (3) SV SP 2012/114 "Biomedical engineering systems VIII"; (4) TACR TA01010632 "SCADA system for control and measurement of process in real time. The paper has been elaborated in the framework of the IT4 Innovations Centre of Excellence project, reg. no. CZ.1.05/1.1.00/02.0070 supported by Operational Programme 'Research and Development for Innovations' funded by Structural Funds of the European Union and state budget of the Czech Republic.

References

1. Burakowski, W., Beben, A.: Wireless Networks, Analysis and Design of Advanced Multiservice Networks Supporting Mobility, Multimedia, and Internetworking, pp. 115–148 (2006)
2. Liu, L.S., Zimmermann, R.: Measured end-to-end delay. Multimedia Systems 11(6), 497–512 (2005)
3. Lee, P.S.N., Leung, L., Lo, V., Xiong, C., Wu, T.: Social Indicators Research. Internet Communication Versus Face-to-face Interaction in Quality of Life 100(3), 375–389 (2011)
4. Klir, G.J., Yuan, B.: Fuzzy Sets and Fuzzy Logic: Theory and Applications. Prentice Hall P T R, Upper Saddle River (1995) ISBN 0-13-101171-5
5. Li, X., Er, M.J., Lim, B.S., Zhou, J.H., Gan, O.P., Rutkowski, L.: Fuzzy Regression Modeling for Tool Performance Prediction and Degradation Detection. International Journal of Neural Systems 20(5), 405–419 (2010), doi:10.1142/S0129065710002498

6. Borrajo, M.L., Baruque, B., Corchado, E., Bajo, J., Corchado, J.M.: Hybrid Neural Intelligent System to Predict Business Failure in Small-To-Medium-Size Enterprises. International Journal of Neural Systems 21(4), 277–296 (2011), doi:10.1142/S0129065711002833
7. Li, T., Ren, J., Tang, X.: Secure Wireless Monitoring and Control Systems for Smart Grid and Smart Home. IEEE Wireless Communications 19(3), 66–73 (2012)
8. Novosád, T., Martinovič, J., Scherer, P., Snášel, V., Šebesta, R., Klement, P.: Mobile Phone Positioning in GSM Networks Based on Information Retrieval Methods and Data Structures. In: Snasel, V., Platos, J., El-Qawasmeh, E. (eds.) ICDIPC 2011, Part II. CCIS, vol. 189, pp. 349–363. Springer, Heidelberg (2011)
9. Krömer, P., Snášel, V., Platoš, J.: Learning Patterns from Data by an Evolutionary-Fuzzy Approach. In: Corchado, E., Snášel, V., Sedano, J., Hassanien, A.E., Calvo, J.L., Ślęzak, D. (eds.) SOCO 2011. AISC, vol. 87, pp. 127–135. Springer, Heidelberg (2011)

Concept of the Personal Devices Content Management Using Modular Architecture and Evaluation Based Design

Miroslav Behan and Ondrej Krejcar

University of Hradec Kralove, FIM, Department of Information Technologies,
Rokitanskeho 62, Hradec Kralove, 500 03,
Czech Republic Miroslav
Behan@uhk.cz, Ondrej.Krejcar@ASJournal.eu

Abstract. Personal devices as smart phones, smart watches, and smart glasses will be considered as natural cyberspace interface. The content will be valuable more without fix relation to single device. Therefore increasing amount of personal devices will evolve open standards for content exchange over network and through different application providers. The personal productivity will be more or less influenced by comprehensive form of management over multiple device's types or platforms. The proposed concept is considered as modular where possible changes of system key functionalities are various modules dependable on behavior or type of person.

Keywords: Mobile, Device, Management, Smart, Sensor, Content.

1   Introduction

The increasing mobile devices computing power influences development of smart environment solutions and propose more human productivity possibilities. We acknowledged that nowadays the current market with mobile devices is more and more fragmented and therefore we propose personal device content management as alternative to overflowed types and kinds of devices. Also remote device control area in approach to management device groups by remote interface are known as challenge nowadays. We would like to present concept of personal device content management as a future vision of multi device environment approach.

Personal content delivery based information system to develop is complex task where are different resources over different platforms. The beneficial approach in development such a kind of private cloud service or application is in modular scalable architecture where separate parts are built and tested separately and are customizable within system.

As a device we define all that devices, which are able to connect to network resp. to the internet sources using an online or offline mode. The multi device environment from single person point of view naturally underline future realistic scenario where user would own or have to manage more than one device. We

P.C. Vinh et al. (Eds.): ICCASA 2012, LNICST 109, pp. 151–159, 2013.
© Institute for Computer Sciences, Social Informatics and Telecommunications Engineering 2013

acknowledge multi-vendor environment and multi-platform environment as Android [8], iOS, Mango and others. Currently many users have more than one device which would be as an interface to cyberspace or which would be as an extension to visualize electronic world. The scenario would be about connectivity with cyberspace and user in conventional way more and more. The basic idea of multiple device management is based on simplify and user friendly environment, where the same user interface (UI) for different devices or type of devices from multiple vendors or manufactures, is presented. What could happen when user reclaims the same type of device interface for instance mobile phones where the same functionality and content basically is? The user has to know as many device interfaces as many types of platforms exist. What if exists one customize able device interface which accessible the most common features for devices. Is that would be good experience in evaluation of human productivity? What if user could be independent on platforms and type of devices and in case of device crash or device lost, it could be easily recovered by one button click? Even more when user realizes that there is a possibility to multiply devices with same content and when expecting precise content from one device it would be accessed from different device. Of course it is all about capability of devices which could in future leads more and more in massive usage of mobile device smart solutions and mobile device could be as natural connection between the rests others types of devices (e.g. car, fridge or boat).

The Apple platform provides for developers fundamental and well prepared design support with framework named COCOA, which is basically using Object-C as programmatic language. There are others extensions from point of developers view where Java or others scripting languages could be used. The mobile devices are using as operation systems the iOS and the most convenient way for developing application is at using common system calls as application interfaces, application services and core services [2]. The advantages of apple platform are basically comprehensive, publishable and distributive application channel over internet.

Another plus of this platform architecture [10] is one vendor device based solution where the certainty of proper system calls and their behavior is well defined and supported. As well as device hardware access in terms of mobile device development the screen resolution where is ratio between height and width constantly 5:3 could be announced another beneficial aspect in rapid application development (RAD). Apple platform establish fundamentals of mobile application eco-system environment. The increase of usability of mobile device is enormous. Identity of application is consists of small image and short term expression with remote update framework possibility known as application market.

The mobile platform as Android is due to self inter open ability suitable for 3rd party solutions where partial problems are solved [3]. The security and stability of system which is based on open source concept is outstanding [4]. A device types which are currently running under Android platform are well-known smartphones and tablets but other types of devices are suitable caused by advantages of platform for instance laptop, netbooks, smart books, e-book readers, smart TVs, wristwatches, headphones, car players, smart glasses, vehicle navigating systems, refrigerators, home automation systems, games consoles, mirrors, cameras or portable media players. The architecture of Java based platform fully provides multithreading environment where gathering precise data form sensors are required. The architecture [5] allows services which are running on background to provider or consume external services or content dependable on version [6].

2 Problem Definition of Remote Device Management

In this chapter we summarized problematic areas in device management in consideration of possible remote use. We focused on cross device features which are main base upon which the management provides measurement, controlling and maintenance over sensors or content of device. Other point of view would consider the platforms aspect which are supportive to some key benefits in remote device management. At last the focus would consider the network access and its capabilities in terms of usability and sustainable processing. For better overview we outline ideas expressed in mind map on following figure (see Fig.1)

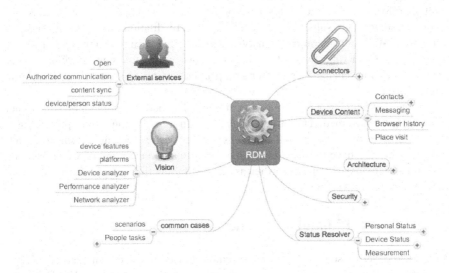

Fig. 1. Mind map – Remote Device Management

2.1 Content Problematic

The core feature of remote device management is multiply, sync or backup device content. Content would be any kind of information but in terms of device management we defined content as end-user data which are important to keep on mobile device caused by daily usage bases or offline mode of device connectivity. As main we recognized Contacts, Photos, Messages or History of communication. Such content would be synchronized over end-user owned devices or be backed up automatically before some of device is lost. Management of content would be more convenient on desktop device rather than small screen device. On the other hand in time or in location tasks are required event from nonconforming user interfaces for specific tasks of content management.

2.2   Sensor Problematic

The sensors which are informational providers over types of devices would be more in future used due to cost-effective available solutions for daily tasks. As a correct way of gathering sensor data is by using allowed platform system calls where access is authorized by end-user. The other way would be over device management provided by platform or by overriding manufactured firmware by dedicated customized distribution of open platforms which would be available as an open source. We are focusing on allowed 3rd party sensor access which is available through framework API for example in android sensors for smart and ambient environments [Table 1] [12].

The measurement requires at least separate thread to perform precise measured result therefore architecture suites to producer and consumer concept. In case of remote consumer the results wouldn't be influenced by dilation of time of transport or transaction. With consideration of network latency the result would be notified or expected in correct time form. We recognized two groups of sensors where one of them are real-time changed and other group is consisting of state full or long-time change sensors.

We consider as contributory following article [11] where the domain of sensor data gathering is well defined. The informational system as extension would provide user status resolution over sets of gathered sensor data; where sleeping, sitting, running, walking or driving have informational value in current context point of view. Also the environment context is valuable in terms of user productivity for instance vacation, work or distance movement.

3   Concept of Modular Architecture

This article describe solution concept of remote device management focused mainly on server side architecture, where a modular architecture is used [17], [18]. Designed concept is variable in terms of technology use case. We suppose to use as development framework all Java based technology. The reason why is hidden in effectiveness in productivity, scalability and reuse available open source components. The following figure (See Fig. 2) highlighted important parts of architecture which are required for specific needs especially from network connectivity characteristics [1], [22]. The informational system consists of three main parts which are remote client part, core system part and end-user interface part. We starts describe remote part where all possible devices potentially could be connected to system. The devices are highly fragmented hardware area due to competition of manufactures and vendors about end-user goodwill. We recognize basically two sets of devices from system point of view.

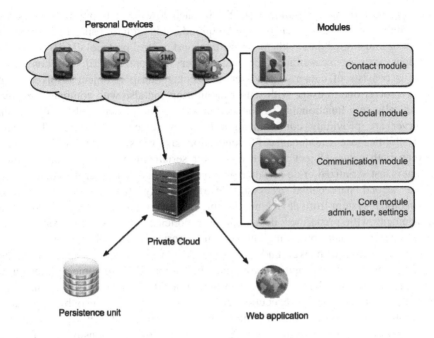

Fig. 2. System architecture – Remote Device Management

The first are all mobile devices which have to care about power supply management and without power saving management the unnecessarily draining battery would lead to uselessness of developed application. The second group of devices is all with an independent power supply where we for instance we classify cars because of their external engine power supplier [19]. For these reasons each of group would behave differently in terms of kind of connectivity mode. The devices which could be connected to system over any kind of network and could provide peer-peer internet connectivity instantly or for exact amount of time we called as active devices. Others we called as passive where which would not be all time online or connected to dedicated server. The passive mode would respect user's defined network connectivity due to cost effectiveness or power management. The connectivity of devices and their statuses accordingly to active or passive device policy are presented in [Table 2][12].

Explicitly defined states of connectivity wouldn't get rid of some cases where the uncertain behavior of network connectivity could appear. The problem would be eliminated by control queuing management based on messages. The messages of events and data would be handled on client side as well as on server side in correct time frame where is explicitly defined. In case of network unavailability the queue substitute consumer and when network status changed and reconnects the message queue processed all FIFO messages in time order. The sentinel measurement data which are with low level importance and are not supposed for real-time processing are lastly consumed. From technical point of view the messages are sent from client to server by user datagram protocol (UDP) in such low level importance cases and where high measurement precision is not required but is preferred speed of delivery or amount of transmitted data. Otherwise the transport control protocol (TCP) is used for confident types of measurement or data delivery of content [20]. The connection server is consists of datagram resolver and socket transport object resolver where socket resolver due to usage with sensor monitoring and also with command executor is practically core functionality of connection server. The socket resolver either client or server are providing communication between device and system. The main responsibilities are maintenance of connection and transportation of data objects between both sides. Object are transport over serialization Java technology where content is fast serialized or de-serialize on binary code and send over network.

The second part called as system part basically handles core features of informational system from device monitoring, device command execution and device management with predefined device or user policies up to system external data storing, system content providing and system authorized access ability for all kind of requests from front or background processing. Also as a connection server we would use Java programing language for implementation due to object inter-server exchange. What and when would be transported decide application server and client application service. Device execution commands are initiated also by application server where are authorizations of requests dispatched from end-user actions or device routines with associated permissions. Application server is responsible for all other types of requests from device or end-user. The calls consist of group with data visualization calls, group of background routine calls based on time triggering settings and maintenance group or administration group of calls. All calls are related to specific tasks or concrete device or group of devices therefore also security and authorizations is part of responsibility of application server. Last component is data management of informational system based on Java Persistence API (JPA) technology which is being used due to extraordinary developing capability and time development saving. The data objects are defined in Java classes and relations between entities are expressed as member of concrete class with specific annotation which specific cardinality and type of relation. The objects are transformed to database thought persistent commands and after commitment are saved to hard file on disk.

The last part of system is focused on web content delivery and interactions with end-user. The web content is hosted on external web server as a cloud solution where the user identity and cloud services could be used. The web client is connected to web cloud services either to application server over secure channel. Web cloud is used due to implicit network traffic monitoring tool and cost-effective load balancing for web clients with minimal impact to maintenance. Basically is used as secured fast traffic response container for web client which mainly communicate with application server in global world scale where continental redistribution is a case. Web client itself implements data visualization, requests posting and corresponding response handling. The client is based on Hypertext Markup Language (HTLM) version 5 and JavaScript (JS) concept and communication with application server is over transmission protocol (TCP) by Web Socket technology due to convenient and fast responsive way than classical Asynchronous JavaScript and XML (AJAX) technology. The Web Socket technology provides persist communication channel over well-known port 80 with advantages of socket connectivity. Therefore the reaction time of committed commands in live online mode increases usability entire system where round trip to server is multiple times faster than common XmlHttpRequest (XHR).

4   Evaluation

The evaluation of the proposed concept of system is based on partial implementation where modules are representing key functionality in terms of personal content. The first contact management module using as resource for data minding embedded contact lists of device, social connectors which are accessible over OAuth [21], [22] and other external services based on Restful architecture. The merging process of identities over resources is done on client side and by uniform content provider where data are scored over informational massiveness, social relevancy and frequency of usage.

Table 1. Evaluation of modules functionalities

Module name	Functionality description	Status
Personal	All personal details which are provided for identification, autocomplete and distribute functionalities.	Not implemented yet
Contacts	Contact management module for gathering available resources and merging identities from different providers into comprehensive visual form with smart attributes behavior.	Implemented Android > 2.0
Messages	Communication over message base delivery with fast and full text search history where the smart attributes are included in conversation as location and context is provided.	Not implemented yet
Files	Files synchronization capabilities over USB cable access where device provide memory stick.	Not implemented yet
Apps	Application management and related data are able to be resynchronized	Not implemented yet
Images	Images management with resynchronization capabilities, where optimal filter will be used [23]	Not implemented yet

The evaluation is considered as part of development where increasing quality of result is beneficial. There are numerous evaluation techniques which will be used when concept of system is fully implemented where testers and real users are involved in process of evaluation and usability measurement.

5   Conclusions

The concept of modular personal content devices management is proposed, problematic related to device content is defined and technology principals are designed with evaluation of design. The further discovery would revile capabilities over different platforms with usability of key functionalities for uniform comprehensive device management. Future works will implement proposed concept and test productivity with real users. Benefits of concept are more significant in deployment within real scenario. We considered as mandatory provide uniform access to personal content as private cloud service which would be device or platform independent and accessible anywhere anytime.

Acknowledgment. The work and the contribution were partially supported by the project (1) "SMEW – Smart Environments at Workplaces", the Grant Agency of the Czech Republic, GACR P403/10/1310; (2) specific research project "Smart Solutions in Ambient Intelligent Environments", University of Hradec Kralove under the project SP/2012/6.

References

1. Conder, S., Darcey, L.: Android Wireless Application Development. Addison-Wesley (2009) ISBN 978-0-321-62709-4
2. Hall, S.P., Anderson, E.: Operating Systems for Mobile Computing. Journal of Computing Sciences in Colleges (2009) ISSN:1937-4771
3. Murphy, M.L.: Android Programming Tutorials. CommonsWare (2009) ISBN 978-0-9816780-2-3
4. Yamakami, T.: Foundation-based Mobile Platform Software Engineering: Implications to Converge to Open Source Software. In: ACM International Conference Proceeding Series, vol. 403 (2009) ISBN:978-1-60558-710-3
5. Android. What is Android? http://developer.android.com/guide/basics/what-is-android.html (retrieved May 23, 2012)
6. Android, Platform versions, http://developer.android.com/resources/dashboard/platform-versions.html (retrieved May 23, 2012)
7. Open Handset Alliance Overview, http://www.openhandsetalliance.com/oha_overview.html(retrieved May 23, 2012)
8. Wikipedia, Android OS, http://en.wikipedia.org/wiki/Android_operating_system (retrieved May 23, 2012)
9. Android Developer Site, Sensors, http://developer.android.com/reference/android/hardware/Sensor.html (retrieved May 23, 2012)
10. Apple Developer Site, iOS, https://developer.apple.com/library/ios/#documentation/ (retrieved May 24, 2012)
11. Blazquez, G.G., Berlanga, A., Molina, J.M.: InContexto: multisensor architecture to obtain people context from smartphones. International Journal of Distributed Sensor Networks 2012, Article ID 758789, 15 pages (2012), doi:10.1155/2012/758789

12. Behan, M., Krejcar, O.: The Concept of the Remote Devices Content Management. Journal of Computer Networks and Communications 2012, Article ID 194284, 7 (2012), doi:10.1155/2012/194284
13. Vybiral, D., Augustynek, M., Penhaker, M.: Devices for position detection. Journal of Vibroengineering 13(3), 531–535 (2011)
14. Espada, J.P., Crespo, R.G., Martınez, O.S., Pelayo, B.C., Bustelo, G., Lovelle, J.M.C.: Extensible architecture for context-aware mobile web applications. Expert Systems with Applications 39(10), 9686–9694 (2012)
15. Kasik, V., Penhaker, M., Novak, V., Bridzik, R., Krawiec, J.: User interactive biomedical data web services application. Communications in Computer and Information Science 171, 223–237 (2011)
16. Penhaker, M., Krejcar, O., Kasik, V., Snášel, V.: Cloud Computing Environments for Biomedical Data Services. In: Yin, H., Costa, J.A.F., Barreto, G. (eds.) IDEAL 2012. LNCS, vol. 7435, pp. 336–343. Springer, Heidelberg (2012)
17. Pittera, T., D'Errico, M.: Multi-purpose modular plug and play architecture for space systems: Design, integration and testing. Acta Astronautica 69(7-8), 629–643 (2011), doi:10.1016/j.actaastro.2011.04.002
18. Sojka, M., Pisa, P., Faggioli, D., Cucinotta, T., Checconi, F., Hanzalek, Z., Lipari, G.: Modular software architecture for flexible reservation mechanisms on heterogeneous resources. Journal of Systems Architecture 57(4), 366–382 (2011), doi:10.1016/j.sysarc.2011.02.005
19. Rodriguez-Ascariz, J.M., Boquete-Vazquez, L.: Transforming PC Power Supplies Into Smart Car Battery Conditioners. IEEE Transactions on Education 54(3), 366–373 (2011), doi:10.1109/TE.2010.2059704
20. Horalek, J., Sobeslav, V.: Datanetworking Aspects of Power Substation Automation. In: International Conference on Communication and Management in Technological Innovation and Academic Globalization, Puerto De La Cruz, Spain, November 30-December 02, pp. 147–153 (2010)
21. Tomaszuk, D., Rybiński, H.: OAuth+UAO: A Distributed Identification Mechanism for Triplestores. In: Jędrzejowicz, P., Nguyen, N.T., Hoang, K. (eds.) ICCCI 2011, Part I. LNCS, vol. 6922, pp. 275–284. Springer, Heidelberg (2011)
22. Jung, J.J., Ou, C.M., Nguyen, N.T., Kim, C.G.: Advances on agent-based network management. Journal of Network and Computer Applications 35(6), Special Issue: SI, 631–632 (2010), doi:10.1016/j.jnca.2010.07.009
23. Sharmin, N., Brad, R.: Optimal Filter Estimation for Lucas-Kanade Optical Flow. Journal Sensors 12(9), 12694–12709 (2012)

Functional Stream Derivatives
of Context-Awareness on P2P Networks

Phan Cong Vinh[1], Nguyen Thanh Tung[2], Nguyen Van Phuc[1],
and Nguyen Hai Thanh[2]

[1] Department of IT, NTT University, 300A Nguyen Tat Thanh St., Ward 13,
District 4, HCM City, Vietnam
pcvinh@ntt.edu.vn, phuc.tsu@gmail.com
[2] International School, Vietnam National University in Hanoi, 144 Xuan Thuy St.,
Cau Giay District, Hanoi, Vietnam
{tungnt,thanh.ishn}@isvnu.vn

Abstract. This paper will be both to give an in-depth analysis as well as
to present the new material on the notion of context-awareness process on
P2P networks, an idea that networking can both sense and react accor-
dantly based on external actions. The paper formalizes context-awareness
process using the notion of *functional stream derivative*, including P2P
networks, context-awareness and the functional stream derivatives of
context-awareness on P2P networks. A brief summary of this approach
is also given.

Keywords: Context-awareness, Context-awareness process, Functional
stream derivative, P2P networks.

1 Introduction

In development of P2P networks, one of the limitations of the current approaches
is that when increasing (fully or partially) the context-awareness of networking,
the semantics and understanding of the context-awareness process become difficult to capture for the development. As motivation, the context-awareness process on P2P networks should be carefully considered under a suitably rigorous
mathematical structure to capture its semantics completely, and then support an
automatic developing process, in particular, and applications of context-aware
networking, generally.

Both initial algebras and final coalgebras are mathematical tools that can
supply abstract representations to aspects of the context-awareness process on
P2P networks. On the one hand, algebras can specify the operators and values.
On the other hand, coalgebras, based on a collection of observers, are considered
in this paper as a useful framework to model and reason about the context-
awareness process on P2P networks. Both initiality and finality give rise to a
basis for the development of context-awareness calculi on P2P networks directly
based on and driven by the specifications. From a programming point of view,

P.C. Vinh et al. (Eds.): ICCASA 2012, LNICST 109, pp. 160–167, 2013.
© Institute for Computer Sciences, Social Informatics and Telecommunications Engineering 2013

this paper provides coalgebraic structures to develop the applications in the area of context-aware computing on P2P networks.

A coalgebraic structure provides an expressive, powerful and uniform view of context-awareness, in which the observation of context-awareness processes on P2P networks plays a central role. The concepts of bisimulation and homomorphism of context-awareness are used to compute the context-awareness process on P2P networks.

2   Outline

The paper is a reference material for readers who already have a basic understanding of P2P networks and are now ready to know the novel approach for formalizing context-awareness process on such P2P networks using coalgebraic language.

Formalization is presented in a straightforward fashion by discussing in detail the necessary components and briefly touching on the more advanced components. The notion of functional stream derivatives, including justifications needed in order to achieve the particular results, is also presented.

The rest of this paper is organized as follows: Section 3 briefly describes related work and existing concepts. P2P networks and context-awareness are the subjects of Section 4. Section 5 presents functional stream derivatives of context-awareness. Finally, Section 6 is a brief summary.

3   Related Work and Existing Concepts

In our previous paper [15], we have rigorously approached to the notion of context-awareness in context-aware systems from which coalgebraic aspects of the context-awareness emerge. The coalgebraic model is used to formalize the unifying frameworks for context-awareness and evolution of the context-awareness processes, respectively.

Most notions and observations of this paper are instances of a theory called universal coalgebra [10,4]. In [9,11], some recent developments in coalgebra are presented.

The programming paradigm with functions called functional programming [1,5,2,3,7] treats computation as the evaluation of mathematical functions. Functional programming emphasizes the evaluation of functional expressions. The expressions are formed by using functions to combine basic values.

The notion of bisimulation is a categorical generalization that applies to many different instances of infinite data structures, various other types of automata, and dynamic systems [10,9,4]. In theoretical computer science, a bisimulation is an equivalence relation between abstract machines, also called the abstract computers or state transition systems (i.e., a theoretical model of a computer hardware or software system) used in the study of computation. Abstraction of computing is usually considered as discrete time processes. Two computing systems are bisimular if, regarding their behaviors, each of the systems "simulates" the other and vice-versa. In other words, each of the systems cannot be distinguished from the other by the observation.

Homomorphism is one of the fundamental concepts in abstract algebra [8], which scrutinizes the sets of algebraic objects, operations on those algebraic objects, and functions from one set of algebraic objects to another. A function that preserves the operations on the algebraic objects is known as a homomorphism. In other words, if an algebraic object includes several operations, then all its operations must be preserved for a function to be a homomorphism in that category [13,6].

4   P2P Networks and Context-Awareness

4.1   P2P Networks

A network, which consists of the set of peers (considered as nodes) together with morphisms $\_ \parallel \_$ in the set of parallel compositions (considered as edges), generates P2P structure [14]. The P2P structure is dynamic in nature because peers can be dynamically added to or dropped from the network. For such every action, *context-awareness* for the P2P structure occurs.

4.2   Context-Awareness

Let PEER be the set of peers and SYS= $\{\parallel_{i \in \mathbb{N}_0} a_i$ with $a_i \in$ PEER$\}$ be the set of parallel compositions on the P2P network.
Let $T = \{add, drop\}$ be the set of actions making a P2P structure on the network change, in which add and $drop$ are defined as follows:

add is a binary operation

$$add : \text{SYS} \times \text{PEER} \longrightarrow \text{SYS} \tag{1}$$

(sometimes specified as SYS $\xrightarrow{add(\text{PEER})}$ SYS or $add(\text{PEER}) :$ SYS $\longrightarrow$ SYS)

obeying the following axioms: For all $i \in \mathbb{N}_0$,

$$add(\parallel_i a_i, b) = \begin{cases} (\parallel_{1 \leqslant i \leqslant n} a_i) \parallel b & \text{for } i \geqslant 1 \\ (\parallel_0) \parallel b = skip \parallel b = b & \text{when } i = 0 \end{cases} \tag{2}$$

or, also written as

$$\begin{cases} \parallel_{1 \leqslant i \leqslant n} a_i \xrightarrow{add(b)} (\parallel_{1 \leqslant i \leqslant n} a_i) \parallel b & \text{for } i \geqslant 1 \\ \parallel_0 \xrightarrow{add(b)} (\parallel_0) \parallel b = skip \parallel b = b & \text{when } i = 0 \end{cases}$$

or

$$\begin{cases} add(b) : \parallel_{1 \leqslant i \leqslant n} a_i \longrightarrow (\parallel_{1 \leqslant i \leqslant n} a_i) \parallel b & \text{for } i \geqslant 1 \\ add(b) : \parallel_0 \longrightarrow (\parallel_0) \parallel b = skip \parallel b = b & \text{when } i = 0 \end{cases}$$

Example:

$$add(\|_0, a) = a$$
$$add(a, b) = a \parallel b$$
$$add(a \parallel b, c) = a \parallel b \parallel c$$

drop is also a binary operation

$$drop : \mathsf{SYS} \times \mathsf{PEER} \longrightarrow \mathsf{SYS} \tag{3}$$

(sometimes specified as $\mathsf{SYS} \xrightarrow{drop(\mathsf{PEER})} \mathsf{SYS}$ or $drop(\mathsf{PEER}) : \mathsf{SYS} \longrightarrow \mathsf{SYS}$)

obeying the following axioms: For all $i \in \mathbb{N}_0$,

$$drop(\|_i \, a_i, b) = \begin{cases} \|_{1 \leqslant i \leqslant (n-1)} \, a_i & \text{when there exists } a_i = b \\ \|_{1 \leqslant i \leqslant n} \, a_i & \text{for all } a_i \neq b \end{cases} \tag{4}$$

or, also written as

$$\begin{cases} \|_{1 \leqslant i \leqslant n} \, a_i \xrightarrow{drop(b)} \|_{1 \leqslant i \leqslant (n-1)} \, a_i & \text{when there exists } a_i = b \\ \|_{1 \leqslant i \leqslant n} \, a_i \xrightarrow{drop(b)} \|_{1 \leqslant i \leqslant n} \, a_i & \text{for all } a_i \neq b \end{cases}$$

or

$$\begin{cases} drop(b) \; : \; \|_{1 \leqslant i \leqslant n} \, a_i \longrightarrow \|_{1 \leqslant i \leqslant (n-1)} \, a_i & \text{when there exists } a_i = b \\ drop(b) \; : \; \|_{1 \leqslant i \leqslant n} \, a_i \longrightarrow \|_{1 \leqslant i \leqslant n} \, a_i & \text{for all } a_i \neq b \end{cases}$$

It follows that $drop(\|_0, b) = \|_0 = skip$.

Example:

$$drop(a, a) = \|_0$$
$$drop(a \parallel b \parallel c, b) = a \parallel c$$
$$drop(a \parallel b \parallel c, d) = a \parallel b \parallel c$$

A context-awareness process is completely defined when actions *add* and *drop* are executed on a P2P network as illustrated in the following diagram:

In consideration of P2P networks, context-awarenesses are known as *homomorphisms* from a P2P network to another P2P network to preserve the P2P structure. In other words, context-awareness is a map from a set of parallel compositions to another set of parallel compositions of the same type that preserves all the P2P structures.

Definition 1 (Context-Awareness). *Let* $T = \{add, drop\}$ *be a set of actions. A context-awareness with set of actions* T *is a pair* $\langle SYS, \langle o_{SYS}, e_{SYS} \rangle \rangle$ *consisting of*

- *a set* SYS *of* P2P *networks,*
- *an* output *function* $o_{SYS} : SYS \longrightarrow (T \longrightarrow 2)$, *and*
- *an* evolution *function* $e_{SYS} : SYS \longrightarrow (T \longrightarrow SYS)$.

where

- $\mathbf{2} = \{0, 1\}$,
- o_{SYS} assigns, to a network c, a function $o_{SYS}(c) : T \longrightarrow \mathbf{2}$, which specifies the value $o_{SYS}(c)(t)$ that is reached after an action t has been executed. In other words,

$$o_{SYS}(c)(t) = \begin{cases} 1 \text{ when } t \text{ becomes fully available, or} \\ 0 \text{ otherwise} \end{cases}$$

- Similarly, e_{SYS} assigns, to a network c, a function $e_{SYS}(c) : T \longrightarrow SYS$, which specifies the network $e_{SYS}(c)(t)$ that is reached after an action t has been executed. Sometimes $c \xrightarrow{t} c'$ is used to denote $e_{SYS}(c)(t) = c'$.

Generally, both the network space SYS and the set T of actions may be infinite. If both SYS and T are finite, then we have a finite context-awareness, otherwise we have an infinite context-awareness.

5   Functional Stream Derivatives of Context-Awareness

The notion of *functional stream derivative* is Rutten's new contribution in [12]. This concept is defined for functions on streams over arbitrary inputs. Hence if the operators of any algebra of stream functions can be defined by notion of *stream differential equations* then all of them are available to apply Rutten's functional stream derivative.

Here the application of this functional stream derivative is found in our algebra of context-awareness involving two actions: *add* and *drop*. Therefore, a network can be changed to become another one in the set of parallel compositions SYS= $\{\|_{i \in \mathbb{N}_0} a_i\}$ (see diagram 5). In other words, the set of parallel compositions SYS is closed under the actions in T. Below are some basic Rutten's stream concepts [12] manipulated on context-awareness.

- A *stream* over a set of actions T is an infinite sequence of consecutive actions in T, obtained by repeatedly applying the evolution function e_{SYS}. Let σ denote a stream that is described as

$$\sigma = (\sigma(0), \sigma(1), \sigma(2), ...) : \{0, 1, 2, ...\} \longrightarrow T$$

- A set of *streams*, denoted by T^ω, over a set of actions T is determined by $T^\omega = \{\sigma \mid \sigma : \{0,1,2,...\} \longrightarrow T\} = \{(\sigma(0),\sigma(1),\sigma(2),...) \mid (\sigma(0),\sigma(1),\sigma(2),...) : \{0,1,2,...\} \longrightarrow T\}$. Similarly, another set of streams $\mathbf{2}^\omega$ over the boolean set $\mathbf{2} = \{0,1\}$ is determined by $\mathbf{2}^\omega = \{\sigma \mid \sigma : \{0,1,2,...\} \longrightarrow \mathbf{2}\} = \{(\sigma(0),\sigma(1),\sigma(2),...) \mid (\sigma(0),\sigma(1),\sigma(2),...) : \{0,1,2,...\} \longrightarrow \mathbf{2}\}$
- The *stream derivative* of a stream σ is defined by $\sigma' = (\sigma(1),\sigma(2),\sigma(3),...)$ and $\sigma(0)$ is called the *initial value* of σ.
- A function $f : T^\omega \longrightarrow \mathbf{2}^\omega$ is called *causal* if for any $\sigma, \tau \in T^\omega$, $i \geqslant 0, t_0, ..., t_i \in T$, and with $t_0 : ... : t_i : \sigma$ denoting $(t_0, ..., t_i, \sigma(0), \sigma(1), ...)$, then

$$f(t_0 : ... : t_i : \sigma)(i) = f(t_0 : ... : t_i : \tau)(i)$$

That is, the ith element of the stream $f(\sigma)$ depend only on the i elements early in σ.
- For a causal function $f : T^\omega \longrightarrow \mathbf{2}^\omega$, action $t \in T$ and $\sigma \in T^\omega$,
  (*i*) The initial output of f is defined by $f(t : \sigma)(0)$ and denoted by $f[t]$.
  (*ii*) The functional stream derivative of f, denoted as $f_t : T^\omega \longrightarrow \mathbf{2}^\omega$, is defined by a causal function $f_t(\sigma) = f(t : \sigma)'$. That is, f_t acts as f on the rest of σ after the first t.

Let f be causal and $\Gamma = \{f \mid f : T^\omega \longrightarrow \mathbf{2}^\omega\}$. For f in Γ and t in T, the function $\langle o_\Gamma, e_\Gamma \rangle : \Gamma \longrightarrow (\mathbf{2} \times \Gamma)^T$ is defined by $\langle o_\Gamma, e_\Gamma \rangle = \langle f[t], f_t \rangle$. This notion offers a context-awareness process $\langle \Gamma, \langle o_\Gamma, e_\Gamma \rangle \rangle$ with evolution as follows:

$$f \xrightarrow{\;t \mid f[t]\;} f_t$$

As mentioned in our other publication [15], a homomorphism between $\langle \mathsf{SYS}, \langle o_{\mathsf{SYS}}, e_{\mathsf{SYS}} \rangle \rangle$ and $\langle \Gamma, \langle o_\Gamma, e_\Gamma \rangle \rangle$ is any function $h : \mathsf{SYS} \longrightarrow \Gamma$ such that

$$c \xrightarrow{\;t \mid o_{\mathsf{SYS}}(c)(t)\;} e_{\mathsf{SYS}}(c)(t) \implies h(c) \xrightarrow{\;t \mid o_\Gamma(h(c))(t)\;} e_\Gamma(h(c))(t)$$

Theorem 1. *The context-awareness $\langle \Gamma, \langle o_\Gamma, e_\Gamma \rangle \rangle$ is final among all context-awarenesses; i.e., for any context-awareness $\langle \mathsf{SYS}, \langle o_{\mathsf{SYS}}, e_{\mathsf{SYS}} \rangle \rangle$, there exists a unique homomorphism $h : \langle \mathsf{SYS}, \langle o_{\mathsf{SYS}}, e_{\mathsf{SYS}} \rangle \rangle \longrightarrow \langle \Gamma, \langle o_\Gamma, e_\Gamma \rangle \rangle$.*

Proof. For $\langle \mathsf{SYS}, \langle o_{\mathsf{SYS}}, e_{\mathsf{SYS}} \rangle \rangle$, we define a function $h : \langle \mathsf{SYS}, \langle o_{\mathsf{SYS}}, e_{\mathsf{SYS}} \rangle \rangle \longrightarrow \langle \Gamma, \langle o_\Gamma, e_\Gamma \rangle \rangle$, whose commutative diagram is as follows:

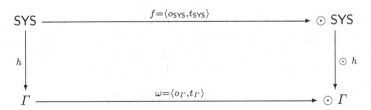

In other words, for c in SYS, we must define a function $h(c) : T^\omega \longrightarrow 2^\omega$ by considering, for σ in T^ω and $n \geqslant 0$, a stream of consecutive actions in T obtained by repeatedly applying the evolution function e_{SYS}.

$$c \xrightarrow{\;\sigma(0)|o_{\mathsf{SYS}}(c)(\sigma(0))\;} c_1 \xrightarrow{\;\sigma(1)|o_{\mathsf{SYS}}(\sigma(1))(t)\;} \cdots \xrightarrow{\;\sigma(n)|o_{\mathsf{SYS}}(c_n)(\sigma(n))\;} c_{n+1}\cdots$$

and assigning $h(c)(\sigma(n)) = o_{\mathsf{SYS}}(c_n)(\sigma(n))$. In this way, h is a homomorphism and unique. In addition, $h(c)$ is also causal.

The stream function $h(c)$ is called the context-awareness process of c. For a causal function f in Γ, network c in SYS is called an *implementation* of f if $f = h(c)$ [12].

From the universal view, for a network c in SYS of $\langle \mathsf{SYS}, \langle o_{\mathsf{SYS}}, e_{\mathsf{SYS}} \rangle \rangle$, $\langle c \rangle \subseteq \langle \mathsf{SYS}, \langle o_{\mathsf{SYS}}, e_{\mathsf{SYS}} \rangle \rangle$ denotes the smallest subset containing c and closed under evolutions for any actions in T. Hence $\langle c \rangle$ is also a subcontext-awareness of $\langle \mathsf{SYS}, \langle o_{\mathsf{SYS}}, e_{\mathsf{SYS}} \rangle \rangle$ generated from c by applying its evolution function e_{SYS} restrictively over the set $\langle c \rangle$.

As considered in [12], the two following corollaries are also true for our context-awareness.

Corollary 1. *Subcontext-awareness* $\langle f \rangle \subseteq \langle \Gamma, \langle o_\Gamma, e_\Gamma \rangle \rangle$ *implements any causal function f in Γ.*

Proof. As in [12], this is trivial because it follows that the inclusion function $i : \langle f \rangle \longrightarrow \Gamma$ (i.e., $i(f) = f$) is homomorphism.

Corollary 2. $\langle f \rangle$ *is a minimal context-awareness process containing the smallest number of networks that implements f.*

Proof. As in [12], for context-awareness $\langle \langle c \rangle, \langle o_{\langle c \rangle}, e_{\langle c \rangle} \rangle \rangle$ and h in theorem 1, the network c in $\langle c \rangle$ implements f; therefore $h(c) = f$. Because h is a homomorphism, it implies that $h(\langle c \rangle) = \langle h(c) \rangle = \langle f \rangle$. Hence the size of $\langle h(c) \rangle$ is the size of $\langle f \rangle$.

6   Conclusions

In this paper, the notion of Rutten's functional stream derivatives is used to formalize the evolution of the context-awareness process on P2P networks. In addition, as our future work, based on functional stream derivatives, a coalgebraic implementation procedure of context-awareness on P2P networks can also be developed.

Acknowledgements. Thank you to NTTUFSTD[1] for the constant support of our work which culminated in the publication of this paper. As always, we are deeply indebted to the anonymous reviewers for their helpful comments and valuable suggestions which have contributed to the final preparation of the paper.

---

[1] The NTTU foundation for Science and Technology Development.

References

1. Barbosa, L.S.: Components as Processes: An Exercise in Coalgebraic Modeling. In: Smith, S.F., Talcott, C.L. (eds.) 4th International Conference on Formal Methods for Open Object-Based Distributed Systems, IFIP TC6/WG6.1, Stanford, CA, USA, September 6-8, pp. 397–417. Kluwer Academic Publishers (2000)
2. Cockett, R., Spencer, D.: Strong Categorical Datatypes I. In: Seely, R.A.G. (ed.) International Summer Meeting on Category Theory, Montréal, Québec, Canada, June 23-30, pp. 141–169. AMS Canadian Mathematical Society (1991)
3. Hagino, T.: A Typed Lambda Calculus with Categorical Type Constructors. In: Pitt, D.H., Rydeheard, D.E., Poigné, A. (eds.) Category Theory and Computer Science. LNCS, vol. 283, pp. 140–157. Springer, Heidelberg (1987)
4. Jacobs, B., Rutten, J.: A Tutorial on (Co)Algebras and (Co)Induction. Bulletin of EATCS 62, 222–259 (1997)
5. Kieburtz, R.B.: Reactive Functional Programming. In: Gries, D., de Roever, W.P. (eds.) Programming Concepts and Methods (PROCOMET), IFIP International Federation for Information Processing, Shelter Island, NY, USA, June 8-12, pp. 263–284. Chapman and Hall (1998)
6. Levine, M.: Categorical Algebra. In: Benkart, G., Ratiu, T.S., Masur, H.A., Renardy, M. (eds.) Mixed Motives. Mathematical Surveys and Monographs, vol. 57, I, II, II, Part II, pp. 373–499. American Mathematical Society, USA (1998)
7. Meijer, E., Fokkinga, M., Paterson, R.: Functional Programming with Bananas, Lenses, Envelopes and Barbed Wire. In: Hughes, J. (ed.) FPCA 1991. LNCS, vol. 523, pp. 124–144. Springer, Heidelberg (1991)
8. Rotman, J.J.: Advanced Modern Algebra, 1st edn. Prentice Hall, USA (2002)
9. Rutten, J.J.M.M.: Automata and Coinduction (an Exercise in Coalgebra). In: Sangiorgi, D., de Simone, R. (eds.) CONCUR 1998. LNCS, vol. 1466, pp. 194–218. Springer, Heidelberg (1998)
10. Rutten, J.J.M.M.: Universal Coalgebra: A Theory of Systems. Theoretical Computer Science 249(1), 3–80 (2000)
11. Rutten, J.J.M.M.: Algebra, Bitstreams, and Circuits. Technical Report SEN-R0502, CWI, Amsterdam, The Netherlands (2005)
12. Rutten, J.J.M.M.: Algebraic Specification and Coalgebraic Synthesis of Mealy Automata. In: Barbosa, L.S., Liu, Z. (eds.) 2nd International Workshop on Formal Aspects of Component Software (FACS), UNU/IIST, Macao, October 24-25, ENTCS (2005)
13. van Oosten, J.: Basic Category Theory. Department of Mathematics, Utrecht University, The Netherlands (July 2002)
14. Vinh, P.C.: Formal and Practical Aspects of Autonomic Computing and Networking: Specification, Development, and Verification. In: Formal Specification and Verification of Self-Configuring P2P Networking: A Case Study in Mobile Environments, 1st edn., pp. 170–188. IGI Global (2011)
15. Vinh, P.C., Tung, N.T.: Coalgebraic aspects of Context-Awareness. Mobile Networks and Applications (August 2012), doi:10.1007/s11036-012-0404-0

Efficient Space Exploration through Laziness

Emil Vassev and Mike Hinchey

Lero—the Irish Software Engineering Research Centre,
University of Limerick, Limerick, Ireland
{Emil.Vassev,Mike.Hinchey}@lero.ie

Abstract. Autonomous behavior and onboard decision making is the backbone of robotic space exploration. The enormous distance and communication latency make such missions hardly controllable from Earth and external decision making may overlap and often contradict with the onboard decision making. We propose a behavior model based on some sort of "laziness" that helps spacecraft evaluate external instructions and eventually postpone their execution, or even discard some, when those are considered inappropriate by the internal spacecraft decision making.

Keywords: decision making, space exploration, autonomous spacecraft.

1   Introduction

Robotic space exploration helps NASA perform unmanned missions to reach deep space where no human can go. The enormous distance and communication latency make such missions hardly controllable from Earth. Hence, autonomous behavior and onboard decision making is the "backbone" of robotic space exploration. Contemporary robotic spacecraft have onboard intelligence based on structured knowledge and reasoning capabilities. This artificial intelligence helps spacecraft make decisions driven by factors like mission goals, safety, performance, efficiency, resource consumption, etc. Similar to the human mind, such intelligence cannot exist isolated on its own and must cope with external control provided by other sources of intelligence – human pilots, mission ground stations, or other sources of artificial intelligence like spacecraft and unmanned space stations. Therefore, external decision-making processes may overlap and often contradict with the internal spacecraft decision making. "Blind" execution of all the external control instructions might be harmful and will often lead to insufficient performance, simply because the external decision making is not that well informed about all the spacecraft issues and parameters. We propose a behavior model for spacecraft based on some sort of "laziness" that helps spacecraft evaluate external instructions and eventually postpone their execution, or even discard some, when those are considered inappropriate by the internal spacecraft decision making. Discarded or postponed external instruction may require feedback sent to the initial instruction source. Moreover, high-priority external instructions should not be evaluated, but executed immediately to assure

P.C. Vinh et al. (Eds.): ICCASA 2012, LNICST 109, pp. 168–175, 2013.

high-authority control over the functionality of smart spacecraft. A postponed external instruction might be delayed by spacecraft just to reach a state where its execution might lead to the best possible performance.

2   Model for Efficient Space Exploration through Laziness

The basic idea behind this behavior model is to allow smart spacecraft act as "lazy workers" having their own interest and goals and often reluctant to perform external instructions if the latter do not conform to their goals. Instead of immediately performing any newly received external instruction, smart spacecraft will evaluate that instruction and decide whether to perform, postpone, or discard the same. Presuming that 1) the spacecraft goals are set by their mission objectives or driven by their safety policies; and 2) the external instructions might be obsolete due to communication delay (coming from Earth and thus travelling a long distance) and eventually incorrect, because the sender does not have complete and recent information about all the spacecraft parameters; the overall result of such behavior could be a significant performance gain. The behavior model for such *Efficient Space Exploration through Laziness* (for short *efficiency with laziness* (EL)) can be presented as a function accepting two parameters – *system knowledge* and a set of *external instructions*, and determining the spacecraft behavior concerning the incoming set of external instructions.

2.1   Formal Model for Efficiency with Laziness

Formally, the behavior model for EL can be presented as following:

$$R_{EL}: K \times L_I \to B_{EL} \tag{1}$$

Here, R_{EL} is the EL function computing the *possible behavior* for each external set of instructions L_I considering the system knowledge K. The knowledge K of smart spacecraft capable of reasoning and decision making can be formally presented as a tuple of three main knowledge components (knowledge models):

$$K = \langle K_I, K_C, K_E \rangle \tag{2}$$

where K_I is *internal knowledge*, K_C is *control knowledge*, and K_E is *external knowledge*. The internal knowledge K_I carries information about the internal structure and capabilities of the system and it can be presented as a tuple of three components:

$$K_I = \langle C, F, R \rangle \tag{3}$$

where C states for system components, F is system functionality, and R is system resources. There could be added more parameters to this tuple, such as *interdependencies* (if not present in the knowledge about the system components C), *system architecture*, etc. Further, the control knowledge K_C gives the system knowledge about its control parameters and mission and it can be presented as a tuple of a few parameters:

$$K_C = \langle \Pi, M\langle G, T\rangle, S, A, H_{Si}\langle S_H, A_H\rangle, L\rangle \tag{4}$$

where:

- Π states for behavior policies (safety, performance, etc.) driving the system in particular situations.
- M is the mission knowledge such as goals G (or objectives, e.g., service-level objectives), time constraints T, etc.
- S is a set of all known possible states the system can take.
- A is a set of all possible actions the system can undertake (actions are functions over system's functionality involving consumption of system resources).
- H_{Si} is a history of situations the system ended up in. A situation connects past states S_H to past actions A_H performed by the system to get out from those states. Note that H_{Si} provide the necessary information for *reinforcement learning*.
- L is alphabet of an interface language used to communicate with the system.

Finally, the external knowledge K_E is to provide the spacecraft with information about the surrounding environment (environmental factors), e.g., solar system, solar storms, planetary systems, asteroids, gravity force of the near space objects, etc. Considering all the knowledge elements, we further reveal Definition (2):

$$K = \langle K_I \langle C, F, R\rangle, K_C \langle \Pi, M\langle G, T\rangle, S, A, H_{Si}\langle S_H, A_H\rangle, L\rangle, K_E\rangle \tag{5}$$

Further, the set of external instructions in Definition (1) shall be expressed with the alphabet provided by the interface language L. The determined by the function R_{EL} (see Definition (1)) EL behavior B_{EL} can be one of the following:

- *execute* – all the external instructions are immediately executed with the highest possible priority;
- *postpone* - the external instructions are scheduled for execution but after the execution of more important and locally decided instructions;
- *discard* – the external instructions are discarded.

When the spacecraft postpones or discards external instructions, it may notify the instructions' sender about this behavior with the appropriate reasons. In order to decide on the behavior B_{EL}, the function R_{EL} follows the following algorithm:

1) Check whether the external instructions L_I are high priority instructions:

- Yes – perform.
- No - continue with 2).

2) Check whether the external instructions L_I are obsolete:

- Yes – discard.
- No – continue with 3).

3) Check whether the external instructions L_I require the execution of actions $A' \subset A$ that will harm the mission goals G or contradict with the spacecraft policies Π (e.g., for safety). To do that, the spacecraft must compute the probability of the spacecraft occupying one of the undesired states $S' \subset S$ (where some of the mission goals or spacecraft policies are violated) after the execution of actions A'. Here,

$$N: S \times A \rightarrow P(S) \tag{6}$$

is a *state-transition function* giving for each state $s \in S$ and action $a \in A$ a probability distribution. Here, $N(s; a; s')$ computes the probability of ending in state s', given that the start state is s and the spacecraft takes action a, $p(s' \mid s; a)$. Therefore, the spacecraft knows the probability of ending in one of the undesired states S' if actions A' are executed from the current state s. The computed probability p is a scalar value in the range $[0..1]$. A special EL policy may decide on the two thresholds: 1) what probability level is sufficient a set of external instructions L_I to be postponed, e.g., $p \in [0..0,5)$; and 2) what probability level is sufficient a set of external instructions L_I to be discarded, e.g., $p \in [0,5..1]$.

There could be different "levels of laziness" depending on the probability ranges, which determine those two thresholds. The theoretical foundation for the probability assessment is the so-called Markov Chains [1].

2.2   Probability Assessment

The EL model requires computation of probability values for ending in possible undesired states when particular actions are executed. In this subsection, we present a *model for assessing probability* applicable to the computation of EL probability values. In our approach, the *probability assessment* is an indicator of the number of possible execution paths spacecraft may take, meaning the amount of certainty (excess entropy) in the spacecraft behavior. To assess that behavior prior to implementation, it is important to understand the interactions among the *spacecraft components* and also the complex interactions with the surrounding environment (space). This can be achieved by modeling the behavior of the *individual reactive spacecraft components* and the behavior of the *environmental factors* (e.g., solar storm, gravity of a planet, etc.), together with the *global system behavior* as *Discrete Time Markov Chains* [1], and by assessing the level of probability through calculating the probabilities of the state transitions in the corresponding models. We assume that the component interactions and the environment-system interaction are stochastic processes where the events are not controlled by the spacecraft and thus, their probabilities are considered equal.

The theoretical foundation for our Probability Assessment Model is the property of Markov chains, which states that, *given the current state of the whole spacecraft system, its future evolution is independent of its history*, which is also the main characteristic of a reactive and autonomic spacecraft [2, 3].

An algebraic representation of a Markov chain is a matrix (called *transition matrix*) (see Table 1) where the rows and columns correspond to the states, and the entry p_{ij} in the ith row, j^{th} column is the transition probability of being in state s_j at the stage following state s_i.

Table 1. Transition matrix P

	s_1	s_2	...	s_j	...	s_n
s_1	p_{11}	p_{12}	...	p_{1j}	...	p_{1n}
s_2	p_{21}	p_{22}	...	p_{2j}	...	p_{2n}
...	...	...	...	...	...	...
s_i	p_{i1}	p_{i2}	...	p_{ij}	...	p_{in}
...	...	...	...	...	...	...
s_n	p_{n1}	p_{n2}	...	p_{nj}	...	p_{nn}

We need to build such a transition matrix taking into account both the system components and environmental factors influencing the system behavior. The following property holds for the calculated probabilities:

$$\Sigma_j \, p_{ij} = 1 \tag{7}$$

We contend that probability should be calculated from the *steady state* of the Markov chain. A steady state (or *equilibrium state*) is one in which the probability of being in a state before and after a transition is the same as time progresses. Here, we define probability for a spacecraft system composed of k components and taking into account x environmental factors as the level of certainty quantified by the source excess entropy, as follows.

$$P = \Sigma_{i=1,k} H_i + \Sigma_{e=1,x} H_e - H \tag{8}$$

$$H_i = -\Sigma_j \, p_{ij} \, log_2(p_{ij}) \tag{9}$$

$$H_e = -\Sigma_j \, p_{ej} \, log_2(p_{ej}) \tag{10}$$

$$H = -(\Sigma_i \, v_i \, \Sigma_j \, p_{ij} \, log_2(p_{ij}) + \Sigma_e \, v_e \, \Sigma_j \, p_{ej} \, log_2(p_{ej})) \tag{11}$$

Here,

- **H** is an entropy that quantifies the level of uncertainty in the Markov chain corresponding to the entire spacecraft system;
- **H_i** is a level of uncertainty in a Markov chain corresponding to a spacecraft component;
- **H_e** is a level of uncertainty in a Markov chain corresponding to an environmental factor, e.g., distance to ground base, solar storm, gravity force of a planet, etc.;
- **v** is a steady state distribution vector for the corresponding Markov chain;
- **p_{ij}** values are transition probabilities in the extended state machines modeling the behavior of the ith component;
- **p_{ej}** values are transition probabilities in the extended state machines modeling the behavior of the eth environmental factor.

Note that for a transition matrix P, the steady state distribution vector v satisfies the property $v*P = v$, and the sum of its components v_i is equal to 1.

Interpretation. The level of uncertainty H is exponentially related to the number of *statistically typical paths* in the Markov chain. Having an entropy value of 0 means that there is no level of uncertainty in a Markov system for a specific unit's behavior. A higher value of probability implies less uncertainty in the model.

2.3   Modeling the Behavior Policies with Probability

To allow for EL-driven behavior, we need to develop the behavior policies Π (see Definition 5) taking into consideration the probability distribution for the possible state transitions (see Section 2.2). Note that in another project of ours, we have developed a model for *autonomic policies* that uses probability distributions to rate the probability of policies being executed in specific situations and under specific conditions [4]. Because, each policy is associated with possible actions, the behavior realized by the actions executed in the environment will be guided by the policies with the highest probability where the probability rates are recomputed after every action execution.

We can elaborate on this approach to adapt it to the EL model where policies should consider both the internal components and environmental factors.

2.4   Awareness for EL

In general, an EL-based system engages in interactions with the ground base on Earth and with its operational environment. When interacting with the environment, the EL spacecraft also perceive important structural and dynamic aspects of the same [3]. To become interaction-aware, such a system needs to be aware of its physical environment and whereabouts and its current internal status. This ability is defined as *awareness* and it helps intelligent computerized systems to sense, draw inferences for their own behavior and react. The notion of awareness should be generally related to perception, recognition, thinking and eventually prediction [5]. Recall that the EL mechanism requires relevant knowledge (see Definitions 1 and 2) that helps the system autonomously determine states. For example, the EL approach requires the system to be aware about the environmental factors such as gravity, solar storms, etc. This can be achieved via a mechanism called "Pyramid of Awareness" [5] where a complex chain of functions shall be implemented to control the EL awareness process via monitoring, recognition, assessment, and learning.

3   Example of Efficient Space Exploration through Laziness

In this short example, we use as a case study the prospective NASA's Autonomous Nano-Technology Swarm (ANTS) space exploration mission [6], which is a novel approach to asteroid-belt resource exploration (see Figure 1).

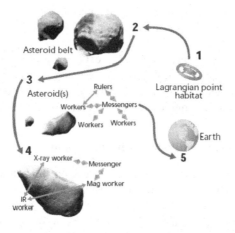

Fig. 1. ANTS mission concept [6]

An ANTS system is composed of individual spacecraft where each spacecraft is equipped with a solar sail and relies primarily on power from the sun, using only tiny thrusters to navigate independently. Moreover, each spacecraft also has onboard computation, artificial intelligence, and heuristics systems for control at both the individual and system levels. To explore a new asteroid, ANTS needs to form a team of spacecraft units called *workers* and carrying special instruments. A team is formed and coordinated by a special spacecraft unit called *ruler* [6]. Special messengers are needed to connect the team members when they cannot connect directly, due to long distances or a barrier. To form a team, a ruler broadcasts instructions to workers.

In our approach, the EL mechanism helps workers evaluate those instructions and make their decision how to proceed, so the overall ANTS goals are not harmed and the overall efficiency is the highest possible. For example, EL will help 1) only idle workers join the team; and 2) to complete the team with the sufficient number of workers. When the team is complete, the other idle workers will not join the team, because the EL mechanism will evaluate this as an act harming the overall ANTS goals. Moreover, the EL mechanism will prevent workers from joining the team if the probability of having a solar storm is high which can jeopardize the overall mission.

4   Conclusion

In this paper, we proposed a behavior model for efficient space exploration through laziness. The basic idea is to allow smart spacecraft act as "lazy workers" having their own interest and goals and often be reluctant to perform external instructions if the latter do not conform to spacecraft goals and if the environment imposes considerable hazards. The approach requires the spacecraft to compute the probability of occupying an undesired state after following external instructions. Note that as undesired state is considered a situation where either mission goals or spacecraft behavior policies are violated. Based on the computed probability, the external instructions can be immediately executed, postponed for later execution or completely discarded. The probability assessment is an indicator of the number of possible execution paths spacecraft may take, meaning the amount of certainty in the spacecraft behavior. In our approach the probability assessment is based on Markov Chains. Finally, the EL approach requires an awareness mechanism to keep the EL knowledge relevant and up-to-date by taking into consideration internal, control and environmental factors. The proposed awareness mechanism is the so-called "Pyramid of Awareness", which we are currently developing for another project of ours.

Future work is concerned with further and complete development of the EL mechanism, including knowledge representation for modeling EL behavior, probability assessment and awareness for EL.

Acknowledgment. This work was supported by Science Foundation Ireland grant 03/CE2/I303_1 to Lero—the Irish Software Engineering Research Centre at University of Limerick, Ireland and by the European Union FP7 Integrated Project Autonomic Service-Component Ensembles (ASCENS).

References

1. Ewens, W.J., Grant, G.R.: Stochastic processes (i): poison processes and Markov chains. In: Statistical Methods in Bioinformatics, 2nd edn. Springer, New York (2005)
2. Vassev, E., Sterritt, R., Rouff, C., Hinchey, M.: Swarm Technology at NASA: Building Resilient Systems. IT Professional 14(2), 36–42 (2012)
3. Vassev, E., Hinchey, M.: The Challenge of Developing Autonomic Systems. IEEE Computer 43(12), 93–96 (2010)
4. Vassev, E., Hinchey, M., Gaudin, B.: Knowledge Representation for Self-Adaptive Behavior. In: Proceedings of C* Conference on Computer Science & Software Engineering (C3S2E 2012), pp. 113–117. ACM (2012)
5. Vassev, E.: Building the pyramid of awareness. Awareness Magazine - Self-awareness in Autonomic Systems (July 2012), doi: 10.2417/3201207.004320
6. Truszkowski, W., Hinchey, M., Rash, J., Rouff, C.: NASA's swarm missions: The challenge of building autonomous software. IT Professional 6(5), 47–52 (2004)

Efficient Reasoning with Ambient Trees
for Space Exploration

Emil Vassev and Mike Hinchey

Lero—the Irish Software Engineering Research Centre,
University of Limerick, Limerick, Ireland
{Emil.Vassev,Mike.Hinchey}@lero.ie

Abstract. Modern reasoning is based on inference techniques such as induction, deduction, abduction, subsumption, classification and recognition. These inference techniques are very inefficient when applied to large amounts of knowledge such as ones employed by contemporary unmanned spacecraft. For efficient reasoning, we aim at knowledge representation based on special ambient trees determining special knowledge contexts to help such spacecraft retrieve context-relevant knowledge and perform deductive reasoning, which would not be otherwise highlighted. Contexts via their ambient trees provide a sort of a condensed and explicit symbolic representation of the world. This representation is cleaned from the overwhelming information that is non-relevant to the context and thus, it provides for efficient models of situations to reason about.

Keywords: reasoning, knowledge representation, space exploration, autonomous spacecraft.

1 Introduction

Modern unmanned spacecraft have *onboard intelligence* that helps them reason about situations in space where autonomous decision making is required [1]. The basic compound in the reasoning process is *knowledge*. Smart spacecraft employ appropriately structured knowledge that is used by onboard inferential engines. The knowledge is integrated in the spacecraft system via *knowledge representation* techniques to build a computational model of the space-mission domain of interest in which symbols serve as *knowledge surrogates* for real world artifacts, such as spacecraft components and functions, mission details, space objects such as planets, satellites, asteroids, etc. The domain of interest can cover any part of the real world or any hypothetical system about which one desires to represent knowledge for computational purposes. Modern reasoning is based on inference techniques such as *induction*, *deduction*, *abduction*, *subsumption*, *classification* and *recognition*. Although efficient on small knowledge models, those inference techniques are very inefficient when applied to large amounts of knowledge such as ones employed by modern unmanned spacecraft. Therefore, for efficient reasoning, it should be possible to reason by emphasizing on relevant knowledge by ignoring selected parts that are

P.C. Vinh et al. (Eds.): ICCASA 2012, LNICST 109, pp. 176–182, 2013.

not relevant to the particular situation of interest. In our approach, special ambient trees define *knowledge contexts* that help spacecraft retrieve context-relevant knowledge and perform deductive reasoning, which would not be otherwise highlighted. Contexts via their ambient trees provide a sort of a condensed and explicit symbolic representation of the world. This knowledge representation is *cleaned* from the overwhelming information that is non-relevant to the knowledge context and thus, it provides efficient models of situations to reason about.

2   Theoretical Model for Efficient Reasoning with Ambient Trees

The most prominent and powerful knowledge-representation technique is ontology [2]. A space-mission ontology gives a *formal* and *declarative representation* of the knowledge domain in terms of explicitly described domain concepts, individuals and the relationships between those concepts/individuals. The Theoretical Model for Efficient Reasoning with Ambient Trees (for short Efficient Reasoning with Ambient Trees (ERAT)), relies on the ontology technique to represent knowledge in smart spacecraft. According to ERAT, the knowledge K of smart spacecraft, capable of reasoning and decision making, can be formally presented as a tuple of three main knowledge components (knowledge models):

$$K = \langle K_I, K_C, K_E \rangle \qquad (1)$$

where K_I is *internal knowledge*, K_C is *control knowledge*, and K_E is *external knowledge*. The internal knowledge K_I carries information about the internal structure and capabilities of the system. The control knowledge K_C gives the system knowledge about its control parameters and mission. Finally, the external knowledge K_E is to provide the spacecraft with information about the surrounding environment, e.g., solar system, solar storms, planetary systems, asteroids, gravity force of the near space objects, etc. Each one of the K components is presented by an ontology O and a set of special contexts C_X.

$$K_X = \langle O, C_X \rangle \qquad (2)$$

This way of structuring knowledge is a sort of *context-oriented knowledge structuring* and it helps us to decompose complicated intelligent behavior into many "simple" and context-dependent behavior modules. Furthermore, an ontology is composed of hierarchically organized sets of *meta-concepts* C_M, special *concept trees* C_T, *object trees* O_T, *relations* R, predicates V and facts F.

$$O = \langle C_M, C_T, O_T, R, V, F \rangle \qquad (3)$$

Meta-concepts C_M provide a context-oriented *interpretation* of concepts. Concept trees C_T consist of semantically related *concepts* C. Every *concept tree* $c_T \in C_T$ has a *root concept* r_C, because the architecture ultimately must reference a single concept that is the connection point to concepts that are outside the concept tree. A root concept may *optionally* inherit a meta-concept, which is denoted $[r_C \rightarrow c_M]$ (see Formula 5). Every concept c has a set of *properties* P and optional sets of functionalities A, *parent concepts* C_P and *children concepts* C_H. Figure 1 depicts a sample *concept tree* structuring the capabilities of a space robot (e.g., automatic probe).

$$C_T = \langle r_C, C \rangle \tag{4}$$

$$r_C \in C, [r_C \rightarrow c_M] \tag{5}$$

$$c_M \in C_M$$

$$c = \langle P, [A], [C_P], [C_H] \rangle \tag{6}$$

$$C_P \subset C, C_H \subset C$$

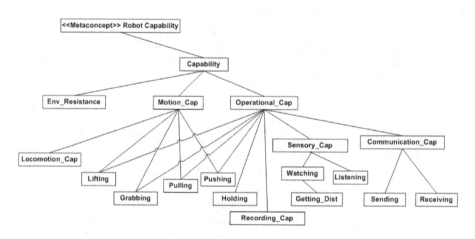

Fig. 1. Concept Tree: Robot Capability

Object trees O_T are conceptualization of how objects existing in the world of interest are related to each other. The relationships are based on the principle that objects are concepts realization and have properties where sometimes the value of a property is another object, which in turn also has properties. Such properties are termed as *object properties* P_O. An object tree consists of a root object r_O and an optional set of nested object trees O_T' formed by those object properties. An *object* is an instance of a concept.

$$o_T = \langle r_O, [O_T'] \rangle \tag{7}$$

Relations R connect two concepts/objects (only binary relations are considered), and facts F define true statements in an ontology O. Predicates V are special knowledge structures that specify distinct *interstate relations* or schemes for evaluation of complex states (e.g., context states). For example, we can specify a predicate that verifies whether the system is fully functional or to verify whether there is an upcoming high-energy solar storm. A predicate might be used whether a specific object, the environment or the entire system is in a specific state. Thus, a predicate v formally can be presented as a tuple of predicate concepts C_V, predicate states S_V and a Boolean expression over ontology ($bf(O)$) that determines what conditions must be held to conclude that the predicate states are active (see Formula 8). Note that a state (including a predicate state s_V) can be presented as a Boolean expression over ontology that holds (see Formula 9). A Boolean expression determining a state may involve *concept properties*, *object properties* and *concept functionalities*. Predicates might be used to determine if a specific context is present based on state evaluation.

$$v = \langle C_V, S_V, bf(O) \rangle \tag{8}$$

$$v \in V, C_V \subset C, S_V \subset S$$

$$s_V = \langle bf(O) \rangle \tag{9}$$

$$s_V \in S_V, S_V \subset S \; (S_V \text{ - predicate states})$$

Here, a state-determination function N shall determine for each state $s \in S$ the Boolean expression that must hold in order to consider a state "active".

$$N: S \times O \rightarrow \langle bf(O), S \rangle \tag{10}$$

Contexts C_X are intended to extract the relevant knowledge from an ontology O. Moreover, contexts carry interpretation for some of the meta-concepts (see Formula (11)), which may lead to new interpretation of the *descendant concepts* (derived from a meta-concept – see Formula 5). We consider a very broad notion of context, e.g., the space environment in a fraction of time or a generic situation such as currently-ongoing important system function, such as observing, listening, etc. Thus, a context must emphasize the key concepts in an ontology O, which helps the inference mechanism narrow the domain knowledge by exploring the concept trees down to the emphasized key concepts only. Thus, depending on the context, some low-level concepts might be subsumed by their upper-level parent concepts, just because the former are not relevant for that very context. For example, the planet Mars can be considered as a natural space object with gravity and spin orbit or as an important exploration target, which requires knowledge in great details about Mars. As a result, context interpretation of knowledge will help the system deal with "clean" knowledge and the reasoning shall be more efficient.

A context $c_X \in C_X$ consists of:

- special *ambient trees* A_T
- a set of context states S_{CX} determining when a context is present;
- optional *context interpretations* I_{CX}.

An ambient tree $a_T \in A_T$ consists of a *concept tree* c_T, a set of *ambient concepts* C_A, part of the concept tree c_T, and optional *context interpretation i*.

$$C_X = \langle A_T, S_{CX}, [I_{CX}] \rangle \tag{11}$$

$$A_T = \langle c_T, C_A, [i] \rangle \tag{12}$$

$$c_T \in C_T, \ C_A \subset C, \ i \in I_{CX}$$

$$s_{CX} = \langle bf(O) \rangle \tag{13}$$

$$s_{CX} \in S_{CX}, \ S_{CX} \subset S \ (S_{CX} \text{ - context states})$$

The ambient concepts C_A are concepts, which explicitly determine a new level of deepness for their concept tree, i.e., ambient concepts subsume all of their child concepts (if any). As result, when the spacecraft reasons about a particular context (expressed with the ambient trees), the reasoning process does not consider those child concepts, but their ambient parents, which are far more generic, and thus less detailed. This technique reduces the size of the relevant knowledge, by temporarily removing from the concept trees all the ambient concepts' children (child concepts). We may think about ambient trees as filters the system applies at runtime to reduce the visibility (the amount of concepts) of a concept tree.

A context state s_{CX} determines when the context is present and thus, the ambient trees might be applied to hide the irrelevant knowledge. A context can be associated with multiple states where each state is a sufficient guarantee that the context is present. For example, we may have a state "*the spaceship is currently receiving signals from Earth*" that may uniquely identify that the *message-receiving context* is present.

Here, a context-aware function E is required to determine at runtime the current context. This function should operate on both predicates V (see Definition 8) and contexts C_X to determine the current context via the evaluation of the current system state, which eventually is a context state as well (s_X) (see Definition 14).

$$E: V \times C_X \overset{s_X}{\to} c_X \tag{14}$$

Finally, we need a function F that will apply the discovered context over the ontology and force the system use the reduced in size context ontology O_X.

$$F: c_X \times O \to O_X \tag{15}$$

3   Context Awareness

In general, autonomous spacecraft engage in interactions with the ground base on Earth and with the operational environment (space). When interacting with the environment, such spacecraft also perceive important structural and dynamic aspects of the same [3]. To become interaction-aware, such a system needs to be aware of its physical environment and whereabouts and its current internal status. This ability is defined as *awareness* and it helps intelligent computerized systems to sense, draw inferences for their own behavior and react. The notion of awareness should be generally related to perception, recognition, thinking and eventually prediction [4]. Recall that this approach requires relevant knowledge (see Definitions 1) that helps the system autonomously determine contexts (see Definition 14). This can be achieved via a mechanism called "Pyramid of Awareness" [4] where a complex chain of functions shall be implemented to control the *context awareness* process via monitoring, recognition, assessment, and learning.

4   Example of Efficient Reasoning with Ambient Trees

This technique could be successfully used to refining spacecraft knowledge that is relevant to a specific context. For example, let us suppose a spacecraft is using its radio to listen to its communication channels and to space sounds and noise. In such a case, we have a "listening" context, i.e., only knowledge relevant to speech, sounds and noise should be considered. The expressed with the ontologies spacecraft knowledge has concepts related to "sound" knowledge, e.g., concepts like "vocal commands", "speech", "sound", "noise", etc. The listening context defines all the ambient concepts, which should be used to subsume parts of their concept trees that are not relevant to sound knowledge. Figure 2, shows the application of an ambient tree from the listening context to a concept tree. The resulted concept tree is smaller in terms of concepts, which leads to faster and more efficient reasoning about situations in the listening context.

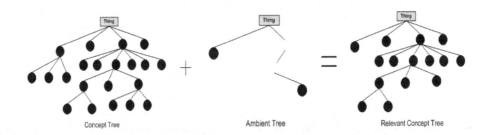

Concept Tree   Ambient Tree   Relevant Concept Tree

Fig. 2. Reducing knowledge size through ambient trees

5   Conclusion

In this paper, we outlined an approach to a knowledge representation technique helping unmanned spacecraft perform efficient reasoning by emphasizing context-relevant knowledge. The approach is based on special ambient trees intended to hide irrelevant knowledge by reducing the size of the ontology trees used to represent that knowledge. A special context-aware function is required to determine at runtime the current context and another function is required to automatically apply that context. Finally, the approach requires a context-awareness mechanism to keep the knowledge relevant and up-to-date by taking into consideration internal, control and environmental factors. The proposed awareness mechanism is the so-called "Pyramid of Awareness", which we are currently developing for another project of ours.

Currently, the approach is under development within the mandate of the ASCENS FP7 Project [5].

Acknowledgment. This work was supported by Science Foundation Ireland grant 03/CE2/I303_1 to Lero—the Irish Software Engineering Research Centre at University of Limerick, Ireland and by the European Union FP7 Integrated Project Autonomic Service-Component Ensembles (ASCENS).

References

1. Vassev, E., Sterritt, R., Rouff, C., Hinchey, M.: Swarm Technology at NASA: Building Resilient Systems. IT Professional 14(2), 36–42 (2012)
2. Vassev, E., Hinchey, M.: Knowledge Representation and Reasoning for Intelligent Software Systems. IEEE Computer 44(8), 96–99 (2011)
3. Vassev, E., Hinchey, M.: The Challenge of Developing Autonomic Systems. IEEE Computer 43(12), 93–96 (2010)
4. Vassev, E.: Building the pyramid of awareness. Awareness Magazine - Self-awareness in Autonomic Systems (July 2012), doi: 10.2417/3201207.004320
5. ASCENS – Autonomic Service-Component Ensembles (2012), http://www.ascens-ist.eu/

Power Save Protocol Using Chain Based Routing

Nguyen Thanh Tung[1], Nguyen Van Duc[2], Nguyen Hai Thanh[1],
Phan Cong Vinh[3], and Nguyen Dai Tho[4]

[1] International School, Vietnam National University
{tungnt,thanh.ishn}@isvnu.vn
[2] Hanoi University of Technology
ducnv-fet@mail.hut.edu.vn
[3] Nguyen Tat Thanh University
pcvinh@ntt.edu.vn
[4] University of Engineering and Technology,
Vietnam National University
nguyendaitho@vnu.edu.vn

Abstract. Sensor networks are deployed in numerous military and civil applications, such as remote target detection, weather monitoring, weather forecast, natural resource exploration and disaster management. Despite having many potential applications, wireless sensor networks still face a number of challenges due to their particular characteristics that other wireless networks, like cellular networks or mobile ad hoc networks do not have. The most difficult challenge of the design of wireless sensor networks is the limited energy resource of the battery of the sensors. This limited resource restricts the operational time that wireless sensor networks can function in their applications. Routing protocols play a major part in the energy efficiency of wireless sensor networks because data communication dissipates most of the energy resource of the networks. In many situations, a base station only needs a summary of the gathered information. For example, the base station might only require the maximum temperature of all sub-regions, each covered by a sensor or the average temperature of all sensors in the network. For similar types of application, data aggregation can be applied at all sensor nodes before the data is forwarded to the base station. The above discussions imply a new family of protocols called chain-based protocols. In the protocols, all sensor nodes sense and gather data in an energy efficient manner by cooperating with their closest neighbors. The gathering process can be done until an elected node calculates the final data and sends the data to the base station.

Keywords: Sensor, Routing, Chain based Routing, Linear Programming.

1 Introduction

Lindsey et al. [5] proposed one type of chain-based protocol called PEGASIS (Power-Efficient Gathering in Sensor Information Systems), which is near optimal for gathering data in sensor networks. PEGASIS forms a chain among sensor nodes so that each node will receive data from a close neighboring node and transmit data to

P.C. Vinh et al. (Eds.): ICCASA 2012, LNICST 109, pp. 183–191, 2013.
© Institute for Computer Sciences, Social Informatics and Telecommunications Engineering 2013

another close neighbor. Gathered data moves from a sensor node to the nearest neighbor, is aggregated with the neighbor's data, and eventually reaches a determined Cluster-Head (CH) before finally being transmitted to the Base Station (BS). Fig. 1 illustrates the ideas of the PEGASIS protocol. In this round of data transmission, Node 3 is elected as the CH. Node 5 transmits data to Node 4, and Node 4 fuses the data with its own data and transmits the fused data to Node 3. Similarly, Node 1 transmits data to Node 2, and Node 2 transmits the fused data to Node 3. Finally, Node 3 fuses the data of the other nodes with its own data and transmits the final fused data to the base station. The data fusion function can be any function e.g. minima, maxima and average, depending on the specific applications as discussed in [1],[2],[3]. Nodes take turns equally to be the CH so that the energy spent by each node is balanced. In other words, each node becomes a CH once for every n rounds of data transmission, where n is the number of sensor nodes.

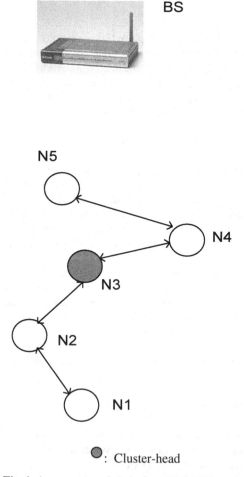

Fig. 1. A reconstructed chain from PEGASIS method

The authors in [5] showed that building a chain to minimize the energy consumption is similar to the traveling salesman problem [6], which is known to be NP-complete. They proposed a greedy algorithm starting from the furthest node from the base station until a near optimal chain is built as follows:

1) Add the node furthest from the base station to the chain

2) This node finds a closest node from it that is not already in the chain

(Closest Euclidean distance)

3) Repeat until all nodes are added to the chain.

Fig. 2 shows the formation of a chain with five sensor nodes. Node 1 connects to Node 2, Node 2 connects to Node 3, Node 3 connects to Node 4 and Node 4 connects to Node 5.

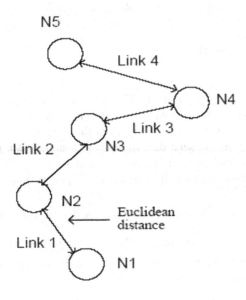

Fig. 2. Greedy algorithm to build a chain by PEGASIS method

In each round, a sensor node must be selected as the CH. Each sensor node receives data from its downstream neighbor, fuses with its own data to generate a single packet of the same length, and transmits the fused data to its upstream neighbor on the chain. This process is illustrated in Fig. 3 below. When Node 4 is selected as the CH, Node 3 fuses data with Node 5. Node 2 fuses its data with Node 1. Node 4 fuses its data with Node 2 and Node 3 and transmits the data to the base station.

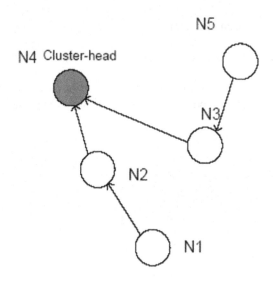

Fig. 3. Data moving from all sensor nodes to the CH node

2   Problem Formulation

In many applications, the data reporting of all sensor nodes is critical as in medical applications or in security applications. The above PEGASIS protocol tries to ensure that every node can become a CH equally. This is not appropriate for optimum system lifetime. Sensor nodes that are far away from the base station will consume more energy than closer nodes to send data to the base station. Also, nodes that have too little energy should not become CHs. As an equal selection of CHs will result in a reduced lifetime, a formulation to determine the CH pattern among all sensor nodes is presented below.

Let us define n to be the number of sensor nodes, and x_j to be the number of rounds node j becomes a CH. In chain-based routing, only one CH is selected each round. Therefore, there are n possible choices of CHs. The problem for the selection of the CHs is formulated as follows:

Maximize:

$$\sum_{j=1}^{n} x_j$$

Subject to:

$$\sum_{j=1}^{n} c_j^i x_j \le E_i : \forall i \in [1...n] \qquad (1)$$

$$x_j \in Z^+ : \forall j \in [1...n]$$

,where c_j^i is the energy usage of Node i to send a unit of data in a round, when Node j becomes CH and E_i to be the initial energy storage of Node i

The above Linear Programming problem tries to maximize the total number of rounds of transmitting data by all sensor nodes under the battery-constraint of all sensor nodes. The energy coefficients c_j^i of each non CH node include the energy dissipation for the node to receive data from its downstream neighbor and to send the fused data to its upstream neighbor in the chain. The energy coefficients of each CH node in the formula include the energy dissipation for the node to receive data from its downstream neighbors and to send the fused data to the base station. The diagram in Fig. 4 shows that when Node 4 becomes a CH, c_4^2 includes the energy dissipation to receive data from Node 1 and to send the fused data to Node 4. c_4^4 includes the energy dissipation to receive data from Node 3 and Node 2 and to send the fused data to the base station.

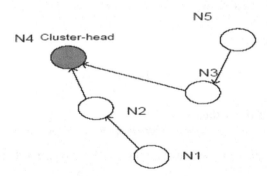

Fig. 4. Energy consumption coefficients of every sensor depends on the position of the CH

3   A New Heuristic Solution

Problem formulation (1) can be solved by Linear Programming solvers. These solvers are not always available and it is not easy to build these solvers inside sensors.

Therefore, the heuristic RE_chain algorithm is proposed. In the RE_chain algorithm, the CH positions are reallocated among the sensor nodes so that the minimum residual energy of all sensor nodes is maximized. The heuristic algorithm (RE_chain) is given as below:

RE_chain:

In every round of data transmission to the base station, select a sensor node as a leader for the chain in order to maximize the minimum residual energy of all sensor nodes after sending data for the round.

Given:

N : the number of sensor nodes indexed from 1 to N

s : A current CH solution

$f(s)$: The minimum residual energy of all nodes with solution s

s_0 : Best solution so far

RE_chain algorithm:

Initialization: $s_0 \leftarrow 0$

For (s from 1 to N)

$$\delta = f(s) - f(s_0)$$

If $\delta > 0$ **then** $s_0 = s$

Result: s_0 is the CH solution obtained from the RE_chain algorithm

4   Simulation Results

To evaluate the performance of RE_chain and compare the performance with that of PEGASIS and LEACH protocol [1], a number of simulators in Visual C++ were developed. The comparison between the system lifetime from Problem formulation (1) and that of RE_chain is also performed. In the first set of simulations, the performance of RE_chain is compared to the solution given by Formulation (1). In the simulations, 100 random 100-node sensor networks are generated. Each node begins with 1 J of energy. The network settings for the simulations in this section are given below. The energy model was used in [1],[3],[9],[10],[11].

Network size $(100m \times 100m)$

Base station $(50m, 300m)$

Number of sensor nodes   100 nodes

Data message size: 4000 bits

Broadcast message: 200 bits

Energy message: 20 bits

Position of sensor nodes: Uniform placed in the area

Energy model: $E_{elec} = 50*10^{-9}$ J, $\varepsilon_{fs} = 10*10^{-12}$ J/bit/m^2 and

$\varepsilon_{mp} = 0.0013*10^{-12}$ J/bit/m^4

Fig. 5 shows the ratio of the number of rounds of RE_chain and the Linear Programming solution of Formulation (1). From the simulation result, it can be said that RE_chain performs within 1% of the Linear Programming solution.

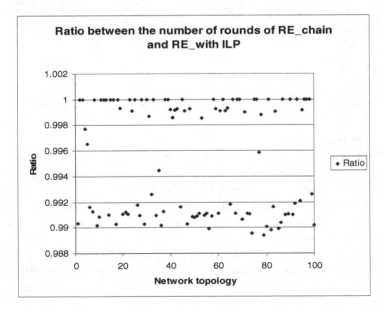

Fig. 5. Ratio of the number of rounds between RE_chain and RE_chain_with_ILP

It is also of interest to compare the performance of RE_chain, PEGASIS, and LEACH on the network topologies. On average, LEACH, PEGASIS, and RE_chain perform 602, 890, and 1305 rounds respectively.

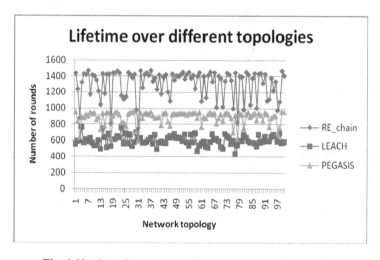

Fig. 6. Number of rounds over 100 random 100-node networks

Table 1. Results for Fig. 6

Protocol	PEGASIS	RE_chain	LEACH
Mean	890.3	1305.4	602.3
Variance	84.9	174.5	62.5
90 % confidence interval of the sample means	(876, 904)	(1276, 1335)	(592, 613)

5   Conclusion

This paper has focused on a new family of routing protocols for sensor networks: chain-based routing protocols. In chain-based routing, nodes form a chain connecting all nodes in the network. Data are gathered from all sensor nodes and move along the chain toward an elected sensor. The role of the elected node is rotated between all sensor nodes to increase the network lifetime. Chain-based routing exploits the data aggregation capability of sensor networks at maximum. When data are gathered from all sensor nodes, the data are aggregated with the data from their neighbors into a single message. The process is repeated until a single message is collected at the elected sensor node.

The previous chain-based routing (PEGASIS) selects the CH nodes uniformly among all sensor nodes. It is demonstrated in this chapter that the selection is a bad practice to ensure a good lifetime. Depending on the energy usage of each sensor to send data to its neighbors and to the base station, the sensor nodes should be elected as a leader differently. The paper has then proposed a method to optimize the selection of the CH among all sensor nodes using Linear Programming formulations. As it is not always practical to do the Linear Programming formulation, a simple heuristic method called RE_chain is proposed to calculate the selection. Simulations showed that RE_chain performs very closely to the Linear Programming formulation. The performance of RE_chain was then compared to that of LEACH, PEGASIS. This was shown that RE_chain improves the system lifetime significantly than that of PEGASIS. Also, it was observed that RE_chain performs about 3 times better than LEACH.

References

1. Heinzelman, W.B., Chandrakasan, A.P., Balakrish, H.: Energy-Efficient Communication Protocol for Wireless Microsensor Networks. In: 33rd Hawaii International Conference Systems Sciences (January 2000)
2. Al-Karaki, J.N., Kamal, A.E.: Routing techniques in wireless sensor networks: a survey. IEEE Wireless Communications, 6–28 (December 2004)
3. Tung, N.T.: Energy-Efficient Routing Algorithms in Wireless Sensor Networks: PhD thesis, Monash University, Australia (July 2009)
4. Heinzelman, W.B., Chandrakasan, A.P.: An Application Specific Protocol Architecture for Wireless Microsensor Networks. IEEE Transaction on Wireless Communications 1(4), 660–670 (2002)
5. Lindsey, S., Raghavendra, C.: Power-Efficient Gathering in Sensor Information Systems. In: IEEE Aerospace Conference (2002)
6. Traveling sale problem (2007), http://en.wikipedia.org/wiki/Travelling_salesman_problem
7. GLPK programming (2007), http://www.gnu.org/software/glpk/
8. Linear Programming (2007), http://en.wikipedia.org/wiki/Linear_programming
9. Tung, N.T., Vinh, P.C.: The Energy-Aware Operational Time of Wireless Ad-hoc Sensor Networks. ACM/Springer Mobile Networks and Applications (MONET) Journal 17 (August 2012), doi:10.1007/s11036-012-0403-1
10. Tung, N.T.: The power-save protocol of wireless ad-hoc sensor networks. Mediterranean Journal of Computers and Networks 4 (October 2012) ISSN: 1744-2397
11. Tung, N.T.: Heuristic Energy-Efficient Routing Solutions to Extend the Lifetime of Wireless Ad-Hoc Sensor Networks. In: Pan, J.-S., Chen, S.-M., Nguyen, N.T. (eds.) ACIIDS 2012, Part II. LNCS, vol. 7197, pp. 487–497. Springer, Heidelberg (2012)

Object Detection and Tracking
in Contourlet Domain

Nguyen Thanh Binh and Tran Anh Dien

Faculty of Computer Science and Engineering,
Ho Chi Minh City University of Technology, Vietnam
ntbinh@cse.hcmut.edu.vn, dientrananh@gmail.com

Abstract. This paper describes a method for the moving object detection and tracking in video sequences using contourlet transform. For the contourlet transform to be translation-invariant a 2D cycle spinning is implemented on subbands Δ_1 and Δ_2. Cycle spinning for edge detection is implemented. The shape of object may change from this frame to other frame. The 3D moving object is combined two parts: a 2D shape change and 2D motion. The 2D motion of the object, we use the minimum Hausdorff distance from the model to the image to find where object moved to. With 2D shape change of the object, we use distance from the image to the transformed model to select set of image pixels of the next model. For performance evaluation, we compared the proposed method based on the contourlet transform using cycle spinning with the similar methods based on the complex wavelet transform and wavelet transform.

Keywords: edge detection, contourlet tranform, cycle spinning, object tracking.

1 Introduction

Wavelet transforms domain methods are used for object tracking. Several algorithms have been proposed to solve the problem of tracking [3, 4]. Every tracking method requires an object detection mechanism either when the object first appears in the video. A common for object detection is to use information of single frame.

Y. Wang [17] proposed an algorithm that derives the objects based on the motion between frames. This tracking is limited and not able to handle some complex situations such as object starts moving, object stops moving and objects move together. A lot of existing methods first perform computationally expensive spatial segmentation based on a moving object region tracking [15]. This is not necessary in a lot of applications, where only moving objects need to be tracked.

The Discrete wavelet transform (DWT) provides a fast, local, sparse and decorrelated multiresolution analysis of images. DWT have limited such as shift-sensitivity and poor directionality [9]. Several researchers have provided solutions for minimizing these disadvantages. Recently new X-let multiscale transforms have been developed such as curvelet, contourlet [1,2,5,6,7,13,14] which integrate the concept of directionality in better way. Techniques to reduce these drawbacks have been proposed; new multiscale transforms have been designed such as the contourlet transform to integrate the concept of directionality in a more useful fashion.

P.C. Vinh et al. (Eds.): ICCASA 2012, LNICST 109, pp. 192–200, 2013.

We propose an implementation of the contourlet transform and described a method for moving object tracking, using contourlet transform with cycle spinning. The shape of object may change from this frame to other frame. The approach consists of two steps. First contourlet coefficients are used for detection of object and second tracking of object in the sequence of frames. The rest of the paper is organized as follows: In section 2, we described the basic concepts of contourlet transform. Details of the proposed algorithm are given in section 3. In section 4, the results of the proposed method for detection, tracking are shown and compared to other methods and finally in section 5, we presented our conclusions.

2   The Contourlet Transform

The contourlet construction presented here is based on the work of Do and Vetterli [1]. Contourlets constitute a new family of frames that are designed to represent smooth contours in different directions of an image. Contourlet is easily applied in image processing because its representation is a fixed transform. Contourlet allows for a different number of directions at each scale and aspect ratios. This feature allows an efficient contourlet-based approximation of a smooth contour at multiple resolutions. The discrete contourlet transform is a multiscale and directional decomposition using a combination of Laplacian pyramid (LP) and directional filter bank (DFB) [1].

The idea of the contourlet construction [1] is: let $a_0[n]$ be the input image, the output after the LP step is I bandpass images $b_i[n]$, $i = 1, 2,..., I$ and a lowpass image $a_I[n]$. Each bandpass image $b_i[n]$ is decomposed by an ℓ_i-level DFB into 2^{ℓ_i} bandpass directional images $c_{i,k}^{(\ell_i)}[n]$, for $k = 0, 1,..., 2^{\ell_i}\text{-}1$.

In the discrete contourlet transform, the multiscale and directional decomposition steps are decoupled. So, we have different numbers of directions at different scales.

Contourlet decomposition proceeds through two main steps: first, Laplacian pyramid multiscale decomposition is performed; then directional filter bank decomposition is used to link point discontinuity to linear structures. In more detail, an image is decomposed into a low pass image and bandpass images by the LP decomposition. Each bandpass output is further decomposed by the DFB step. The output of the DFB step consists of smooth contours and directional edges. In this paper, each directional subband at each level consists of 2^n element, where n is a positive integer. Fig 1 shows a contourlet decomposition.

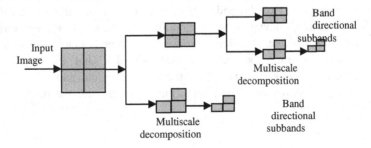

Fig. 1. Contourlet decomposition

3   The Proposed Method

In this section, we present an approach to implement of the contourlet transform and described a method for moving object tracking, using contourlet transform. The shape of object may change from this frame to other frame. The approach consists of two steps. First contourlet coefficients are used for detection of object and second tracking of object in the sequence of frames. A video sequence contains a series of frames. Each frame can be considered as an image. If an algorithm can track moving objects between two digital images, it should be able to track moving objects in a video sequence. The algorithm starts with two steps.

3.1   The Detection of Object Algorithm

The goal of edge detection is to divide the given image into regions that belong to distinct objects in the depicted scene. This process consists of three steps [1,2,13] apply contourlet transform to the image, retain the coefficients where the signal-to-noise ratio is high, and reduce the coefficients where the signal-to- noise ratio is low.

A 2-D cycle spinning is implemented on subbands Δ_1 and Δ_2 so that the contourlet transform is translation-invariant. The transformed data are shifted, edge detected, and unshifted. Applying the following procedure,

$$\hat{s} = \frac{1}{K_1 K_2} \sum_{i=1, j=1}^{K_1, K_2} S_{-i,-j}(T^{-1}(\theta[T(S_{i,j}(x))])) \tag{1}$$

where K_1 and K_2 are the maximum number of shifts, we expect an improvement for the estimation $\hat{s}$ compared to the image without cycle spinning. For the contourlet transform, if the input image has size $N \times N$, with $N = 2^K$, then after K shifts in each direction, the output becomes repetitive and so the maximum numbers of shifts will be K in each direction. If one decomposes an image of size $N \times N$ using the contourlet transform, then the number of decomposition levels in the Δ_1 stage will be at most K, and therefore, the maximum number of shifts is K in the row and column directions.

The threshold for the contourlet coefficients can be calculated using statistical properties of noise or blur. After thresholding the contourlet coefficients, the image can be reconstructed. Donoho and Johnstone [10] have described a threshold that depends on standard deviation of contourlet coefficients. Here, to compute the threshold value for image edge detection, we use a combination of three parameters: the contrast ratio (ratio between standard deviation and mean of contourlet coefficients), the absolute median of contourlet coefficients, and a level dependent parameter. Fig. 2 shows the detection in duck images with the method presented above.

(a) Original image.   (b) Detected image

Fig. 2. Duck image

3.2   The Tracking Algorithm

In all the computations, the frame rate is adequate and the shape change from one time frame to the next is required to be small. The 3D moving object is combined two parts: a 2D shape change and 2D motion. To change 2D shape in image frame, we use 2D geometric models to capture them. With 2D motion of the object, we use the minimum Hausdorff distance [11] from the model to the image to find where object moved to.

Hausdorff distance [11] defined distance between two point sets P and Q as

$$H(P, Q)=\max(h(P, Q), h(Q, P)) \tag{2}$$

where $h(P,Q) = \max_{p\in P}\min_{q\in Q}\|p-q\|$ and $\|.\|$ denotes Euclidean distance.

Daniel[11] defines the partial distance as:

$$h_k(P,Q) = \underset{p\in P, q\in Q}{K^{th}\min}\|p-q\|$$

For some transformation group G [11], the natural definition of a distance is simply the minimum with respect to that group action $D_G(P,Q) = \min_{g\in G} H(g(P),Q)$, if $D_G(P,Q)=0$, two shapes are same otherwise change in shape is measured.

With 2D shape change of the object, we use distance from the image to the transformed model to select set of image pixels of the next model. The model M_t consist of m point moved to next time frame I_{t+1}. The location of the object in the new image frame is computed by the minimum valued d of distance from M_t to the frame I_{t+1}

$$d = \min_{g\in G} h_k(g(M_t), I_{t+1}) = \min_{g\in G} \underset{p\in M_t, q\in I_{t+1}}{K^{th}\min}\|g(p)-q\|$$

which d identifies the transformation $g^*\in G$ of M_t which minimizes the rank order.

4 Experiments and Results

We have applied the procedure described in section 3 and observed good performance in our detection and tracking experiments as briefly demonstrated in this section.

Hard thresholding is applied to the coefficients after decomposition in contourlet domain. In case of contourlet transform with cycle spinning, the input image is of size $N \times N$, with $N = 2^K$. In the case $K = 8$ (i.e., $N = 256$) after 8 shifts in each direction, the transform output repeats and so the maximum number of shifts will be 8 in each direction. We apply the same approach to the contourlet transform.

For the tracking part, we determine the object in each frame of the movie. The object area is determined in the first frame by hand. In this experiment, we use mouse to select the object area in the first frame. The object area is determined in the first frame, the tracking algorithm need to track the object from frame to frame.

For performance evaluation, we compared the proposed method based on the contourlet transform with the similar methods based on the complex wavelet transform and wavelet transform. The comparison of results with other methods has been done using our program on the same video and at similar scales. Here, we report the results on some video clips. Our experimental approach was as follows.

Our experiment is on car and player video clips with frame size 288 by 352. The proposed method processes this video clip at 28 frames/second. We have experimented on the video up to 1000 frames. Here, we report the results upto 1000 frames and starting from frame number: 100, 200, 300, 400, 500, 600, 700, 800, 900 and 1000. Some results achieved as shown in fig. 3 and fig 4.

Frame No	Wavelet Domain	Complex wavelet Domain	Proposed method
100			
200			
300			

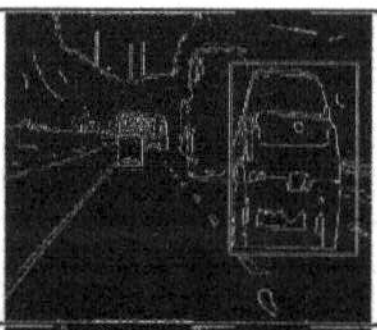

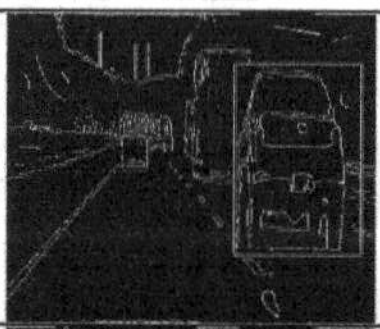

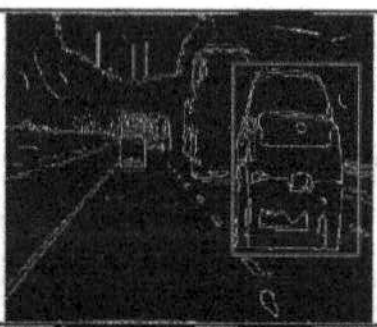

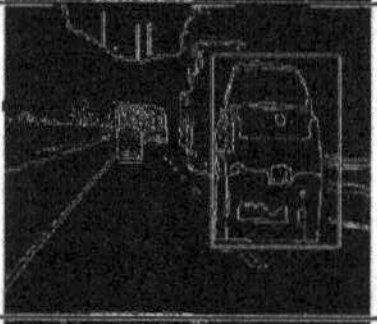

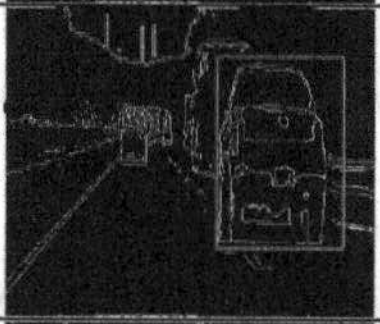

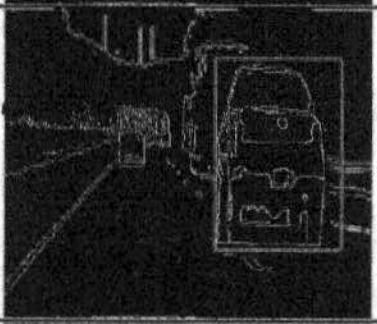

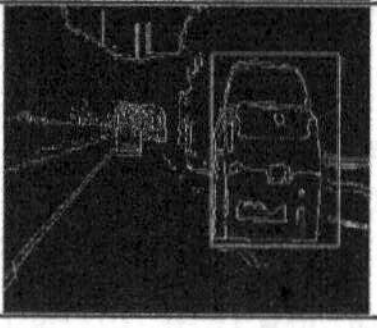

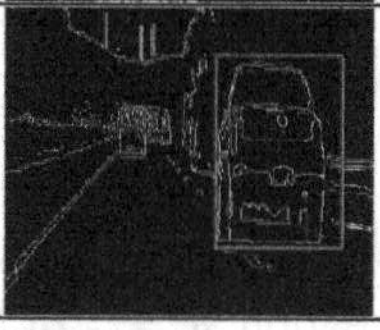

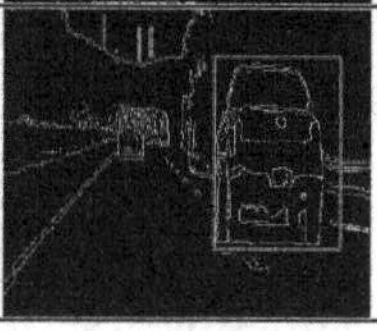

Fig. 3. Tracking in Car video clips upto 1000 frames

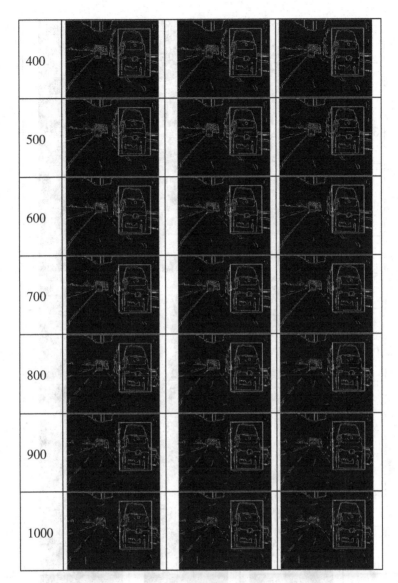

Fig. 3. (*Continued*)

Frame No	Wavelet Domain	Complex wavelet Domain	Proposed method
100			

Fig. 4. Tracking in Play video clips upto 1000 frames

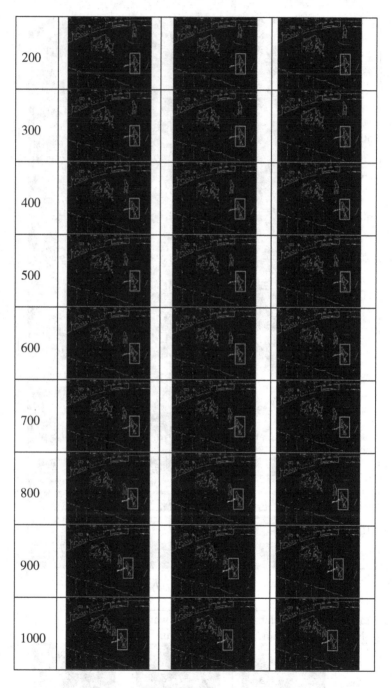

Fig. 4. (*Continued*)

In these figures, we observe that the proposed method performs better than the other two methods. Other experiments also show that the proposed method works well and better than the other ones. In wavelet domain, tracking is high execution time. In complex wavelet domain, tracking is more accurate but is also medium execution time. The proposed method is also more accurate and faster other method. As above mentioned, contourlet allows for a different number of directions at each scale and aspect ratios. This feature allows an efficient contourlet-based approximation of a smooth contour at multiple resolutions.

5   Conclusions

In this paper we have constructed a method for detection and tracking of object that provides a sparse expansion for typical images having smooth contours. We use contourlet coefficients and cycle spinning to detection and tracking the object in the sequence of frames. We compared the proposed method based on the contourlet transform with the similar methods based on the complex wavelet transform, and wavelet transform. The proposed method is more accurate and faster other method. However, if the quality of the frame in video is very bad, such as strong noise, blur, etc., then the estimation ability is reduced. To avoid this problem, we should try to reduce noise and blur before the application of the proposed algorithm. Unlike the other methods, the algorithm does not rely upon many properties of object such as size, shapes, colors, etc.... In all of computations, it has been assumed that the frame rate is adequate and the size of the object may be change between adjacent frames.

References

1. Do, M.N., Vetterli, M.: The Contourlet Transform: An Efficient Directional Multiresolution Image Representation. IEEE Transactions on Image Processing 14, 2091–2106 (2005)
2. Eslami, R., Radha, H.: Translation-invariant contourlet transform and its application to image denoising. IEEE Transactions on Image Processing 15(11), 3362–3374 (2006)
3. Stamou, G., Krinidis, M., Loutas, E., Nikolaidis, N., Pitas, I.: 2D and 3D motion tracking in digital video. In: Bovik, A.C. (ed.) Handbook of Image and Video Processing. Academic Press (2005)
4. Moeslund, T.B., Granum, E.: A survey of computer vision based human motion capture. Computer Vision and Image Understanding 81, 231–268 (2001)
5. Liu, K., Guo, L., Chen, J.: Contourlet transform for image fusion using cycle spinning. Journal of Systems Engineering and Electronics 22(2), 353–357 (2011)
6. Raghavendra, B.S., Bhat, P.S.: Contourlet Based Multiresolution Texture Segmentation Using Contextual Hidden Markov Models. In: Das, G., Gulati, V.P. (eds.) CIT 2004. LNCS, vol. 3356, pp. 336–343. Springer, Heidelberg (2004)
7. Li, Y.-Q., He, M.-Y., Fang, X.-F.: SAR Image Segmentation Algorithm Using Mean Shift on Contourlet Domain. Computer Engineering 33(22), 48–50 (2007)
8. Contourlet Toolbox, Matlab source code, http://www.ifp.uiuc.edu/~minhdo/software/
9. Gopinath, R.A.: The Phaselet Transform – An Integral Redundancy Nearly Shift-Invariant Wavelet Transform. IEEE Trans. on Signal Processing 51, 1792–1805 (2003)

10. Donoho, D.L., Johnstone, I.M.: Ideal spatial adaptation by wavelet shrinkage. Biometrika 8, 425–455 (1994)
11. Huttenlocher, D.P., Noh, J.J., Rucklidge, W.J.: Tracking Non-Rigid Objects in Complex Scenes. In: Proceedings of 4th International Conference on Computer Vision, Berlin, May 11-14, pp. 93–101 (1993)
12. Stamou, G., Krinidis, M., Loutas, E., Nikolaidis, N., Pitas, I.: 2D and 3D motion tracking in digital video. In: Bovik, A.C. (ed.) Handbook of Image and Video Processing. Academic Press (2005)
13. Binh, N.T., Minh, L.N.: Adaptive medical image edge detection in contourlet domain. In: Proceedings of the 4th International Conference on the Development of Biomedical Engineering, pp. 238–241 (2012)
14. Binh, N.T., Khare, A.: Object tracking of video sequences in curvelet domain. International Journal of Image and Graphics 11(1), 1–20 (2011)
15. Masoud, O., Papanikolopoulos, N.P.: A novel method for tracking and counting pedestrians in real-time using a single camera. IEEE Transactions on Vehicular Technology 50, 1267–1278 (2001)
16. Prakash, O., Khare, A.: Tracking of Non-Rigid Object in Complex Wavelet Domain. Journal of Signal and Information Processing 2, 105–111 (2011)
17. Wang, Y., Van Dyck, R.E., Doherty, J.F.: Tracking Moving Objects in Video Sequences. In: Proc. Conference on Information Sciences and Systems, Princeton, NJ (March 2000)

User Preferences Elicitation and Exploitation in a Push-Delivery Mobile Recommender System

Quang Nhat Nguyen, Thuan Minh Hoang, Lan Quynh Thi Ta, Cuong Van Ta, and Phai Minh Hoang

Hanoi University of Science and Technology, Hanoi, Vietnam
quangnn-fit@mail.hut.edu.vn

Abstract. Most existing recommender systems follow the pull-delivery approach, where the user must explicitly make request before receiving some product or service recommendations. However, in application domains where the availability of items changes quickly and often (e.g., recommendation of relevant promotions, events, etc.), the pull-delivery recommendation approach seems not effective in helping users keep track of their desired and interested items. In this paper, we present our proposed push-delivery mobile recommendation methodology that is capable of proactively delivering personalized recommendations to mobile users at appropriate context. The proposed recommendation methodology has been implemented in *Prom4U* - a push mobile recommender system that helps users timely receive their interested promotions of commercial products from supermarkets and stores. We present here the experimental results of a live-user evaluation of *Prom4U* that show the appropriateness of the proposed recommendation approach and the effectiveness of the system *Prom4U*.

Keywords: mobile recommender system, push delivery, user preferences elicitation, critique-based recommendation, live-user evaluation.

1 Introduction

Recommender systems (RSs) aims at solving the information overload problem by providing product and service recommendations personalized to a given user's needs and preferences [1], [2]. Most existing RSs follow the pull-delivery approach, where the user must explicitly make request for some product or service recommendations. However, in some application domains (e.g., the problem of providing interested product promotions to a given user), the availability of items changes quickly and often. In such application domains, the pull-delivery approach seems less effective in helping users keep track of their interested items, i.e., at the time of a user's request some of his interested items are not available, but when they are available (often in short durations) the user does not know.

In this paper, we present our proposed mobile push-delivery recommendation methodology that is capable of proactively (i.e., automatically) providing relevant recommendations to users at right contexts. To provide push-delivery recommendations to users, the system must decide: *what recommendations should be*

P.C. Vinh et al. (Eds.): ICCASA 2012, LNICST 109, pp. 201–211, 2013.
© Institute for Computer Sciences, Social Informatics and Telecommunications Engineering 2013

pushed to a given user, and *when the system should push these recommendations to the user*. To tackle the first problem, our proposed recommendation methodology integrates both long-term and session-specific user preferences and exploits a critique-based conversational approach [3]. The long-term user preferences are inferred from past recommendation sessions, whereas the session-specific user preferences are derived from the user's critiques to the provided recommendations in the current session. To deal with the second problem, the system models a push context as a case, and uses the Case-Based Reasoning (CBR) problem-solving strategy [4], i.e., a machine learning approach, to exploit (i.e., reuse) the knowledge contained in the past push cases to determine the right push context for the current case.

Our proposed recommendation methodology has been implemented in *Prom4U* - a mobile push recommender system that helps users timely receive their interested product promotions. We conducted an evaluation of the system *Prom4U* with real test users. This live-user evaluation aims at testing the appropriateness of the proposed recommendation approach and the effectiveness of the implemented system. We present in this paper the experimental results of this live-user evaluation.

The remainder of the paper is organized as follows. In Section 2, we discuss some related work on recommender systems and push-delivery information systems. In Section 3, we introduce the formal representations of product promotions, the user profile and the user query. In Section 4, we present our proposed mobile push-delivery recommendation methodology. In Section 5, we report the experimental results of the live-user evaluation. Finally, the conclusion and future work are given in Section 6.

2   Related Work

Recommender Systems (RSs) are intelligent decision support tools that help users find and select their desired products and services when there are too many options to consider or when users lack the domain-specific knowledge to make selection decisions by themselves. Traditional recommendation approaches include: collaborative, content-based, and knowledge-based [1], [2]. RSs have been very effective and popular tools in well-known commercial websites, such as Amazon.com, Barnes&Noble.com, eBay.com, Yahoo! news, iTunes Genius, TripAdvisor.com, MyProductAdvisor.com, etc.

A push-delivery information system is a system that automatically delivers (i.e., pushes) the information to users without their request. The push-delivery model appears to be effective in application domains where the availability of items changes often and quickly, because it helps users timely receive their interested information. However, if the system pushes uninterested information to a user, or even pushes interested information to the user but at inappropriate contexts, there is a high risk that this push-based delivery will annoy the user (i.e., considered as a spam). Hence, for push-delivery RSs, to provide personalized recommendations and reduce the spamming issue, the system must push *only relevant and targeted* information to the user *at right time.* In some previous approaches, the system just pushes all objects (or items) that locate near the user's position, without regarding his preferences [5], [6]. In other previous approaches, the system, though takes into account the user's preferences, but does not estimate right contexts to push, i.e., the system always pushes advertisements to the user when he is close to (or inside) the store [7], [8]. Ciaramella et al. [9] presented a mobile services RS that uses a rules table to determine a user's situation, but the system pushes all services associated with the determined situation to the user without regarding his preferences. The information service system presented in [10] determines the push time based on a decision table that is the same for all users.

In our proposed approach, the pushed recommendations are personalized for each user (i.e., suitable for his preferences), and the push context is determined based on the system's learning from past push cases. Hence, the system's push-context determination is personalized for each user. Moreover, all the push-delivery information systems mentioned above follow the single-shot strategy, where the system computes and pushes to the user the information, and the session ends. In our proposed approach, a push session, after the user accepts to view the pushed recommendations, evolves in a dialogue where the system's recommendations interleave with the user's critiques to these recommendations [3]. Such critiques enable the system to better understand the user's preferences, and hence to provide more suitable recommendations to the user.

3 Formal Representations

3.1 Promotion Representation

In our recommendation problem, a promotion, *represented hierarchically*, consists of the three main components: the promotion's information, the promotion's promoted product(s) and the promotion's gift(s). In this hierarchical representation, each component is represented by its own sub-components and features. Because of the limited paper space, we elaborate here only the first and second levels of the hierarchical representation of a promotion.

$$X = (PROM\_INFO, PROM\_PRODUCTS, GIFTS)$$

The component $PROM\_INFO$ stores the information of the promotion:

$$PROM\_INFO = (Prom\_Types, DURATION, PROVIDER);$$

where the feature $Prom\_Types$ represents the types of the promotion, the sub-components $DURATION$ and $PROVIDER$ represent the promotion's available duration and provider, respectively.

The component $PROM\_PRODUCTS$ represents the set of the promoted products, where each promoted product is represented by the product identifier, its category and price.

$$PROM\_PRODUCTS = \{(Product\_Id, Category, Price)\}$$

The component $GIFTS$ represents the set of the gifts of the promotion, where each gift is represented by the gift identifier and its type.

$$GIFTS = \{(Gift\_Id, Gift\_Type)\}$$

3.2 User Profile Representation

The user profile stores *the user's long-term preferences* that are exploited by the system to build the initial representation of the user query. The user profile, *hierarchically represented*, consists of the three components that represent the user's long-term preferences on promotions, promoted products and gifts.

$$U = (PROM\_PREF, PRODUCT\_PREF, GIFT\_PREF);$$

where the component $PROM\_PREF$ stores the user's long-term preferences on promotions types and providers; the component $PRODUCT\_PREF$ stores his long-term preferences on category and price of promoted products; and the component $GIFT\_PREF$ stores his long-term preferences on gift types.

3.3 User Query Representation

The user query (Q) representation encodes the system's understanding of *the user's session-specific preferences*. In a recommendation session, at every recommendation cycle the system uses this query Q to compute the promotions recommendation list for the user. The user query Q consists of the two structured components: the favorite pattern (FP) and the component and feature importance weights (W).

$$Q = (FP, W)$$

The favorite pattern FP, hierarchically represented, consists of the three components that represent the user's session-specific preferences on promotions, promoted products and gifts. The structure of FP is similar to the structure of the user profile (U) representation, except that FP includes additionally the sub-component $DURATION$ (i.e., to represent the user's session-specific preference on promotion available duration) and the feature $Distance$ (i.e., to represent the user's session-specific preference on distance to promotion provider).

The weights vector W is *represented hierarchically* corresponding to the representation of FP. For each representation level, the weight of a sub-component (or a feature) models how much important the sub-component (or the feature) is for the user with respect to the others.

4 Proposed Recommendation Methodology

In our approach, a recommendation session starts when the system shows a notification screen (i.e., of new interesting promotions) on the user's mobile device, and ends when he quits the session. The overview of the recommendation process is shown in Figure 1.

When the session starts, the system builds the initial query representation (Q^0) exploiting the user's contextual information and long-term preferences stored in the user profile. In particular, the values of the features of FP^0 are set

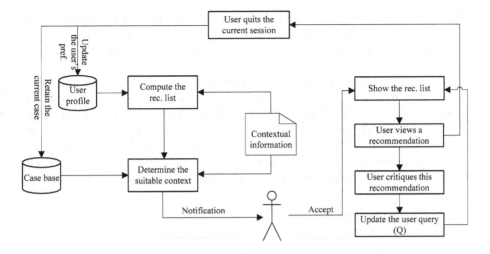

Fig. 1. The overview of the recommendation process

by the values of the corresponding features in the user profile (U). In addition, the values of $DURATION$ and $Distance$ are set to unknown to indicate that the system, at the beginning of the session, does not know about the user's session-specific preferences on promotion available period and distance to provider.

The importance weights vector W is initialized by exploiting the history of user critiques. The intuitive idea is that a feature (or sub-component)'s initial importance weight is proportional to the frequency of the user critiques expressed on that feature (or sub-component) [11]. We note that in our current approach, *at a recommendation cycle the user can make critique to a number of (i.e., more than one) features* of the item; whereas in our previous work [11] the system allows the user to make critique to only one feature per cycle.

The system uses this initial query Q^0 to compute the initial recommendation list for the user, by ranking the available promotions to their similarity to (FP^0, W^0). The ranking is done, using a similarity function computed over the hierarchical representation described in Section 3, so that the more similar to (FP^0, W^0) a promotion is the higher it appears in the ranked list. In case of ties, the promotion provided by the provider closer to the user's position is ranked higher. Only k (i.e., a predefined cut-off parameter) best promotions in the ranked list, i.e., those most similar to (FP^0, W^0), are included in the recommendation list.

After computing the recommendation list, the system must determine when it should push this list to the user. In our proposed approach, this push-context determination is done based on the Case-Based Reasoning (CBR) problem-solving strategy [4]. The CBR is used to exploit (i.e., reuse) the knowledge contained in the past push cases. In our recommendation methodology, each push case is modeled by two parts: *problem description* and *solution*. In particular, the problem description of a case contains information of: 1) the time-slot of the push, 2) the list of providers that provide promotions contained in the recommendation list,

3) the user's distances to those providers, and 4) the user's long-term preferences to those providers. The solution of a case indicates the decision of the user, i.e., either the user accepts to receive (i.e., view) the recommendation list or the user rejects to receive.

To estimate (i.e., predict) an appropriate push context, the system identifies the set of m past push cases most similar to the current one in that the users accepted to receive the recommendation list (denoted as $C^{Accepted}$) and the set of m past push cases most similar to the current one in that the users rejected to receive the recommendation list (denoted as $C^{Rejected}$). Then, the system computes the *acceptance degree* (i.e., the confidence level to push) and the *rejection degree* (i.e., the confidence level to not push) for the current case.

$$acceptance\_degree(C^*) = \frac{1}{m} \sum_{C \in C^{Accepted}} sim(C^*, C); \qquad (1)$$

$$rejection\_degree(C^*) = \frac{1}{m} \sum_{C \in C^{Rejected}} sim(C^*, C); \qquad (2)$$

where C^* is the current case, C is a past one, and $sim(C^*, C)$ is the similarity between C^* and C.

If $(acceptance\_degree(C^*) - rejection\_degree(C^*)) \geq \theta$ (i.e., θ is a predefined push-confidence threshold value), then the system sends a push notification to the user. Otherwise, the system does not, and the recommendation list is saved in the pending list for him (i.e., at the next time-slot, the system re-estimates whether or not to send the push notification to him).

We note that in our proposed approach, at the predicted push time the system does not immediately show the recommendation list. Instead, the system just shows a notification on the screen of the user's mobile device and lets him make the final decision (i.e., to accept or reject the push). In this way, we get the two advantages. First, in case the system's predicted time is not (really) appropriate for the user, showing just a notification screen makes him less annoying compared to showing immediately the recommendation list. Second, showing the notification screen allows the system to collect the user's decision (i.e., to accept or reject the push) that is recorded as the solution part of the current push case.

Given the push notification sent to the user's mobile device, he can decide to accept the push, or postpone it, or reject it (see Figure 2-a). If he accepts the push, then the system stores the current push case in its case base (for the future uses) and shows the recommendation list to him (see Figure 2-b). If he rejects to receive the push, then the system stores the current push case in its case base, and the session ends. If he postpones the push, then he specifies a later appropriate time slot (see Figure 2-a). At that indicated (postponed) time the system re-sends the push notification to him. Until the end of the current day, if he has not accepted the postponed push, then the system records the postponed push case as a rejection one in its case base.

When the recommendation list is shown to the user (see Figure 2-b), he can select a recommended promotion to see its details (see Figure 2-c). After the user

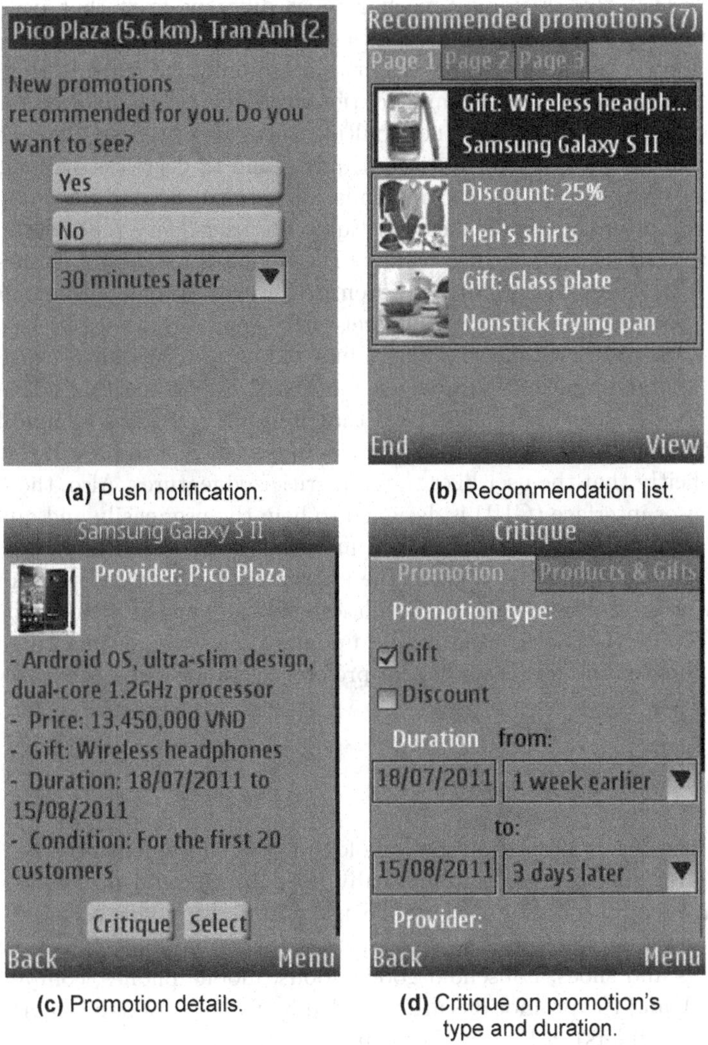

(a) Push notification.

(b) Recommendation list.

(c) Promotion details.

(d) Critique on promotion's type and duration.

Fig. 2. The user interface of the system *Prom4U*

views a promotion's details, if he accepts the promotion, then this promotion is added to his Selection List, and he can view another recommended one or quit the session. If he is somewhat interested in the promotion, but some of its features do not completely satisfy him, then he critiques the promotion to specify his preferences on these unsatisfactory features (see Figure 2-d). Such critiques help the system adapt its current understanding of the user's preferences (i.e., encoded in Q), and re-compute a new list of recommended promotions shown to the user, and the system proceeds to the next recommendation cycle.

We note that this critiquing mechanism is different from that used in our previous work [3] in two aspects. First, in our previous approach [3], at a recommendation cycle the user can make a critique to only one feature. However, in our current approach, at a recommendation cycle the user is allowed to make a critique to a number of features (i.e., multi features are criticized per cycle). This helps to increase the convenience in critiquing, and to decrease the length (i.e., the number of cycles) of the recommendation session. Second, in our previous approach [3], after the user makes a critique, the user-query representation (Q) is updated exploiting solely the critique (i.e., not exploiting the values of the uncriticized features of the criticized item). However, in our current approach, after the user makes a critique, the user-query representation (Q) is updated exploiting both the critique and the values of the uncriticized features of the criticized item. Our current approach is motivated by the fact that a user makes a critique to an item when: 1)he likes that item, but 2)wants to modify some unsatisfactory features of that item. Hence, in our current approach the system infers implicitly that the user likes those uncriticized features. Also, the system's graphical user interface (GUI) is designed to help the user easily and quickly see all the features of the promotion before making critique (see Figure 2-c).

When the user quits the session, the system exploits the information of his expressed critiques and selected promotions in the current session to update the user profile (U). This user profile update allows the system to refine its understanding of the user's long-term preferences, and hence better serve him in the future.

5   Live-User Evaluation

The proposed recommendation methodology has been implemented in *Prom4U* - a mobile RS that aims at automatically (i.e., proactively) providing relevant promotion recommendations to mobile users at appropriate contexts. In the current version of *Prom4U*, the system provides promotions of five categories (i.e., clothes and shoes, household goods, foods, mobile phones, computers and accessories), and the promotions are provided by five biggest super markets (i.e., promotion providers) in Hanoi, Vietnam.

We conducted a live-user evaluation of *Prom4U* to evaluate the appropriateness of the proposed recommendation approach and the usability of the system. This live-user evaluation lasted in more than two months and involved seven test users[1], i.e., three men and four women, in the ages of from 20 to 30 years old. All of the test users were interested in receiving suitable product promotions from super markets. In this live-user evaluation, we used the Vietnamese user-interface version of *Prom4U*, since all the test users are Vietnamese and for some of them their English are not good. (Note that Figure 2 shows the English user-interface version of *Prom4U*.)

---

[1] In fact, there were twenty two persons registering to join in this evaluation. But unfortunately, we had to exclude fifteen of them, because their mobile phones do not support running J2ME application and/or do not have a GPS built-in receiver.

After the client side of *Prom4U* (i.e., a J2ME midlet application) was installed on the mobile phone of a test user, he (or she) was introduced by the use guide of *Prom4U* and the test scenario, and then started using the system (in about two months). The test scenario, which every test user followed, consists of four main steps.

- Step 1. Given the push notification shown on the mobile phone's screen, the test user can either accept, postpone or reject to see the recommended promotions list (see Figure 2-a).
- Step 2. If the user accepts to see the recommended promotions list, it is shown on his/her mobile phone's screen. He/she can view the details of any of the recommended promotions.
- Step 3. After viewing a recommended promotion, the user can either selects it (i.e., if it satisfies him/her) or make a critique.
- Step 4. If the user likes a recommended promotion, but is not satisfied with it, then he/she uses the critiquing function to indicate his/her preferences to the promotion's unsatisfactory features. After the user makes a critique (to a number of features), the system exploits the critique to compute a new recommendation list and shows it to him/her.

The live-user evaluation collected both objective measures and subjective comments. The objective measures include the following metrics.

- *Push Acceptance Rate*: The number of the sessions in that the test users accept to see the recommendation list (after the system shows the push notification).
- *Recommendation Success Rate*: The number of the sessions in that the test users select some promotion(s).
- *Average Recommendation Length*: The average number of cycles of a recommendation session.
- *Average Number of Criticized Features Per Cycle*: The average number of features that are criticized per cycle.

In total, we collected 32 recommendation sessions from the test users' use of *Prom4U*. Regarding the push acceptance rate, among 32 sessions there were 30 ones in that the test users accepted to see the recommendation list after receiving the notification screen (i.e., the push acceptance rate of 93.75%). This objective result shows that in many cases the context (i.e., time) when the system automatically pushes the recommendation list to the user is appropriate (or at least acceptable) for him/her.

Regarding the recommendation success rate, among 30 sessions (i.e., those in that the user accepted to see the recommendation list) there were 27 successful recommendation sessions (i.e., 90% of the recommendation sessions in that the user selected some recommended promotions). This objective result is very promising, which shows that the system is capable of providing good recommendations for the users.

The average recommendation length was 1.67, which means that on average the test users could find their desired promotions within 1-2 recommendation cycles. Recall that in our proposed recommendation approach, at each recommendation cycle the user can make critique to a number of features of the criticized item. Given the simple and easy user-system interactions (see Figure 2-c,d), this average recommendation length is really acceptable for mobile users.

The average number of criticized features per cycle was 2.56. This result shows our proposed approach's effectiveness of allowing to make critique to more than one feature per cycle. If the user is limited to make critique to only one feature per cycle (e.g., as in [3]), then certainly the average recommendation length would be (much) longer than the reported value of 1.67.

At the end of this live-user evaluation (i.e., after more than two months of using *Prom4U*), the subjective comments and suggestions were collected from each test user, in form of free-text writing, regarding the effectiveness and usability of *Prom4U*. All the test users found that: 1)the system was effective in helping them receive their interested promotions, and 2)the system was easy to use and fast in the system-user interactions. However, by exploiting the test users' comments and suggestions, we found some possible improvement aspects of *Prom4U*. First, at first some test users did not find how to execute the screen-embedded commands (e.g., the buttons "Critique" and "Select" in Figure 2-c). (To execute such a screen-embedded command, the user has first to navigate through several display objects and then to activate that command.) For them, soft-button or menu commands are more traditional and easier to use. Second, some test users wanted to see again those promotions that they had previously criticized (in their current recommendation session). Third, some test users suggested that visualizing the recommended promotions on an electronic map, i.e., corresponding with their providers' locations, facilitates their promotions selection. In the next improvement version of *Prom4U* we should take into account these comments and suggestions.

6   Conclusion and Future Work

Mobile recommender systems aim at providing recommendations to users at anytime and anywhere, exploiting the popularization of mobile devices and their unique features like mobility, high targeting and personality. In this paper, we have presented our proposed methodology for proactively providing personalized recommendations to mobile users at appropriate contexts. The integration of the user's long-term and session-specific preferences enables the system to provide relevant recommendations, and the appropriate push-context prediction helps the system deliver these recommendations to him at right time. This mobile push recommendation methodology has been implemented in a recommender system called *Prom4U* that helps users timely receive their interested product promotions. In this paper, we have also presented the experimental results of the live-user evaluation of *Prom4U*, which show that our proposed approach is a good and promising solution for the mobile push-delivery recommendation problem.

For future work, we plan to do some tasks. First, we would like to run an empirical study to understand if users see all the features of the item before making a critique. This strongly influences the update method of the user query representation (Q). Second, we need to exploit all the test users' comments and suggestions to improve the usability of *Prom4U*. Third, we will need to find the best way to visualize the push notification on the screen of the user's mobile device. In the current design of *Prom4U*, this notification occupies the whole screen (see Figure 2-a), and it should be reduced much smaller (e.g., like the way of visualizing an incoming SMS message); so the notification causes less interruption and becomes more friendly for mobile users.

Acknowledgement. The financial support for this research work from the Vietnam National Foundation for Science and Technology Development (NAFOSTED) under the grant number 102.01.14.09 is gratefully appreciated.

References

1. Burke, R.: Hybrid Web Recommender Systems. In: Brusilovsky, P., Kobsa, A., Nejdl, W. (eds.) The Adaptive Web 2007. LNCS, vol. 4321, pp. 377–408. Springer, Heidelberg (2007)
2. Ricci, F., Rokach, L., Kantor, P.B.: Recommender Systems Handbook. Springer (2010)
3. Ricci, F., Nguyen, Q.N.: Acquiring and Revising Preferences in a Critique-Based Mobile Recommender System. IEEE Intelligent Sys. 22(3), 22–29 (2007)
4. Aamodt, A., Plaza, E.: Case-Based Reasoning: Foundational Issues, Methodological Variations, and System Approaches. AI Communications 7(1), 39–59 (1994)
5. Aalto, L., Göthlin, N., Korhonen, J., Ojala, T.: Bluetooth and WAP Push-Based Location-Aware Mobile Advertising System. In: 2nd International Conference on Mobile Systems, Application, and Services, pp. 49–58 (2004)
6. Hristova, N., O'Hare, G.: Ad-me: Wireless Advertising Adapted to the User Location, Device and Emotions. In: 37th Annual Hawaii International Conference on System Sciences, pp. 285–294 (2004)
7. de Castro, J.E., Shimakawa, H.: Mobile Advertisement System Utilizing User´s Contextual Information. In: 7th International Conference on Mobile Data Management, p. 91 (2006)
8. Kurkovsky, S., Harihar, K.: Using Ubiquitous Computing in Interactive Mobile Marketing. Personal and Ubiquitous Computing 10(4), 227–240 (2006)
9. Ciaramella, A., Cimino, M.G.C.A., Lazzerini, B., Marcelloni, F.: Situation-Aware Mobile Service Recommendation with Fuzzy Logic and Semantic Web. In: 9th International Conference on Intelligent Systems Design and Applications, pp. 1037–1042 (2009)
10. Pinyapong, S., Shoji, H., Ogino, A., Kato, T.: A Mobile Information Service Adapted to Vague and Situational Requirements of Individual. In: 7th International Conference on Mobile Data Management, pp. 20–22 (2006)
11. Nguyen, Q.N., Ricci, F.: User Preferences Initialization and Integration in Critique-Based Mobile Recommender Systems. In: 5th International Workshop on Artificial Intelligence in Mobile Systems, pp. 71–78 (2004)

Research on Innovating, Evaluating and Applying Multicast Routing Technique for Routing Messages in Service-Oriented Routing

Nguyen Thanh Long[1], Nguyen Duc Thuy[2], and Pham Huy Hoang[3]

[1] Informatic Center of Ha noi Telecommunications
75 Dinh Tien Hoang, Hoan Kiem, Ha Noi, Viet Nam
longptpm@vnpt-hanoi.com.vn
[2] Research Institute of Posts and Telecommunications
122 Hoang Quoc Viet, Nghia Tan, Cau Giay, Hanoi, Viet Nam
thuynd@ptit.edu.vn
[3] Hanoi University of Science and Technology
1 Dai Co Viet Road, Hanoi, Viet Nam
hoangph@soict.hut.edu.vn

Abstract. MANET (short for Mobile Ad-Hoc Network) consists of a set of mobile network nodes, network configuration changes very fast. Each node will act as a router to maintain network operation. There is no central node for controlling entire network. So routing in MANET is very important.

In content based routing, data is transferred from source node to requested nodes is not based on destinations addresses. Therefore it is very flexible and reliable, because source node does not need to know destination nodes. As some standard content based routing protocols, when a node publishes its content, It will broadcast data to network. The published content will be cached at all routes on the network. So when a node publish a request to get some content, it will prepare a subscription message then broadcast it to network. When any node on network received that subscription, it matches subscriptions content with published content that have been cached on it. If found then matched content will be transferred to requested node. There is another routing model when nodes have content requests, they broadcast subscription messages to network. When nodes receive subscriptions, they cache these messages. When a node publish its content by broadcast protocol, any node receives that content, it will match received content with subscriptions cached on it to find all nodes have requested that content, then forwarding that content to these nodes.

Service Oriented Routing is inherited from the model of content based routing (CBR) [3, 4], combined with several advanced techniques such as Multicast increase the data rate [6], and data encryption to ensure information security.

This article presents some techniques to support multicast packet forwarding from one network node to a set of nodes with guaranteed quality

P.C. Vinh et al. (Eds.): ICCASA 2012, LNICST 109, pp. 212–228, 2013.
© Institute for Computer Sciences, Social Informatics and Telecommunications Engineering 2013

of service. By using these techniques can decrease network load, congestion, use network resources efficiently.

Keywords: Ad hoc network, MANET, QoS, bandwidth guarantee, time slot assignment, routing, service, content.

1 Introduction

Publish/Subscription Model (abbreviated P/S) is the interaction model is performed asynchronously in the content based routing systems [3].

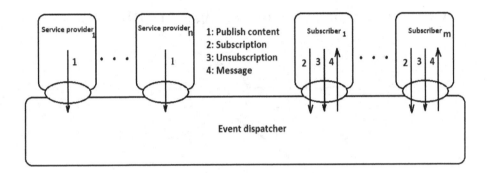

Fig. 1. Service based routing model

Each network node must undertake the following roles: service provider, content receiver, router. To perform these tasks efficiently at each node of the network We have to install a specific routing protocol. Currently there are many routing protocols developed for MANET such as OLSR, CBR, DSR, DSDV, AODV, ODMRP, in which there are some content based protocols. In the article We will make use of the advantages of these routing protocols and customize some important characteristics to construct novel routing protocol that is oriented service and guarantees quality of service, for example bandwidth and latency, failover, etc.

Service oriented architecture allows flexible communication, the ability to provide location transparency for the transmission of information between applications. Position transparency is defined as the connection to avoid the point - to - point because the application is separated with the data transmission services below, will undertake the implementation when the applications require communicating with each other.

Service-based network infrastructure is a new network interface in which the flow of messages is controlled by class of service that generated it. Next is its content, improved shipping address specified by the sender and attached to the message. Networks based on services complement for networks based on traditional unicast and multicast addresses, which provides support for communication patterns based on the service class of large-scale applications, loose

connections, multiple partitions and scattered like auctions, information sharing, combined, distributed, sensor networks, distributed according to personal
information, service discovery, multi-player game.

In the SBR routing, the sender does not indicate message receiver by the
unicast or multicast use. Instead it simply pushes messages to the network. It
defines the routing based on the messages it cares. It determines the appropriate
message class based on message content based on its key-value pairs or regular
expressions. Therefore, in SBR routing the receiver determines the transmission
of messages, not the sender. Communication based on content services increases
the independence, flexibility in the distributed architecture.

2   Organization of Types of Messages in SBR Network

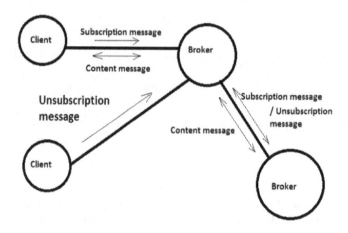

Fig. 2. Message transmission model in service-oriented routing network

2.1   Introduction of Message Types [3,4,6]

In order to perform service based routing, We have to organize data into messages, there are some message types will been constructed. That are:

Subcription/Unsubcription Message. Use this message type to regis-
ter/unregister nodes requested content.

Content Message. Use this message type to publish nodes content.

Advertisement Message. Use this message type in order to advertise nodes
content, to direct subscriptions from subscribers to matched publishers, avoid
to flood subscriptions all over networks. When a node need to advertise its
content: i) Make an advertisement message; ii) It will broadcast this content
advertisement message to network. iii) Its content advertisement will be cached

on nodes of network. When a subscription message happen on a node: a) Firstly It check that if subscription is matched with its published content. If it is true matched content will be sent to requested node immediately. b) Secondly, it will be matched with content advertisements on that node. Then this subscription will be transmitted to a set of matched advertisement nodes. So that We have to build multicast tree from requested node to the set of matched advertisement nodes to decrease latency and bandwidth required.

Update Request and Reply Sender Message Pair. In order to update routing table of content based routing protocol. By using minimum spanning tree (established by PRIM algorithm) to forward data from source node to a set of destination nodes in service based routing. To maintain this multicast tree, the source node periodically has to send an update request message to destination nodes. When destination node receive this request, it will reply with a reply sender message.

Route Request and Route Reply Message Pair. In order to detect routes (network topology), We use a pair of messages: route request and route reply message. When We want to forward data from one source node to a set of destination nodes in case of transmitting matched content to subscribers. We have to build a multicast tree with root is current node, leaf nodes are destination nodes. We have to make update request message, broadcast this message to network. When this message reaches destination nodes or forwarding nodes that have up-to-date route information, a reply message is created to send to source node. After specified time-out the source node have received enough route information from destination nodes to source node. We use these received routes to build multiple multi-cast trees.

2.2   The Request/Cancel Request (subscription/unsubscription) [3, 4] Messages

Subscription (registration) / unsubscription (unregistration) message is emitted from the application service classes to subscribe/ unsubscribe content requests. The message is structured with: the address of the subscriber and binding on the list of services and content requirements (constraints). In particular, each constraint is a set of 3 components, has the form: key+operator+value. For example, the contents of the registration message: [service_ class= "Network monitor" alert-type = "intrusion" severity> 2] or [service_ class = "Network monitor" class = "alert" device-type = "web-server"], these are 2 request messages of Network monitor service class.

Structure of Subscription/ Unsubscription Messages. Of which: Subscriber address is the address of required node. The service and content searching predicate: is a set of constraints. The first constraint is service binding, followed

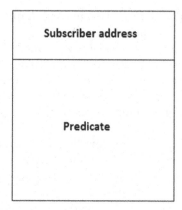

Fig. 3. Structure of subscription

by the content constraints. 1) Each constraint consists of 3 components: key, operator, value. 2) In which key is a string, the operator is subject to value. 3) If the value is the number then operators are: $=, <, >, <=, >=$, in. 4) If the value is a string then operators are : $=, <, >, <=, >=$, substring (sb), prefix (pf), postfix (ps). 5) If operator is sb, need to declare 2 parameters: start index v stop index specify start position and stop position for a string is extracted from value of a property to compare with value of constraint. 6) If operator is pf, need to declare number of beginning characters are extract from value of property to compare with value of constraint. 7) If operator is ps, need to declare number of ending characters are extracted from value of property to compare with value of constraint.

2.3   The Content [3, 4] Message

Content messages are transmitted from the host service provider. These messages will be transmitted to the network, it will be transmitted to the nodes based on the subscription request messages received from those nodes.

Content Message Structure. Of which: Source node address is the address of the node that generate message. The next $attribute_1$, $attribute_2$, ..., $attribute_n$ are the attributes of the message. The first attribute1 is the service information, the remaining attributes define the content of the message.

Components of a Content Message. Content Message includes nodes address that generated message and a set of attributes (properties), each attribute is a pair of name and value that are separated by a sign "=". The name attribute is a string. Possible type of values is string or numeric. For example, a message content: Node_a, [service_class = "Network monitor", class = "alert", severity = 6, device-type = "web-server", alert-type = "Hardware failure"].

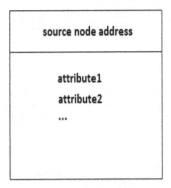

Fig. 4. Content message structure

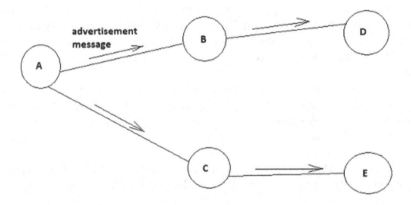

Fig. 5. Process of transmitting advertisement messages

2.4   The Advertisement Message [3, 4]

Advertisement message is the message advertises the basic content that applications for certain services provided. i) To direct the subscription requests to the right offer places. ii) Prevents spread of the subscription messages throughout the network. Naturally, subscription messages are partitioning to some smaller areas. So that We can acquire: i) decrease time to find subscription matched a content message and ii) lower cost to maintain routing table.

The advertising message is passed under the minimum spanning tree from the source node.

Advertisement message is also structured similar content message, including a set of attributes. So this kind of message is to expand the content of advertising messages. Generally use advertising message to advertise the most common content.

Advertisement message is transmitted from the service delivery system.

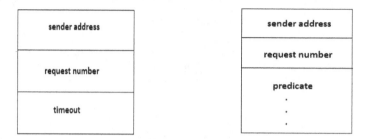

Fig. 6. Structures of the sender request and update reply message pair

2.5   Update Request and Reply Sender Message Pair [3, 4]

Sender request: request from the router, the structure including 3 fields. Two fields: sender address and request number determine the uniqueness of an sender request message. Timeout determines the longest time the sender wait for an answer. This message is transmitted by the Minimum Spanning Tree (established by PRIM algorithm) starting from the source router to the other routers in the network.

When the leaf router nodes of MST tree receive this sender request message, it will respond with a reply update (UR) message. The UR message consists of three fields, two fields from the sender request, the field no.3 contains its all content based addresses (content based routing table). The UR message spreads back the sender router.

On the way to the sender router, the intermediate routers will incorporate their content based address routing table and of the message then push it to the sender router.

When the sender router receives UR message, it updates its routing table. End of the implementation process.

2.6   Route Request and Route Reply Message Pair [6]

This pair of messages is used to detect routes on the network to a set of destination addresses from a source node for building multicast trees with root is source node and leaf nodes are this set of destination nodes.

Route request message: use to make a request from the source router, the message structure consists of eight fields. Two fields: 1) Source Address and 2) Request Number determine the uniqueness of the message. 3) The Type field identifies of the kind of message, is set to 1; 4) the Timeout field determines the longest time the sender node waits for a response. 5) The Time To Live (TTL) field determines the maximum number of HOPs of the route that message is passed on. 6) The Route field records addresses of the hops on the route the message passes through. 7) The Free Time Slots field records free bandwidth at the nodes of the route that message is transmitted on. 8) The Destination List field saves address list that contains addresses of the set of destination

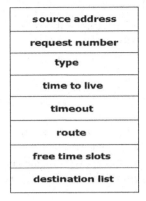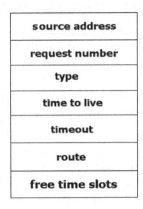

Fig. 7. Structures of route request and route reply message pair

nodes that are the leaf nodes of multicast trees that we need to build. The message is transmitted by broadcast protocol to other routers in the MANET. The message transmission process is indicated as following: 1) This message is transmitted from source node to any node on the network. 2) At any node (N) that message has been received: i) if Timeout is less than current time then drop this message, ii) otherwise the node will update the 3 fields of the message: Route (Route=Route U $Address_N$), Free Time Slots , Time To Live (TTL=TTL-1), assume previous node is Np, TS denote Time Slot. 3) If TTL=0: drop this message. 4) If number of free common Time Slots between current node and last hop-sender is equal to 0 then this node cannot be in route from source to any destination node: drop this message. 5) Otherwise: i) if the node firstly receives message then: a) if the node is not a destination node, node will forward this message to network; b) if node address is in destination list, create reply message to transmit to the source node. ii) If node have received this message, it will immediately make route reply message (RREP) to transmit to the source node.

The RREP message contains almost information from RREQ message, besides the type field is set to 2 and doesnt have destination list field. RREP message is sent back to the source router.

3   Some Channel Access Techniques

In order to build multicast tree with guaranteed bandwidth and latency. We have to use specific techniques to measure link bandwidth between any two nodes in networks.

Channel access technique is the main task of the MAC protocol. There are some channel access techniques for wireless networks: TDMA, CSMA and polling, etc.

3.1   FDMA (Frequency Division Multiple Access)

FDMA is primary channel access technique, in which a subscriber is regulated a frequency to be recognized by Mobile Switching Office. One inadequate problem is when two subscribers use a common frequency, tend to one subscriber can not call.

3.2   TDM (Time Division Multiplexing)

An subscriber is assign one specific time slot, by which subscribers data is transferred. After time slot run out, the subscriber will have to wait. For TDM, a dedicated time slot always is assigned to any subscriber, even if that subscriber does not use it. For example ISDN is ground digital telephone network that uses TDM channel access technique.

3.3   TDMA (Time Division Multiplex Access)

Operation Time Division Mechanism:

It is very similar to above TDM, an subscriber is assigned a specific time slot, through which subscribers data can be transmitted. After time slot run out, the subscriber have to wait. When assigned time slots run out, these time slots are released and can be assigned for another subscribers. Typically, time slots are assigned dynamically, a node can be received different time slots once accessing network.

A specific node (base station), is responsible for coordination of the network nodes. Channel time is divided into time slots, one time slot has a fixed size. Each node is granted a fixed number of time slots in which it can transmit. GSM uses TDMA in combining with FDMA technique to access network.

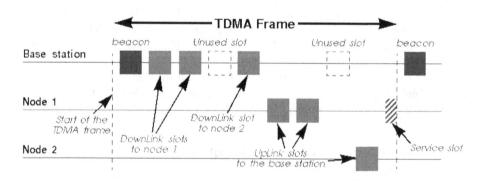

Fig. 8. TDMA channel access technique

Operating Principles:

All exchanges are made through this base station. TDMA is used in the mobile phone standard. TDMA allows for low latency and guaranteed bandwidth.

TDMA is not well-suited for applications that transfer data, because it's tight and inflexible. TDMA depends on the spectrum quality. TDMA can not cope with and matches the strong interference sources such as the unlicensed band.

3.4   CDMA (Code Division Multiplex Access)

CDMA employs a spread-spectrum technology and a special coding scheme, where each transmitter is assigned a code to allow multiple users to be multi-plexed over same physical channel. TDMA divides access by time, while FDMA divides it by frequency. CDMA is a form of spread-spectrum signalling, since the modulated coded signal has a much higher data bandwidth than the data being communicated.

3.5   CSMA / CA (Carrier Sense Multiple Access / Collision Avoidance)

This is a channel access technique is used by most wireless LAN under ISM band. This channel access technique is a part of the protocol that shows how to use the media, when listening and communicating to avoid conflict.

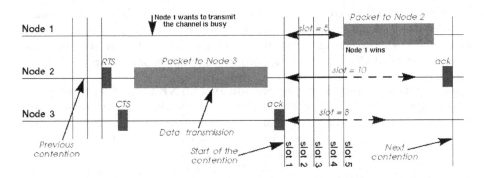

Fig. 9. CSMA/ CA channel access technique

After waiting for a data transfer session ends, the node waiting a period of a random integer number of time units is specified. Node has waited completely first that will have right to transfer.

3.6   POLLING

This is the main channel access technique, the networking standard using polling success is 100vg (IEEE 802.12), a wireless standard also uses it. For example, the 802.11 standard recommends the use of polling channel access technique with CSMA/CA.

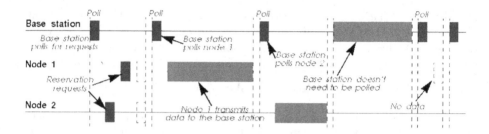

Fig. 10. Polling channel access technique

This channel access technique is between TDMA and CSMA/CA techniques, the base station to maintain control over the entire channel. No fixed-size packets are sent over the network. Base station sends the packet to ask (poll packet) to request node that it can send. Polling can be implemented as connection-oriented services, almost like TDMA but with more flexible packet size, or can be connectionless.

Therefore in this paper We use TDMA channel access technique to calculate link bandwidth as presented in the following section.

3.7 Quality of Service (QoS) Requirements

Nowaday, MANET often has been used to transmit multimedia data of online transactions in commercial applications. So We have to guarantee bandwidth and latency when transmitting data. But by mobile and loosely structure, infrustructure of MANET is often violated by many kinds of malware.

Some Causes of Network Congestion in MANET (a) A new route has admitted a node that is a part of other routes are overloaded with traffic at the network layer. (b) Data speed of channel or application is greater than the queue size of MAC layer (Media Access Control) (cause congestion at the MAC layer). (c) Many neighboring nodes attack network. (d) Denial of Service (DoS) attacks can occur at any layer in the network [2]. (e) The node with malicious intents can push up the network with the routing information is not correct, or delete all the packets passing through it. Node can also depend on MAC layer to make the network to be always busy or make a maximum throughput of the channel [2].

Some Quality of Service Requirements [6] To transmit data in Manet network effectively, to avoid congestion. We have to build a multicast tree with quality of services assurance from the source node of the message to the set of required destination nodes. The information for building tree is taken from Response Packet - Route Reply packet pair for detecting route.

These factors ensure service quality in service-oriented routing:

a) BANDWIDTH Using time slot [6] parameter to calculate bandwidth in Manet network using Time Division Multiplex Access denoted by TDMA. Divide the time interval regulated in each node as a number of equal time units,

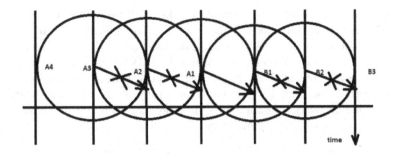

Fig. 11. Interference range and transmission range

each unit is called a time slot. Because the use of time slots at different nodes is very different hence to find routes that are ensured bandwidth is difficult. We have to assign time slots for all links of a route to make sure to avoid radio interference between the nodes to transmit and receive data efficiently. When time slot of one node of a link is assigned at order x (x is integer), We cant assign time slot at the same order x for 1-hop or 2-hop neighbors.

We define link bandwidth is a number of common free time slots of two nodes that form the link [6]. For example, link bandwidth between two nodes A and B [5] is as following figure:

Bandwidth of a route is defined by minimum bandwidth of all links that form the route [6].

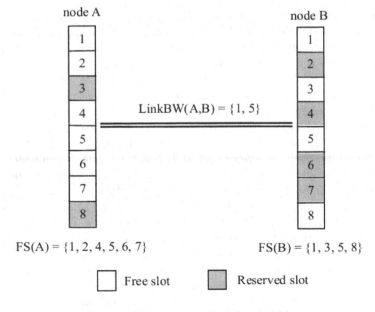

Fig. 12. An example of link bandwidth

Assume We have a route consists of N links, each time cycle has definite K time slots, therefore each link has maximum K free time slots. Status of each time slot at the moment of assignment is denoted by a(i,j), x(i,j) denotes time slot assignments result of time slot j of link i. a(i,j) has two values: 0 if slot is free, 1 if slot is not free. x(i,j) has two values: 1 if this time slot is assigned for the route, 0 if otherwise. Hence, in order to have route has maximum bandwidth, We have to assign maximum number of time slots for each link. We have several conditions that time slot assignment has to satisfy:

$$1. \sum_{j=1}^{K} x(i,j) = \sum_{j=1}^{K} x(i+1,j)(1 \leq i \leq N-1) \ 2.$$
$$x(i,j) + x(i+1,j) + x(i+2,j) \leq 1(1 \leq j \leq K) \ 3. \ a(i,j) + x(i,j) \leq 1 \ (1) \ -$$
Conditions for time slot assigning algorithm

Calculation of route bandwidth based on the assigned time slots for each link. The route bandwidth calculation is performed by the following principles [5]: 1. The calculation starts from the link that is in a state of worst bottle-neck, that is, have some at least time slots. If there are more than one link that have equal minimum number of time slots, We use the following formula to select link to start the algorithm:

a) Assume We have defined k constant numbers that have descending order: $W_1 > W_2 > \ > W_k$. b) We have k values $numberTS_h(1 \leq h \leq k)$, where $numberTS_h$ is the number of free time slots at time h. All these numbers are free for just k times in each of its concerned links. c) Calculate:
$$\text{CALCULATE\_INDEPENDENCE} = \sum_{h=1}^{K}(W_h * numberTS_h) \ (2) \ - \text{Formula to}$$
check link independence

for all links that have equal minimum time slots. d) We choose link that has CALCULATE_INDEPENDENCE is maximum. 2. Estimate bandwidth w of a route by formula: w=min(t/3,g), in which: t is the total of time slots, g is total of free time slots of start link. 3. We call that link is L_min that connects two nodes A, B. Select w time slots from free time slots of this link which are not used by its 1-hop and 2-hop neighbors links. Then continue the bandwidth calculation (assign free timeslots) for other links in the two directions of the route. 4. Calculate bandwidth of next links for nodes from B to destination node of the route. 5. Calculate bandwidth of previous links for nodes from A to source node of the route. *The algorithm to calculate link bandwidth of two nodes A and B [5] is:* 1. Find all common free time slots between two nodes A and B, we have a set T of time slots. Select w time slots from T by the following algorithm: Suppose current link is denoted by li, it has four 1-hop, 2-hop neighbors links that are $l_{i-2}, l_{i-1}, l_{i+1}, l_{i+2}$. We choose w time slots from T according to the order of their free times in five successive links $l_{i-2}, l_{i-1}, l_i, l_{i+1}, l_{i+2}$. The time slot of fewest free times will be chosen. 2. Delete above selected w time slots from the free time slots of 1-hop and 2-hop neighbor links. 3. If We cant choose w time slots from T, the estimated routes bandwidth is decremented by Then We repeat to assign bandwidth for this link. *The algorithm to calculate bandwidth of next links for nodes from B to destination node [5] is:* 1. Assume current link between two nodes Bi and B_{i+1} exists. 2. Find all common free time slots between two nodes B_i and B_{i+1}, we have a set T_i of time slots. 3. We choose w time slots from Ti according to above algorithms. If it cant be chosen then the estimated routes bandwidth is decremented by 1 and repeat bandwidth assignment from the beginning. 4. We remove above w selected time slots that are free time slots between two nodes B_{i+1} and B_{i+1}'s 1-hop neighbor from the set T_{i+1}. And We update state for that free time slots for calculating bandwidth of link between B_{i+1} and B_{i+1}'s 1-hop neighbor. 5. Remove w above selected time slots that are free time slots between two nodes B_{i+1}'s 1-hop neighbor and B_{i+1}'s 2-hop neighbor from the set T_{i+2}. And We update state for that free time slots for calculating bandwidth of link between B_{i+1}'s 1-hop neighbor and B_{i+1}'s 2-hop neighbor. *The algorithm to calculate bandwidth of previous links for nodes from A to the source node [5] is:* 1. Assume current link between two nodes A_i and A_{i-1}. 2. Find all common free time slots between two nodes A_i and A_{i-1}, we have a set T_{i-1} of time slots. 3. We choose w time slots from T_{i-1} according to above algorithms. If it cant be chosen then the estimated routes bandwidth is decremented by 1 and repeat bandwidth assignment from the beginning. 4. We remove time slots that are free time slots between two nodes A_{i-1} and A_{i-1}'s one-hop neighbor from the set T_{i-1}. And We update state for that free time slots for calculating bandwidth of link between A_{i-1} and A_{i-1}'s one-hop neighbor. 5. Remove time slots that are free time slots between two nodes A_{i-1}'s one-hop neighbor and A_{i-1}'s two-hop neighbor from the set T_{i-2}. And We update state for that free time slots for calculating bandwidth of link between A_{i-1}'s 1-hop neighbor and A_{i-1}'s 2-hop neighbor. s b) LATENCY Use hop count on a route to determine latency for that route. We define latency of the multicast tree is the length of the longest route from one of the leaves to the root of the tree. c) ERROR FAILOVER (The ability to overcome errors) This is important characteristic for the network remains stable operation in case of node errors or link errors / broken.

4   Algorithms for Building Minimum Spanning Tree

4.1   Build Shortest Path Tree Based Multiple Paths[6](SPTM)

Building Multicast-tree that has the shortest path by hop on the multi-path route from the root node to the leaf nodes. That can guarantee the bandwidth and latency. Because It is hard to find any route to be sure guaranteed bandwidth. We should include the concept of multiple-paths routing, in every part of the route We find all possible paths. So the bandwidth of the route will equal to the total bandwidth of all possible paths:$BW_{route} = \sum_{i=1}^{n} BW_{path_i}$. If there are multiple candidate paths to each path segment, they are sorted by shortest-path-first rule. So it is easy to find Multicast Tree that ensures bandwidth and latency requirements.

4.2   Build Least Cost Tree Based Multiple Paths (LCTM)

Building multicast tree that has the total cost of all paths is minimum which is calculated by summing the cost of the links which form quality of service

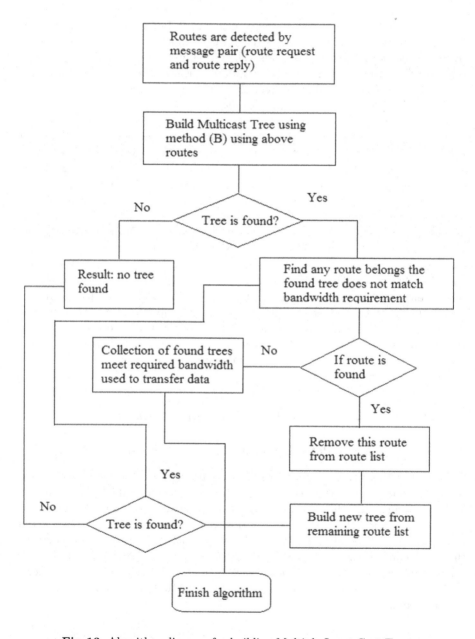

Fig. 13. Algorithm diagram for building Multiple Least Cost Trees

multicast tree. This kind of Multicast Tree can be built by PRIM algorithm. Hence the cost of the tree is equal to total cost of the links that have made tree: $C_t ree = \sum_{i=1}^{n} C_{link_i}$. Cost of link is evaluated based on bandwidth, latency. To ensure the required bandwidth, We also introduce the concept of multi-path routing for each part of the route. On each part of route, We will find all possible paths based on the route detected messages pair as shown above. This method has the advantage of guaranteed bandwidth but greater latency at the destination node.

4.3   Build Multiple Least Cost Trees (MLCT)

Building many multicast trees that have the lowest cost, the cost of tree is equal to total cost of the links that have made the tree. In which cost of links is calculated by criterion of quality of service. a) The routes of tree are detected by message pair (route request and route reply). Therefore, We can use these discovered trees to transmit messages, increase the ability to overcome errors, use load balancing, utilise bandwidth available. b) Each tree is built by the algorithm LCTM, browse through the trees routes, find any route does not meet bandwidth requirement. Removing this route, and build new tree by the algorithm LCTM. c) Algorithm stops when no tree is found or the collection of trees found if they meet the bandwidth requirements on any route that will be used to transmit data, if that are not satisfy then data transmission will be stopped. d) Split large data block into several small packets of data, the packets are transmitted on different trees, small packets are eventually combined to form the original package at the destination node. This method ensures the network is able to overcome errors, load balancing and the effective use of bandwidth. Following is the algorithm diagram:

5   Conclusions

We can improve the routing process in content based routing by using Multicast Tree. We can build Multicast Tree by process of transmitting route requests and receiving route reply messages shown above. By using TTL (time to live) parameter so We can build trees that have bound delay by hop count. Otherwise by calculating route bandwidth, We can use one of three strategies presented above to build trees with guaranteed bandwidth. By using timeout parameter can avoid flooding data to network. Multicast Trees can reduce network load, avoid flooding data all over network, balance network load, failover, etc. The complexity of three strategies to build multicast trees depend on number of routes detected (R_SET_RESULT) received by route reply messages. Each route has maximum of TTL hops and bandwidth is more than 0. Hence complexity to find a multicast tree from source node to a set of destination nodes is O(R_SET_RESULT). If We concern only finding multicast tree is bounded by delay (hop count), complexity is O(R_SET_RESULT). After a delay bounded multicast tree is found, We can compute bandwidth of every route from source node to each destination nodes by above presented link bandwidth calculating algorithm. The complexity of this algorithm is depended on length of the route L_R and estimated routes bandwidth W, that is $O(L_R * W)$. If We can find any route or any part of a route of tree that does not meet bandwidth requirement, the source will run an algorithm according to one of three multicast tree building algorithms presented above to find another route or paths of current route in addition to this route or current path of it to meet bandwidth requirement. Or We can find another least cost trees from the source node to all the destination nodes in addition to this tree. If We can find multiple multicast trees that aggregated tree satisfies bandwidth requirement, split original message into multiple small messages to transmit concurrently on these multicast trees. On destination nodes We combine separated messages into original message. Hence We can utilise better network resources, it causes data transfer rate be higher, load balancing, failover.

Acknowledgements. I would like to thank the dedicated instructors, teachers for help and support. My office, family, brothers and friends have made many favorable conditions for studying and researching to complete this research paper.

References

1. Cao, F., Singh, J.P.: Efficient Event Routing in Content-based Publish-Subscribe Service Networks. In: Proc. IEEE Infocom (2004)
2. Kalaiarasi, R., Getsy, S., Sara, S., Pari, N., Sridharan, D.: Performance Analysis of Contention Window Cheating Misbehaviors in Mobile Ad Hoc Networks. International Journal of Computer Science & Information Technology (IJCSIT) 2(5) (October 2010)
3. Carzaniga, A., Wolf, A.: Forwarding in a Content-Based Network. In: Proc. SIGCOMM (2003)
4. Carzaniga, A., Rutherford, M.J., Wolf, A.L.: A Routing Scheme for Content-Based Networking. In: Proc. IEEE Infocom (2004)
5. Li, J., Wakahara, Y.: Time Slot Assignment for Maximum Bandwidth in a Mobile Ad Hoc Network. Journal of Communications 2(6) (November 2007)
6. Wu, H., Jia, X.: QoS multicast routing by using multiple paths/trees in wireless ad hoc networks. Research supported by a grant FFCSA. Elsevier BV (2006)

HMM Modeling of User Mood through Recognition of Vocal Emotions

Krishna Asawa and Raj Vardhan

Department of CSE & IT, JIIT-Noida, India
krishna.asawa@jiit.ac.in, me@rajvardhan.co.in

Abstract. This paper aims at defining a real-time probabilistic model for user's mood in its dialect with a software agent, which has a long-term goal of counseling the user in the domain of "coping with exam pressure". We propose a new approach based on Hidden Markov Models (HMMs) to describe the differences in the sequence of emotions expressed due to different moods experienced by users. During real time operation, each user move is passed on to a vocal affect recognizer. The decisions from the recognizer about the kind of emotion expressed are then mapped into code-words to generate a sequence of discrete symbols for HMM models of each mood. We train and test the system using corpora of the temporal sequences of tagged emotional utterances by six male and six female adult Indians in English and Hindi language. Our system achieved an average f-measure rating for all moods of approximately 78.33%.

Keywords: Mood detection, Hidden Markov models, affective computing.

1   Introduction

The examination of different software in various application areas like virtual training environments, portable personal guides, storytelling systems and interfaces of consumer electronics reveals that embodied conversational agents are widely used to provide users with a more human-like interface. But the ECA face the fundamental challenge of better understanding and integrating the affective cues used in communication by a user [8]. During an interaction with the agent, a user may be confident, ignorant, aggressive, cheerful, excited, bored, etc. The capability to recognize the current mood of the user could potentially assist the agent in better communication via selecting the appropriate words, phrases, dialog strategies etc. Here we attempt to integrate and model two major affective characteristics: emotions and moods [9] of an individual experienced and expressed in dynamic social interactions.

Emotion [4] is the complex psycho physiological experience of an individual's state of mind as interacting with biochemical (internal) and environmental (external) influences. A mood is a medium-term emotional state. Moods differ from emotions in that they are less specific, less intense, and less likely to be triggered by a particular stimulus or event. According to [3] conditions for mood-changes can be divided into (a) the onset of a mildly positive or negative event, (b) the offset of an emotion-inducing event, (c) the recollection or imagining of emotional experience, and (d) the

P.C. Vinh et al. (Eds.): ICCASA 2012, LNICST 109, pp. 229–238, 2013.
© Institute for Computer Sciences, Social Informatics and Telecommunications Engineering 2013

inhibition of emotional responding in the presence of an emotion-inducing event, (e) the personality traits such as optimism and neuroticism. Mood is an internal subjective state, but the emotions expressed by a user during an interaction can be monitored and analyzed to indicate the current mood. We classify an expressed fixed duration temporal pattern of emotions into one of the three classes of mood – Positive, Negative and Neutral.

In the first category of Positive mood (POS) [3], the user is in a desirable state of mind. Users seem to experience positive mood when they feel no sense of stress. Positive mood is usually considered a displaced state; users cannot pinpoint exactly why they are in a good mood. POS users are easier to interact with as compared to users in a negative or neutral mood. They have high probability of expressing emotions of happiness for longer durations during an interaction with the agent. Negative mood (NEG) [3], our second category is for the class of users that are in an undesirable state. Negative mood can be a consequence of chronic unresolved stress. We identify NEG users as those with high probability of expressing emotions of sadness for long durations. Finally, a third category of Neutral mood (NEUT) [3] is defined for users who display neutral emotions. Emotions expressed by NEUT users are generally neutral and the overall degree of happiness or sadness in an interaction is low.

Although the primary support of voice is to communicate, it can be also seen as an indicator of the psychological and physiological state of the speaker. Prosodic elements [2] transmit essential information with regard to the speaker's attitude, emotion, intention, context, gender, age and physical condition. The various prosodic features that characterize the emotions are variation in syllable length, loudness, pitch, formant frequencies of speech sound, accent, stress, rhythm, tone, and intonation. The discrete basic emotions considered in our study are happiness, surprise, sadness, anger and neutral.

In this paper, we investigate the issue of detecting the user's mood based on vocal emotions expressed by a user in due course of conversational speech with a software agent. We choose a three layered SVM classifier [5], having 85% recognition accuracy, to understand the kind of emotion carried by the utterance uttered by users during an interaction with the agent. Hidden Markov Models (HMMs) [1] are used as a suitable formalism to represent relationship of these temporal vocal emotion patterns with the user's mood. During real time operation, each user move is passed on to the vocal affect recognizer. The decisions from the recognizer about the kind of emotion expressed are then mapped into code-words to generate a sequence of discrete symbols for HMM models of each mood. The HMM model selected is the one that is more likely to produce the emotion sequence given as input.

2   Related Work

Embedding an affect-recognition component in an intelligent interactive system will enhance its ability to provide the necessary guidance, and make the chat sessions more interactive and thus effective. Affect, however is difficult to model because of its inherent complexity. Affect is a construct that subsumes heterogeneous group of processes and there are many ways by which those emotions particular to a mood can be parsed at the human level [7]. One can argue that a computer cannot model emotions and feelings or general subjective impressions precisely because these are subjective entities.

The proven efficiency of identifying various differences in wide varieties of patterns encourages researchers to gauge the effectiveness of HMM modeling in the field of affect recognition from extracted low level feature classification and coded features classification to fusion of heterogeneous affective features.   Other than several machine learning approaches like NNs (neural networks), k-NN (nearest neighbor) algorithm and SVM (support vector machines), HMM is also attempted to classify the given affect in the several emotions. In [13] speech data are parameterized with prosody related features and spectral features together with their first and second order derivatives. The temporal patterns of the emotion dependent prosody contours are modeled with the HMM structures. In an earlier work [17] author has proposed an expert-critic system based on HMMs to combine multiple modalities. The work reported by [16] has used HMM based head-nod and head-shake detection system, which provides the likelihoods of head-nods and head-shakes on the basis of tracked pupil positions. In the studies done in [18] Hidden Markov Models (HMM) are used to handle the temporal properties of the gesture(s). Levin et al. [10] proposed to use this formalism in dialogue pattern modeling: system's moves are represented in states while the user's moves are associated with arcs. Their goal is to solve the problem of defining the minimal cost dialogue strategy to adopt. Stolcke et al. [11] defines a discourse grammar using HMMs for Dialogue Act (DAs) prediction: they associate user moves with states in a HMM based dialogue structure in which transitions represent the likely sequencing of user moves. Evidence about DAs is expressed in terms of their lexical and prosodic manifestations. Novielli N. [12] studied on how the behavior of users changes according to their own goals and to their level of involvement in the advice-giving task using HMMs. In their models, states represent aggregates of either system's or user's moves, each with a probability to occur in that specific phase of the dialogue while the transitions represent the possible dialogue sequences.

For an agent to lively communicate with people in a natural way, it requires its understanding of human mood and personality. The research in the direction of detecting mood from perceived emotions by a software agent is very limited. In this study we have attempted to model the relationship of temporal expressed vocal emotions and its corresponding mood by wide range of personalities during interaction of a user with a software agent.

3   Architecture

During an interaction with the agent, each user move is classified into a discrete emotion value by the vocal affect recognizer, which is streamed to a decision pool. Figure 1 shows the overall architecture of our system for mood detection. Section IV and section V describe details of the emotion recognition phase and HMM modeling respectively.

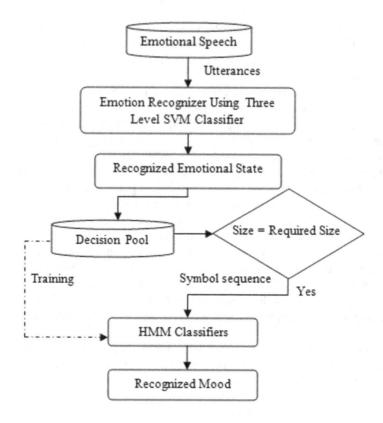

Fig. 1. Architecture of the mood detection system

4   Recognition of Vocal Emotions

The vocal emotion recognizer [5] proposed in our previous research recognizes discrete basic five emotions (anger, sadness, happiness, neutral, and fear) expressed in arbitrary duration utterances which may be language, cultural and subject independent. The various prosodic features used that characterize the emotions are variation in syllable length, loudness, pitch, formant frequencies of speech sound, accent, stress, rhythm, tone, and intonation. These features convey paralinguistic information such as emphasis, intent, attitude, and emotion of a speaker. Fusion of vocal segments with respect to classification and combination of diverse timing level are done at the pre-processing stage.

A three layered SVM classifier having RBF kernel is used that utilizes the dominant prosodic discriminant features at different layers. At the starting level, the features in consideration are intensity, shimmer, LPC and zero crossing rate so as to differentiate between high energy emotions (anger and happiness) with low energy emotions. At second level the various features considered are MFCC, pitch, jitter, harmonics. Along with MFCC and pitch, jitter distinguishes between anger and happiness and shimmer distinguishes neutral from fear and sadness. The third level is used to differentiate sadness and fear since they are relatively similar and hence more specific features like fundamental frequency used to discriminate them.

The experiments are conducted on both the standard Berlin Database of Emotional Speech (EMO-DB) and self-recorded portrayed audio by Indians in the Hindi and English Language. Results obtained reveal that the system performed well with an average accuracy for all discrete basic five emotions of approximately 85%. A sample voice utterance which was tagged as 'Happy' by the affect recognizer can be seen in Figure 2.

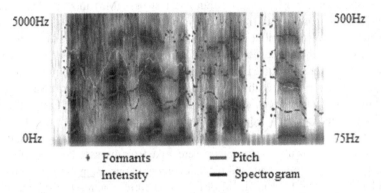

Fig. 2. Various prosodic features captured through Prat tool for a voice utterance corresponding to emotion 'happy'

5   HMM Modeling of User Mood

We decided to model the current mood of a user, by looking at differences in the emotion pattern obtained by analyzing their voice utterances. By using the formalism of HMMs, we are able to represent differences in the whole structure of these patterns among subjects with the kinds of mood we mentioned above.

5.1   User Mood Representation

Formally an HMM can be defined as a tuple: (Q, V, π, A, B), where:

- N = number of states in the model
- M = number of observation symbols
- $Q = \{q_1, q_2, \ldots, q_N\}$ is the set of states in the model
- $V = \{v_1, v_2 \ldots, v_M\}$ is the set of observations or output symbols
- $\pi = \{\pi_i\}$, $\pi_i = P_r(q_i$ at t=1), i $\in$ S, is the initial state distribution
- $A = \{a_{ij}\}$, aij = $P_r(qj$ at t+1 | q_i at t), i, j $\in$ S, is the state transition probability distribution
- $B = \{b_j(k)\}$, $b_j(k) = P_r$ (v_k at t|q_j at t), observation symbol probability distribution in state j

In our models states represent user moves, such that emission probability of the emotion e is probability of that emotion e being expressed in that state. The transitions represent the possible emotion sequences.

5.2   Learning the Model

The publicly available Berlin Database of Emotional Speech (EMO-DB) is used for the training of the affect recognizer model [5]. We used a database [19] of portrayed mood audio utterances from by six males and six females adult Indians in two languages viz. English and Hindi, to train and test the HMM models. This database was created with the help of a wizard of Oz experiment.

The database covers several different aspects including age, gender and background in computer science of the participating actors. During the building phase of the database in [19], 10 sessions were conducted, each on a different day with conditions suitable for recording. In every session, each actor had an interaction with the software agent for 15-20 minutes. To suite our requirements for testing, this database was further annotated. Each voice utterance was labeled with a discrete emotion value by 2 raters. Further the overall mood of users during a session interaction was annotated as per our definitions of positive, negative or neutral. The raters were asked to discuss the cases for which different annotations were given, and reach a common conclusion. These sequences of emotion labels are used to train HMM of the mood corresponding to the annotation of those interactions. For example, the set of sequences of emotion labels for interactions which were annotated with positive user mood will train the positive mood HMM, and so on. The corpus contains voice samples for 24 speech-based interactions with a total of 720 tagged voice utterances. 41% of this set of voice utterances was labeled positive, 27% as negative and 32% as neutral.

The Baum-Welch algorithm [6] is used to find the maximum-likelihood estimate of the parameters of a hidden Markov model given a set of observation sequences. The algorithm starts by assigning random parameters, which are iteratively adjusted according to the maximization function.

5.3   Model Description

Figures 3(a), (b) and (c) show respectively, the best 5-state HMMs for Positive, Negative and Neutral mood subjects. Tables 1, 2 and 3 show other parameters like emission and initial probabilities for the learnt HMMs. Abbreviated emotion labels {H-happy, Su-surprise, S-sad, A-anger, N-neutral} have been used in the tables. For instance, in Table 1 the value 0.149 at the intersection of the column H and the row $U1$ gives the emission probability of emotion happiness at state U1. In Table 2, the value 0.65 at the intersection of the column P_i and the row $U2$ indicates the initial probability of state U2 for the negative mood HMM.

In Figure 3(a) it can be seen that transition probabilities to U0, having the highest emission probability for emotion happiness, is relatively high. Clearly, a user in a positive mood will express emotions of joy for longer durations and if sad or angry, will have high probability of again starting to express neutral or happy emotions.

In Figure 3(b), states U2 and U3 have the highest emission probability of sadness and anger respectively. Transition probabilities to U2 and U3 being high explains why duration of emotions such as sadness and anger for a negative mood user are greater as compared to that of happiness, surprise or neutral. Similarly, in Figure 3(c), it can be seen that NEUT users show emotions of happiness or sadness for shorter durations as compared to neutral emotions.

Table 1. Emission and initial probabilities for positive mood HMM

State	H	Su	S	A	N	P_i
U0	.646	.150	.052	.047	.106	0.72
U1	.149	.609	.154	.073	.015	0.14
U2	.018	.085	.743	.057	.097	0.05
U3	.008	.016	.226	.734	.016	0.07
U4	.169	.029	.160	.027	.615	0.01

Table 2. Emission and initial probabilities for negative mood HMM

State	H	Su	S	A	N	P_i
U0	.700	.077	.036	.047	0.142	0.03
U1	.162	.549	.162	.101	.025	0.07
U2	.021	.087	.685	.091	.117	0.65
U3	.014	.040	.198	.738	.010	0.10
U4	.115	.018	.141	.028	.699	0.15

Table 3. Emission and initial probabilities for neutral mood HMM

State	H	Su	S	A	N	P_i
U0	.581	.164	.052	.062	.141	0.04
U1	.115	.621	.152	.095	0.016	0.03
U2	.015	.098	.682	.111	.095	0.03
U3	.006	.039	.201	.747	.007	0.08
U4	.148	.025	.149	.028	.650	0.83

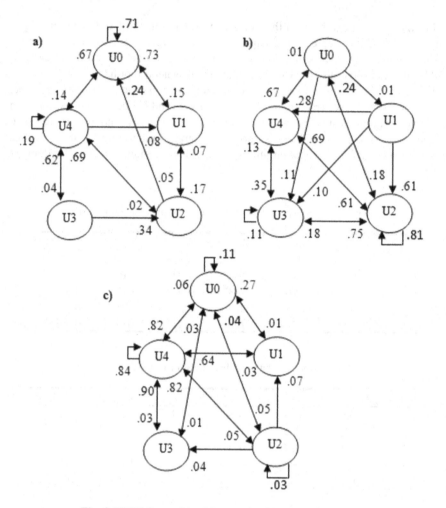

Fig. 3. HMM for *positive* (a), *negative* (b), *neutral* (c) mood

6   Testing

To evaluate the classification performance of the HMM models learnt, a 10-fold leave one out cross validation was performed on the annotated corpus. At every iteration *i*, the *i*-th instance of the data set is classified by choosing the model from all trained HMMs which maximizes the following:

$$loglik = \log P(i\text{-th case} | HMM_x), \text{ with } x \in \{POS, NEG, NEUT\}, \tag{1}$$

The HMM model selected is the one that is more likely to produce the emotion sequence given as input. For example, if we get that the positive HMM is most likely to produce the sequence of emotions: {H, H, H, Su, S......, N, N, H}, it means that user is more likely to be in a positive mood. The probability is computed by using the forward algorithm [6]. All computations have been done using the open source JAHMM library [20] with programming done in java. Table 4 shows the results in terms of precision, recall and balanced f1 measure.

Table 4. Confusion matrix for positive, negative and neutral mood users

	Positive	Negative	Neutral	Precision	Recall	F-measure
Positive	.83	.05	.12	.83	.89	.86
Negative	.07	.74	.19	.74	.77	.75
Neutral	.09	.13	.78	.78	.71	.74

One of the reasons for robustness of the system being different for different classes of mood is the unequal distribution of training dataset. Some negative mood user interactions being confused for neutral mood can be attributed to certain similarities in behavior of negative and neutral mood users. Users of both these classes were found to have lower interest in the on-going interaction with the agent. While the negative mood users as a consequence of their mood tend to show more of emotions of sadness and anger, neutral users on the other hand are less engaged in the conversation and prefer to stay neutral.

We have discussed previously that in real-time mood detection, the voice inputs from a user first passes through a pre-processing phase where the emotion recognizer gives a resultant emotion label to it. The emotion recognizer used in our work has an accuracy of 85%, which further affects the accuracy of the overall system. Till now, we have limited our work to recognizing vocal emotions, however a multi-modal approach can be used to attain more efficiency as the attributes of HMM models are independent of the pre-processing done.

7   Conclusion

In this paper we model a problem of mood recognition faced by a software agent giving a session of dialect with a user. This study is based on temporal sequences of vocal emotions expressed by the user in different situations and context. The HMM model shows good recognition accuracy over wide varieties of emotional patterns corresponding to a mood. A pre-built 3 layer SVM based vocal emotion classifier which produces the input sequence to the HMM has been used to tag the emotion of the speech spoken by a user.

Acknowledgments. The work reported in this paper is supported by the grant received from All India Council for Technical Education; A Statutory body of the Govt. of India. vide f. no. 8023/BOR/RID/RPS-129/2008-09.

References

1. Charniak, E.: Statistical language learning. MIT Press, Cambridge (1993)
2. Fox, A.: Prosodic Features and Prosodic Structure. Oxford University Press (2000)
3. Morris, W.N.: Mood: The frame of mind. Springer, New York (1989)
4. Becker, P.: Structural and Relational Analyses of Emotion and Personality Traits. In: Zeitschrift für Differentielle und Diagnostische Psychologie (2001) (in German)
5. Asawa, K., Verma, V., Aggrawal, A.: Recognition of Vocal Emotions from Acoustic Profile. In: Proceedings of International Conference on Advances in Computing, Communications and Informatics, Chennai (2012)
6. Rabiner, L.R.: A tutorial on hidden Markov models and selected applications in speech recognition. Proc. IEEE 77(2), 257–286 (1989)
7. Davidson, R.: Honoring biology in the study of affective style. In: Ekman, P., Davidson, R. (eds.) The Nature of Emotion: Fundamental Questions, pp. 321–328 (1994)
8. Picard, R.W.: Affective computing: challenges. Int. J. Human- Comput. Stud 59(12), 55–64 (2003)
9. Batliner, A., Steidl, S., Hacker, C., Noth, E., Niemann, E.: Private emotions vs social interaction: towards new dimensions in research on emotions. In: Carberry, S., De Rosis, F. (eds.) Procs. of the Workshop on Adapting the Interaction Style to Affective Factors (2005)
10. Levin, E., Pieraccini, R., Eckert, W.: Using Markov decision process for learning dialogue strategies. In: Proceedings of the IEEE International Conference on Acoustic, Speech and Signal Processing, vol. 1, pp. 201–204 (1998)
11. Stolcke, A., Coccaro, N., Bates, R., Taylor, P., Van Ess-Dykema, C., Ries, K., Shriberg, E., Jurafsky, D., Martin, R., Meteer, M.: Dialogue act modeling for automatic tagging and recognition of conversational speech. Comput. Linguist 26(3) (2000)
12. Novielli, N.: HMM modeling of user engagement in advice-giving dialogues. J. Multimodal User Interfaces 3, 131–140 (2010)
13. Schuller, B., Rigoll, G., Lang, M.: Hidden Markov Model-Based Speech Emotion Recognition. In: ICASSP, vol. 1, pp. 1–4 (2003)
14. Vlasenko, B., Wendemuth, A.: Tuning Hidden Markov Models for Speech Emotion Recognition. In: 33rd German Annual Conference on Acoustics, Stuttgart, Germany (2007)
15. Pantic, M., Bartlett, M.S.: Machine Analysis of Facial Expressions. In: Delac, K., Grgic, M. (eds.) Face Recognition, pp. 377–416. I-Tech Education and Publishing, Vienna
16. Kapoor Ashish Picard R.: Multimodal Affect Recognition in Learning Environments, Singapore (2005)
17. Kapoor, A., Picard, R.W., Ivanov, Y.: Probabilistic combination of multiple modalities to detect interest. In: ICPR (August 2004)
18. Elgammal, A., Shet, V., Yacoob, Y., Davis, L.S.: Learning dynamics for exemplar based gesture recognition. In: Proc. of the IEEE Conf. on Computer Vision and Pattern Recognition, pp. 571–578 (2003)
19. Vardhan, R., Asawa, K., Goel, S.: Emotion elicitation in a virtual dialog agent of an interactive counseling system. In: National Conference on Advances in Computer Sciences, Communication and Information Technologies, New Delhi (2012)
20. Jahmm – Hidden Markov Model (HMM): An Implementation of HMM in java, http://www.run.montefiore.ulg.ac.be/~francois/software/jahmm

Genetic Based Interval Type-2 Fuzzy C-Means Clustering

Dzung Dinh Nguyen, Long Thanh Ngo, and Long The Pham

Department of Information Systems, Faculty of Information Technology,
Le Quy Don Technical University, No 100, Hoang Quoc Viet, Hanoi, Vietnam
{dinhdung1082,ngotlong}@gmail.com

Abstract. This paper deals with a genetic-based interval type 2 fuzzy c-means clustering (GIT2FCM), which automatically find the optimal number of clusters. A heuristic method based on a genetic algorithm (GA) is adopted to automatically determine the number of cluster based on the validity index. The proposed algorithm contains two main steps: initialize randomly the population of the GA and use the GA to adjust the cluster centroids based on the validity index which is computed by interval type 2 fuzzy c-means clustering (IT2FCM). The experiments are done based on datasets with the statistics show that the algorithm generates good quality of clusters.

Keywords: fuzzy clustering, interval type-2 fuzzy c-means, genetic algorithm.

1 Introduction

Clustering is used to detect any structures or patterns in the data set, in which objects within the cluster level data show certain similarities. Clustering algorithms have different shapes from simple clustering as k-means and various improvements [2,3,4,5], development of family of fuzzy c-mean clustering (FCM) [11]. In addition, genetic algorithms (GAs) have been proposed as alternatives to carry out optimization search due to its prosperities of multi-objective, coded variables and global optimization. The GA [20] is an artificial genetic system based on the principle of natural selection where stronger individuals are likely the winners in a competing environment. GA as a tool for search and optimization has reached a mature stage with the development of low cost and speedy computers. Thus, many studies have proposed an algorithm which integrated GA and FCM called genetic fuzzy c-mean algorithm (GFCM). GFCM has been successfully applied to several data analysis problems such as image processing [24], bio informatics [23]...

However, the general clustering algorithms and GFCM often have difficulty in determining the number of clusters and choosing the initial centroids of the clusters. They have limitation in the handling of the uncertainty and the combination between FCM and GA. Recently, type-2 fuzzy sets are extensions of original fuzzy sets, have the advantage of handling uncertainty, which have been developed and applied to many different problems [6,7,8,9] including data clustering problems. In addition, interval type-2 fuzzy c-means clustering (IT2FCM) [1] has developed a step in the clustering

P.C. Vinh et al. (Eds.): ICCASA 2012, LNICST 109, pp. 239–248, 2013.

method in which FOU (footprint of uncertainty) is created for the fuzzier m using two parameters for handling of uncertainty, making clustering more efficiently

Therefore, This paper proposes a genetic interval type 2 fuzzy c-mean clustering algorithm (GIT2FCM) based on a validity index to automatically find the optimal initial centroids of the clusters and determine the number of clusters. The proposed algorithm uses the cluster validity measure proposed by Ramze Rezaee [10] to evaluate the clustering results. By minimizing this validity measure by GA through adjusting the initial centroids of the clusters and the number of clusters, the proposed algorithm will find the optimal number of clusters. The algorithm consists of two steps. The first step, we randomly initiate the population of the GA. The second step, a GA adjusts the cluster centroids based on the validity index as a fitness function which is computed by IT2FCM. The proposed algorithm also automatically determine the optimal number of clusters. Experiments are implemented based various datasets of classification to show the advantage of proposed approach.

Remain of the paper is organized as follows: Section II briefly introduces about type-2 fuzzy sets, IT2FCM clustering and GA. Section III describes the proposed algorithm; Section IV offers some experimental results and section V concludes the paper.

2   Preliminaries

2.1   Type-2 Fuzzy Sets

A type-2 fuzzy set [6] in X is denoted $\tilde{A}$, and its membership grade of $x \in X$ is $\mu_{\tilde{A}}(x, u), u \in J_x \subseteq [0, 1]$, which is a type-1 fuzzy set in $[0, 1]$. The elements of domain of $\mu_{\tilde{A}}(x, u)$ are called primary memberships of x in $\tilde{A}$ and memberships of primary memberships in $\mu_{\tilde{A}}(x, u)$ are called secondary memberships of x in $\tilde{A}$.

Definition 1. *A type-2 fuzzy set, denoted $\tilde{A}$, is characterized by a type-2 membership function $\mu_{\tilde{A}}(x, u)$ where $x \in X$ and $u \in J_x \subseteq [0, 1]$, i.e.,*

$$\tilde{A} = \{((x, u), \mu_{\tilde{A}}(x, u)) | \forall x \in X, \forall u \in J_x \subseteq [0, 1]\} \tag{1}$$

or

$$\tilde{A} = \int_{x \in X} \int_{u \in J_x} \mu_{\tilde{A}}(x, u)) / (x, u), J_x \subseteq [0, 1] \tag{2}$$

in which $0 \leq \mu_{\tilde{A}}(x, u) \leq 1$.

At each value of x, say $x = x'$, the 2-D plane whose axes are u and $\mu_{\tilde{A}}(x', u)$ is called a *vertical slice* of $\mu_{\tilde{A}}(x, u)$. A *secondary membership function* is a vertical slice of $\mu_{\tilde{A}}(x, u)$. It is $\mu_{\tilde{A}}(x = x', u)$ for $x \in X$ and $\forall u \in J_{x'} \subseteq [0, 1]$, i.e.

$$\mu_{\tilde{A}}(x = x', u) \equiv \mu_{\tilde{A}}(x') = \int_{u \in J_{x'}} f_{x'}(u)/u, J_{x'} \subseteq [0, 1] \tag{3}$$

in which $0 \leq f_{x'}(u) \leq 1$.

Type-2 fuzzy sets are called an interval type-2 fuzzy sets [8] if the secondary membership function $f_{x'}(u) = 1 \ \forall u \in J_x$ i.e. a type-2 fuzzy set are defined as follows:

Definition 2. *An interval type-2 fuzzy set $\tilde{A}$ is characterized by an interval type-2 membership function $\mu_{\tilde{A}}(x, u) = 1$ where $x \in X$ and $u \in J_x \subseteq [0, 1]$, i.e.,*

$$\tilde{A} = \{((x, u), 1) | \forall x \in X, \forall u \in J_x \subseteq [0, 1]\} \tag{4}$$

Uncertainty of $\tilde{A}$, denoted FOU, is union of primary functions i.e. $FOU(\tilde{A}) = \bigcup_{x \in X} J_x$. Upper/lower bounds of membership function (UMF/LMF), denoted $\overline{\mu}_{\tilde{A}}(x)$ and $\underline{\mu}_{\tilde{A}}(x)$, of $\tilde{A}$.

2.2 Interval Type-2 Fuzzy Clustering Algorithm

IT2FCM is extension of FCM clustering by using two fuzziness parameters m_1, m_2 to make FOU, corresponding to upper and lower values of fuzzy clustering (detail in [1]). The use of fuzzifiers gives different objective functions to be minimized as follows:

$$\begin{cases} J_{m_1}(U, v) = \sum_{k=1}^{N} \sum_{i=1}^{C} (u_{ik})^{m_1} d_{ik}^2 \\ J_{m_2}(U, v) = \sum_{k=1}^{N} \sum_{i=1}^{C} (u_{ik})^{m_2} d_{ik}^2 \end{cases} \tag{5}$$

in which $d_{ik} = \| x_k - v_i \|$ is Euclidean distance between the pattern x_k and the centroid v_i, C is number of clusters and N is number of patterns. Upper/lower degrees of membership, $\overline{u}_{ik}$ and $\underline{u}_{ik}$ are determined as follows:

$$\overline{u}_{ik} = \begin{cases} \dfrac{1}{\sum_{j=1}^{C} (d_{ik}/d_{jk})^{2/(m_1-1)}} & \textit{if } \dfrac{1}{\sum_{j=1}^{C} (d_{ik}/d_{jk})} < \dfrac{1}{C} \\ \dfrac{1}{\sum_{j=1}^{C} (d_{ik}/d_{jk})^{2/(m_2-1)}} & \textit{if } \dfrac{1}{\sum_{j=1}^{C} (d_{ik}/d_{jk})} \geq \dfrac{1}{C} \end{cases} \tag{6}$$

$$\underline{u}_{ik} = \begin{cases} \dfrac{1}{\sum_{j=1}^{C} (d_{ik}/d_{jk})^{2/(m_1-1)}} & \textit{if } \dfrac{1}{\sum_{j=1}^{C} (d_{ik}/d_{jk})} \geq \dfrac{1}{C} \\ \dfrac{1}{\sum_{j=1}^{C} (d_{ik}/d_{jk})^{2/(m_2-1)}} & \textit{if } \dfrac{1}{\sum_{j=1}^{C} (d_{ik}/d_{jk})} < \dfrac{1}{C} \end{cases} \tag{7}$$

in which $i = \overline{1, C}$, $k = \overline{1, N}$.

Because each pattern has membership interval as the upper $\overline{u}$ and the lower $\underline{u}$, each centroid of cluster is represented by the interval between v^L and v^R. Cluster centroids is computed in the same way of FCM as follows:

$$v_i = \frac{\sum_{k=1}^{N} (u_{ik})^m x_k}{\sum_{k=1}^{N} (u_{ik})^m} \tag{8}$$

in which $i = \overline{1, C}$.

After obtaining v_i^R, v_i^L, type-reduction is applied to get centroid of clusters as follows:

$$v_i = (v_i^R + v_i^L)/2 \tag{9}$$

For membership grades:

$$u_i(x_k) = (u_i^R(x_k) + u_i^L(x_k))/2, j = 1, ..., C \qquad (10)$$

in which

$$u_i^L = \sum_{l=1}^{M} u_{il}/M, u_{il} = \begin{cases} \overline{u}_i(x_k) \text{ if } x_{il} \text{ uses } \overline{u}_i(x_k) \text{ for } v_i^L \\ \underline{u}_i(x_k) \qquad otherwise \end{cases} \qquad (11)$$

$$u_i^R = \sum_{l=1}^{M} u_{il}/M, u_{il} = \begin{cases} \overline{u}_i(x_k) \text{ if } x_{il} \text{ uses } \overline{u}_i(x_k) \text{ for } v_i^R \\ \underline{u}_i(x_k) \qquad otherwise \end{cases} \qquad (12)$$

Next, defuzzification for IT2FCM is made as if $u_i(x_k) > u_j(x_k)$ for $j = 1, ..., C$ and $i \neq j$ then x_k is assigned to cluster i.

2.3 Genetic Algorithm

The GA [20] is an artificial system based on the principle of natural selection. As a stochastic algorithm, GA is a robust and powerful optimization method for solving problems with a large search space which are not easily solved by exhaustive methods. Usually, a basic GA consists of three operators: selection, crossover, and mutation [19].

3 Genetic-Based Interval Type-2 FCM Clustering

3.1 Chromosome Representation

In GA applications, the unknown parameters are encoded in the form of strings, so-called chromosomes. A chromosome is encoded with binary, integer or real numbers. In this research a chromosome is encoded with a unit which represents a potential cluster centroid. The length of the chromosome, K, is equivalent to the number of clusters in the classification problem. K takes value in the range $[K_{min}, K_{max}]$, where K_{min} is usually assigned to 2 and K_{max} describes the maximum chromosome length, which means the maximum number of possible cluster centroids. Therefore, K_{max} must be selected according to experience. Without assigning the number of clusters in advance, a variable string length is used. Invalid (non-existing) clusters are represented with negative integer "-1". The values of the chromosomes are changed in an iterative process to determine the correct number of clusters (the number of valid units in the chromosomes) and the actual cluster centroids for a given classification problem.

3.2 Population Initialization

In genetic algorithm, the population size of P is needed. In the proposed method, all values are chosen randomly from the data space. Such a chromosome belongs to the so-called parent generation. One (arbitrary)chromosomes of the parent generation is of size K. Each chromosome of the population is a potential solution by IT2FCM algorithm with number of clusters $C = K$.

3.3 Selection

This fitness level is used to associate a probability of selection with each individual chromosome. Roulette wheel selection is applied, a proportional selection algorithm where the number of copies of a chromosome, that go into the mating pool for subsequent operations, is proportional to its fitness. If f_i is the fitness of individual P_i in the population, its probability of being selected is as follows:

$$p_i = \frac{f_i}{\sum_{i=1}^{P} f_i} \tag{13}$$

where P is the number of individuals in the population.

3.4 Crossover

The purpose of the crossover operation is to create two new individual chromosomes from two existing chromosomes selected randomly from the current population. Typical crossover operations are one-point crossover, two-point crossover, cycle crossover and uniform crossover. In this research, only the simplest one, the one-point crossover with a fixed crossover probability of μ_c is used; For the one-point crossover, two chromosomes are randomly chosen from the population. Assuming the length of the chromosome to be k, this process randomly chooses a point between 1 and $k - 1$ and swaps the content of the two chromosomes beyond the crossover point to obtain the offspring. A crossover between a pair of chromosomes is affected only if they satisfy the crossover probability.

3.5 Mutation

During mutation, all the chromosomes in the population are checked unit by unit and according to a fixed probability μ_m. All values of a specific unit may be randomly changed. In this paper, a number σ in the range $[0, 1]$ is generated with uniform distribution. If the value at a gene position is v, after mutation it becomes

$$v = v + \sigma * v, if \quad v > 0$$
$$v = v + \sigma, if \quad v = 0$$

3.6 Validity Index and Fitness Computation

The cluster validity measure used in this paper is the one proposed by Ramze Rezaee [10]. It aims at minimizing the validity index given by the function

$$V_{CWB} = \alpha Scat(C) + Dis(C) \tag{14}$$

The term $Scat(C)$ of V_{CWB} is the average of scattering within clusters, which is defined as

$$Scat(C) = \frac{\frac{1}{C}\sum_{i=1}^{C} ||\sigma(v_i)||}{||\sigma(X)||} \tag{15}$$

in which $||X|| = (X^T.X)^{1/2}$ and

$$\sigma(v_i) = \frac{1}{n} \sum_{k=1}^{n} u_{ik}(x_k - v_i)^2 \qquad (16)$$

$$\sigma(X) = \frac{1}{n} \sum_{k=1}^{n} (x_k - \bar{x})^2 \qquad (17)$$

with $\bar{x} = \sum_{k=1}^{n} x_k/n$ and $x_k \in X$.

The $Scat(C)$ term is used to measure the compactness of the clusters. The $Dis(C)$ term is the total separation between the clusters which is defined as follows:

$$Dis(C) = \frac{D_{max}}{D_{min}} \sum_{k=1}^{C} (\sum_{z=1}^{C} \| v_k - v_z \|)^{-1} \qquad (18)$$

where $D_{max} = maximum(\| v_i - v_j \|)$ and $D_{min} = minimum(\| v_i - v_j \|), \forall i, j \in 1, ..., C$. Lastly, α is a weighting factor, given as

$$\alpha = Dis(C_{max}) \qquad (19)$$

From validity index, fitness computation is implemented in three following steps.

Step 1: The pixel dataset is clustered according to the centroid encoded in the considered chromosome, such that each pattern $x_i, i = \overline{1, N}$ is assigned to cluster with centroid $v_j, j = \overline{1, K}$ according to the equations (6), (7), (10) in IT2FCM.

Step 2: This step adjusts the values of centroids encoded in the chromosome and replaces them by the mean points of clusters, respectively. The new center v_i^* for the cluster C_i is given by iterative algorithm for finding centroids (9) in IT2FCM.

$$v_i^* = \frac{v_i^R + v_i^L}{2} \qquad (20)$$

Step 3: Validity index is computed as above description to obtain V_{CWB}. The goal for achieving a proper clustering is to minimize the V_{CWB}. Thus, the fitness function for chromosome j is defined as $1/V_{CWB}^j$, which is equivalent to the cluster with the smallest inner-cluster scatter and the largest cluster separation.

Therefore, the fitness function is defined as

$$f = \frac{1}{V_{CWB}} \qquad (21)$$

3.7   Algorithm

Performance this algorithm is given by a sequence of steps, which are:
   1. Generate initial population.
   REPEAT

2. Evaluate population followed fitness function by IT2FCM. In this step, We do an IT2FCM step to cluster the processing data. After IT2FCM step, we can calculate the fitness function of the chromosomes following the subsection Validity index and fitness computation 21.

3. Selection.

4. Crossover.

5. Mutation.

6. Reinsertion of new individuals to the population.

UNTIL Termination criterion is met

Termination criterion: We execute the processes of fitness computation, selection, crossover, and mutation for a predetermined number of iterations or the difference between these two fitness values lies below a pre-defined threshold. In every generational cycle, the fittest chromosome till the last generation is preserved. Thus on termination, this chromosome gives us the best solution encountered during the search.

4   Experiments

Experiments are implemented with the following parameters of the GIT2FCM are set: The size of population, P, is taken 30, selection is roulette wheel, crossover rate, $\mu_c = 0.9$ and mutation rate, $\mu_m = 0.01$ [14]. Over the experimental results, the algorithm uses the terminating condition with the number of iterations is set to 20 or the difference between these two fitness values (error) is smaller than 0.00001. Because the experiments are well-known with the number of clusters smaller than 10, we choose the value of chromosome length K is 11.

The results of the proposed algorithm will be compared with the results of the FCM, IT2FCM with the number of the clusters is optimal obtained by GIT2FCM and the initial centroids are randomly selected. Besides, the results of GFCM with the similar combination between GA and FCM with the same parameters such as $P = 30$, $\mu_c = 0.9$, $\mu_m = 0.01$, $K = 11$ also are compared.

In addition, we measured results on the basis of several validity indexes to assess performance of the algorithms.

The first experiment is done with image segmentation on the Wolf Image by GFCM algorithm and GIT2FCM (the proposed algorithm). In Fig. 1, we computed the validity index [10] on this image with different number of clusters. We can see that the number of clusters is 4 in which has the minimum validity index with both GFCM and GIT2FCM. However, the value of validity index of GIT2FCM is smaller than the one of GFCM on the same number of clusters. Fig. 4 shows that image segmentation by GIT2FCM gives the better clustering by separating three clusters clearer involving the wolf, the grass and background.

In the second experiment, the well-known datasets consisting IRIS, Wisconsin Diagnostic Breast Cancer (WDBC), Wine [25] are considered. Implementation is performed to find the optimal number of clusters for these data by two algorithms: GFCM and GIT2FCM (the proposed algorithm) with validity index V_{CWB}. The optimal number of clusters C_{opt} is input of FCM and IT2FCM to cluster and compute validity indices. The considered validity indices consist the Bezdeks partition coefficient (PC-I), the Dunns

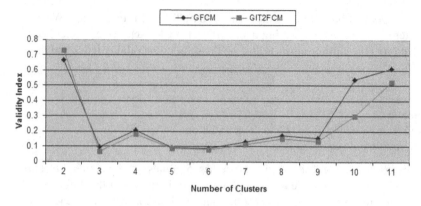

Fig. 1. Validity index is achieved by GFCM and GIT2FCM on Wolf Image

| (a) Wolf image | (b) GFCM result | (c) GIT2FCM result |

Fig. 2. Clustering results of GFCM with the number of clusters is 6 and the validity index is 0.085446; GIT2FCM with the number of clusters is 3 and the validity Index is 0.064709364

Table 1. The validity indices V_{CWB} on various algorithms. The optimal clusters C obtained is 3 for Iris data and Wine data, $C = 2$ for WDBC.

Data + Algorithm	2	3	4	5	6	7	8	9	10	11
Iris,GIT2FCM	0.2424	**0.2044**	0.2669	0.2831	0.3066	0.3546	0.2202	0.4893	0.3982	0.2973
Iris,GFCM	1.6326	**1.4228**	2.8368	2.4591	1.6975	2.3160	4.1007	4.1276	3.9259	2.2807
WDBC,GIT2FCM	**0.0015**	0.0018	0.0017	0.0018	0.0020	0.0019	0.0020	0.0021	0.0021	0.0023
WDBC,GFCM	**0.0020**	0.0045	0.0074	0.0075	0.0114	0.0024	0.0075	0.0027	0.0029	0.0205
Wine,GIT2FCM	0.0045	**0.0035**	0.0036	0.0047	0.0048	0.0051	0.0054	0.0058	0.0059	0.0059
Wine,GFCM	0.0099	**0.0043**	0.0095	0.0087	0.0198	0.0172	0.0101	0.0254	0.0166	0.0231

separation index (Dunn-I), the Davies-Bouldins index (DB-I), and the Separation index (S-I), Xie and Beni's index (XB-I), Classification Entropy index (CE-I) [22], Turi's index (T-I) [17], Yuangang Tang's Index (YT-I) [21], CBW index (CBW-I). Results on validity indices are shown in the table 1.

Table 2. The various validity indices on WDBC, Wine and IRIS data by algorithms (1): FCM, (2): GFCM, (3): IT2FCM and (4): GIT2FCM

Validity index	WDBC data ($C = 2$)				Wine data ($C = 3$)				IRIS data ($C = 3$)			
	(1)	(2)	(3)	(4)	(1)	(2)	(3)	(4)	(1)	(2)	(3)	(4)
T-I	1.5713	0.8231	0.5131	0.4481	0.7721	0.3986	0.2356	0.1468	0.6423	0.3667	0.3582	0.0970
DB-I	4.1590	4.1590	1.2750	1.0359	5.6337	4.7694	0.7972	0.5326	4.9394	2.9907	1.3350	1.2805
XB-I	0.0103	0.0060	0.0026	0.0021	0.0159	0.0116	0.0067	0.0060	0.0137	0.0115	0.0113	0.0040
S-I	0.0597	0.0597	0.0024	0.0001	0.0441	0.0421	0.1732	0.0008	0.0374	0.0349	0.0195	0.0006
CE-I	0.1809	0.1809	0.1722	0.0612	0.3804	0.3733	0.1943	0.0815	0.3986	0.2211	0.0943	0.0909
PC-I	0.8969	0.8969	0.9059	0.9394	0.7948	0.7993	0.8083	0.9265	0.7832	0.7876	0.9516	0.9897
YT-I	8.7454	8.7453	7.8837	1.0003	7.7540	7.4410	6.3607	2.0046	5.9636	5.5663	4.7094	1.6805
CWB-I	0.0020	0.0020	0.0017	0.0015	0.0099	0.0044	0.0081	0.0035	1.5687	0.7467	0.7073	0.2635

Various validity indices are calculated with the optimal number of clusters that are shown in the tables 2.

Because, the validity indices are proposed to evaluate the quality of clustering. The better algorithm gives the smaller value of T-I, DB-I, XB-I, S-I, CE-I, YT-I ,CWB-I and the larger value of PC-I. The summarized results show that the GIT2FCM clustering (the proposed algorithm) have a better performance or higher quality clustering than the other typical algorithm such as FCM, IT2FCM and GFCM. Besides, GIT2FCM can automatically obtains the optimal number of clusters.

5 Conclusion

One of the priori inputs traditionally needed for unsupervised classification is the number of clusters in the data set. In many cases, however, this number of classes is not available. This paper presents a clustering algorithm based on genetic technique which determines the required number of clusters as part of the algorithm. The proposed approach do not need to predict the optimal number of clusters, required to partition the dataset. The experiments are done based on well-known dataset with the statistics show that the algorithm generates clusters with better quality.

The next goal is some studies related to speed-up algorithms for processing huge data based parallel architecture of GPU computing and applying the algorithm to problems.

References

1. Hwang, C., Rhee, F.C.H.: Uncertain Fuzzy clustering: Interval Type-2 Fuzzy Approach to C-Means. IEEE Tran. on Fuzzy Systems 15, 107–120 (2007)
2. Kanungo, T., Mount, D.M., Netanyahu, N.S., Piatko, C.D., Silverman, R., Wu, A.Y.: An Efficient k-Means Clustering Algorithm: Analysis and Implementation. IEEE Trans. on Pattern Analysis and Machine Intelligence 24(7), 881–893 (2002)

3. Hung, M.C., Wu, J., Chang, J.H., Yang, D.L.: An Efficient k-Means Clustering Algorithm Using Simple Partitioning. J. of Info. Science and Engineering 21, 1157–1177 (2005)
4. Zalik, K.R.: An efficient k-means clustering algorithm. Pattern Recognition Letters 29, 1385–1391 (2008)
5. Abdul Nazeer, K.A., Sebastian, M.P.: Improving the Accuracy and Efficiency of the k-means Clustering Algorithm. In: Proceedings of the World Congress on Engineering (2009)
6. Mendel, J.M., John, R.I.: Type-2 fuzzy set made simple. IEEE Trans.Fuzzy Syst. 10(2), 117–127 (2002)
7. Karnik, N., Mendel, J.M.: Operations on Type-2 Fuzzy Sets. Fuzzy Sets and Systems 122, 327–348 (2001)
8. Liang, Q., Mendel, J.M.: Interval Type-2 Fuzzy Logic Systems: Theory and Design. IEEE Trans. on Fuzzy Systems 8(5), 535–550 (2000)
9. Mendel, J.M., John, R.I., Liu, F.: Interval Type-2 Fuzzy Logic Systems Made Simple. IEEE Trans. on Fuzzy Systems 14(6), 808–821 (2006)
10. Rezaee, M.R., Lelieveldt, B.P.F., Reiber, J.H.C.: A new cluster validity index for the fuzzy c-mean. Pattern Recognition Lett. 19, 237–246 (1998)
11. Bezdek, J.: Pattern Recognition with Fuzzy Objective Function Algorithms. Plenum, New York (1981)
12. Alata, M., Molhim, M., Ramini, A.: The Optimizing of Fuzzy C-Means Clustering Algorithm Using GA. World Academy of Science, Engineering and Technology 2, 224–229 (2008)
13. Abraham, A., et al.: Foundations of Computer Intelligent. SCI, vol. 4, 204, pp. 167–195 (2009)
14. Srinivas, M., Patnaik, L.M.: Genetic Algorithms: A Survey. IEEE Computer 27(6), 17–26 (1994)
15. Steinley, D., Brusco, M.J.: Initialization k-means batch clustering: a critical evaluation of several techniques. J. Classif. 24, 99–121 (2007)
16. Cheug, Y.M.: On rival penalization controlled competitive learning for clustering with automatic cluster number selection. IEEE Trans. Knowledge Data Eng. 17, 1583–1588 (2005)
17. Roberts, S.J., Everson, R., Rezek, I.: Maximum certainty data partitioning. Pattern Recognition 33, 833–839 (2000)
18. Turi, R.H.: Clustering-Based Color Image Segmentation, PhD Thesis, Monash University, Australia (2001)
19. Haykin, S.: Neural Networks: A Comprehensive Foundation. Prentice-Hall, Inc. (1999)
20. Holland, J.H.: Adaptation in Natural and Artificial Systems. MIT Press (1975)
21. Tang, Y., Sun, F.: Improved Validation Index for Fuzzy Clustering. In: American Control Conference (2005)
22. Wang, W., Zhang, Y.: On fuzzy cluster validity indices. Fuzzy Sets and Systems 158, 2095–2117 (2007)
23. Cao, H., Deng, H., Wang, Y.: Segmentation of M-FISH Images for Improved Classification of Chromosomes With an Adaptive Fuzzy C-means Clustering Algorithm. IEEE Transactions on Fuzzy Systems 20(1), 1–8 (2012)
24. Wei, C., Tingjin, L., Jizheng, W., Yanqing, Z.: An improved genetic FCM clustering algorithm, An improved genetic FCM clustering algorithm. In: International Conference on Future Computer and Communication, ICFCC, pp.V1-45–V1-48 (2010)
25. Datasets, http://www.ics.uci.edu/mlearn/mlrepository.html

Emotion Analysis of the Text Using Fuzzy Affect Typing over Emotions

Krishna Asawa, Vikrant Verma, and Surbhi Dhupar

Department of CSE & IT,
JIIT-Noida,
India
krishna.asawa@jiit.ac.in,
{vik.vikrantverma,surbhi.dhupar11}@gmail.com

Abstract. This paper presents a novel approach of emotion estimation in the affective content of the textual messages or dialogues. The individual words in a sentence has been chopped and mapped onto the corresponding affective categories. An affective category is assigned to its membership value in the all basic 5 emotions viz. happy, surprise, neutral, anger and sad. To analyze the affective content effectively we use natural language processing for the lexical analysis and thereafter fuzzy affect typing over basic emotions with the membership modifier rules to handle various modifiers of affective contents. Machine learning based prediction approach has been suggested for new encountered words.

Keywords: Emotion prediction, Affective content, Hebbian learning, Natural language processing.

1 Introduction

In order to deal with the increasing demands of today's dialogue management systems introducing a human dimension into automatic text understanding and representation has become necessary. Recent work shows the importance of emotions in decision making, perception and learning [1]. Affect information thus becomes critical to Human Machine Interaction (HMI) for a quick identification and analysis of particular affect in the text and its intuitive presentation to the user.

The present work deals with the inherent ambiguities in the text due to the kind of emotions and words in the natural languages. Here we experiment with qualitative analysis of affect-related information in free textual dialogues. Affect-related information includes words describing primitive emotions in the following categories i.e. happy, surprise, neutral, anger and sad.

For any relevant word that appears in a textual dialogues, we include all of its possible meanings and connotations in our analysis by assigning it a corresponding weight of meta linguistic domain from 0 to 1 in all the 5 categories i.e. happy, surprise, neutral, anger and sad. We create a realistic picture of the textual dialogue's affective content by cumulative effect of all the related words in it.

P.C. Vinh et al. (Eds.): ICCASA 2012, LNICST 109, pp. 249–257, 2013.

Fuzzy techniques provide an excellent framework for computational management of the ambiguity and imprecision those are pervasive in the words of the natural languages. The ambiguity due to the presence of certain modifiers in the text is addressed by constructing fuzzy modifier rules which improves on the whole affect estimation of the text.

The machine learning has been employed to predict the affect of the new encountered word in the text whenever the meta linguistic domain database becomes constraint. It trains the model using Hebbian learning rule for future affective context prediction based on past affective context. It not only improves our efficiency but at the same time also reduces the database dependency to a great extent.

2   Related Work

Achievements in this domain can be used in next generation intelligent robotics, artificial intelligence, psychology, blogs, product reviews, and finally development of emotion-ware applications. A variety of approaches, methodologies and techniques have been used by researchers in order to analyze affect communicated through text. Kamps and Marx [2] evaluated subjective aspects of meaning expressed in written texts, such as the attitude or value expressed in them. Kim and Hovy [3] developed a module for determining word sentiment and another for combining sentiments within a sentence by integrating various models of classifying and finally combining sentiment at word and sentence levels. Statistical language modeling techniques [4] have been applied by researchers to analyze moods conveyed through online diary posts. However, the main limitation of those "bag-of-words" approaches to textual affect classification is that they neglect the negation constructions and syntactical relations in sentences. Some researchers employed keyword-spotting technique [9]; they reported that textual recognition rate is lower than speech based recognition. According to their work, emotion recognition performance of multimodal system is better than performance of individual modalities. Liu et al. [5] employed a commonsense knowledgebase OMCS (Open Mind Common Sense) having 400,000 facts about everyday world to classify sentences created affect sensing engine into an affectively responsive email composer called Empathy Buddy. M. Shaikh, H. Prendinger, and M. Ishizuka [1] used semantic parsers to categorize the themes of the news using news fetched from different news sources. M. Shaikh, H. Prendinger, and M. Ishizuka [6], developed an ALICE chat-bot based on Artificial Intelligence markup language (AIML) script to improve interaction in a text based instant messaging system that uses emoticons or avatar that the sensed emotion to express the emotional state. The affective information present in the input sentences sensed using OCC model of cognitive theory. Emotion analysis of news headlines and blog posts produced on the data set developed for the Sem Eval 2007 task on "Affective Text". For this purpose Strapparava and Mihalcea, [7] employ a range of techniques including keyword-spotting, Latent Semantic Analysis (LSA), Naïve Bayes, rule based analysis and Pointwise Mutual Information (PMI). A. C. Boucouvalas and X.Zhe, [8] described Emotion Extraction Engine that can analyze the input text in a chat dialogue, extract the emotion and displays the expressive image on the communicating users display. He focused on parsing technique that considers sentences in present continuous tense, sentences without starting auxiliary verbs positive sentences, etc. Taner Danisman and Adil Alpkocak Feeler [10] shown automatic classification of anger, disgust, fear, joy and sad emotions in news head- lines using Vector- Space Model.

3   Affect Lexicon and Fuzzy Affect Typing over Emotions

The affect lexicon is a compendium of lexical entries for words having affectual connotation, with their corresponding parts of speech, affect category. An affect lexicon, which characterizes a large vocabulary of affectual words in terms of a small set of basic categories, such as love, hate, happiness, ecstatic, burdened, anxious, each to some numerical fuzzy membership value in the basic 5 emotions: happy, surprise, neutral, sad and anger.

Assigning category labels to a lexicon entries and emotion membership degrees to an affect category is a very subjective process. During the present proof-of concept phase, the assignments have been made by a single linguist. They are obviously influenced by the linguist's own experience, reading background, and (since affects are in question) personal/emotional background and prejudices. Though subjective, the process is not completely arbitrary—the assignments are general enough to yield useful results. The different fuzzy membership values assigned to each categories for each emotion is given below in the table1.

The 2000 words having affectual connotation have been mapped onto one of the 40 emotion oriented affect categories, as listed below.

angry, sad, happy, ecstatic, irresistible, powerless, out_of_control, apathetic, adequate, alone, independent, attached,   codependent, hatred, love, belittled, embarrassed, average, esteemed, cheated, singled_out, justified, entitled, trapped, burdened, free, derailed, lost, focused, obsessed, demoralized, bored, attracted, lustful, fearful, anxious, fearless, safe, surprise and unsorted.

Entries in the affect lexicons and its probable emotional content are represented in the form:

(lexical entry) (POS_tag) (affect category)(Centrality Score) (Intensity Score)
(lexical entry) (affect category) (Happy membership) (Surprise membership) (Neutral membership) (Sad membership) (Anger membership)

Eg: 'annoyed' 'vb' 'angry' '0.6' '0.5' and 'annoyed' 'vb' 'hatred' '0.8' '0.6'

'annoyed' 'hatred' '0.1' '0.2' '0.3' '0.8' '0.5'

In a sentence affectual connotations usually are represented by a verb and an adjective. The POS tagger has been used to tag the Verbs and Adjectives. As of natural constraint all words cannot be completely classified into different categories, so few words were listed under the 'Unsorted' Category. Each word is associated with centrality and intensity score [11] which could help in selecting the best affect category, in case it is listed in more than one affect categories.

Table 1. Different fuzzy membership values assigned to affect category into basic five Emotions

Affect Category	Happy	Surprise	Neutral	Sad	Anger
angry	0.1	0.2	0.5	0.3	1.0
sad	0.1	0.1	0.3	1.0	0.4
happy	1.0	0.7	0.3	0.1	0.1
ecstatic	1.0	0.7	0.3	0.1	0.2
irresistible	0.1	0.2	0.4	0.5	0.9
powerless	0.1	0.2	0.4	0.9	0.5
out_of_control	0.2	0.3	0.4	0.7	0.5
adequate	0.8	0.3	0.6	0.1	0.2
alone	0.1	0.2	0.4	0.9	0.3
attached	0.7	0.4	0.5	0.2	0.3
hatred	0.1	0.2	0.3	0.8	0.5
love	0.8	0.3	0.4	0.2	0.1
belittled	0.1	0.2	0.3	0.9	0.5
Embarrassed	0.1	0.2	0.3	0.9	0.5
Average	0.2	0.1	0.9	0.3	0.4
Esteemed	0.8	0.6	0.4	0.1	0.2
Cheated	0.2	0.6	0.3	0.7	0.9
Justified	0.7	0.1	0.5	0.3	0.2
Trapped	0.2	0.1	0.3	0.7	0.4
Burdened	0.2	0.1	0.3	0.7	0.4
Free	0.7	0.5	0.4	0.2	0.3
Lost	0.2	0.1	0.3	0.7	0.4
Focused	0.5	0.3	0.7	0.1	0.2
Demoralized	0.1	0.3	0.2	1.0	0.4
Bored	0.3	0.2	0.3	0.8	0.5
Attracted	0.7	0.6	0.5	0.1	0.2
Fearful	0.1	0.2	0.3	0.8	0.5
Anxious	0.1	0.2	0.3	0.8	0.5
Fearless	0.8	0.6	0.5	0.2	0.4
Safe	0.7	0.4	0.5	0.2	0.3
Surprise	0.7	1.0	0.3	0.5	0.4
Unsorted	0.3	0.4	0.8	0.6	0.5

4   Architecture of Fuzzy Affect Typing over Emotions

The process for tagging a dialogue with an emotion is shown in figure1. It includes the following processes:

1. Parts of speech tagging
2. Checking for emotion membership value modifier rule applicability.
3. Retrieving fuzzy membership values of each lexical word.
4. Training the model of emotion prediction.

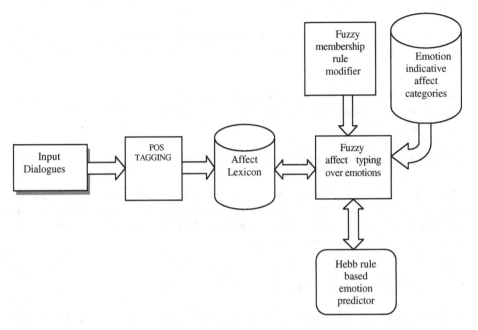

Fig. 1. Architecture for Emotion Prediction

The fuzzy membership values for a lexical entry are retrieved from the database using the table 1 shown above. It may be possible that one word can be listed in two categories. In that case the context sensitive information indicated by centrality score and intensity score [11] are used to assign the best match. Centrality and intensity score of an affect lexicon within an emotion oriented affect category addresses the key issues - *To what extent an affect word X related to category C? To what extent can affect word X be replaced with category C in the text, without changing the meaning?* For example as shown in table 2, the word "Discouraged" is found in categories "*Sad*", "*Demoralized*" and "*Powerless*". But the meaning is different in these three categories, which makes the emotion membership values assigned to this word different depending on the contextual relationship of the word in the affect categories.

5   Hebbian Learning for Emotion Prediction

Hebbian learning which states that with each input value, the model vector will tend to get updated towards the goal value with a constant learning rate, not too high and not too low. The fuzzy membership values assigned to a lexicon have been used to train a neural network model. The hebb rule is used to find weights for each emotion 'i' and updates itself after each iteration 'j' as follows-

$$W[i][j+1] = w[i][j] + alpha*(p[i]-w[i][j]) \qquad (1)$$

where:

'w[j]' is the previous weight of the 'i'th emotion
'w[i][j+1]' is the updated weight of the (j+1)th iteration for 'i'th emotion
'alpha' is the learning rate
'p[i]' is the input value for 'i'th emotion
'i' is one emotion belongs to the set of all basic five emotions.

This trained model is used to predict the overall emotional content of a dialogue as well it also helps to predict emotional values of words whose corresponding affect category is not in the affect category database. Thus, it helps in overcoming the dependency on the affect category database.

6   Rules for Modifying Membership Value

Following modifier rules have been proposed to modify the membership value assigned to a word to get the impact of the fuzzified affective word at sentence level.

A. Non-Arousal Modifiers -- {shall, can, will, could, would}
All of these words depict a permission seeking quality (politeness) contributing to Non-Arousal quality. Hence, we reduce the overall membership value of the word by a small factor.

B. Dominance Modifiers -- {shouldn't, can't, won't, don't}
All of these words depict a dominating characteristic thus not asking for a favour but giving an order. Therefore we increase the angriness membership value of the word by a small factor.

C. Quantifier Modifiers -- {very, little}
Both these words act as quantifiers. Thus enhancing or attenuating the emotion respectively.

- 'Very' modifier rule: increases the overall membership value of the word significantly.
- 'Little' modifier rule: decreases the overall membership value of the word significantly.

D. Negation Modifiers -- {not}
'Not' changes the emotion to the opposite affect content. Thus, overall membership value of the word should be complemented.

E. Tense Modifiers -- {was, is}

- 'Is' modifier rule: 'Is' represents the present emotion of the speaker and thus increases the overall membership value of the word because of present tense.
- 'Was' modifier rule: 'Was' represents the event has happened in the past, hence emotion has attenuated in the present by some amount. Therefore we decrease the overall membership value of the word because of past tense.

After applying these rules, the final values of different emotions for this word are used to update the prediction model.

These calculated values as well as the predicted values are plotted on a graph by GNU Plot and the dialogue's context based prediction by Hebbian learning is compared with the mean value approach.

7   Results and Conclusion

As an example, let us consider the following paragraph:

I was feeling astonished and ecstatic after seeing such a bright, sunny and cheerful festive season all around. Everyone was so excited and sparkling looking really enthusiastic and high-spirited which made me feel delighted and overjoyed. I was also welcomed and loved. At the same time I was shocked at the people's response. But as soon as I remembered what happened the previous day I was grief-stricken and started feeling guilty. I was depressed to be a part of the act and felt awkward to face them. I started feeling hopeless but suddenly I was outraged and decided to face it how bitter it may be.

The result for the overall emotion prediction of the speaker based on the above example shown in table2.

Table 2. Emotion Prediction

Method	Happy (%)	Surprise (%)	Neutral (%)	Sad (%)	Anger (%)
Our Prediction	5.58	9.50	22.08	21.75	41.09
Mean	31.06	23.05	15.51	17.18	13.20

The mean method result gives very different results from what was expected and on the other hand the prediction approach understands the mood swing of the speaker very efficiently and provides realistic results. Few other samples were collected from movie reviews and analyzed for emotional content to form a summarization of common emotions used in a particular type of movies: Romance, Action, Sci-Fi, Family and Comedies, with 10-15 reviews in each group.

The common categories of emotional words and their relative frequency found in the above reviews are shown in the table 3. These results conforms the nature of dominant emotional content present in them.

Table 3. Affect categories observed in various kinds reviews

	High (0.7-1.0)	Medium (0.4-0.7)	Low (0.1 – 0.4)
Movies – Romance	love, attached, happy, ecstatic, free	Justified, Average, irresistible, lost, out_of_control	adequate, sad, alone, trapped, embarrassed, burdened, unsorted
Movies – Action	Angry, Hatred, cheated, out-of-control, trapped, fearless	fearful, safe, Powerless, lost, belittled, irresistible	justified, lost, anxious, unsorted
Movies – Sci-Fi	irresistible, focused, out_of_control	trapped, justified, free, lost	happy, love, average, adequate, unsorted
Movies – Family	attached, love, esteemed, safe, happy, ecstatic	adequate, burdened, average, sad, free, cheated	alone, embarrassed, justified, unsorted
Movies – Comedy	happy, ecstatic, surprise, free, out_of_control	average, adequate, Justified, focused	Belittled, sad, embarrassed, Lost, unsorted

Acknowledgement. The work reported in this paper is supported by the grant received from All India Council for Technical Education; A Statutory body of the Govt. of India. vide f. no. 8023/BOR/RID/RPS-129/2008-09.

References

[1] Shaikh, M., Prendinger, H., Ishizuka, M.: Emotion sensitive news agent: An approach towards user centric emotion sensing from the news. In: The 2007 IEEE/WIC/ACM International Conference on Web Intelligence (WI 2007), Silicon Valley, USA, pp. 614–620 (November 2007)

[2] Kamps, J., Marx, M.: Words with Attitude. In: Proceedings of BNAIC 2002, pp. 449–450 (2002)

[3] Kim, S.-M., Hovy, E.: Automatic Detection of Opinion Bearing Words and Sentences. In: Proceedings of IJCNLP 2005 (2005)

[4] Neviarouskaya, A., Prendinger, H., Ishizuka, M.: Textual Affect Sensing for Sociable and Expressive Online Communication, pp. 220–231. Springer, Heidelberg (2007)

[5] Liu, H., Lieberman, H., Selker, T.: A model of textual affect sensing using real-world Knowledge. In: Proceedings of International Conference on Intelligent User Interfaces (IUI 2003), pp. 125–132 (2003)

[6] Shaikh, M., Prendinger, H., Ishizuka, M.: A cognitively based approach to affect sensing from text. In: Proceedings of 10th Int'l Conf. on Intelligent User Interface (IUI 2006), Sydney, Australia, pp. 349–351 (2006)

[7] Strapparava, C., Mihalcea, R.: Learning to identify emotions in text. In: SAC (2008)

[8] Boucouvalas, A.C., Zhe, X.: Text-to-Emotion. Engine for Real Time Internet Communication. In: Proceedings of the 3rd International Symposium on CSNDSP, pp. 164–168. Staffordshire University, UK (2002)

[9] Chuang, Z.J., Wu, H.: Multi-Modal Emotion Recognition from Speech and Text. International Journal of Computational Linguistics and Chinese Language Processing 9(2), 1–18 (2004)

[10] Danisman, T., Alpkocak, A.: Feeler: Emotion Classification of Text Using Vector Space Model. In: AISB 2008 Convention, Communication, Interaction and Social Intelligence, Affective Language in Human and Machine, Aberdeen, UK, vol. 2, pp. 53–59 (April 2008)

[11] Subasic, P., Huettner, A.: Affect Analysis of Text Using Fuzzy Semantic Typing. IEEE Transactions on Fuzzy Systems 9(4), 483 (2001)

Compare Effective Fuzzy Associative Memories for Grey-Scale Image Recognition

Pham Viet Binh and Nong Thi Hoa

Thainguyen University of Information Technology and Communication
pvbinh@ictu.edu.vn, nongthihoa@gmail.com

Abstract. Pattern recognition (PR) is the most important field of image processing that is widely developed by many scientists. Reason is that PR provides complete information of objects from noisy inputs. Several types of approach have been proposed to solve this problem, such as recognition base on key features, recognition base on the distribution of histogram. In studies about recognition using key features, Fuzzy Associative Memory (FAM) is an artificial neural network that solve effectively for PR. Advantages of FAM consist of compressing data and recalling from noisy inputs (noise tolerance). Therefore, FAM stores many patterns and retrieves stored patterns. In this paper, we present designs of effective FAM models and experiments to compare the ability of recall with nine types of noise. From results of experiments, we propose useful comments to choose an effective FAM model for pattern recognition applications.

Keywords: Fuzzy Associative Memory, Pattern Recognition, Associative Memory.

1 Introduction

Pattern recognition, a sub-branch of image processing, have attracted many scientists because of many applications in today life such as face recognition, reading bar-code, detecting mistakes on products, action recognition. The most important advantage that a application of PR must possess is correctly recognizing objects from noisy inputs. FAM is a artificial neural network that solve effectively for PR. FAM has two key advantages, including learning capacity of neural network, recalling from noisy inputs by using operators of Fuzzy logic and mathematical morphology (MM).

Thus, studies of FAM are various and can be divided into two categories, including developing the design of models and using models for applications. In the first category, operators of fuzzy set and MM are widely used in designing models [12,2,5,7]. Scientists also use operators of math for computing of models to suite for specific problems [17,15]. In the second category, FAMs are applied for many fields, including pattern recognition [13,12,14,17,15], control [10,18], estimation [16,1], prediction [19,11] and inference [6,3]. Previous studies show FAMs are widely apply for pattern recognition.

P.C. Vinh et al. (Eds.): ICCASA 2012, LNICST 109, pp. 258–267, 2013.

In this paper, we present designs of effective FAM models and experiments in grey-scale image recognition with nine types of noise in two working modes, including auto-association and hetero-association. These models possess three important advantages, including (i) learning and recalling process in an iteration, (ii) unlimited storage capacity, and (iii) high noise tolerance. The design of each model is presented the easy way to understand and compare. Experiments are conducted with nine types of noise of grey-scale images to compare the ability of recall among models. Then, we sum up useful comments to choose an effective model for an application of PR.

The rest of the paper is organized as follows. Back grounds of fuzzy set and MM are presented in Section 2. In section 3, we present the design of effective FAMs for PR. Section 4 shows experiments to compare noise tolerance among models. Then, we propose meaningful comments for choosing a effective model for applications. Conclusions and developing this study are written in Section 5.

2   Back Ground

2.1   Fuzzy Set [8]

Definition

Let X be a non-empty set. A fuzzy set A in X is characterized by its membership function $\mu_A : X \to [0,1]$ and $\mu_A(x)$ is interpreted as the degree of membership of element x in fuzzy set A for each $x \in X$.

Operators of Fuzzy Logic

Let A and B are fuzzy subsets of a non-empty set X.

The *intersection* of A and B is defined as $A \wedge B(x) = min\{\mu_A(x), \mu_B(x)\}$ for all $x \in X$

The *union* of A and B is defined as $A \vee B(x) = max\{\mu_A(x), \mu_B(x)\}$ for all $x \in X$

The *complement* of fuzzy set A is defined as $]A(x) = 1 - \mu_A(x)$ for all $x \in X$

The *fuzzy conjunction* of A and B is an increasing mapping $C : [0,1] \times [0,1] \longrightarrow [0,1]$ that satisfies $C(0,0) = C(0,1) = C(1,0) = 0$ and $C(1,1) = 1$. For example, the minimum operator and the product are typical examples.

A fuzzy conjunction $T : [0,1] \times [0,1] \longrightarrow [0,1]$ that satisfies $T(x,1) = x$ for $x \in [0,1]$ is called *triangular norm* or *t-norm*. The fuzzy conjunctions C_M, C_P , and C_L are examples of t-norms.

$$C_M(x,y) = x \wedge y \tag{1}$$

$$C_P(x,y) = x.y \tag{2}$$

$$C_L(x,y) = 0 \vee (x+y-1) \tag{3}$$

A *fuzzy disjunction* is an increasing mapping $D : [0,1] \times [0,1] \longrightarrow [0,1]$ that satisfies $D(0,0) = 0$ and $D(0,1) = D(1,0) = D(1,1) = 1$.

A fuzzy disjunction $S : [0,1] \times [0,1] \longrightarrow [0,1]$ that satisfies $S(1,x) = x$ for every $x \in [0,1]$ is called *triangular co-norm* or *short s-norm*. The following operators represent s-norms:

$$D_M(x,y) = x \vee y \tag{4}$$

$$D_P(x,y) = x + y - x.y \tag{5}$$

$$D_L(x,y) = 1 \wedge (x+y) \tag{6}$$

An operator $I : [0,1] \times [0,1] \longrightarrow [0,1]$ is called a *fuzzy implication* if I extends the usual crisp implication on $[0,1] \times [0,1]$ with $I(0,0) = I(0,1) = I(1,1) = 1$ and $I(1,0) = 0$. Some particular fuzzy implications:

$$I_M(x,y) = \begin{bmatrix} 1, x \leq y \\ y, x > y \end{bmatrix} \tag{7}$$

$$I_P(x,y) = \begin{bmatrix} 1, x \leq y \\ y/x, x > y \end{bmatrix} \tag{8}$$

$$I_L(x,y) = 1 \wedge (y - x + 1) \tag{9}$$

2.2   The Complete Lattice Framework of MM [4]

A Complete Lattice of MM

Mathematical morphology is a theory which is concerned with the processing and analysis of objects by using operators and functions based on topological and geometrical concepts. The most general mathematical framework of MM is given by complete lattices.

A complete lattice is defined as a partially ordered set L in which every (finite or infinite) subset has an infimum and a supremum in L. For any $Y \subseteq L$, the infimum of Y is denoted by the $\bigwedge Y$ and the supremum is denoted by the $\bigvee Y$. The class of fuzzy sets inherits the complete lattice structure of the unit interval $[0,1]$.

Basic Operators of MM

Erosion and dilation are two basic operators of mathematical morphology. An *erosion* is a mapping ε from a complete lattice L to a complete lattice M that satisfies the following equation:

$$\varepsilon(\bigwedge Y) = \bigwedge_{y \in Y} \varepsilon(y) \tag{10}$$

Similarly, an operator $\delta : L \longrightarrow M$ is called *dilation* if it satisfies the following equation:

$$\delta\left(\bigvee Y\right) = \bigvee_{y \in Y} \delta(y) \tag{11}$$

3 Effective FAMs for PR

Assuming that FAM stores p fuzzy pattern pairs that are noted (A^k, B^k) where $A_k = (A_1^k, ..., A_1^m)$ and $B_k = (B_1^k, ..., B_1^n)$.

3.1 Kosko's Model [7]

The associative matrix W^k of the pattern pair (A^k, B^k) are computed by the following equation:

$$W_{ij}^k = min\{A_i^k, B_j^k\} \tag{12}$$

and the general weight matrix W that stores all pattern pairs is formulated by below equation:

$$W_{ij} = \bigvee_{k=1}^{p} W_{ij}^k \tag{13}$$

With an input X, the output Y is calculated by the output function:

$$Y_j = \bigvee_{i=1}^{m} min\{X_i, W_{ij}\} \tag{14}$$

3.2 The Model of Junbo et al. [5]

The associative matrix W_k of the pattern pair (A_k, B_k) are computed by the following equation:

$$W_{ij}^k = I_M(A_i^k, B_j^k) \tag{15}$$

and the general weight matrix W that stores all pattern pairs is formulated by below equation:

$$W_{ij} = \bigwedge_{k=1}^{p} W_{ij}^k \tag{16}$$

With an input X, the output Y is calculated by the output function:

$$Y_j = \bigvee_{i=1}^{m} min\{X_i, W_{ij}\} \tag{17}$$

3.3   Models of Fulai and Tong [2]

The associative matrix W_k of the pattern pair (A_k, B_k) are computed by the following equation:

$$W_{ij}^k = I_M(A_i^k, B_j^k) \tag{18}$$

and the general weight matrix W that stores all pattern pairs is formulated by below equation:

$$W_{ij} = \bigwedge_{k=1}^{p} W_{ij}^k \tag{19}$$

With an input X, the output Y is calculated by the output function:

$$Y_j = \bigwedge_{k=1}^{p} \varphi(X_i, W_{ij}) \tag{20}$$

where φ is a t-norm.

3.4   Models of Ping Xiao et al. [17]

The associative matrix W^k of the pattern pair (A^k, B^k) are computed by the following equation:

$$W_{ij}^k = \varphi(A_i^k, B_j^k) \tag{21}$$

where φ is formulated as

$$\varphi(\mathbf{x}, \mathbf{y}) = \left[\begin{array}{l} 1, x = y \\ \frac{min\,A_i^k, B_j^k)}{max(A_i^k, B_j^k)}, x \neq y \end{array} \right. \tag{22}$$

and the general weight matrix W that stores all pattern pairs is formulated by below equation:

$$W_{ij} = \bigwedge_{k=1}^{p} W_{ij}^k \tag{23}$$

With an input X, the output Y is calculated by the output function:

$$Y_j = \bigvee_{i=1}^{m} X_i.W_{ij} \tag{24}$$

3.5   Models of S.T.Wang et al. [15]

The associative matrix W_k of the pattern pair (A_k, B_k) are computed by the following equation:

$$W_{ij}^k = B_i^k / A_j^k \tag{25}$$

and the general weight matrix W that stores all pattern pairs is formulated by below equation:

$$W_{ij} = \bigwedge_{k=1}^{p} W_{ij}^k \tag{26}$$

OR

$$W_{ij} = \bigvee_{k=1}^{p} W_{ij}^k \tag{27}$$

With an input X, the output Y is calculated by the output function:

$$Y_j = \bigvee_{i=1}^{m} (X_j + W_{ij}) \tag{28}$$

OR

$$Y_j = \bigwedge_{i=1}^{m} (X_j + W_{ij}) \tag{29}$$

3.6   Models of Sussner and Valle [11]

The associative matrix W_k of the pattern pair (A_k, B_k) are computed by the following equation:

$$W_{ij}^k = \varphi(B_i^k, A_j^k) \tag{30}$$

where φ be I_M or I_P or I_L

and the general weight matrix W that stores all pattern pairs is formulated by below equation:

$$W_{ij} = \bigwedge_{k=1}^{p} W_{ij}^k \tag{31}$$

OR

$$W_{ij} = \bigvee_{k=1}^{p} W_{ij}^k \tag{32}$$

With an input X, the output Y is calculated by the output function:

$$Y_j = \varphi(X_j, W_{ij}) \vee \theta_j \qquad (33)$$

where φ be s-norm.

θ is computed by:

$$\theta_j = \bigwedge_{k=1}^{p} B_j \qquad (34)$$

4 Experiments and Summarise Useful Comments

We make experiments with grey-scale images to test noise tolerance of models. In each experiment, models of FAM are test with two working modes, including auto-association and hetero-association. Moreover, nine types of noise are applied for training inputs to make noisy inputs. We use the peak signal-to-noise ratio (PSNR) to measure quality between the training and a output image [9]. The higher the PSNR, the better the quality of the output image.

We choose 4 images from the grey-scale image database of tests in Mathlab, including Cameraman, Pepper2, Zelda, Lena. Normal images are training patterns and nine noisy images are inputs for experiments. Noisy inputs are made from the training images by using Mathlab's function. Nine types of noisy inputs, including on and off pixels, Gaussian white noise, dilate image with structure DISK, erode image with structure DISK, morphological open image with structure DISK, morphological close image with structure DISK, erode image with structure BALL, erode image with structure LINE, and dilate image with structure LINE.

Six models of FAM are similar in both learning and recalling process. Therefore, we only interest noise tolerance of models. Studies of Sussner and Valle, Fulai and Tong, and S.T.Wang et al. proposed a family of FAM but we only show results of best models.

4.1 Experiments

Experiment 1: FAMs in Auto-association Mode

In auto-association mode, $B_k = A_k$ with all pattern pairs. Thus, this experiment suits to applications such as face recognition, bar-code recognition. Table 1 presents PSNR of models with nine types of noisy inputs.

Bold numbers in Table 1 show models that are the best for each type of noise. In summary, two models of Wang are the best models for four types of noise (respectively 1, 2, 3, 9) and models of Sussner are the best models for types of noise from 4 to 8 in auto-association mode.

Table 1. PSNR of models with nine noisy types in Experiment 1

Noise	Type1	Type2	Type3	Type4	Type5	Type6	Type7	Type8	Type9
Fulai1	8.9	18.7	18.7	32.2	33.2	23.4	29.1	31.6	18.5
Fulai2	14.9	28.6	25.9	**51.9**	**62.5**	36.9	**1000.0**	**52.7**	24.8
Junbo	14.9	28.6	25.9	**51.9**	**62.5**	36.9	**1000.0**	**52.7**	24.8
Kosko	**23.1**	23.4	23.5	25.0	24.6	23.8	23.8	24.6	23.8
Ping	16.6	**28.9**	**29.0**	49.5	59.6	**39.0**	656.2	51.3	**28.8**
Sussner1	11.7	24.1	24.1	**59.8**	**68.9**	34.8	651.2	**61.7**	22.5
Sussner2	14.9	29.6	26.3	45.0	58.5	**40.5**	**1000.0**	47.2	25.0
Sussner3	14.9	28.6	25.9	51.9	**62.5**	36.9	**1000.0**	**52.7**	24.8
Wang1	**30.1**	**30.1**	**30.1**	30.1	30.1	30.1	30.1	30.1	**30.1**
Wang2	**30.1**	**30.1**	**30.1**	30.1	30.1	30.1	30.1	30.1	**30.1**

Experiment 2: FAMs in Hetero-association Mode

In hetero-association mode, $B_k \neq A_k$ with all pattern pairs. Thus, this experiment suits to applications that provide patterns associated with inputs. For example, proposing the face image of a person from a noisy input of fingerprint image. Table 2 presents PSNR of models with nine types of noisy inputs.

Table 2. PSNR of models with nine noisy types in Experiment 2

Noise	Type1	Type2	Type3	Type4	Type5	Type6	Type7	Type8	Type9
Fulai1	9.0	18.5	18.4	25.4	26.4	21.0	25.3	25.9	18.8
Fulai2	14.8	**27.8**	25.8	35.2	36.0	31.1	37.8	35.5	25.3
Junbo	14.8	**27.8**	25.8	35.2	36.0	31.1	37.8	35.5	25.3
Kosko	**24.2**	24.7	24.7	27.9	26.7	25.4	25.4	26.9	25.4
Ping	**21.4**	**31.3**	**30.9**	35.7	**38.2**	35.3	**41.1**	**37.3**	30.9
Sussner1	12.7	25.2	25.0	**42.5**	**45.4**	31.9	47.6	**43.1**	24.4
Sussner2	14.8	27.9	25.6	31.6	33.7	31.3	35.7	32.5	25.1
Sussner3	14.8	27.8	25.8	35.2	36.0	31.1	37.8	35.5	25.3
Wang1	13.5	13.5	**78.8**	17.4	27.8	**87.4**	**366.8**	17.7	**212.3**
Wang2	**30.1**	**30.1**	**30.1**	30.1	30.1	30.1	30.1	30.1	**30.1**

Bold numbers in Table 2 show models that are the best for each type of noise. To sum up, models Wang are the best models for types of noise (respectively 1, 3,6, 7, 9), the first model of Sussner for three types (respectively 4, 5, 8), and the model of Ping for Type 2 in hetero-association mode. However, the model of Ping is good for all types of noise.

4.2   Summarise Useful Comments

Each application features by data, algorithm. Moreover, the most important advantage of PR is providing complete information of objects from noisy inputs. Therefore, each application should choose a best model base on noisy types of inputs and working mode. We propose following useful comments:

1. In auto-association mode with each type of noise, we sort models of authors by the descending order of the ability of recall in each column of Table 3. When PSNR of the best model of each type of noise is low, use the second model because testing data are abnormal.

Table 3. Choose a suitable model for each type of noise in auto-association mode

Type1	Type2	Type3	Type4	Type5	Type6	Type7	Type8	Type9
Wang	Wang	Wang	Sussner	Sussner	Sussner	Sussner	Sussner	Wang
Kosko	Ping	Ping	Junbo	Junbo	Ping	Junbo	Junbo	Ping
			Fulai	Fulai		Fulai	Fulai	

2. Similarly, we list comments to choose an effective model in hetero-association mode in Table 4. Data show the model of Ping is the best models for all types of noise.

Table 4. Choose a suitable model for each type of noise in hetero-association mode

Type1	Type2	Type3	Type4	Type5	Type6	Type7	Type8	Type9
Wang	Ping	Wang	Sussner	Sussner	Wang	Wang	Sussner	Wang
Kosko	Wang	Ping	Ping	Ping	Ping	Sussner	Ping	Ping
Ping	Junbo					Ping		

3. Select models of Sussner or Wang in auto-association mode and select the model of Ping in hetero-association for applications that have to work with complex or unknown types of noise.

5 Conclusion

In this paper, we summarise studies about the design of effective FAMs for PR in the simple way to understand and compare by describing equations in a clear way and using uniform signs. With each model, we propose equations to compute the associative weight matrix of each pattern pair, the general weight matrix of all pattern pair, and outputs of the given input. Moreover, we conduct many sub-experiments to measure the ability of recall of models with two working modes. In each working mode, nine types of noise are used to test. From results of experiment, we propose three meaningful comments to choose a effective model for an application of PR.

FAMs also apply for medicine, economy, and machine because FAMs work well with uncertain data for tasks such as estimation, prediction and inference. Moreover, on-line learning rule is an idea method that allows FAMs meet the need of real-time application. We will investigate to develop an on-line learning rule of FAM for estimation and prediction in the future.

References

1. Chang, H.C., Chen, H.C., Fang, J.H.: Lithology Determination from Well Logs with fuzzy associative memory neural network. IEEE Transactions on Geoscience and Remote Sensing 35(3), 773–780 (1997)
2. Chung, F.I., Lee, T.: Towards a High Capacity Fuzzy Associative Memory Model. In: IEEE World Congress on Computational Intelligence (1994)
3. Chung, F.I., Lee, T.: On fuzzy associative memories with multiple-rule storage capacity. IEEE Transactions on Fuzzy System 4(3) (1996)
4. Serra, J.: Image Analysis and Mathematical Morphology. Academic Press, London (1982)
5. Junbo, F., Fan, J., Yan, S.: A learning rule for FAM. In: 1994 IEEE International Conference on Neural Networks, pp. 4273–4277 (1994)
6. Kim, M.J., Han, I., Lee, K.C.: Fuzzy Associative Memory-Driven Approach to Knowledge Integration. In: 1999 IEEE International Fuzzy Systems Conference Proceedings, pp. 298–303 (1999)
7. Kosko, B.: NeuralNetworks and Fuzzy Systems: A Dynamical Systems Approach to Machine Intelligence. Prentice Hall, Englewood Cliffs (1992)
8. Zadeh, L.A.: Fuzzy sets and information granularity. Advances in Fuzzy Set Theory and Applications Book. North Holland, Amsterdam (1979)
9. MathWorks: Product Documentation in Blocks/Statistics, http://www.mathworks.com/help/toolbox/vision/ref/psnr.html
10. Shahir, S., Chen, X.: Adaptive fuzzy associative memory for on-line quality control. In: Proceedings of the 35th South-eastern Symposium on System Theory, pp. 357–361 (2003)
11. Sussner, P., Valle, M.E.: Implicative Fuzzy Associative Memories. IEEE Transactions on Fuzzy System 14(6), 793–807 (2006)
12. Sussner, P., Valle, M.E.: Fuzzy Associative Memories and Their Relationship to Mathematical Morphology. In: Handbook of Granular Computing, pp. 1–41 (2008)
13. Valle, M.E.: A New Class of Implicative FAM for the Reconstruction of Gray-Scale Images Corrupted by Salt and Pepper Noise. In: 2010 Eleventh Brazilian Symposium on Neural Networks (2010)
14. Valle, M.E., Sussner, P., Gomide, F., El, F., Eng, C.: Introduction to implicative fuzzy associative memories. IEEE Transactions on Fuzzy System 14(6) (2006)
15. Wang, S.T., Lu, H.J.: On New Fuzzy Morphological Associative Memories. IEEE Transaction on Fuzzy Systems 12(3), 316–323 (2004)
16. Wang, Z., Zhang, J.: Detecting Pedestrian Abnormal Behavior Based on Fuzzy Associative Memory. In: Fourth International Conference on Natural Computation, pp. 143–147 (2008)
17. Xiao, P., Yang, F., Yu, Y.: Max-Min Encoding Learning Algorithm for Fuzzy Max-Multiplication Associative Memory Networks. In: 1997 IEEE International Conference on Systems, Man, and Cybernetics (1997)
18. Yamaguchi, T., Wakamatsu, Y.: Creativity Support Using Chaotic Retrieval Fuzzy Associative Memory System. In: IEEE International Conference on Systems, Man, and Cybernetics, pp. 1966–1971 (1996)
19. Zhang, C., Sun, H., Zhou, H., Li, R.: A Method of FAM for Pedestrian Behaviour Classification. In: 2009 Second International Symposium on Electronic Commerce and Security, pp. 150–154 (2009)

Applying Multi Support Vector Machine for Flower Image Classification

Thai Hoang Le[1], Hai Son Tran[2], and Thuy Thanh Nguyen[3]

[1] Computer Science Department, University of Science, Ho Chi Minh City, Vietnam
lhthai@fit.hcmus.edu.vn
[2] Informatics Technology Department, University of Pedagogy, Ho Chi Minh City, Vietnam
member of AICSIT
haits@hcmup.edu.vn
[3] VNU University of Engineering and Technology, Ha Noi City, Vietnam
nguyenthanhthuy@vnu.edu.vn

Abstract. Image classification is the significant problems of concern in image processing and image recognition. There are many methods have been proposed for solving image classification problem such as k nearest neighbor (K-NN), Bayesian Network, Adaptive boost (Adaboost), Artificial Neural Network (NN), and Support Vector Machine (SVM). The aim of this paper is to propose a novel model using multi SVMs concurrently to apply for image classification. Firstly, each image is extracted to many feature vectors. Each of feature vectors is classified into the responsive class by one SVM. Finally, all the classify results of SVM are combined to give the final result. Our proposal classification model uses many SVMs. Let it call multi_SVM. As a case study for validation the proposal model, experiment trials were done of Oxford Flower Dataset divided into three categories (lotus, rose, and daisy) has been reported and compared on RGB and HIS color spaces. Results based on the proposed model are found encouraging in term of flower image classification accuracy.

Keywords: image classification, flower image classification, multi Support Vector Machine.

1 Introduction

Image classification is the significant problem of concern in image processing and image recognition. The aim of image classification is to identify the right categories of images based on image features. The first problem in image classification is image feature extraction and the second problem is to classify image into the suitable classes.

Many transformations such as Fourier, Wavelet [1,2], Hough [3], Principal Component Analysis (PCA) [4], Independent Component Analysis (ICA) [5], curvelet and ridgelet [6]… can be used to extract the image's features. Every transformation has some advantages and dis advantages. The researchers need to choose to the suitable transformation for their interesting problem.

P.C. Vinh et al. (Eds.): ICCASA 2012, LNICST 109, pp. 268–281, 2013.
© Institute for Computer Sciences, Social Informatics and Telecommunications Engineering 2013

Classification problem can be solved by various techniques such as k nearest neighbor (K-NN)[7], Bayesian Network [8], Adaptive boost (Adaboost), Artificial Neural Network (NN), and Support Vector Machine (SVM)...

The k-NN classifier identifies the categories of the input image based on the distance between the feature vector of the input image and the feature vector dataset of training images.

Adaboost classifier is a fast classifier based on the set of weak classifiers. It uses an iterative learning algorithm to create one classifier by using a training dataset and a "weak" learning algorithm. The disadvantages of Adaboost classifier is the non- high classification precision. This classifier need to integrate with another technique for improving the precision [9].

Artificial Neural Network (ANN) has been built for many applications. There are many ANN's structures which have been designed suitable with their problem. The difficulty of using ANN is how to develop good ANN structure for the application. For an example, the number of node of the hidden layer is not easily to identify in the specific context [10].

SVM is one the feasible method applying for pattern classification and can be used for image classification. SVM separates of a training dataset two classes and builds the optimal separating hyperplanes. The feature vector of image in one category lies on one side of the hyperplanes, and the others lie on the opposite side of the hyperplanes [11].

2   Background and Related Work

SVM is one of popular kernel based classification learning algorithm that can apply for pattern classification and image classification. The researchers often use the Gaussian or Polynomial kernel function in developing SVM. The number of hyperplanes of a SVM is dependent on the number of classes. For example, if we use one vs. one strategy for classifying into L different classes, then the number of hyperplanes is L-1. If we use one vs. rest strategy for classifying into L different classes, then the number of hyperplanes is $L(L-1)/2$.

The aim of Classification via SVM [12] is to find a computationally efficient way of learning good separating hyperplanes in a hyperspace, where 'good' hyperplanes mean ones optimizing the generalizing bounds and by 'computationally efficient' we mean algorithms able to deal with sample sizes of very high order.

Devis Tuia has suggested an algorithm with margin rescaling applying for remote sensing image classification [13]:

In this research, we suggest a model using multiple SVM to apply for image classification. For example, every image is extracted to m feature vectors and need to classify into L different classes. Our proposed model use m SVM(s) with kernel function Gauss or Polynomial.

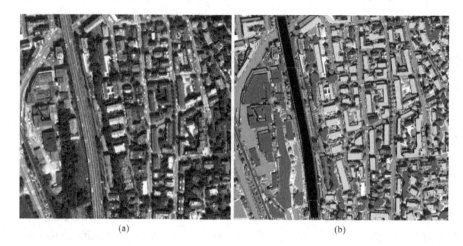

Fig. 1. Multispectral very high resolution Quickbird image acquired over Zurich. A RGB composition of the image and b ground survey of the seven classes of interest identified: 'trees'(Dark green), 'meadows' (light green), 'highway' (black), 'road' (brown), 'residential' (orange), 'commercial' (red) 'and shadow' (blue) [13].

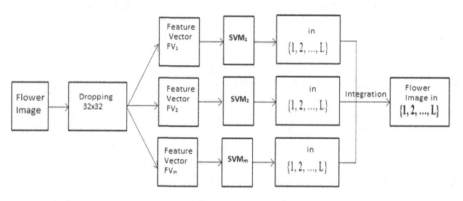

Fig. 2. Multi SVM model (m,L)

Where m = the number of image feature vectors = the number of SVM(s)

L = the number of classes

The number of hyperplanes of one SVM is dependent on L and what kind of hyperplane building strategy (one vs. one, or one vs. rest…) has been used.

3   Multi SVM Apply for Flower Image Classification

Color is the critical feature of images, especially in flower images. It does not require the careful preprocessing. Thus color is one the popular feature using in image classification. There are many color spaces in image processing and image classification. Some color spaces orient to devices such as RGB, CMYK, YIQ... and other color space orient to user such as HSI, HSV, HCV...

In this research, we use two typical color spaces which are RGB and HSI to check the feasibility of multi_SVM model for flower image classification. The input flower image must be classified into L=3 categories (rose, lotus, and daisy).

3.1   Multi SVM Model Apply for Flower Image Classification

3.1.1   Flower Image Classification Based on RGB Color Space

The flower image's size is dropped 32x32 and represent in RGB color space. We set the average threshold to transform the image to the digital matrix based on every component color (R, G, B) like below:

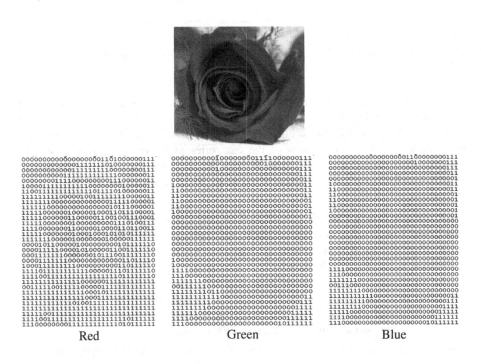

Red   Green   Blue

Fig. 3. Flower image color extraction using RGB color space

The red feature of flower image is the digital matrix 32x32 with the value 0 or 1. The value of an element in the matrix set to 0 if its red color value is lower than the average threshold. The SVM_R get the red feature of an image to identify the category of the image. We do the same to SVM_G and SVM_B.

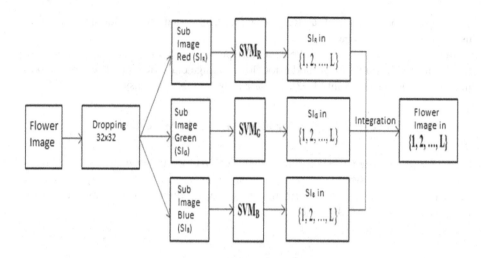

Fig. 4. Flower image classification using RGB color space

The input flower image are extracted to 3 sub-image based on each R, G, B component color. Let them denote SI_R, SI_G, and SI_B. Thus the multi_SVM system must have three SVM components SVM_R, SVM_G, and SVM_B. Each of three SVM components gives the conclusion of the categories of flower images. We need to integrate three results of classification. We can use majority or average to integrate all SVM(s) result to give the final result of the multi_SVM classification system.

3.1.2 Flower Image Classification Based on HSI Color Space

The flower image's size is dropped 32x32 and represent in HSI color space. We set the average threshold to transform the image to the digital matrix based on every component color (H, S, I) like below:

The hue feature of flower image is the digital matrix 32x32 with the value 0 or 1. The value of an element in the matrix set to 0 if its red color value is lower than the average threshold. The SVM_H get the red feature of an image to identify the category of the image. We do the same to SVM_S and SVM_I.

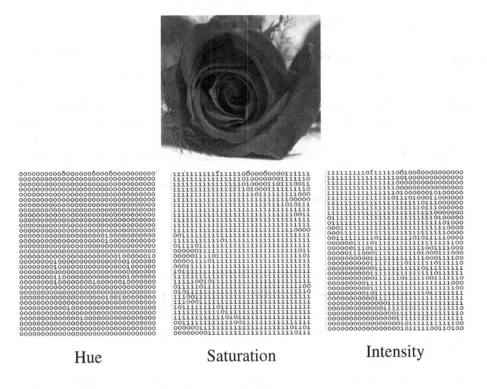

Fig. 5. Flower image color extraction using HSI color space

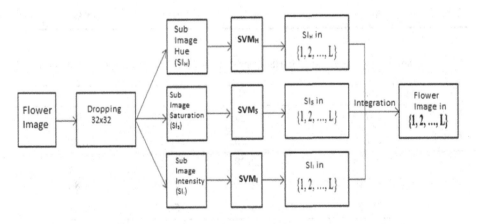

Fig. 6. Flower image classification using HSI color space

The mechanism of flower image classification system using HIS color space is the same to using the above RGB color space. The detail of integration method will explain in the next section.

3.2   Integration of Multi SVM Classification Result

3.2.1 Majority Integration Method

Majority Integration Method is a simple and easy to implementation method. The final result is the highest consensus result. In this problem, we have three results of three SVM components (SVM_R, SVM_G, SVM_B or SVM_H, SVM_S, SVM_I). The final conclusion is the result having the same of two or three classification results. For example in using RGB color, if both of SVM_R and SVM_B show that the flower image is lotus and the SVM_G shows that the flower image is the rose, then the final result is lotus.

In order to test the feasibility of the majority integration method, we have tested in the 80 flower images of three categories consisting 27 rose images, 25 lotus images and 28 daisy images. The kernel functions of SVM (Gaussian, and Polynomial kernel) have been used in the implementing experiments.

Table 1. Majority integration method in RGB color space and SVM using Gaussian kernel function

Flower Image	SVM_R	SVM_G	SVM_B	Majority
Rose	13/27	22/27	20/27	17/27
Lotus	20/25	23/25	25/25	24/25
Daisy	14/28	25/28	27/28	24/28
All	**47/80**	**69/80**	**72/80**	**64/80**
Precision	**59%**	**86%**	**90%**	**80%**

Table 2. Majority integration method in HSI color space and SVM using Gaussian kernel function

Flower Image	SVM_H	SVM_S	SVM_I	Majority
Rose	14/27	16/27	11/27	9/27
Lotus	22/25	24/25	20/25	17/25
Daisy	26/28	22/28	14/28	12/28
All	**62/80**	**62/80**	**45/80**	**38/80**
Precision	**78%**	**78%**	**56%**	**48%**

Table 3. Majority integration method in RGB color space and SVM using Polynomial kernel function

Flower Image	SVM_R	SVM_G	SVM_B	Majority
Rose	14/27	26/27	15/27	14/27
Lotus	19/25	16/25	25/25	16/25
Daisy	15/28	25/28	27/28	23/28
All	**48/80**	**67/80**	**67/80**	**53/80**
Precision	**60%**	**84%**	**84%**	**66%**

Table 4. Majority integration method in RGB color space and SVM using Polynomial kernel function

Flower Image	SVM_R	SVM_G	SVM_B	Majority
Rose	17/27	12/27	13/27	9/27
Lotus	20/25	21/25	19/25	20/25
Daisy	28/28	23/28	17/28	23/28
All	**65/80**	**56/80**	**49/80**	**52/80**
Precision	**81%**	**70%**	**61%**	**65%**

The experimental results show that the precision of the majority integration method is low and does not improve the classification result of each SVM component. Although we use Gaussian or Polynomial kernel function for SVM component, RGB color space are more suitable for improving the precision of flower image classification than HIS color space.

In the special case, there is no majority result. The final result is not identification. For example in using RGB color, SVM_R shows that the flower image is lotus, SVM_G shows that the flower image is the rose and SVM_B shows that the flower image is the daisy. We can choose any majority result. Thus the final result is not identification. This is a disadvantage of majority integration method. To overcome this disadvantage, the majority integration method need to combine average method and will be explained in the section 3.2.3.

3.2.2 Average Integration Method

Average Integration Method is a natural and simple integration method. The final result is the average of result of all components. The distance between the sub images and the hyperplanes of SVM component are used to calculate the average distance.

The final classification result is identified based on this distance. In order to test the feasibility of the average integration method, we have also tested in the 80 flower images of three categories (rose, lotus, and daisy) and two kernel functions (Gaussian, and Polynomial). The experimental results show in the below tables:

Table 5. Average integration method in RGB color space and SVM using Gaussian kernel function

Flower Image	SVM_R	SVM_G	SVM_B	Average Method
Rose	13/27	22/27	20/27	25/27
Lotus	20/25	23/25	25/25	25/25
Daisy	14/28	25/28	27/28	26/28
All	**47/80**	**69/80**	**72/80**	**76/80**
Precision	**59%**	**86%**	**90%**	**95%**

Table 6. Average integration method in HSI color space and SVM using Gaussian kernel function

Flower Image	SVM_H	SVM_S	SVM_I	Average Method
Rose	14/27	16/27	11/27	20/27
Lotus	22/25	24/25	20/25	22/25
Daisy	26/28	22/28	14/28	26/28
All	**62/80**	**62/80**	**45/80**	**68/80**
Precision	**78%**	**78%**	**56%**	**85%**

Table 7. Average integration method in RGB color space and SVM using Polynomial kernel function

Flower Image	SVM_R	SVM_G	SVM_B	Average Method
Rose	14/27	26/27	15/27	24/27
Lotus	19/25	16/25	25/25	22/25
Daisy	15/28	25/28	27/28	27/28
All	**48/80**	**67/80**	**67/80**	**73/80**
Precision	**60%**	**84%**	**84%**	**91%**

Table 8. Average integration method in RGB color space and SVM using Polynomial kernel function

Flower Image	SVM_R	SVM_G	SVM_B	Average Method
Rose	17/27	12/27	13/27	23/27
Lotus	20/25	21/25	19/25	21/25
Daisy	28/28	23/28	17/28	25/28
All	**65/80**	**56/80**	**49/80**	**69/80**
Precision	**81%**	**70%**	**61%**	**86%**

The experimental results show that the precision of the average integration method have improved the precision of the classification result of each SVM component. Although Gaussian or Polynomial kernel function for SVM component has been used, the precision of average integration method is stable and does not change too much.

3.2.3 Fusion of Majority and Average Integration Method

Fusion of Majority and Average Integration Method is an integration method overcoming the disadvantage of the majority integration method in the special case (not identify). The final result is the same to the majority integration method in the normal case. In the not identify case, the final result is the same to the average integration method. In order to test the feasibility of this integration method, we have also tested in the 80 flower images and two kernel functions like above. The experimental results show in the below tables:

Table 9. Fusion of Majority and Average integration method in RGB color space and SVM using Gaussian kernel function

Flower Image	SVM_R	SVM_G	SVM_B	Fusion Method
Rose	13/27	22/27	20/27	25/27
Lotus	20/25	23/25	25/25	25/25
Daisy	14/28	25/28	27/28	26/28
All	**47/80**	**69/80**	**72/80**	**76/80**
Precision	**59%**	**86%**	**90%**	**95%**

Table 10. Fusion of Majority and Average integration method in HSI color space and SVM using Gaussian kernel function

Flower Image	SVM_H	SVM_S	SVM_I	Fusion Method
Rose	14/27	16/27	11/27	19/27
Lotus	22/25	24/25	20/25	23/25
Daisy	26/28	22/28	14/28	26/28
All	**62/80**	**62/80**	**45/80**	**68/80**
Precision	**78%**	**78%**	**56%**	**85%**

Table 11. Fusion of Majority and Average integration method in RGB color space and SVM using Polynomial kernel function

Flower Image	SVM_R	SVM_G	SVM_B	Fusion Method
Rose	14/27	26/27	15/27	24/27
Lotus	19/25	16/25	25/25	22/25
Daisy	15/28	25/28	27/28	27/28
All	**48/80**	**67/80**	**67/80**	**73/80**
Precision	**60%**	**84%**	**84%**	**91%**

Table 12. Fusion of Majority and Average integration method in RGB color space and SVM using Polynomial kernel function

Flower Image	SVM_R	SVM_G	SVM_B	Fusion Method
Rose	17/27	12/27	13/27	21/27
Lotus	20/25	21/25	19/25	22/25
Daisy	28/28	23/28	17/28	26/28
All	**65/80**	**56/80**	**49/80**	**69/80**
Precision	**81%**	**70%**	**61%**	**86%**

The experimental results show that the precision of the fusion of majority and average integration method have improved the precision of the classification result of each SVM component. This method gets precision more than the average integration method. The experimental results show that this integration method is suitable to use Gaussian kernel function than Polynomial kernel function.

4   Analysis of Experiments

The flower images database get from The Oxford Flower Dataset (www.flowers.vg) are used for our experiments.

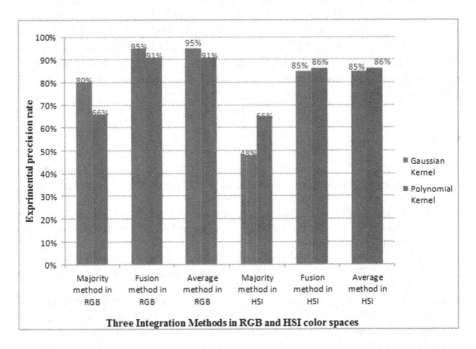

Fig. 7. Overview of experimental results in flower image classification

The majority method is very easy to develop, but the average and fusion methods are better method than majority method in general. The precision of average method are minor higher than fusion method. The Gaussian kernel function of SVM is suitable to RGB color features, while the Polynomial kernel function of SVM is suitable to HIS color features.

All experimental results show that the feature of RGB color are better than HSI color when we use it to apply for flower image classification. The image in the flower dataset often focuses on the flower object and changes the intensity a little. So that HIS color with the Intensity element does not support much the classification processes.

5   Conclusion

In this paper, we propose and implement a multi Support Vector Machines model having two parameters (m and L) to apply for image classification, called multi_SVM. Where, L = the number of categories of images = the number of hyperplanes of one SVM; m = the number of a flower image's feature vectors = the number of SVM(s).

Multi_SVM model is easy to design and deploy for the specific image classification application with high precision. We can apply multi_SVM for the complex image such flower or facial images. When the number of categories of images increases, we just increase the number of hyperplanes of one SVM. It means that the developer only update the SVM component. Multi_SVM model has been applied for three categories of flower image classification in Oxford Flower Dataset and the precision rate can reach 95% in the best case. The experimental results show the feasibility of our proposal model. Multi_SVM model require that the number of image's feature vectors must be a constant.

References

1. Yang, Z., Rongyi, H., Muwei, J.: Comparison of Two Methods for Texture Image Classification. In: Second International Workshop on Computer Science and Engineering, WCSE 2009, vol. 1, pp. 65–68. IEEE Press (2009)
2. Linlin, S., Li, B., Picton, P.: Facial recognition/verification using Gabor wavelets and kernel methods. In: International Conference on Image Processing, ICIP 2004, vol. 3, pp. 1433–1436. IEEE Press (2004)
3. White, K.P., Kundu, B., Mastrangelo, C.M.: Classification of Defect Clusters on Semiconductor Wafers Via the Hough Transformation. IEEE Transactions on Semiconductor Manufacturing 21(2), 272–278 (2008)
4. Zhao, L., Guo, Z.: Face Recognition Method Based on Adaptively Weighted Block-Two Dimensional Principal Component Analysis. In: Third International Conference on Computational Intelligence, Communication Systems and Networks (CICSyN), pp. 22–25. IEEE Press (2011)
5. Xingfu, Z., Xiangmin, R.: Two Dimensional Principal Component Analysis based Independent Component Analysis for face recognition. In: International Conference on Multimedia Technology (ICMT), pp. 934–936. IEEE Press (2011)
6. Wakin, M.B.: Sparse Image and Signal Processing: Wavelets, Curvelets, Morphological Diversity. Signal Processing Magazine 28(5), 144–146 (2011)
7. McSherry, D., Stretch, C.: An Analysis of Order Dependence in k-NN. In: Coyle, L., Freyne, J. (eds.) AICS 2009. LNCS, vol. 6206, pp. 207–218. Springer, Heidelberg (2010)
8. Madden, M.G.: A New Bayesian Network Structure for Classification Tasks. In: O'Neill, M., Sutcliffe, R.F.E., Ryan, C., Eaton, M., Griffith, N.J.L. (eds.) AICS 2002. LNCS (LNAI), vol. 2464, p. 203. Springer, Heidelberg (2002)
9. Li, S., Zhu, L., Jiang, T.-Z.: Active Shape Model Segmentation Using Local Edge Structures and AdaBoost. In: Yang, G.Z., Jiang, T.-Z. (eds.) MIAR 2004. LNCS, vol. 3150, pp. 121–128. Springer, Heidelberg (2004)
10. Yong, L., Xin, Y.: Negatively correlated neural networks for classification. Artificial Life and Robotics 3(4), 255–259 (1999)
11. Rud, S., Yang, J.-S.: A Support Vector Machine (SVM) Classification Approach to Heart Murmur Detection. In: Zhang, L., Lu, B.-L., Kwok, J. (eds.) ISNN 2010, Part II. LNCS, vol. 6064, pp. 52–59. Springer, Heidelberg (2010)

12. Agrawal, S., Verma, N.K., Tamrakar, P., Sircar, P.: Content Based Color Image Classification using SVM. In: Eighth International Conference on Information Technology: New Generations (ITNG), pp. 1090–1094. IEEE Press (2011)
13. Devis, T., Jordi, M., Mikhail, K., Gustavo, C.V.: Structured Output SVM for Remote Sensing Image Classification. Journal of Signal Processing Systems 65(3), 301–310 (2011)
14. Demir, B., Erturk, S.: Improving SVM classification accuracy using a hierarchical approach for hyperspectral images. In: 16th IEEE International Conference on Image Processing (ICIP), pp. 2848–2852. IEEE Press (2009)

Clustering Hierarchical Data Using SOM Neural Network

Le Anh Tu[1], Nguyen Quang Hoan[2], and Le Son Thai[1]

[1] Thai Nguyen University of Information and Communication Technology
[2] Posts and Telecommunications Institute of Technology
{anhtucntt,lesonthai}@gmail.com, quanghoanptit@yahoo.com.vn

Abstract. This paper proposes a solution for clustering hierarchical data using SOM neural network. The training process that combines data-partition and network-partition allows forming an automated hierarchical tree structure representing the clustering process more detailed from the root node to the leaf node. In which the root node and intermediate nodes act as the orientation for data distribution, and the leaf nodes represent real clusters of data. This training tree structure allows programming parallel processing to speed up network training. In addition, applying the trained network could be more efficient because the search process performed on the tree structure.

Keywords: neural network, kohonen, self organizing map, clustering data, data mining.

1   Introduction

Teuvo Kohonen developed SOM neural network in the 80s. This is the feed-forward neural network using of the competitive learning, unsupervised (or self-organizing), allowing mapping data from a multi-dimensional space to two–dimensional space, thereby creating a feature map of the data [7]. SOM is an appropriate tool to solve the problem of data clustering, an important preprocessing step in data mining [1]. When applying the SOM neural network for clustering data, it consists of three phases:

-   Phase 1: Training the network with sample data set.
-   Phase 2: Applying the trained network.
-   Phase 3: Visualize network (usually using the gray level map, U-Matrix, to present data distribution image [6])

However, the standard SOM model requires computation time relatively long (both training time and applying the trained network). The main reason is Kohonen matrix must be large enough to describe all features of the data (usually thousands of neurons), while with each input vector, the network will perform sequential search across the entire Kohonen matrix. Currently, there have been many studies on this issue, for example: Batch SOM algorithm [2] speeds up training by deferring the updates of weights to the end of a learning epoch (after browsing all the training samples); Tree-Structured SOM algorithm (TS-SOM) [4] builds a training tree

P.C. Vinh et al. (Eds.): ICCASA 2012, LNICST 109, pp. 282–289, 2013.

structure, in which each node on the tree is a neuron. The numbers of sub-nodes of each node are equal and increase according to exponential function. The nodes at the same level forms a layer, upper layer trains the underlying one. For example, the first layer has four nodes (neuron), each node has 4 sub-nodes, so the second layer has 16 nodes, and the third layer has 64 nodes... The training time is faster because finding the winning neuron (Best Matching Unit - BMU) at each step of the training process is performed following the branches of the tree. Alfredo F. Costa proposed a tree structure representing the clusters, in which each node of the tree is a Kohonen map [3]. Each node is fully trained as standard SOM, then builds the U-Matrix and uses this information to form the sub-nodes. This solution is not effective because the fact that at the root node has finished training and U-Matrix of the root node completely visualized input data (step 3 above). However, data analysis (data-partition) following tree structure is a good idea to program processing in parallel.

After studying the standard model and some improved models of SOM, we found that there are two issues needed to be considered in order to improve the efficiency of SOM neural network when applied to large data sets. Firstly, reducing the size of Kohonen matrix but still fully describing the features of data. Secondly, having mechanisms to search and process data in parallel on different parts of the network.

This paper proposes a hierarchical training technique based on threshold T, non-similar on the features of the data, which allows segmenting data (data-partition) according to the hierarchy tree structure. Each node of the tree is a Kohonen matrix, in which the root node and the intermediate nodes (branch nodes) only serve to orient the data segmenting, leaf nodes represent real clusters of data. Thus, the size of the original Kohonen matrix will reduce, and the size of sub Kohonen will reduce gradually after each branching. At each node, threshold T clusters the neurons in the process of training. Each cluster in the parent node is the basis for establishing a child node. All data vectors that belong to a cluster of the parent node will be used to train the child node corresponding to that cluster. At the next training level, when threshold T declines α value, repeat the training and develop the children nodes for all the current leaf nodes. Training process will stop when the threshold T reduces to a minimum value ε.

The rest of the paper include: Section 2 presents the standard SOM model and U-Matrix, Section 3 presents the principle of neural clustering in the training process based on the threshold T, Section 4 provides a hierarchical tree training architecture, Section 5 presents the experimental results and the final section concludes and comments on the presented solution in the articles.

2   SOM Neural Network and U-Matrix

SOM neural network includes an input layer and a output layer called Kohonen layer. Kohonen layer is often organized as a two dimensional matrix of neurons. Each unit i (neurons) in the Kohonen layer is attached a weight vector $w_i=[w_{i1}, w_{i2},... ,w_{in}]$, with n is the input vector size, w_{ij} is the weight of neuron i corresponding to the input j. Network training process is repeated several times, at iteration t, three steps are done:

- Step 1- find the BMU: randomly select an input v from the data set, find b neuron that has the smallest *dist* distance function in the Kohonen matrix (frequently use functions Euclidian, Manhattan or Vector Dot Product). b neuron is called BMU.

$$dist = \| v - w_b \| = \min_i \{ \| v - m_i \| \} \qquad (1)$$

- Step 2- determine the neighborhood radius of the BMU:

$\sigma(t) = \sigma_0 \exp\left[-\dfrac{t}{\lambda}\right]$ is interpolation function of radius (decreasing as the numbers of iterations), where σ_0 is the initial radius; time constant $\lambda = \dfrac{K}{\log(\sigma_0)}$, where K is the total number of iterations.

- Step 3- update the weights of the neurons in the neighborhood radius of the BMU in a trend closer to the input vector v :

$$w_i(t+1) = w_i(t) + \alpha(t) h_{bi}(t)\left[v - w_i(t)\right] \qquad (2)$$

where $\alpha(t) = \alpha_0 \exp\left[-\dfrac{t}{\lambda}\right]$ is the learning speed interpolation function, with α_0 is the initial value of the learning rate; $h_{bi}(t)$ is the interpolation function over learning times, shows the effect of distance to the learning process, can be calculated by the formula $h_{bi}(t) = \exp\left[-\dfrac{\| r_b - r_i \|^2}{2\sigma^2(t)}\right]$ where r_b and r_i position of the neuron b and neuron i in the Kohonen matrix.

To observe the feature map of the data, visual matrix using gray level (U-Matrix) is often used (Figure 1). The bright region in the matrix represents the clusters (the distance between the weight vectors of neurons is small), dark areas (large distance) which is used to separate areas between clusters. Agglomerative algorithm [8] is used to determine the boundary between the clusters.

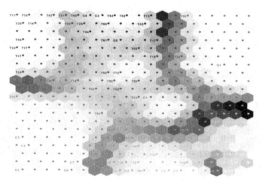

Fig. 1. Illustration of U-Matrix

Indeed, each neuron in the Kohonen layer represents one or several data samples, therefore the clustering data is clustering the neurons. The paper [5] we proposed improved SOM algorithm that allowed us to identify data clusters (clusters of neurons) and labeled on each neuron on Kohonen matrix in the process of network training without a visual matrix. Applying standard SOM to cluster data, it has computing complexity is $O(n^4)$, whereas using improved SOM, it is $O(n^3)$. The principles identifying clusters will be presented in the next section.

3   Principles of Neuron Cluster in the Training Process

For each neuron in the neighborhood radius of the BMU (including BMU), besides updating the weight vector (step 3), we labeled neurons with clustered index based on the following four principles:

- *Principles of cluster formation:* if BMU does not yet belong to any cluster, a new cluster is formed, which include BMU and neurons in the neighborhood radius of the BMU if these neurons are also not members of any clusters. Figure 2, BMU and N_1 do not belong to any cluster, N_1 is within the impact of BMU, therefore forming a new cluster of BMU and N_1.

- *Principle of neurons dispute:* A neuron M is deemed to be a dispute if it was attached to a cluster G_1 and located in the radius of the impact of the BMU. Let k_1 be the feature difference between the M and G_1; k_2 is the feature difference between the M and BMU. If $k_1 < k_2$, M belongs to cluster G_1, otherwise, M belongs to the cluster of the BMU. Figure 2, N_2 is of cluster 1 but located within a radius of the impact of the BMU, so disputes occur between cluster of the BMU and cluster 1.

- *Principle of cluster splitting:* If BMU belongs to a certain cluster, check splitting condition: let k be the different feature value of BMU from its cluster. If $k >= T$ (splitting threshold), BMU will form a new cluster, similarly to principles of cluster formation; otherwise, BMU will extend cluster

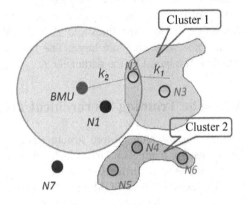

Fig. 2. Illustration of the principle of the cluster formation and neurons dispute

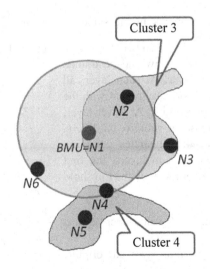

Fig. 3. Illustration of the principle of the cluster formation and neurons dispute

which contain it using the principle of extension. Figure 3, the BMU is the neuron of cluster 3, splitting condition should be considered.

- *Principle of cluster extension:* If BMU is a member of a cluster, and splitting condition is false, it will consolidate its cluster by admitting more neurons in its radius impact as the principle of cluster formation. Figure 3, if the BMU does not satisfy the splitting condition (but still in cluster 3), it will admit N_6 to cluster 3 and N_4 will be disputed with the cluster 4.

The four principles above did not entirely alter the data feature results of network, because in fact they only assigned cluster index for each neuron. Therefore, the quality of the Kohonen map is constant. However, the numbers of clusters formed depend on the splitting threshold T. If T is large, the numbers of clusters formed is small. Otherwise, they are large. The next section presents the training hierarchical tree structure based on the parameter T.

4   The Training Hierarchical Tree Structure

The training hierarchical tree structure comes from the idea of dividing the data into large clusters, from each large cluster further divided into smaller clusters, and from the small cluster is further subdivided into smaller clusters. In which, each node of the tree is designed as a SOM neural network, allowing to cluster data more detail gradually from the root node to the leaf node. A parent node after having been trained will be used to divide its data into subsets. Each subset of data continues to be used to train the corresponding child nodes generated. This division process is based on the threshold T, with $\varepsilon \leq T < \max_{i,j}\left\{\| v_i - v_j \|\right\}$, where ε is the limit on the value of non-similar elements in the same cluster, $\max_{i,j}\left\{\| v_i - v_j \|\right\}$ is the value of the largest difference between two certain elements in the entire data set.

Tree will grow and be trained on each layer. At each layer, all the leaf nodes are trained with the same threshold T. At lower layer, T decreases a value α until T=ε. Figure 4 illustrates training structure with m layers, the first layer is trained with threshold $T = T_1 < \max_{i,j}\left\{\| v_i - v_j \|\right\}$, on each layer, T value decreases α until it reachs ε value.

On the first layer, all original data are trained by only a single Kohonen whose size is $n x n$, and uses splitting threshold T_1. Results

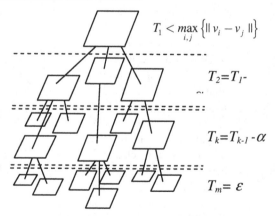

$$T_1 < \max_{i,j}\left\{\| v_i - v_j \|\right\}$$

$$T_2 = T_1 -$$

$$T_k = T_{k-1} - \alpha$$

$$T_m = \varepsilon$$

Fig. 4. Illustration of the training hierarchical tree structure

were k subsets of $I=\{I_1, I_2, ..., I_k\}$. On the second layer, each subset $I_1, I_2,..., I_k$ will be trained by each corresponding Kohonen $K_{I1}, K_{I2}, ..., K_{Ik}$ and uses splitting threshold $T_2=T_1-\alpha$. Thus each set I_i (where $i=1..k$) trained by K_{Ii} was divided into subsets $I_{i1}, I_{i2},...$ On the next layers, repeat the reduction T and train each child node with the corresponding subset of it, until $T=\varepsilon$.

The size of the child nodes will be reduced gradually depending on the size of the parent node and the ratio of the number of elements in the subset used to train it with the number of elements used to train the parent node.

Let n_{child} be size of child node: $n_{child} = \left(\dfrac{\mid I_{child} \mid}{\mid I_{parent} \mid} \right)^{\beta} n_{parent}$, where $\mid.\mid$ represents the cardinality of the set, β is used to limit the child node size reduction in compared with the parent node size (we tested with $\beta=0.3$).

Because the role of the root node and the intermediate nodes are data oriented division, the root node size does not need to be large enough to describe all features of the data set. This significantly reduces the training time at each node. In addition, data is divided as tree structure to train in parallel on many Kohonen networks, so training time and application time of the trained network are faster than standard SOM model.

To test these evaluations, we have written the test program on a personal computer, using multithreaded programming technique combining recursion. These experimental results will be presented in the next section.

5   Experimental Results

To facilitate the visual observation and evaluate research results, we choose the problem of color image segment. The input data set is the pixels. Each pixel is considered as a vector of input data including three elements corresponding to three colors R, G, B. Thus, the network has three inputs and the size of the data set is the size of an image (up to hundred thousands of pixels).

We adjust the training parameters for both models training hierarchical tree and standard SOM model (applying the four principles presented in the section 3) to reach the similar result of the formation of clusters and evaluate the effectiveness of execution time.

The standard SOM model: size of Kohonen is 30x30, splitting threshold T=30.

The training hierarchical tree model: size of original Kohonen is 11x11, splitting threshold $30<=T<=120$ (with $\varepsilon=30$, $T_1=120<$ $\max_{i,j}\{\parallel v_i - v_j \parallel\} = \sqrt{255^2 + 255^2 + 255^2} \simeq 442$), at each layer, T reduces $\alpha=20$.

We tested four different sized images, each image ran 5 times. The table below presents the test results.

In all cases, the training time and time applying trained network to cluster of hierarchical tree model are faster. The first two images with the size of about 26

Original image	Times	Standard SOM model			Hierarchical tree model		
		Time (ms)		Image result/ numbers of clusters	Time (ms)		Image result/ numbers of clusters
		Training	Applying clustering		Training	Applying clustering	
	1	4747.27	1813.10		1974.32	623.03	
	2	4627.26	1897.45		2012.35	708.25	
	3	4759.54	1854.32		1987.32	732.12	
	4	4813.65	1864.35		2103.54	698.65	
	5	4687.25	1824.54		2014.36	743.25	
163X159	avg	4726.99	1850.75	111-130	2018.38	701.06	127-155
	1	4655.26	1592.35		1163.06	679.03	
	2	4568.25	1685.32		1254.32	684.35	
	3	4687.26	1672.32		1198.32	687.32	
	4	4756.21	1612.32		1245.35	702.35	
	5	4587.25	1586.21		1234.15	624.21	
160X160	avg	4650.85	1629.70	22-29	1219.04	675.45	29-35
	1	19665.56	6833.26		4025.32	2313.25	
	2	19565.69	6696.21		4059.23	2268.12	
	3	19615.58	6787.65		3998.26	2298.32	
	4	19625.76	6681.84		4065.32	2274.54	
	5	19584.84	6904.65		4100.23	2289.78	
350x300	avg	19611.49	6780.72	32-36	4049.67	2288.80	31-36
	1	41307.32	14346.54		7738.44	4107.23	
	2	42563.24	14687.25		7954.32	4321.25	
	3	43124.87	14753.24		7542.21	4215.36	
	4	40154.65	13968.24		7652.32	4198.25	
	5	42564.65	14885.98		7764.24	4253.35	
550x382	avg	41942.95	14528.25	80-110	7730.31	4219.09	77-109

Fig. 5. Comparison of experimental results of the two models

thousand pixels, hierarchical tree model has training time of approximately 2.3 to 3.8 times faster, and application time is about 2.5 times faster. Two next images (the numbers of pixels are over 100 thousands) hierarchical tree model has faster training time of approximately 4.8 to 5.4 times, and faster application time 3 to 3.5 times. This shows that the speed advantage of the hierarchical tree model increases when the data size is large. We have tested with variety of input images and received the similar results.

6   Conclusions

The training hierarchical tree structure significantly reduces the network training time by two main reasons. Firstly, the size of Kohonen matrix reduced (due to the features of the data are not represented on a Kohonen matrix, but represented on the sub Kohonen matrixes which are the leaf node of the training tree). Secondly, allowed segmenting the data to train in parallel by many SOM neural networks. In addition, the training model is represented by a tree structure so the application time of trained network to cluster data is also dramatically reduced.

In terms of the quality, data features are completely unchanged since the hierarchical tree model does not change the standard SOM algorithm but only segments data for parallel processing.

However, as a standard SOM model, proposing a suitable configuration for the network is difficult. It is needed to test several times to select the parameters (original Kohonen matrix size and scope of the threshold T and the reduced value of T after each layer) best suited to each type of data. In principle, the smaller the matrix size is, the faster the original Kohonen network runs, but if it is too small , the efficiency of the characterization data of the network will decrease like the standard SOM model; if T_l is too large, this will affect the efficiency of data segmenting of the original Kohonen and Kohonens in the first layers.

References

[1] Han, J., Kamber, M.: Data Mining - Concepts and Techniques, ch. 8. Morgan Kaufmann (2001)
[2] Silva, M.: A hybrid parallel SOM algorithm for large maps in data-mining. In: 13th Portuguese Conference on Artificial Intelligence (EPIA 2007), Workshop on Business Intelligence. IEEE, Guimaraes (2007)
[3] Costa, M.: A new tree-structured self-organizing map for data analysis. In: Proceedings of the International Joint Conference on IJCNN (2001)
[4] Laaksonen, J., Koskela, M., Oja, E.: Application of Tree Structured Self-Organizing Maps in Content-Based Image Retrieval. In: Proceedings of 9th ICANN 1999, Edinburgh, UK (1999)
[5] Tu, L.A., Hoan, N.Q.: Improving som neural network algorithm for color image clustering problem. In: Proceedings of VCCA Conference-VietNam (2011)
[6] Ultsch, A., Peter Siemon, H.: Kohonen's self-organizing feature maps for exploratory data analysis. In: Proceedings of the International Neural Network Conference (INNC 1990), pp. 305–308. Kluwer (1990)
[7] Kohonen, T.: Self-Organizing Maps, 3rd edn. Springer (2001)
[8] https://rtmath.net/help/html/29f7cb00-39a1-4fc0-af60-52925f074edd.htm

Modeling and Verifying WS-CDL Using Event-B

Hong Anh Le and Ninh Thuan Truong

VNU - University of Engineering and Technology
144 Xuan Thuy, Cau Giay, Hanoi
{anhlh.di10,thuantn}@vnu.edu.vn

Abstract. The Web Services Choreography Description Language (WS-CDL) is an XML-based language that describes web service composition in the view point of choreography by defining their common and complementary observable behavior, where ordered message exchanges result in accomplishing a common business goal [3]. However, WS-CDL does not come with formal specification, nor with official vefication tools. In this paper, we present an approach to formalize and verify choreography composition described in WS-CDL. In the first phase, we propose to use Event-B as a formal method to model choreography interactions by transforming WS-CDL entities to Event-B elements. We use the Rodin platform, in the next phase, to verify some properties of the translated model. Finally, we run an example to illustrate our approach in detail.

Keywords: WS-CDL, composition, verification, Event-B.

1 Introduction

Building platform-independent and distributed software such as web services is a growing trend in software architecture. A Web service is a software system designed to support machine-to-machine interaction over a network. It is mainly based upon WSDL, UDDI, and SOAP standards to describe data type's exchanges, make services discoverable and specify patterns to invoke specific services respectively. In order to group a number of web services into a complex one, we can use some approaches such as choreography and orchestration composition. Composition of web services is increasingly accepted as a paradigm for integration of applications within and across organization boundaries.

The choreography view focuses on the composition in the global observation, while the orchestration describes the interaction between one participant and the others. There are some XML-based languages such as BPEL[13], WS-CDL [3] which are used to describe the composition. WS-CDL focuses on describing the business protocol among different participant roles and the participants perform all the behaviors. Due to lacking of formal semantics and grounding, ambiguous interpretation of a WS-CDL description possibly occurs. Therefore, research in the verification of choreographies' properties has been a recently emerging topic.

Event-B [2] is an evolution of the B method [1] that is more suitable for developing large reactive and distributed systems. Software development in Event-B

P.C. Vinh et al. (Eds.): ICCASA 2012, LNICST 109, pp. 290–299, 2013.

begins by abstractly specifying the requirements of the whole system and then refining them through several steps to reach a description of the system in such a detail that can be translated into code. The consistency of each model and the relationship between an abstract model and its refinements are obtained by formal proofs. Support tools have been provided for Event-B specification and proof in the Rodin platform.

In this paper, we propose an approach to formalize a choreography model by a formal method, e.g. Event-B. Specifically, we present some rules to transform a WS-CDL package to an Event-B model. Some properties of the model can be automatically (or interactively) proved through proof obligations generated from Rodin platform [2] such as deadlock freeness, order of exchanged messages and some business requirements. The advantage of our approach is that the use of Event-B as a method to model choreography interactions since its strong point is modeling multi-agents and reactive systems. Our main idea comes from the similarity between some parts of WS-CDL and Event-B; hence we can formalize a choreography scenario by an Event-B model naturally. Moreover, the approach is such practical that we can implement a tool transforming a choreography model to an Event-B model (semi-) automatically. It makes sense as we can bring the formal verification to web service implementation. It also overcomes one of disadvantages that make formal methods absent in the web service based software because of the complexity of modeling.

The rest of the paper is structured as follows: Section 2 provides some background of WS-CDL and Event-B. Followed by Section 3, we propose an approach to model a WS-CDL package by formalizing its elements using Event-B method. Section 4 presents an example of Purchase order to illustrate our approach. Section 5 summarizes some related works. We give some conclusion and present future works in Section 6.

2   Backgrounds

As our approach focuses on modeling of web service choreography by using Event-B method, in this section, we introduce briefly background of Event-B and give an overview of WS-CDL.

2.1   Event-B

Event-B is a formal method for system-level modeling and analysis. Key features of Event-B are the use of set theory as a modeling notation, the use of refinement to represent systems at different abstraction levels and the use of mathematical proof to verify consistency between refinement levels [2]. An Event B model encodes a state transition system where the variables represent the state and the events represent the transitions from one state to another. A basic structure of an Event-B model consists of a MACHINE and a CONTEXT.

A MACHINE is defined by a set of clauses which is able to refine another MACHINE. We briefly introduce main concepts in Event-B as follows:

VARIABLES   represent the state variables of the specification model.

INVARIANTS described by first order logic expressions, the properties of the attributes defined in the VARIABLES clause. Typing information, functional and safety properties are described in this clause. These properties are true in the whole model. Invariants need to be preserved by events clauses.

THEOREMS define a set of logical expressions that can be deduced from the invariants. Unlike invariants, they do not need to be preserved by events.

EVENTS define all the events that occur in a given model. Each event is characterized by its guard (i.e. a first order logic expression involving variables). An event is fired when its guard evaluates to true. If several guards evaluate to true, only one is fired with a non deterministic choice. The events occurring in an Event B model affect the state described in VARIABLES clause.

An Event B model may refer to a CONTEXT describing a static part where all the relevant properties and hypotheses are defined. A CONTEXT consists of the following items:

SETS describe a set of abstract and enumerated types.

CONSTANTS represent the constants used by the model.

AXIOMS describe with first order logic expressions, the properties of the attributes defined in the CONSTANTS clause. Types and constraints are described in this clause.

THEOREMS are logical expressions that can be deduced from the axioms.

2.2   WS-CDL

Web services composition integrates the existed available ones in order to form a new functionality. Recall that, choreography composition describes the interactions between collections of services without a central peer and all participants are treated equally. WS-CDL is a mark-up language for choreography composition which is first proposed in 2004. A WS-CDL choreography description is contained in a package which is essentially a container for a collection of activities performed the participants [6]. We introduce some elements of WS-CDL shortly as follows:

InformationType: This element identifies the type of information used within a choreography to avoid referencing directly to data types in an XML schema or a WS-CDL document.

RoleTypes: A RoleType enumerates the potential observable behaviors that a participant can exhibit in order to interact together.

RelationshipType: A Relationship Type describes the relationship between two parties in order to collaborate successfully.

The Choregraphy-Notation part specifies interactions between parties of a choreography. We address some concepts which are used frequently in a choreography:

Table 1. Translation from WSCDL static elements to Event-B

WS-CDL elements	Event-B concepts
informationType, participantType, channelType	Set
roleType	Constant
relationshipType	Axiom

Activities: There are three types of activity such as control-flow activities, Work-unit activities and basic activities. The first ones consist of three types namely sequence, choice and parallel activities. A work-unit activity describes the conditional and repeated execution of an activity. A basic activity includes Interaction, NoAction, SilentAction, Assign, and Perform element. Interaction is the most important element of WS-CDL.

Work-units: A work-unit describes constraints that need to be fulfilled to perform activities. It has guards and repeat conditions optionally. Enclosed activities are performed when the guard condition is evaluated to be true.

Variables: The information sent or received during an interaction is described by a named variable and an optional recordReference element in the exchange description. Variables contain values and have an informationType represented as a type of variables.

3 Formalizing and Verifying WS-CDL

From the similarity between some parts of WS-CDL and Event-B, we propose to use Event-B as a method to formalize a WS-CDL model. Since a WS-CDL package is composed of static and dynamic parts, we translate them to Event-B elements separately. After the transformation, we are able to verify some properties based on achieved Event-B model.

3.1 Formalizing Static Part

Before formalizing choreography interactions, we introduce some definitions related to Event-B specification that are useful in the modeling process.

Definition 1. A choreography scenario is modeled by a pair $ch = <S, In>$ where S is a set of static information, In represents for the dynamic part. S is stated as a 5-tuple: $S = <It, C, Rl, P, R>$, where It is a set of **Information-Type** in a WS-CDL package, C and Rl indicate **Channels** and **Relationship** parts respectively, **Participants** and **Roles** elements are represented by P and R. The definition of In is discussed in Subsection 3.2.

Based on the formal definition, we translate WS-CDL elements in the static part to Event-B concepts as in Table 1.

3.2 Formalizing Dynamic Part

The dynamic part is the most important part of a WS-CDL package as it describes how the participants interact with each other to form a web service composition. In order to make the approach more clear, we first model interactions in the choreography by an Event-B model. After that, we translate elements in the dynamic part of a WS-CDL package to an Event-B model.

Modeling Choreography Interactions: Interaction is the essential part of the composition which shows how a new functionality is composed from existing web services. We tranlsate the interaction among two colaboration parties to an Event-B EVENT and formalize the exchanged message by a pair $\{n \mapsto MSG\}$ where n is the order of message MSG. The guard of the translated event is also the order of the message as illustrated in Figure 1

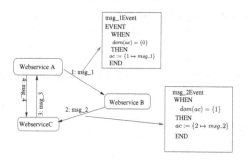

Fig. 1. Transformation from choregraphy interactions to Event-B EVENTs

Formalizing Interaction Part of a WS-CDL Package: We divide the choreography part of a WS-CDL file into two parts: variables and interactions description. Hence, we model In as a tuple $S = <Var, Ac>$, where Var specifies WS-CDL variables, Ac denotes WS-CDL interactions. We translate the former into Event-B variables, while, followed the approach of modeling interactions in the choreography, we formalize the later by Event-B events. In order to do the translation, we present some rules to transform most important WS-CDL entities involving in the dynamic part such as $Work - unit$, $Activity$ to Event-B concepts.

Activities: An activity entity comprises of several components including basic and ordering activities and work-units.

- Basic activities: A basic activity represents the lowest actions performed in a choreography such as an interaction, an assign, a silent, a noAction and a finalize activity. We encode a basic activity by a Event-B Event, more speficialy, the syntax of translation is prensented in Table 2.
- Structured activities:
  A structured activity can be a sequence, parallel or choice activity. We model it by a set of Event-B events, for instance, a sequence activity is transformed to a set of Event-B events. We use an Event-B VARIABLE for representing

Table 2. Translation of WS-CDL basic activities to Event-B

WS-CDL basic activity	Event-B concepts
$<$assign $roleType = $ "$qname$" $>$ $<$copy $name = $ "$ncname$" $>$ $<$source $variable = $ "var_name1"$/>$ $<$target $variable = $ "var_name2"$/>$ $</$copy$>$ $</$assign$>$	WHERE Any THEN $var\_name2 := var\_name1$ END
$<$exchange $name = $ "$exchange\_name$" $informationType = infoType$ $action = $ "$request$" $>$ $<$send $variable = var1/>$ $< receivevariable = var2/>$ $</$exchange$>$	INVARIANTS $var1 \in infoType$ and $var2 \in infoType$ EVENT WHEN $dom(msg) = \{i\}$ THEN $msg = \{i + 1 \mapsto exchange\_name\}$ END

Table 3. Transformation of a Workunit to an Event-B Event

WS-CDL work-unit	Event-B Event
$<$workunit $name = $ "$unitname$" $guard = $ "$xsd : booleanXPath - expression$"? $repeat = $ "$xsd : booleanXPath - expression$"? Activity-Notation $< /$workunit$>$	EVENT $unitname$ WHEN $guard$ and $repeat$ THEN body END

the order of each basic activity in the sequence and it is managed inside the body of each event. A parallel activity is formalized by a combination of events by means of parallel operator ∥.

Work-unit: Since a Work-unit acts similarly to an Event-B event, we transform guard and repeatable conditions of a Work-unit to guard clauses of an Event-B event. Activities inside a Work-unit are represented by operations in the body part of an Event-B event. These operations will activate events corresponding to each Activity. The transformation is illustrated in Table 3.

4 An Example

In this section, we describe a well-known example of Purchase order. We then translate the WS-CDL package of this example to an Event-B model according to the rules presented in Subsection 3

4.1 Purchase Order Scenario Description

The scenario involves four participants: Buyer, Seller, CreditCard and Store services. The Buyer initiates the choreography by sending a purchase request to the Buyer with product and credit card information. The Seller then request to check product information with the Store service and the validity of the Buyer's credit card. If both results are positive then the Seller will reply a Purchase Order confirmation, otherwise the Seller rejects the request.

4.2 Mapping Purchase Order Model in WS-CDL to Event-B

In this Subsection, we describe the Purchase order scenario by a WS-CDL package. We then transform the description in the format of WS-CDL into Event-B model following the rules we define in Section 3.

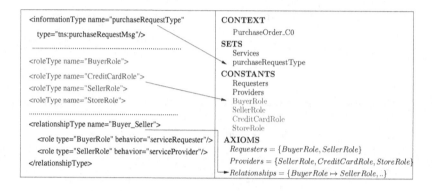

Fig. 2. Transformation from WS-CDL static part to an Event-B model

As illustrated in Figure 2, four participants in the choreography are described by four WS-CDL RoleType elements which are modeled by a set of CONSTANTS such as *BuyerRole, SellerRole, CreditCardRole and StoreRole*. We define two Event-B SETS which are namely *Requesters, Providers* indicating *fromRole* and *toRole* properties of *relationshipType* items in this WS-CDL package. Since *InformationType* elements are variable types, we model them as clauses of Event-B SETs.

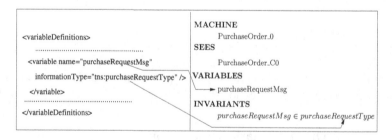

Fig. 3. Transformation from VARIABLES of WS-CDL to an Event-B VARIABLES.

In Figure 3, we model variable *PurchaseRequestMsg* which has type of *PurchaseRequestType* to an Event-B VARIABLE with the same name.

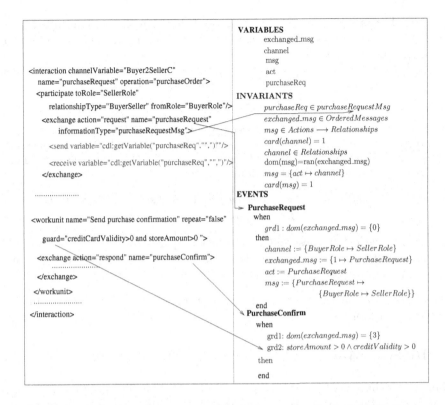

Fig. 4. Transformation from WS-CDL activities to Event-B EVENTS

The choreography part is modeled as depicted in Figure 4, the variable *exchanged_msg* represents messages exchanged between services which is ordered. The variable *channel* present the relationship between services. The exchange action *PurchaseRequest* and Work-unit *PurchaseConfirmation* modeled by two Event-B Events. Guard of this Work-unit is transformed to one of guards of *PurchaseConfirmation* Event-B event.

4.3 Verifying Purchase Order Model

Taking advantages of Event-B method and its support tool, after the transformation, we are able to verify some properties of the choreography interactions model as follows:

- First, we can verify that if the order of messages exchanged between collaboration parties are precise as choreography description . In our example, the order of exchanged messages is represented in the variable *exchanged_messages* and its preserving is showed by the following axiom:

$$exchanged\_messages \in \{0 \mapsto Init, 1 \mapsto PurchaseRequest, 2 \mapsto CheckCreditCard,$$
$$3 \mapsto CheckStore, 4 \mapsto PurchaseConfirm, 4 \mapsto PurchaseReject\}$$

– Second, messages are needed to be proved that they are exchanged between right source and destination web services. This property is modeled by two axioms in our example:

$$dom(msg) = ran(exchanged\_msg)$$
$$msg = \{act \mapsto channel\}$$

– Third, the last message of a choreography usually is the result of the composition, hence it is needed to be verified. In our example, the last message is either "PurchaseConfirm" or "PurchaseReject" but can not be both. This property is described by the axiom such as:

$$ran(last\_msg) = \{PurchaseConfirm\} \lor ran(last\_msg) = \{PurchaseReject\}$$
$$card(last\_msg) = 1$$

– Finally, live lock freeness and no deadlock properties are also proved through this Event-B model since there is at least one event is triggered and is no conflict between guards of the events.

These properties are proved to be preserved through all EVENTS of the model by the Rodin tool.

5   Related Works

Many papers have been proposed for verifying web service composition. G.Salaun *et al.* [15] developed a process algebra to derive the interactive behavior of a business process out from a BPEL specification, while A. Brogi *et al.* [7] presented the formalization of Web Service Choreography Interface (WSCI) using a process algebra approach(CCS), and showed the benefits of the formalization.

More recently, Yahong Li et al. [16] introduced a small language CDL in order to formalize WS-CDL. However, in order to verify the choreography composition, this formal model is translated into notations of SPIN and the general transformation rules are not given yet.

Pengcheng Zhang *et al.* [14] introduced an approach to model and verify WS-CDL using different UML diagrams. Gregorio Diaz *et al.* proposed a method to analyze WS-CDL by translating it into timed automata [10].

Idir Ait-Sadoune *et al.* [4] presented the transformation rules from an orchestration language, namely BPEL to an Event-B model and a support tool called BPEL2B. The structure of WS-CDL is clearly more complicated than the one of BPEL as the collaboration between participants in the choreography model is more complex without a central one.

6   Conclusion

In this paper, we have proposed an approach to formally model and verify web services choreography using Event-B. Our contribution includes the definition of rules to transform WS-CDL entities to Event-B elements and an example to illustrate the approach. The aim of the transformation is automatically verifying some properties such as order of messages, live lock freeness, deadlock, etc. in WS-CDL model. However, our approach is just suitable for a simple collection of interactions but not for complex position one. Our future work is focusing on using Event-B refinement mechanism and handling time out case in choreography. We are building a tool which allows a WS-CDL model to automatically transform to an Event-B model according to our defined rules.

Acknowledgments. This work is partly supported by the research project No. QG.11.32 granted by Vietnam National University, Hanoi.

References

1. B method web site, http://www.bmethod.com
2. Event-b and the rodin platform, http://www.event-b.org
3. Web services choreography description language version 1.0., http://www.w3.org/TR/2004/WD-ws-cdl-10-20041217/
4. Ait-Sadoune, I., Ait-Ameur, Y.: From bpel to event-b. In: IM FMT 2009, Dusseldorf, Germany (February 2009)
5. Ait-Sadoune, I., Ait-Ameur, Y.: Stepwise Design of BPEL Web Services Compositions: An Event_B Refinement Based Approach. In: Lee, R., Ormandjieva, O., Abran, A., Constantinides, C. (eds.) SERA 2010. SCI, vol. 296, pp. 51–68. Springer, Heidelberg (2010)
6. Dumas, M., Barros, A., Oaks, P.: A critical overview of web service choreography description language, ws-cdl (2005)
7. Brogi, A., Canal, C., Pimentel, E., Vallecillo, A.: Formalizing web service choreographies. Electron. Notes Theor. Comput. Sci. 105, 73–94 (2004)
8. Bryans, J.W., Wei, W.: Formal Analysis of BPMN Models Using Event-B. In: Kowalewski, S., Roveri, M. (eds.) FMICS 2010. LNCS, vol. 6371, pp. 33–49. Springer, Heidelberg (2010)
9. Decker, G., Puhlmann, F., Weske, M.: Formalizing Service Interactions. In: Dustdar, S., Fiadeiro, J.L., Sheth, A.P. (eds.) BPM 2006. LNCS, vol. 4102, pp. 414–419. Springer, Heidelberg (2006)
10. Diaz, G., Pardo, J.-J., Cambronero, M.-E., Valero, V., Cuartero, F.: Automatic translation of ws-cdl choreographies to timed automata. In: EPEW 2005/WS-FM 2005, Berlin, Heidelberg, pp. 230–242 (2005)
11. Foster, H., Kramer, J., Magee, J., Uchitel, S.: Model-based verification of web service compositions. In: 18th IEEE International Conference on Automated Software Engineering (ASE), pp. 152–165 (2003)
12. Hoang, T.S., Iliasov, A., Silva, R., Wei, W.: A survey on event-b decomposition. ECEASST 46 (2011)
13. Jordan, D.: Web services business process execution language (ws-bpel). standard version 2.0
14. Zhang, Y.P., Muccini, H., Li, B.: Model and verification of ws-cdl based on uml diagrams. International Journal of Software Engineering and Knowledge Engineering 20, 1119–1149 (2010)
15. Salaün, G., Bordeaux, L., Schaerf, M.: Describing and reasoning on web services using process algebra. In: ICWS 2004, Washington, DC, USA, p. 43 (2004)
16. Yang, H., Zhao, X., Qiu, Z., Pu, G., Wang, S.: A formal model for web service choreography description language (ws-cdl). In: ICWS 2006, pp. 893–894. IEEE Computer Society, Washington, DC (2006)

Aligning Multi Sequences on GPUs

Hong Phong Pham[1], Huu Duc Nguyen[1], and Thanh Thuy Nguyen[2]

[1] Department of Information System, Hanoi University of Science and Technology,
NOT is High Performance Computing Center
[2] Department of Computer Science, VNU - University of Engineering and Technology
{phongph.hut,ducnh.hut}@gmail.com,
nguyenthanhthuy@vnu.edu.vn

Abstract. Implementing Multi Sequence Alignment (MSA) problem using the method of progressive alignment is not feasible on common computing systems; it takes several hours or even days for aligning thousands of sequences if we use sequential versions of the most popular MSA algorithm - Clustal. In this paper, we present our parallel algorithm called CUDAClustal, a MSA parallel program. We have paralleled the first stage of the algorithm Clustal and achieved a significant speedup when compared to the sequential program running on a computer of Pentium 4 3.0 GHz processor. Our tests were performed on one GPU Geforce GTX 295 and they gave a great computing performance: the running time of CUDAClustal is smaller approximately 30 times than Clustal for the first stage. This shows the large benefit of GPU for solving the MSA problem and its high applicability in bioinformatics.

Keywords: Multi sequence alignment, Clustal, CUDA, GPU.

1 Introduction

Bioinformatics is an important field which affects almost sides of people life, it mainly go along with genetics and the science of researching genes. This paper solves problem of multi sequence alignment (MSA) problem [2]. The challenge here is to find out how to align thousands of ADN, ARN or protein sequences to identify similar residues and regions between them. There are methods of resolving this problem such as dynamic programming: Needleman-Wunsch [3], Smith-Waterman [1], progressive alignment methods: Clustal [4], T-Coffee [10].

However, those proposed methods face computational performance problem because the computational complexity of algorithms is very large. In the case of the algorithm Clustal, the complexity is $O(n^2 \times l^2)$, in which n is the number of sequences and l is the average length of sequences. This means that to align multi sequences with a dataset of 1000 sequences with the average length of 500, it takes several hours if using common CPUs. Therefore in this paper, we took advantage of the great computing power of GPU to grow computational performance. Results have shown a significant increase of computational performance when compared to the sequential program, demonstrating GPU's high applicability in bioinformatics field.

P.C. Vinh et al. (Eds.): ICCASA 2012, LNICST 109, pp. 300–309, 2013.
© Institute for Computer Sciences, Social Informatics and Telecommunications Engineering 2013

1.1   Pairwise Sequence Alignment Problem

In bioinformatics fields, one of the most important problems is sequence alignment problem, including two main problems: pairwise sequence alignment (PSA) [15] and multi sequence alignment (MSA) [2]. Firstly, we examine the problem PSA; it is the foundation for the MSA problem. Supposing that we have a pair of sequences {A,B} satisfying the following properties:

- $A = a_1 a_2 \dots a_{l_a},\ B = b_1 b_2 \dots b_{l_b}$
- $a_i, b_j \in R\ (1 \le i \le l_a, 1 \le j \le l_b)$
- R is a set of given characters
- $R \not\ni$ '-' (gap)

An alignment of the pair of sequences {A,B} results in another sequence pair of {A',B'} satisfying all the following properties:

- $A' = a'_1 a'_2 \dots a'_{l'},\ B' = b'_1 b'_2 \dots b'_{l'} (l' \ge l_a, l_b)$
- $a'_i, b'_j \in R \cup \{\text{'-'}\}\ (1 \le i, j \le l')$
- If removing some gaps, A' will become A and B' will be B
- $\not\exists i: a'_i = b'_i = \text{'-'}\ (1 \le i \le l')$

In the pairwise sequence alignment problem, the sum of scores of all character pairs is defined as the score of alignment. The optimal alignment is the one with the highest score. The score of this optimal alignment is called the similarity of the two given sequences. A popular ranking method is using a weight matrix; in this paper, we use the popular weight matrix BLOSUM.

1.2   Multi Sequence Alignment Problem

Supposing that we have n sequences $\{A_1, A_2, \dots, A_n\}$ $(n \ge 3)$ satisfying all the following conditions:

- $A_i = a_{i,1} a_{i,2} \dots a_{i,l_i}\ (1 \le i \le n)$
- $a_{i,j} \in R\ (1 \le i \le n,\ 1 \le j \le l_i)$
- R is a set of given characters
- $R \not\ni$ '-' (Gap)

A solution of aligning multi sequences $\{A_1, A_2, \dots, A_n\}$ is a set of sequences $\{A'_1, A'_2, \dots, A'_n\}$ satisfying all the following conditions:

- $A'_i = a'_{i,1} a'_{i,2} \dots a'_{i,l'}\ (l' \ge l_1, l_2, \dots, l_n)$
- $a'_{i,j} \in R \cup \{\text{'-'}\}\ (1 \le i \le n, 1 \le j \le l')$
- If removing gaps then A'_i will become $A_i\ (1 \le i \le n)$
- $\not\exists j: a'_{1,j} = a'_{2,j} = \dots = a'_{n,j} = \text{'-'}\ (1 \le i \le l')$

```
TTGACATG  CCGGGG---A  AACCG
TTGACATG  CCGGTG--GT  AAGCC
TTGACATG  -CTAGG---A  ACGCG
TTGACATG  -CTAGGGAAC  ACGCG
TTGACATC  -CTCTG---A  ACGCG
```

Fig. 1. An example of aligning multi sequences.

Methods of grading for MSA alignments have the same principles with PSA. Major approaches of solving the MSA problem include:

- The dynamic programming method: this method is not used to directly solve the MSA problem because the size of required memory have the exponential increase.
- The progressive alignment method: the most used method for MSA. This heuristic method uses the approach of "progressive": aligning sequences which are "close" to each other and then adding progressively further sequences into the current alignment. The most used method in progressive alignment is the algorithm **Clustal** [13]. This algorithm includes three steps which are presented in below section. Steps of calculating distances and aligning multi sequences require the large computing power which common computing systems do not meet within an accept time, therefore we implemented these steps on GPU using the parallel programming language CUDA and achieved a very great performance.

2   GPU and Programming Model CUDA

In recent years, the computing power of GPU graphics processors has increased significantly compared to CPU. Until June 2008, NVIDIA's GPU GT200 generation has reached the threshold of 933 GFLOPS, more than 10 times over dual-core processor the Intel Xeon 3.2 GHz at the same time. The computing performance of GPUs is only seen in problems that one certain task can be executed on a lot of independent data concurrently and then each processing core of GPU is assigned to perform one task on a set of data. CUDA [11] is popular software which supports to develop applications on multi cores GPU. A CUDA program includes one or a few special pieces of code, called parallel *kernels*. These kernels can be executed in parallel on the large number of threads on GPUs. Threads are divided into small groups which are executed on the same streaming multiprocessor, called thread *blocks*, these blocks are also designed to a *grid*. GPU's memory is hierarchically organized for effective usage:

- Main memory: the memory area for CPU code. Only this code can access and modify information here.
- Global memory: the memory area that all GPU threads can access to it. Programmers can move data from main memory to global memory by using functions from a CUDA basic library. This memory is often used to store inputs and outputs for parallel threads on GPUs.

- Shared memory: the memory area that only threads in one same block can access. This memory is integrated on-chip; so the speed of accessing data on it is much higher than on global memory. This memory is often used to store temporary shared data among threads in a block to speed up the process of memory usage.
- Local memory: the memory area allocated to local variables of each thread and one GPU thread cannot access to those from others.

With the ability to perform data parallelism on such a lot of threads, GPU is an appropriate choice to solve the multi sequence alignment problem, in which threads can calculate one cell on sub-diagonals of the similarity matrix in parallel or calculate distances between sequences concurrently, as presented in the below section.

3   Parallel Clustal on GPU

3.1   Overview of the Algorithm Clustal

As mentioned above, in the approach of *progressive* alignment to solve the MSA problem, Clustal [13] is one of the most used algorithms. This algorithm includes three stages; the following is details of three stages:

1. *Align Pairwise Sequences*
At first step, we do alignment all pairs of sequences to calculate relative distances about evolution between all sequences. The common method is dynamic programming, in which the value of distance between two sequences is calculated as compensative value of point for these two sequences. The implementation of the algorithm Clustal in this paper uses a simple version of *Smith-Waterman* algorithm. Firstly, the algorithm does alignments for all pairs of sequences $\{A_i, A_j\}$ $(1 \leq i < j \leq n)$ which can be generated from n input sequences $\{A_1, A_2, ..., A_n\}$ and using the score of the optimal alignment to calculate one distance value $dist(A_i, A_j)$ for those pair of sequences. The value of distance is calculated as follows: for a pair of sequences $A_x = a_{x,1}a_{x,2} ... a_{x,l_x}$ and $A_y = a_{y,1}a_{y,2} ... a_{y,l_y}$, we create a similarity matrix H with the size of $(l_x + 1) \times (l_y + 1)$ as follows:

- $H_{i,0} = H_{0,j} = 0$ $(0 \leq i \leq l_x, 0 \leq j \leq l_y)$ (sentries)   (1)

- $H_{i,j} = max \begin{pmatrix} 0, \\ H_{i-1,j} - 1, \\ H_{i,j-1} - 1, \\ H_{i-1,j-1} + sub(a_{x,i}, a_{y,j}) \end{pmatrix} \begin{pmatrix} 1 \leq i \leq l_x, \\ 1 \leq j \leq l_y \end{pmatrix}$ (2)

After building the matrix H, the distance value is calculated as follows:

$$dist(A_x, A_y) = 1 - H_{l_x,l_y}/min(l_x, l_y)$$ (3)

2. *Build the phylogenetic tree*: In this step, distance values are used to create a binary phylogenetic tree by algorithms of clustering. Here we apply a simple version of the popular clustering algorithm *neighbor-joining*.

3. *Perform multi sequences alignment*: the phylogenetic tree is used to perform multi sequences alignment progressively. Aligning multi sequences is executed by using a version of the algorithm Needleman-Wunsch [3].

3.2 Parallel the Algorithm Clustal

In this paper, we show how to use the parallel computing technology CUDA on GPU to accelerate the algorithm by paralleling stages of the algorithm Clustal and evaluate the performance of the GPU-based algorithm.

3.2.1 Basic Strategy of Parallelization

Parallelization strategy of the algorithm can be divided into two directions: paralleling the creation of similarity matrices and paralleling the calculation of distance values between sequences. To calculate distance values, we can see that distances of all pairs of sequences can be calculated independently; therefore we can calculate for all distances in parallel. In parallelization of building similarity matrices, from mathematical formulas of the algorithm Smith-Waterman in part 3.1, calculation of one element in the matrix only depends on values of its left, upper and upper-left neighbors. This is described as Fig.2.

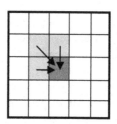

Fig. 2. The dependent relationship between values of elements in a similarity matrix

So all elements on the same diagonal of the matrix are directly or indirectly complete independent to each other. Therefore, calculation of these elements can be executed in parallel theoretically. This leads to basic parallel strategy as follows:

- Calculate all elements on the same diagonal concurrently.
- Diagonals are sequentially calculated in order of from upper-left to down right.

3.2.2 Parallelization Using CUDA on GPU

One significantly modified parallel method from above basic parallel strategy to improve the performance is proposed in the program MSA-CUDA, one parallel implementation of the algorithm Clustal by Yongchao Liu and Maskell in [17]. MSA-CUDA shows two new parallel methods: intra-task parallelization and inter-task parallelization. Here, one task is defined as calculating the distance between a pair of sequences - calculating a similarity matrix of the pair of sequences. In intra-task parallelization, one task is assigned to one block of threads and all threads inside that block combine to perform the assigned task. For inter-task parallelization, one task is assigned to one thread and threads inside a block do not combine to each other. Moreover, calculation of a similarity matrix in MSA-CUDA is also modified with the method of cell block for inter-task parallelization. In this method, each matrix is calculated by units of blocks of elements which are of sub-matrices of the size of n×n of the original matrix instead of every single element.

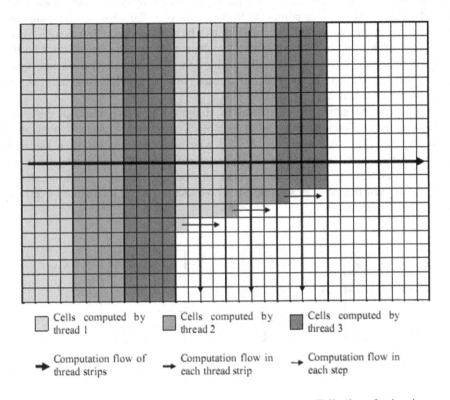

Cells computed by thread 1

Cells computed by thread 2

Cells computed by thread 3

Computation flow of thread strips

Computation flow in each thread strip

Computation flow in each step

Fig. 3. Illustration of calculating the matrix by intra-task parallelization of strip-wise

3.2.3 Parallelization for Stage 1

To parallelize stage 1 of the algorithm Clustal, we utilized an original "strip-wise parallelization" approach on GPUs, based on the idea of "cell block" found in MSA-CUDA and Hirschberg's algorithm [5] for sequence alignment with linear memory. Similar to MSA-CUDA, our approach is split into two flavors: intra-task parallelization and inter-task parallelization.

a) Intra-task parallelization

In intra-task parallelization, each similarity matrix is assigned to a whole block, and all threads in the block cooperate to compute the matrix in question. The similarity matrix is split into vertical "block strips" with fixed horizontal size (about 4-16 cells) and vertical size equal to the matrix's vertical size. Each block strip will be computed almost simultaneously by all threads in the block (except the last strip).

Next, each block strip is spilt into a fixed number of thread strips, each of which corresponds to a thread in the block. Hence, the number of thread strips in each block strip (except for the last) is equal to the number of threads in the block. Each thread strip, in turn, is split into steps. Each step consists of one row of cells in the thread strip.

Since the computation of each cell depends on the cells to its left, above and upper-left, the block strips will be computed from left to right, the steps will be computed from top to bottom and the cells in each step will be computed from left to right. Also, the thread strips will not start computing simultaneously, but the thread strips on the left will start first and work gradually to the right. This can be seen in the figure above. After each step is finished, all threads will be synchronized once before moving on to the next step.

In this way, the similarity matrix can be computed by every thread in the block (except for the beginning and the end of each block strip), which reduces computation time. However, the main advantage of strip-wise intra-task parallelization lies with the fact that the block strips and thread strips are of fixed widths. This means that one can utilize Hirschberg's algorithm to store all the intermediate results on shared memory or even registers, as seen in Fig. 4, without the worry of memory overflow due to their limited sizes.

G											G	
G							S	R	R	R	G	
G			S	R	R	R	S	R	R	R	G	
G	R	R	R	S	R	R	R	S				G
G	R	R	R	S							G	
G											G	

R	Register	S	Shared	G	Global

Fig. 4. Usage of memory in intra-task parallelization

Here only the cells computed in the last step and the cells being computed in the current step are stored. These cells can be stored in register, or in shared memory to take advantage of array structure. The cells on the border with the next thread strip on the right must be stored in shared memory to allow the next thread strip to use the results for the computation of its border cells. Only the cells bordering the next block strip are stored in global memory to be used later. The right-most columns of cells in the matrix will not required global memory as only the cell at the bottom-most does matter at that point.

This way of memory usage should sharply reduce memory latency compared to relying extensively on global memory to store intermediate results (eg. In MSA-CUDA's intra-task parallelization). In the Fig.4, global memory is accessed only once for the computation of 12 cells. And in the actual software the rate is 1:512. This means that for matrix with width of less than or equal to 512 cells, global memory will not be used at all in the computation of the matrix itself, though it is still used to create sentry at the start of the computation in the actual software.

b) Inter-task parallelization

Essentially, inter-task parallelization is a watered-down version of intra-task parallelization, with each similarity matrix being assigned to a thread instead of a whole block. The computation are carried out pretty much the same as intra-task parallelization, albeit with only one thread the "block strip" and "thread strip" become one.

Inter-task parallelization suffers greatly in performance improvement for the computation of a single similarity matrix compared to intra-task parallelization, having all the cells in the similarity matrix computed consequentially, and a higher rate of global memory usage. Nonetheless, it makes up for it in computing more similarity matrices in parallel than intra-task parallelization, since now each thread computes one matrix instead of each block.

Inter-task parallelization, therefore, is more suitable for cases involving larger number of very short sequences. In these cases, because the size of the similarity matrices may be much smaller than the fixed size of one single block strip, many threads will go idle during the computation and are wasted. Intra-task parallelization should be used in cases with small number of very long sequences, in which the huge "jump" of a whole block strip can be fully exploited.

3.2.4 Parallelization for Stage 3

Theoretically, strip-wise parallelization approach can also be applied to the computation of similarity matrices in Stage 3 of the Clustal algorithm. However, due to time constraints, this has not been implemented in the actual software as of yet.

Apart from the parallelization of similarity matrix computation, multiple progressive alignments in multiple internal nodes can be carried out in parallel, as long as these internal nodes are not independent in computation from each other. This has been implemented successfully in MSA-CUDA, so we would not dig further into this.

4   Experiments and Evaluation

Our parallel algorithm - CUDAClustal in this paper were implemented and tested on one GPU Geforce GTX 295 in a PC running the Linux OS. In our tests, we extract data from the database UniProtKB/Swiss-Prot for testing. UniProtKB is a database containing a large amount of biological information about proteins; in which Swiss-Prot is the part evaluated and edited by hand. The algorithm is paralleled on four different datasets, with two cases: a large number of short sequences and a small number of long sequences. Details of data are shown in the Table 1.

CUDAClustal shows a significant improvement of performance when compared to sequential versions of the algorithm Clustal. If evaluating the time of running the entire steps, CUDAClustal is faster two times than Clustal when working with datasets with the large number of sequences (test1.fasta, test2.fasta) and is faster three times than Clustal in the case of datasets with large average lengths of sequences (test3.fasta, test4.fasta). These results are described in Table 1.

Table 1. Comparison of runtime between CUDAClustal and Clustal

Dataset	Number of sequences	Average length of sequences	Runtime	
			CUDAClustal	Clustal
test1.fasta	200	~300	120,13s	220,25s
test2.fasta	300	~300	269,88s	545,25s
test3.fasta	100	~800	110,82	327,51
test4.fasta	50	~1600	121,65s	332,2s

Currently, CUDAClustal has been paralleled for only stage one of the entire algorithm, so to evaluate the computing performance accurately, we consider the runtime of each stages. Results show that for all datasets, CUDAClustal gives a great computational performance: the runtime for stage one of CUDAClustal is smaller approximately 30 times than the sequential Clustal. This result is shown in Table 2. So if only considering parts which have been paralleled then the effect of using GPU is very feasible. This means that if stage three of the algorithm is also paralleled, the total time of the program will be more significantly reduced.

Table 2. Comparison of runtime by stages between CUDAClustal and Clustal

Datasets	Stage 1			Stage 2 & 3	
	CUDAClustal		Clustal	CUDAClustal	Clustal
	Memory Operation	Runtime of kernel			
test1.fasta	0,26s	4,40s	124,13s	115,46s	96,12s
test2.fasta	0,35s	12,16s	304,28s	257,37s	287,88s
test3.fasta	0,04s	8,03s	237,00s	102,48s	90,51s
test4.fasta	0,001s	6,51s	233,05s	115,14s	99,15s

5   Conclusion

The technology GPU shows the ability of improving computational performance for problems which can be paralleled. In this paper, we present our parallel algorithm – CUDAClustal to solve the MSA problem. We have paralleled the first stage of the algorithm and achieved a significant speedup when compared to the sequential program. Here, parallelization for stage one brings increase in performance which is approximately two times for the entire algorithm Clustal and 30 times for stage one. This proves a certain success level of paralleling the algorithm using CUDA on GPU, enabling to parallel the whole three steps. In the future work, we intend to modify our program by parallelizing stage three by performing alignment at nodes with the same height from leaf nodes in parallel. Moreover, we will implement the algorithm on multi GPU and GPU Cluster to increase the computing performance.

References

1. http://docencia.ac.upc.edu/master/AMPP/slides/ampp_sw_presentation.pdf
2. http://en.wikipedia.org/wiki/Multiple_sequence_alignment
3. http://en.wikipedia.org/wiki/Needleman-Wunsch_algorithm
4. http://gpgpu.org
5. http://www.csse.monash.edu.au/~lloyd/tildeAlgDS/Dynamic/Hirsch
6. Cheetham, J., et al.: Parallel ClustalW for PC clusters. In: International Conference on Computational Science and Its Applications (ICCSA), pp. 300–309 (2003)
7. Thompson, J.D., et al.: CLUSTAL W: improving the sensitivity of progressive multiple sequence alignment through sequence weighting, position-specific gap penalties and weight matrix choice. Nucleic Acids Res. 22(22), 4673–4680 (1994)
8. Li, K.B.: Clustal-MPI: ClustalW analysis using parallel and distributed computing. Bioinformatics 19, 1585–1586 (2003)
9. Chaichoompu, K., Kittitornkun, et al.: MT ClustalW: multithreading multiple sequence alignment. In: International Parallel and Distributed Processing Symposium (2006)
10. Notredame, Higgins, Heringa: T-Coffee: A novel method for multiple sequence alignments. JMB 302, 205–217
11. NVIDIA, http://www.nvidia.com/object/cuda_home_new.htm
12. Duzlevski, O.: SMP version of ClustalW 1.82 (unpublished)
13. Sugawara, H., Chenna, R., et al.: Multiple sequence alignment with the Clustal series of programs. Nucleic Acids Res. 31, 3497–3500 (2003)
14. Feng, S., Tan, G., et al.: Parallel multiple sequences alignment in SMP cluster. In: International Conference on HPC in Asia Region, pp. 425–431 (2005)
15. Haque, W., Aravind, A., et al.: Pairwise sequence alignment algorithms: a survey. In: Conference on Information Science, Technology and Application, New York (2009)
16. Liu, W., et al.: Streaming algorithms for biological sequence alignment on GPUs. IEEE Transactions on Parallel and Distributed Systems 18, 1270–1281 (2007)
17. Liu, Y., Schmidt, B., Maskell, D.L.: MSA-CUDA: Multiple Sequence Alignment on Graphics Processing Units with CUDA. In: International Conference on Application-specific Systems, Architectures and Processors, USA (2009)

Performance Evaluation of Virtual Routing Protocol EMRP in WSNs

Thu Ngo, Mai Banh, and Hoa Dam

Hanoi University of Science and Technology
{thunq,maibtq}@soict.hut.edu.vn, vanhoa690@gmail.com

Abstract. Our developed protocol Energy Aware Mesh Routing Protocol EMRP is a robust, cluster-based routing technique used in Wireless Sensor Network (WSN) which provides a reliable, scalable, energy efficient multipath routing mechanism for data transmission to the Base Station (BS). EMRP is classified as a routing technique supporting network virtualization as it reduces energy consumption, improves energy balance and network lifetime of whole WSN by energy aware routing and evenly utilizing available energy each sensor node. In this paper, we clarify the data transmission process of EMRP, how it supports network virtualization and maintains its algorithms to monitor the residual energy of each sensor node to provide such advantages. We then analyze, evaluate and optimized EMRP design parameter that influencing network performance of WSN: total energy consumption, network balance and network lifetime.

Keywords: Cluster based routing, energy aware routing, virtual routing, virtualization, VSN, WSNs.

1   Introduction

Virtualization Sensor Network (VSN) collaborates a dynamic set of sensor nodes belonging to different WSNs that might be controlled or owned by different administrative bodies to perform a specific task [8]. By combining heterogeneous nodes of different WSNs for VSN it provides reliability, flexibility and scalability to WSN especially in the case that links within the network are broken. Figure 1 shows an example of VSN comprising of two sensor networks and other nodes

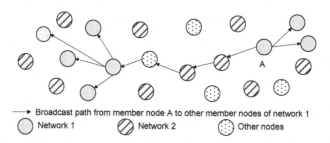

Fig. 1. VSN comprising two networks and other nodes

P.C. Vinh et al. (Eds.): ICCASA 2012, LNICST 109, pp. 310–323, 2013.
© Institute for Computer Sciences, Social Informatics and Telecommunications Engineering 2013

In VSN, network and node resources play very significant roles for the operation of VSN. As power management is one of the most critical issues in WSNs, energy consumption for sending/receiving messages and the residual energy of the nodes and network is taken into account for VSN to work effectively despite the differences of heterogeneous nodes. Moreover, internetworking in VSNs make the energy consumptions of nodes between networks are greatly different therefore routing in VSN needs to work on important missions: energy saving, energy balance and scalability. Cluster-based protocols for heterogeneous networks provide better scalability and higher energy efficiency than other routing protocols. Energy aware routing helps to utilize node and network energy. Our cluster based energy-aware mesh routing EMRP use energy resources efficiently since it not only improves energy efficiency of VSN but also increases lifetime of nodes and of the overall network. The task of energy control and management in EMRP is simple, effective, scalable and involves less control overheads than other routing protocols thus work effectively in WSNs.

Recent research shows that hierarchical cluster-based routing has many advantages in increasing network performance in WSN[1]. Cluster based routing protocols such as LEACH[2], HEED[3] group nodes into clusters in which one or more nodes satisfying evaluation criteria such as highest remaining energy level are selected as Cluster Head (CH). CH aggregates data from its cluster members and sends aggregated data to a base station (BS) in a multi-hop mode. Since these protocols manage WSN nodes in clusters, they offer many advantages necessary for WSNs such as local management of clusters without obtaining information of the whole network, reducing overhead and data redundancy, reducing total consumed energy, distributing energy consumed evenly and finally increasing network lifetime. There are two approaches in hierarchical cluster-based routing protocols: time-driven and event-driven. In time-driven protocols, sensed data is periodically sent to the BS to provide information of the environment all the time whereas in event-driven protocol, sensed data is sent to the BS when an event is detected. Time-driven routing protocols usually form fixed clusters in the initializing stage based on probability formula while event-driven routing protocols only form clusters after detecting an event.

Event-driven hierarchical cluster-based routing protocols such as OEDSR[4], ARPEES[5] and HPEQ[6], EMRP[7] clustering and data transmission to the BS happens only when and where the event occurs (sensed value is greater than predefined threshold). Therefore event-driven approaches in WSNs are more efficient in saving energy, reducing redundant data and increasing network lifetime than time-driven approaches since they involve less overheads, data, energy usage and redundancies. Our recent analyses and simulation results showed that our protocol EMRP outperforms APREES, OESDR, and HPEQ not only in terms of providing reliability but also significant reduction on total energy consumption, improvement on both energy load balance and network lifetime [7]. EMRP provides reliability to the performance of the WSN as it uses alternative multipath for data transmission toward the BS. To make routing decision between these paths, an energy monitoring method is used by estimating and comparing relay node's and backup node's residual energy. A dynamic switch between relay path and backup path is not only done when one path is broken (due to link failure or nodes' out-of-battery) but also to maintain energy load balance among the network.

EMRP Routing Protocol consists of three stages: initializing, cluster forming and data transmission stages. In initializing stage, EMRP uses broadcast processes to find relay nodes toward BS for each node in the network. It selects one main node and backup node based on a link cost factor function where residual energy is the main parameter. At this stage, alternative optimal paths toward the BS are found and stored. In cluster forming stage, EMRP chooses a cluster head for a cluster formed by nodes which could sense an occurring event. The CH sets up a time slot called TDMA schedule for cluster members specifying when to send sensed data to CH and then gathers, aggregates data to a frame for sending to the BS. The final stage is the most important stage in the EMRP routing process. CH uses relay nodes found at the beginning stage to route data to the BS. Each node has two alternative relay paths and EMRP dynamically switch between these two paths based on switch level to route data to the BS. The energy aware switches between two paths help to improve the balance of network thus prolong network lifetime. What is the minimum threshold for the switch to maintain even energy load balance between nodes or how the frequency of the switch could affect network performance is an important issue that is resolved in this paper.

In this paper, we analyze the process of EMRP last stage - data transmission and the mechanism that energy aware multipaths work as a virtualized algorithm that monitor energy balance between nodes and make use of energy resources in the WSN regardless the operation of underlying layers. We then analyze, optimize EMRP design parameter EMRP switch level and evaluate its influence to network performance of WSN: total energy consumption, network balance and network lifetime.

The remainder of the paper is organized as follows: Section 2 discusses virtual routing in EMRP. Section 3 presents our analyses and simulation results of evaluation of EMRP switch levels. The last section is the conclusion of the paper.

2   Virtual Routing in EMRP

The more detailed analysis of EMRP is analyzed in three stages: initialing, clustering and data transmission.

Initializing Stage

In the set up phase of the network, each sensor node broadcasts REQ_RELAY packets containing node ID, residual energy and location to BS to its neighbors. Each node (except node which has direct communication with BS) then uses this information to choose a relay node and a backup node based on maximum values of link cost function F_{RN}.

$$F_{RN}(j) = E_{res}(j) \times \frac{1}{d(j,BS)} \times \cos \alpha_j \qquad (1)$$

where E_{res} (j) is residual energy - available energy of node j, $d(j,BS)$ is the distance from the candidate node j to the BS, α_j is an angle value created by node j, CH and BS.

$$\cos \alpha_j = \frac{d(CH,j)^2 + d(CH,BS)^2 - d(j,BS)^2}{2d(j,BS)d(CH,BS)} \qquad (2)$$

After the initializing stage, we have a meshed hierarchy network topology. Each node has two links one link to its relay node (RN node) and other to its backup node (BN node) as shown in figure 2. Each node stores node ID, residual energy and location of these two nodes.

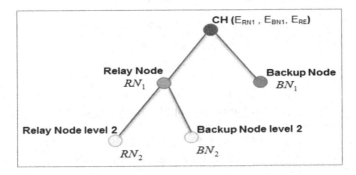

Fig. 2. Each node has two relay nodes RN_1 and BN_1

Cluster Forming Stage

When an event is detected in the network, nodes nearby the event become activated. Those nodes broadcast REQ_CLUSTER message (containing the node ID i, the amount of residual energy $E_{res}(i)$ and descriptive information of the sensed data $I(i)$ from the event) to their neighbors. During a time t_1, each node receiving REQ_CLUSTER messages from all the other nodes and executes the link cost factor function (equation (1)). After t_1, the node which has the maximum value of the cost function sets itself as CH. The CH stores the node ID of all nodes, and then creates a TDMA schedule to assign each node a time slot. All non-CH nodes can use this time slot for transmitting their sensed data to the CH in order to avoid collision in data transmission. The CH receives data from all other nodes and prepare to gather, aggregate data to a frame and then selects relay nodes for creating a route to the BS.

Data Transmission Stage

The main idea of EMRP's transmitting process is energy monitoring method to make routing decision. In this method, each node estimates and compares its relay node's and backup node's residual energy. If either one of the node is out of battery or the difference between residual energy of relay node and backup node is below a predefined switch level, there will be a switch that relay node becomes backup node and backup node becomes relay node. The third stage of EMRP is described as following (illustrated with figure 2):

1th Step: After receiving data from all non-CH nodes, the CH will gather, aggregate and pack processed sensed data to a frame called DATA_TO_BS.

2nd Step: From the initializing stage, the CH saves the residual energy of RN_1 and BN_1 in its two parameters E_{RN1} and E_{BN1}. Then CH starts to send the first data frame DATA_TO_BS to its relay node RN_1.

3^{rd}Step: When RN_1 receives DATA_TO_BS frame for the first time, RN_1 calculates total energy cost for both receiving one DATA_TO_BS frame from CH and relaying this frame to RN_2 using the radio model equation (3):

$$E_{total}(k,d) = E_{Tx}(k,d) + E_{Rx}(k)$$
$$= k\,E_{elec} + k\,E_{fs}d^2 + k\,E_{elec} \tag{3}$$
$$= 2k\,E_{elec} + k\,E_{fs}d^2$$

Where E_{elec} is the power requirement on the electronics devices for transmitting and receiving the data, E_{fs} is the transmission amplification energy. Parameter k is message bit length, d is the transmission distance.

The RN_1 sends back to CH a RELAY_ENERGY message containing the energy cost $E_{Total}(k,d)$ and its current residual energy E_{RN1}. The CH saves this $E_{Total}(k,d)$ in its parameter E_{RE} and update E_{RN1} if needed.

4th Step: After having all three parameters energy residual of $RN_1 E_{RN1}$ and of BN_1 E_{BN1} and estimated spent energy for sending data to RN_1: E_{RE}, CH sends a DATA_TO_BS frame to RN, CH now estimates and updates parameter E_{RN1} corresponding to the residual energy of RN_1 each time a DATA_TO_BS frame is transmitted on the relay path using the below equation:

$$E_{RN1} = E_{RN1} - E_{RE} \tag{4}$$

Thus the CH from now on can continuously send the next DATA_TO_BS frames to $RN_1$for the next round while monitoring the current residual energy of RN_1 without further updating from RN_1

5th Step: At the same time of the 4th step, before transmitting a DATA_TO_BS frame, the CH needs to check two following conditions:

If bothE_{RN1} and E_{BN1} fall below a pre-defined *critical level* (for example 1% of node initial energy), it means that both relay and backup node do not have enough energy in order to continue to send data, the CH will broadcast REQ_RELAY messages again to find new relay and backup node.

If $(E_{BN1} - E_{RN1})$ is less than a pre-defined *switch level* (for example 0.5% node initial energy),RN1 will become a new backup node and the backup node will become the new relay node. For the first switch time, the new switched relay node repeats the 3rd step by sending back to CH total energy cost $E_{Tx}(k,d)$ in RELAY_ENERGY message so that CH can update the parameter E_{RE}.

6th *Step:* In the next hop, the relay node in turn serves as the CH using the same method to relay data to the next relay node, backup node and switch dynamically between them. This process is repeated until data frames reaching to the BS.

Since EMRP is mesh routing protocol it reduces a number of broadcast messages used find relay nodes in data transmission process and costs less control overheads of broadcasting. The task of energy management involves extra energy relay messages RELAY_ENERGY but these messages are only triggered to a specific target when necessary and do not consume a lot of energy (this is discussed in analysis and simulations in more details in section 3). The task of energy management is simple since relay node or backup node only needs to update its energy consumption of data frame to its upper node only one time when first time sending the frame (step 4th). By using residual energy of each node to monitor the switch between two alternative transmission paths and reducing control overhead of broadcasting processes, EMRP helps to utilize the energy resources and thus effectively supports VSN. Moreover, compared with other energy-aware routing protocols in WSNs, EMRP provides reliability, more energy efficiency [7]. The design of EMRP is energy monitoring method where each node is always aware of its relay node's and backup node's energy level. EMRP replaces nodes with new nodes if their energy falls below the critical level. Thus it eliminates the chance a node keeps sending data messages to its relay node when the relay node already runs out of energy, and hence improves the reliability and fault-tolerance of the event-driven cluster-based protocol. Moreover, the dynamic switch levels between relay node and backup node when the difference of their residual energy can reduce the energy consumption deviation of nodes along the transmission paths and achieve better load-balance compared to other event-driven cluster-based protocols. The energy monitoring method and dynamic switch levels better provides energy saving and energy balance therefore strongly supports virtualization sensor networks

3   Evaluation of EMRP Switch Level

EMRP is a mesh routing protocol which stores information of relay nodes at the set up phase of the network thus a number of broadcast messages used find relay nodes are reduced to in data transmission process. Besides, EMRP switch between relay nodes and backup nodes improves energy load balance and network lifetime. These two important issues of EMRP supporting VSN that are reducing control overhead, energy consumptions and providing energy balance due to EMRP switch levels are analyzed.

Since EMRP switch level helps to improve energy load balance between nodes of the network, thus energy consumption is spread evenly and network lifetime is prolonged, this section analyses how the variation of switch levels can influence the performance of EMRP. Switch level is threshold to switch roles between the relay node and the backup node in EMRP. When the energy difference between the residual energy of relay node and backup node is smaller than switch level multiplied by initial energy of a node, the relay node becomes backup node and vice versa.

$$\text{Switch level} = |E_{BN} - E_{RN}| / E_{initial} \ (\%)$$

EMRP energy switches involve a number of relay energy messages. Although these relay messages consume a lot smaller energy than broadcast messages caused by the broadcast process, an appropriate level of switch is important to both reduce total energy consumption and maintain network balance. An appropriate switch level should be chosen to adapt to the length of event and frequency of switches. When the switch level is very low the switches happen so frequently resulting in extra overhead of energy relay messages RELAY_ENERGY. When the switch level is very high, fewer switches are done causing the disparity between relay and backup nodes and thus causing imbalance in node energy distribution. EMRP switch level therefore greatly affects the load balance of sensor networks and thus to network lifetime.

Simulations are setup to measure the weight of relay energy messages RELAY_ENERGY in energy consumption and to evaluate how the variation of switch level could make an impact on network performance and . For each simulated switch level, total remaining energy of network after each event, energy load balance of the network and network lifetime is estimated and evaluated.

Simulation Method and Metrics

EMRP algorithm with different switch levels were implemented in the OMNeT++ simulator [9], which is a public-source, component-based, modular and open-architecture simulation environment with strong GUI support and an embedded simulation kernel. Simulation parameters are the same for different switch levels. Table 1 describes the parameters used in our simulations.

The EMRP protocol is evaluated with different switch levels using the following metrics.

Table 1. Simulation Parameters

Parameter	Value
Initial Energy	1 Joule
Data packet size	500 bytes
Broadcast packet size	25 bytes
E_{elec}	50nJ/bit
E_{fs}	10pJ/bit/m2
Network area	800x800 m
Transmitting range	150 m
Sensing range	70 m
Number of nodes	200
Critical level	1%
Number of transmission rounds per event	5
Number of frames per round	6

In our simulations, we assume that all sensor nodes initially have 1-Joule energy. The simulation network contains 200 sensor nodes that are dispersed onto a field with square dimension. The transmission range is 150m and the sensing range is 70m. Data packet size is fixed at 500 bytes and broadcasting packet size is 25 byte. The low level is 10% of the initial energy. A node will stop participating in routing process if its energy falls below 1% of the initial energy. The simulation is run until all the sensor nodes that have distance to BS less than their transmission range die. That means all the links to BS are failed and data transmission process cannot continue. A round is defined as a complete transmission for one time CH sends all data that aggregates from its cluster. The number of data frames to be transferred in each round is 6 and the number of transmission rounds in each event is set to 5, therefore the number of frames per each event is 30. The switch level is ranging to evaluate its influence to network performance.

Result Analysis

We ran the simulation with 200 sensor nodes uniformly dispersed onto a 800x800 meters square field. The base station is located at co-ordinate (440,800) and 40-meter away from the closest sensor node.

Total Remaining Residual Energy

To compare network performance of each different EMRP switch level, we estimates the total remaining energy of network after each event for each simulated event. The simulation runs for 270 events.

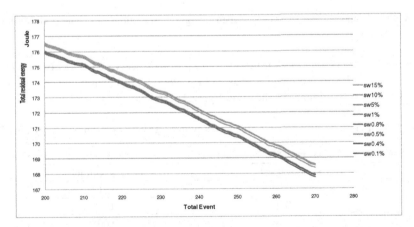

Fig. 3. Total remaining energy of network after each event for each EMRP switch level

The simulation results show that total remaining energy of the network after each event at different switch level cases is almost the same .Figure 3 shows that the total remaining energy of low switch level group is only approximately 0.3 Joule less than compared to that of high switch level group.

The difference of the energy consumptions after each event in different switch level cases is caused by RELAY_ENERGY messages to support the switch. However, the energy consumption of sending and receiving these RELAY_ENERGYmessages is relatively small compared to total network energy. This explains the difference of total remaining energy at different switch level cases is negligible. To clarify this analysis, we also compare the total consumed energy used to send and receive RELAY_ENERGY messages of different switch levels in EMRP after 270 events (shown in figure 4). The number of energy relay messages involved in switch level 15% is the least number among all cases958 messages and this number gradually increases to 5741 messages as switch level decreases to 0.1%. The total energy consumption caused by RELAY_ENERGY messages only varies from roughly 48mJ to 285mJ (a different of 237mJ).

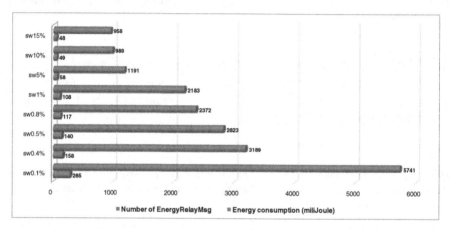

Fig. 4. No. of relay energy messages & their energy consumptions at different switch levels after 270 events

After 270 events, energy consumption to send and receive RELAY_ENERGY of different switch levels are under low as 285 mJ while total remaining energy of those is high as above 165000mJ (as shown in figure 4 and table 2).

Table 2. % of energy consumption of relay energy messages/total remaining energy after 270 events

Switch level	Percentage
0.1%	0.17%
0.4%	0.09%
0.5%	0.08%
0.8%	0.07%
1%	0.06%
5%	0.03%
10%	0.03%
15%	0.03%

Lower switch level involves in larger number of relay energy messages therefore higher energy consumption. Switch level 0.1% achieves highest percentage over total residual energy 0.17% while from switch level 5% and above achieves 0.03%. However, these consumptions are negligible to the total remaining energy of the network. From this simulation, it can be said that the adjustment of diverse switch levels does not make an impact on the total energy of network. The only consideration could be the number of overheads involved due to the number of relay messages although these messages cost low energy levels.

Load Balance

To evaluate the impact of switch level on energy load balance of the network, **three** groups of switch levels are taken to compare load balance of nodes after the network ran for 270 events. The graphs show individual remaining energy of 200 nodes corresponding to different switch levels in groups (0.1%, 0.2%, 0.3%, 0.4% và 0.5%), (0.6%, 0.7%, 0.8% và 0.9%) and (1%, 2%, 5%, 10%,15%) after 270 events

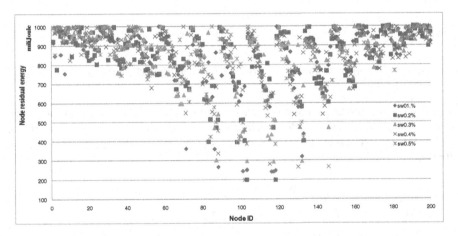

Fig. 5. Node residual energy distribution at switch level 0.1%, 0.2%, 0.3%, 0.4% và 0.5% after 270 events

Figure 5 shows that switch level 0.5% performs the best load balance performance. Nodes which have the lowest residual energy at level 0.5%are approximately 400 mJ at node energy falls under 300mJ, even around 200mJ at all other switch level. The worst switch level on load balance which energy of nodes falls low is 0.1%

Switch level 0.1% of initial energy should provide better load balance among others because the switch level is based on difference residual energy of back up node and relay node. The smaller this difference, the more frequent the switch between relay node and backup node, thus the better load balance of the network. The simulation results show the converse switch level 0.1% is the worst. This could be explained that at switch level 0.1%, the switch between relay node and backup node happens more often, thus resulting in an increase in energy to send and receive

RELAY_ENERGYcompared with other switch levels. Although the energy spent due to RELAY_ENERGY messages is small compared total remaining energy evaluated above, it does make an impact on individual node residual energy. Therefore it makes an impact on load balance thus switch level 0.1% is the worst energy balance case.

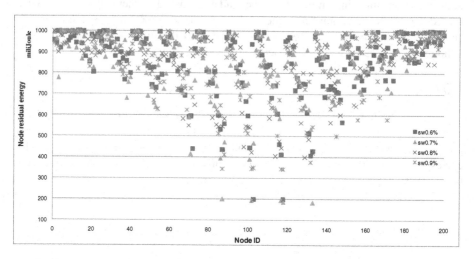

Fig. 6. Node energy distribution atswitch level 0.6%, 0.7%, 0.8%, 0.9% after 270 events

Similarly, as shown in figure 6 in this group of switch levels, the highest switch level 0.9% provides the best load balance among other switch levels 0.6%, 0.7%, 0.8%. The lowest energy level of nodes at switch level 0.9% falls roughly below 400ms.

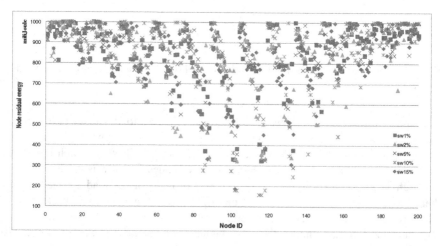

Fig. 7. Node energy distribution at switch level 1%, 2%, 5%, 10%, 15% after 270 events

As shown in figure 7, switch level 1%, 2% provides the better load balance among other switch levels. This could be explained by the higher switch level above 5% leads to lower number of switch between relay nodes and backup nodes thus resulting in smaller number of RELAY_ENERGY messages and smaller values of energy consumptions due to these messages. However, if the switch levels are too high, some nodes continuously became relay nodes thus energy spent mostly on these nodes thus resulting in imbalance of energy distribution. High switch levels therefore are not recommended as switches between relay nodes and back up nodes are done occasionally.

It could be concluded that EMRP switch levels greatly makes an impact on energy balance. Switch levels at the range of 0.4% - 2% initial energy give better load balance (summarized in figure 7) as it balances the number of energy switches and the energy consumptions due to the involvement of energy relay messages. From simulation results, switch level 0.5% gives the best load balance as it involves a reasonable number of switches and reasonable of energy relay messages. EMRP switch between relay nodes and backup nodes clearly improves energy load balance therefore EMRP switch plays an important role in supporting VSN.

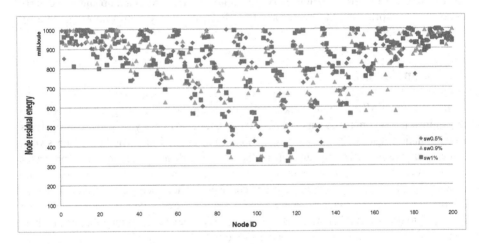

Fig. 8. Node energy distribution at 3 best switch level 0.5%, 0.9%, 1% after 270 events

Network Lifetime

Clearly, when many nodes are dead, then density of nodes decreases significantly, we will get low network connectivity. EMRP is designed to balance the node's energy consumption in order to avoid *hot spot*, which causes quick deaths of the nodes due to their overload. A well distributed energy load balance will make nodes last longer an increase network lifetime. The number of events at which the first node dies in the network and the total live rounds network can operate at different switch levels are

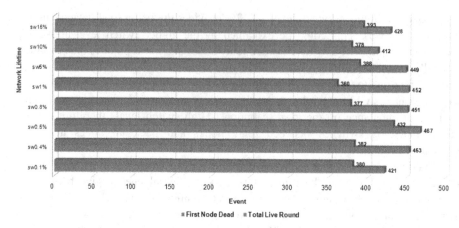

Fig. 9. Network lifetime and first dead node at different switch levels

measured. Switch levels 0.4 to 2% give better load balance therefore at these switch levels event that first node dies last longer and total live rounds (network lifetime) are more extended. EMRP switch between relay nodes and backup nodes clearly improves network lifetime therefore EMRP switch plays an important role in supporting VSN.

4   Conclusion

Virtual reliable EMRP routing concentrates on energy aware routing that reduces total remaining energy, improves energy balance and energy efficiency of VSN. Our analyses and simulation results show that energy monitoring method of EMRP based on switch levels is simple and effective since it involves less overheads of broadcasting processes and less energy consumptions and also greatly make an impact on load balance and network lifetime. By varying different switch levels, better energy balance and network lifetime is achieved. A range of switch level 0.4% - 2% works best for load balance and network lifetime since it balances between frequency of switches and number of involved relay messages, therefore this range better supports VSN.

References

[1] Singh, S.K., Singh, M.P., Singh, D.K.: A Survey of Energy-Efficient Hierarchical Cluster-Based Routing in Wireless Sensor Networks. Int. Journal of Advanced Networking and Applications 02(02), 570–580 (2010)

[2] Heinzelman, W.R., Chandrakasan, A., Balakrishnan, H.: Energy-efficient Communication Protocol for Wireless Microsensor Networks. In: Proceedings of the Thirty Third Hawaii International Conference on System Sciences (HICSS 2000), vol. 8, p. 8020. IEEE Computer Society, Washington, DC (2000)

[3] Younis, O., Fahmy, S.: HEED: A hybrid, Energy-efficient, Distributed Clustering Approach for Ad-hoc Networks. IEEE Transactions on Mobile Computing 3(4), 366–369 (2004)

[4] Ratnaraj, S., Jagannathan, S., Rao, V.: OEDSR: Optimized Energy-Delay Sub-network Routing in Wireless Sensor Network (2006)

[5] Tran Quang, V., Miyoshi, T.: Adaptive Routing Protocol with Energy Efficiency and Event Clustering for Wireless Sensor Networks. IEICE Trans. Commun. E91–B(9) (September 2008)

[6] Boukerche, A., Pazzi, R.W.N., Araujo, R.B.: HPEQ - A Hierarchical Periodic, Event-driven and Query-based Wireless Sensor Network Protocol. In: IEEE Conference on Local Computer Networks 30th Anniversary, LCN 2005 (2005)

[7] Quynh, T.N., Vinh, T.T., Quynh, M.B.: Multipath Routing Protocols for Cluster-based and Event-based Wireless Sensor Network. In: ACM- SoICT International Conference (August 2012)

[8] Elhafsi, E.H., Mitton, N., Simplot- Ry, D.: Cost over Progress Based Energy Efficient Routing over Virtual Coordinates in Wireless Sensor Networks. In: International Symposium on a World of Wireless, Mobile and Multimedia Networks (WoWMoM), Helsinki, Finland, June 18-21, pp. 1–6 (2007)

[9] Omnet++, version 4.2, a discrete event simulation system,
http://www.omnetpp.org

Improving Vietnamese Web Page Classification by Combining Hybrid Feature Selection and Label Propagation with Link Information

Ngo Van Linh, Nguyen Thi Kim Anh, and Cao Manh Dat

School of Information and Communication Technology
Hanoi University of Science
and Technology
{linhnv,anhnk}@soict.hut.edu.vn, caomanhdat317@gmail.com

Abstract. Classification of web pages is essential to many information management and retrieval tasks such as maintaining web directories and focused crawling. One problem in web page classification is that, unlabeled training examples are readily available, while labeled ones are often costly to obtain. Furthermore, the uncontrolled nature of web content presents additional challenges to web page classification, whereas the interconnected characteristic of hypertext can provide useful information for the process. To address these problems, we propose a graph-based semi-supervised classification framework which combines iteratively hybrid semi-supervised feature selection and Label Propagation learning using link information to improve the Vietnamese web page classification. The experimental results show that proposed method outperforms the state-of-the art methods applying to Vietnamese web page classification.

Keywords: Feature Selection, Label Propagation, Web Classification, Web Mining.

1   Introduction

The web has become one of the most important information sources and knowledge base for science, education and research applications. With the exponential growth of information and data in the Internet, people often need to spend a huge amount of time obtaining expected the information even with the help of search engines. Meanwhile, all of the machine learning and data mining methods are aimed to provide more powerful functionalities to meet the needs of users. One way of organizing this overwhelming amount of data is to classify it into descriptive or topical taxonomies. Web page classification can help to improve the quality of the web search results which eventually saves users from a large number of unexpected web pages. Besides, the classification also plays a vital role in many information management and retrieval tasks. On the web, classification of page content is essential to focused crawling, to the assisted development of web directories, to topic-specific web link analysis, and to the analysis of the topical structure of the web.

P.C. Vinh et al. (Eds.): ICCASA 2012, LNICST 109, pp. 324–334, 2013.

Web page classification, as a traditional supervised machine learning task, is to train a classifier with labeled examples, so as to predict the label for any new pages. But in web page classification, just as in many other practical machine learning and data mining applications, unlabeled training examples are readily available, while labeled ones are often laborious, expensive and slow to obtain. This is because labeled examples normally require much efforts and accuracy of experienced annotators. Semi-supervised learning addresses this problem by leveraging a large amount of unlabeled data, together with a small labeled dataset to build better classifiers. However, the limited size of the "labeled" dataset poses hug challenges of selecting an ideal feature subset only based on the "labeled" data.

This practical problem drives the need for "semi-supervised feature selection" to choose the best set of features that produces the most accurate classifier for a learning algorithm given both labeled and unlabeled examples.

Moreover, the uncontrolled nature of web content presents additional challenges to web page classification compared to traditional text classification. To solve this problem, we can refer to the interconnected characteristic of hypertext since the key for implementing effective web page classification is to find intrinsic relationships between web pages. For this purpose, web page content, hyperlinks and usage data (server log files) could be utilized together as important features for the system. Among them, hyperlink analysis has its own advantages, as hyperlinks convey semantics between web pages in most cases.

The motivation for our work is based on the observation that web pages on a particular topic are often linked to other pages on the same topic. In fact, with a few exceptions, the authors of web pages create links to other pages usually with an idea in mind that the linked pages are relevant to the linking pages. If a hyperlink is reasonable, it reflects human semantic judgment and this judgment is objective and independent of the synonymy and polysemy of the words in the pages. This latent semantic, once being revealed, could be employed to find higher-level relationships among the pages. Besides, the hyperlink analysis has also been proven successful in many web-related areas, such as page ranking in the search engine.

In this paper, we propose a graph-based semi-supervised classification framework combined with iteratively hybrid semi-supervised feature selection and Label Propagation learning using link information to improve the accuracy of Vietnamese web page classification. The experimental results show that our algorithm achieves promising results.

The rest of this paper is organized as follows. In section 2, we give a brief review of link-enhanced text classification and clustering methods, semi-supervised learning and semi-supervised feature selection. Section 3 introduces Gini-index-based supervised feature selection method. Section 4 represent the method of constructing integrated graph which combines content-based graph and link-based graph. Section 5 introduces the Label Propagation algorithm in graph. Section 6 proposes a graph-based semi-supervised classification framework which combines iteratively hybrid semi-supervised feature selection and Label Propagation learning using link information. Section 7 reports on the experimental results. Finally, in section 8, we make some conclusions and raise several issues for future work.

2   Related Work

Exploiting link information to enhance text classification has been studied extensively in the research community [1,2,7,9]. Most of these studies fall into two frameworks. One is referred to as relaxation labeling (RL) in which the label of a document is determined by both local content and its neighbors' labels [1,7]. The other improves classification accuracy by incorporating neighbors' content information text into the local content [2,9]. However, Ghani [3] et al. discovered that neighbors' text content information could be useful only when the neighbor link structure exhibits encyclopedia regularity.

In fact, because the availability of labeled examples cannot be taken for granted for many real world applications, semi-supervised learning methods that exploit unlabeled examples in addition to labeled ones have been widely researched. Indeed, for semi-supervised learning methods, when the size of the "labeled" data is limited, it is difficult to select an ideal subset of features based only on the "labeled" data and the effectiveness of semi-supervised learning algorithm, therefore, would be downgraded. Ren et al. proposed a "wrapper-type" forward semi-supervised feature selection framework by using a mechanism of random selection on unlabeled data to extend the initial labeled training set and then, the most frequently selected feature is added to the result feature subset every iteration. Later, Zhong et al. [12] proposed a hybrid graph-based semi-supervised feature selection framework using a confidence-based sampling strategy that provides an improved accuracy over random selection. However, the "Label Propagation" algorithm in [12] use only content-based graph to predict the unlabeled data U. Then, the top $s\%$ of the unlabeled data with the highest confidence are added to the original training data along with their labels to create a new training dataset. In our opinion, the sufficiency and diversity of the new training set can be improved poorly, which in return can help to choose restrictively the most discriminative features.

The work closest to ours is an approach described in [6], which uses a semi-supervised learning algorithm on a K-Nearest Neighbor graph for web page classification. Their algorithm uses a similarity measure between web pages to construct a K-Nearest Neighbor graph. Edge weights of the graph are computed by incorporating text similarity information and link similarity information of web pages. However, using mutual information to measure the correlation between the categories of linked web pages or the class dependency could perform poorly when there isn't class label information of web pages. Furthermore, [9] does not pay attention to feature selection problem when the number of labeled web pages is small and doesn't directly exploit topic-aware characteristic of hyperlinks.

For Vietnamese web page classification, in [8], N.M.Trung et al. proposed to exploit a main content extraction method to improve performance of web classification task using SVM. Their experimental results showed that the proposed method significantly improves the precision of the Vietnamese web page classification from 71% to 80%. However, [8] doesn't deal with the problem of the size of the "labeled" data.

The motivation for our work is based on the observation that the number of labeled web pages is often small; meanwhile, web pages on a particular topic are often linked to other pages on the same topic. Therefore, we propose a graph-based semi-supervised classification framework which combines iteratively hybrid semi-supervised feature selection and Label Propagation learning using link information to improve the accuracy of Vietnamese web page classification using small training set.

3   Gini-Index-Based Supervised Feature Selection

Feature selection is an important data processing step in web page classification because the corpus of web pages is very high dimensional dataset. Traditionally, supervised feature selection methods use information from "labeled data" to find the most informative or most useful feature subsets, but the information in the "unlabeled" data is not used. At present, the feature selection methods are based on statistical theory and machine learning. Some well-known methods are information gain, expected cross entropy, the weight of evidence of text, odds ratio, term frequency, mutual information, CHI, Gini-index and so on. The experiments in [11] show that the quality of Gini-index is comparable with other text feature selection methods. However, its complexity of computing is lower and its speed is higher. Therefore, we chose Gini-index-based supervised feature selection method for Vietnamese web page classification.

The original form of Gini-index is used to measure the impurity of attributes towards categorization. For web page classification, we use *Gini-index* to measure the discriminative quantification of a given word from the set of labeled web pages.

As a feature selection step, we compute Gini-index for each word and further remove the words that have low Gini-index. A Gini-index is regarded as low when its value is smaller than a predefined threshold. However, Gini-index can only be applied effectively when the set of labeled web pages is large since it could unintentionally remove informative and discriminative features. To alleviate the problem, as the set of labeled web pages is small, we pick a set of top *sizeFS* words which have the highest values of $G(w)$ as the features of web pages, where *sizeFS is* size of feature subset and then use them in order to construct our content-based graph.

4   Graph Construction

As with many other graph-based semi-supervised learning methods, we make the assumption that the instance graph is *homophilous* i.e., that instances belonging to the same class tend to link to each other or have higher edge weight between them. When instances are not explicitly linked to each other, usually a similarity function is applied to local features of each pair of instances to derive weighted edges between them. When instances are explicitly linked to each other, the edges simply correspond to the binary presence of a link (or are weighted by the number of links between two instances). For the corpus of web pages, hybrid approaches are used because both local features and explicit links are available.

We construct a graph based on the combination of web page content and links as follows:

1. The first phase, we build two graphs: content-based graph and link-based graph. They share the same set of nodes, but differ from on edges and their corresponding weights.
2. The second phase, we linearly combine the two graphs into an integrated graph.

Content-Based Graph Construction

We build a graph $G^1(V,E^1,W^1)$, in which V is a set of nodes, E^1 is a set of edges and W^1 is the weight matrix of E^1. Each node in V represents a webpage. The relationship between two webpage is represented by an edge in E^1. The weight W^1 could take the form of a matrix or a linked list. In this paper, W^1 is a matrix, each of its elements represent the weight of corresponding edge in the set E^1.

We represent the processed text of each webpage as a feature vector with the set of selected features of web pages based on the TF*IDF model. The weight of the edge between the two page nodes d_i and d_j based on their similarity should be calculated as follows [13]: $w_{ij}^1 = \exp(-(1 - \cos(d_i, d_j))/a)$

To reduce the edge number, we replace the fully connected graph G^1 by a ε-weighted graph that has the same set of vertices with G^1 and allows only the edges with corresponding weights greater than the given threshold ε. The employment of cutting-edge threshold has additional benefit as it could delete cross-topic edge. Although the reduction in the edge set could result in disconnected graph, this is not a problem in Label Propagation if each connected component has some labeled point.

Link-Based Graph Construction

The link-based graph $G^2(V,E^2,W^2)$ shares the same set of nodes with $G^1(V,E^1,W^1)$, and its number of edges depends on the number of hyperlinks between web pages. The reason for the employment of hyperlinks is that any two web pages should likely belong to the same topic if they are connected by a hyperlink. Unfortunately, it is common that there are a large number of noisy links in a web page such as advertisement links and navigation links. To eliminate these noisy links, we measure the similarity between linked web pages and remove the links if their similarity is lower than a threshold γ. It could also argue that the relevant pages would have low similarities due to the diversity of vocabulary used by their different authors. Fortunately, we can hardly find such cases in reality.

Graph Combination

After contracting content-based graph and link-based graph, we combine the two graphs to form a graph G(V,E,W). While the integrated graph has the same set of nodes with two former graphs. Its edge set E and weight matrix W is computed as follow: $E = E^1 \cup E^2$ and $W = \alpha W^1 + (1-\alpha)W^2$

By varying the value of α, it is possible to control the relative importance of content and link in the classification process. Furthermore, thresholds ε and γ as well as similarity measure between web pages have important role in graph construction and affect later classification confidence of graph-based semi-supervised classification algorithm.

5   Label Propagation in Graph

Label Propagation is a semi-supervised classification algorithm that assigns labels for unlabelled examples based on labeled ones. The central idea of Label Propagation algorithm is that the labels of a vertex propagate to other nodes through the edges. The algorithm remains effective when the size of training set is small. In reality, it is costly and laborious to assign labels to a large amount of data so the algorithm is more preferable. The most notable advantage of Label Propagation algorithm is that its convergence is always ensured. However, the accuracy of the algorithm is largely dependent on the similarity matrix built for web pages.

Problem statement: Given a graph G(V,E,W) and a label set C of size m. Let V_l be the subset of labeled data and $V_u = V \setminus V_l$ be the subset of unlabelled data in V. The problem is to assign labels to the unlabelled data based on G and labeled data.

We first transform the problem above into the problem of finding a probability matrix Y of size mxn in which m and n are the number of labels and vertices, respectively. The ith row of the matrix Y represents the probability distribution of vertex i over the label set C. Specifically, the value Y_{ic} corresponds to the probability of vertex i having label c. We could derive label Y_i for each vertex i from matrix Y as follows: $Y_i = \arg\max_c (Y_{ic})$. We first initialize the matrix Y^0: $Y_{ic}^0 = 1$ if vexter i has label c, 0 otherwise.

```
Algothrim 1: Label Propagation
Input: Y⁰, G(V,E,W).
Output: Y
P=D⁻¹W, where D is the diagonal matrix with D(i,i) equal
to the sum of the i-th row of W
Y←Y⁰
t←1
repeat
    Yᵗ ← PYᵗ⁻¹
until convergence to Y˙
Y←Y˙
return Y
```

The convergence of Y is reached when the algorithm executes a fixed number of iterations, *Iteration_prop,* which is usually small compared to the size of dataset.

6   Combining Iteratively Hybrid Semi-Supervised Feature Selection and Label Propagation

In fact, for web page classification, the number of labeled web pages is often small which makes it difficult to generate an ideal subset of features based only on this small labeled dataset. The Label Propagation learning algorithm, as a result, would perform poorly due to the unqualified set of features. Meanwhile, web pages on a particular topic are often linked to other pages on the same topic. Therefore, a hybrid semi-supervised feature selection method combined iteratively with the Label Propagation algorithm using link information would be a reasonable solution.

The framework takes advantages of both the supervised and semi-supervised feature selection paradigms, while can alleviate their deficiencies. Concretely, we first perform the supervised feature selection on the labeled data to obtain an initial "seed" feature subset which is used to represent the processed text of each web page, to measure the content-based similarity between web pages and to construct our content-based graph. Then, to predict the unlabeled data, we apply the Label Propagation learning on the integrated graph which combines content-based graph and link-based graph. The link-based graph is used in label propagation process to directly exploit topic-aware characteristic of hyperlinks. A new training set is built by unifying both the labeled examples and those unlabeled examples whose predicted labels are likely to be correct. After that, feature selection will be carried out on the new training set again, and the selected features will be employed to construct a new graph model for the next iteration. Therefore, during each iteration, we improve this feature subset using the unlabeled data and hence, enhance the performance of the Label Propagation learning. The proposed approach is summarized in Algorithm 2.

Algorithm 2: IterHybridFS& LabelPropagation

Input: L, U, Y^0, sizeFS, s, Iterations
Output: Y
FS = Gini-index-based Feature Selection (L), where $|FS|$ = sizeFS
newL = L; newAvgCon f = 0
G = GraphConstruction(L + U, FS)
$Y^{Predict}$ = Label Propagation (G, Y^0) through **algorithm 1**
For i = 1 **to** Iterations **do**

　　　UwithLabel defined through $Y^{Predict}$
　　　PU= top s% from UwithLabel with highest confidence
　　　AvgCon f = average prediction confidence on PU
　　If AvgCon f >newAvgCon f **then**
　　　newAvgCon f = AvgCon f
　　newL = L + PU
　　　FS = Gini-index-based Feature Selection (newL), where $|FS|$ = sizeFS
　　Else
　　　　Break
　　End if
　　G = GraphConstruction(L + U, FS)
　　$Y^{Predict}$ = Label Propagation (G, Y^0) through **algorithm 1**
End for

Y $=Y^{Predict}$
Result Y

The classification confidence of vertex i being labeled using the Label Propagation algorithm is $Y_i = \arg\max_c (Y_{ic}^{Predict})$.

Following a similar formal performance analysis as [12], the feature selection process depends on the sampled unlabeled data whereas the classification confidence by the Label Propagation algorithm is estimated based on weights of edges or similarity measures between web pages. Therefore, our framework should benefit from a better similarity measure obtained by using a confidence-based sampling strategy that provides an improved accuracy over random selection. Our experimental results corroborate the analysis.

Time complexity of IterHybridFS& LabelPropagation can be obtained as follows. k is the number of features, n is the number of web pages, m is the number of labels and *Iterations_prop* is the number of iterations in label propagation. Gini-index-based feature selection is bounded by $O(k*n+klogk)$. The construction of graph G is bounded by $O(k*n^2)$, while the Label Propagation is bounded by $O(m*n^2*Iterations\_prop)$. The costs for calculating *PU*, *FS*, and *AvgConf* are bounded by $O(nlogn)$, $O(k*n^2)$, and $O(n)$, respectively. These operations need to be performed *Iterations* times. Therefore, the overall time complexity of IteraGraph FS is bounded by $O((k*n^2+m*n^2*Iterations\_prop)*Iterations)$.

7   Experiments and Results

Currently, a standard dataset for Vietnamese web page classification research does not exist. Therefore, to evaluate the performance of our graph-based Vietnamese web Page classification method, we use web pages dataset collected from 11 websites in [8]. The dataset consists of 2500 web pages in 6 categories with nearly 25500 links between pages. These categories can be used as class labels for later evaluation. Since this dataset contains the general categories, it can be used for evaluating the overall performance of classification across websites.

In reality, web pages, especially online web pages, often contains a large amount of redundant and noise information including navigational elements, templates, and advertisements. We use the algorithm devised by Kohlschütter et al. [4] which was reported to remove noise and extract main content of web pages with a high accuracy. After obtaining main content, we perform the word segmentation on the web pages based on the probabilistic model suggested by Phuong [5]. The model could attain the accuracy of 97%.

In natural language, there are many words that convey no or little meaning in a sentence, such as linking words, preposition, conjunctions, etc. These words has no contribution to, even degrade, the classification process. They are called stopwords and we use a stopword list to remove them from the content of web pages. In the first experiment, we perform the Label Propagation algorithm as described in Section 5 to categorize the Vietnamese web pages with a= 0.1, ε= 0.009, γ= 0.001, α=0.9.

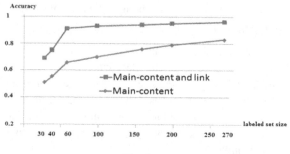

Fig. 1.

Figure 1 depicts the curves of the average accuracy of Label Propagation algorithm on dataset by using two different graph constructions: one is only to consider the content similarity of the web pages; the other is to combine the content similarity with link information. We test this two algorithms on different labeled set sizes. For each labeled set size, we perform 6 trials. In each trial, we randomly sample labeled web pages from the entire dataset, and use the rest of dataset as unlabeled web pages. Figure 1 shows that the classification accuracies are higher when both content similarity and link information are involved. It demonstrates that the exploiting link information allows improving the accuracy of Vietnamese web page classification significantly.

In the second experiment, we perform the IterHybridFS& LabelPropagation algorithm as described in Section 6 to catego-rize the Vietnamese web pages with *sizeFS =3000, %s=30%, Iteration_prop = 20, Iterations = 10.*

The performance of the IterHybridFS& LabelPropagation algorithm is compared with the two Label Propagation algorithms in the integrated graphs in which content-based graph construction uses full text and Gini-index based supervised selection feature. Figure 2 depicts the curves of the average accuracy of classify-cation on the dataset by using three different algorithms and confirms our remark.

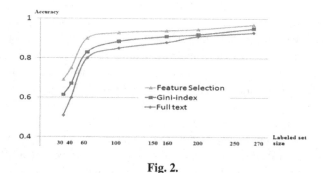

Fig. 2.

The result showed in figure 2 indicates that the mean of the classification accuracies of IterHybridFS& LabelPropagation algorithm are higher than that of two others. In the algorithm based on full text, the high dimensionality of the feature space makes the similarity between any two web pages approximately the same which puts the accuracy of algorithm at the lowest position. Besides, when the number of labeled web pages is small, Gini-index-base supervised feature selection techniques often fails due to the sample selection bias or the unrepresentative sample problem. Experimental results demonstrate that the proposed IterHybridFS& LabelPropagation algorithm outperforms two other algorithms by at least 8% in accuracy.

8   Conclusion

Classification plays a vital role in many information management and retrieval tasks. On the web, classification of page content is essential to focused crawling, to the assisted development of web directories, to topic-specific web link analysis, and to analysis of the topical structure of the web. Web page classification can also help improve the quality of web search.

This paper proposed a graph-based semi-supervised classification framework which combines iteratively hybrid semi-supervised feature selection and Label Propagation

The framework has the following main advantage:

(1) It performs supervised feature selection before predicting on unlabeled data, thereby maintaining the most critical features.
(2) It uses Label Propagation learning with link information, thereby providing a better prediction confidence.
(3) It uses confidence-based sampling strategy through Label Propagation learning with link information, thereby producing better new training dataset. Furthermore, the sufficiency and diversity of the new training set can be improved, which in return helps to choose the most discriminative features.

As the result, our experiments show that the proposed classification method outperforms the state-of-the art methods applying to Vietnamese web page classification.

While our results are encouraging, there are still much improvements to be made. The current training set is still using electronic newspapers. Therefore, it can not represent all types of web page. It is necessary to build a standard Vietnamese web page data set in the future. Another problem is that we can not perform this method on a web page without text such as a flash website or a picture website, so another solution should be used in this case.

References

1. Angelova, R., Weikum, G.: Graph-based text classification: learn from your neighbors. In: SIGIR 2006 (2006)
2. Chakrabarti, S., Dom, B.E., Indyk, P.: Enhanced hypertext categorization using hyperlinks. In: SIGMOD 1998, pp. 307–318 (1998)
3. Ghani, R., Slattery, S., Yang, Y.: Hypertext Categorization using Hyperlink Patterns and Meta Data. In: ICML 2001 (2001)

4. Kohlschütter, C., Fankhauser, P., Nejdl, W.: Boilerplate Detection using Shallow Text Features. In: WSDM 2010 – The Third ACM International Conference on Web Search and Data Mining, New York, City, USA (2010)
5. Hông Phuong, L., Thi Minh Huyên, N., Roussanaly, A., Vinh, H.T.: A Hybrid Approach to Word Segmentation of Vietnamese Texts. In: Martín-Vide, C., Otto, F., Fernau, H. (eds.) LATA 2008. LNCS, vol. 5196, pp. 240–249. Springer, Heidelberg (2008)
6. Liu, R., Zhou, J., Liu, M.: A Graph-based Semi-supervised Learning Algorithm for Web Page Classification. In: Proceedings of the Sixth International Conference on Intelligent Systems Design and Applications, ISDA 2006 (2006)
7. Lu, Q., Getoor, L.: Link-based classification. In: ICML (2003)
8. Trung, N.M., Tam, N.D., Phuong, N.H.: Using main content extraction to improve performance of Vietnamese web page classification. In: SoICT 2011, Hanoi, Vietnam, October 13-14 (2011)
9. Oh, H.J., Myaeng, S.H., Lee, M.H.: A practical hypertext categorization method using links and incrementally available class information. In: SIGIR, pp. 264–271 (2000)
10. Ren, J., Qiu, Z., Fan, W., Cheng, H., Yu, P.S.: Forward Semi-supervised Feature Selection. In: Washio, T., Suzuki, E., Ting, K.M., Inokuchi, A. (eds.) PAKDD 2008. LNCS (LNAI), vol. 5012, pp. 970–976. Springer, Heidelberg (2008)
11. Shang, W., Huang, H., Zhu, H.: A Novel feature selection algorithm for text categorization. Expert System with Application 33, 1–5 (2007)
12. Zhong, E., Xie, S., Fan, W., Ren, J., Peng, J., Zhang, K.: Graph-based Iterative Hybrid Feature Selection. In: Proceeding ICDM 2008 Proceedings of the 2008 Eighth IEEE International Conference on Data Mining (2008)
13. Strehl, A., Ghosh, J., Mooney, R.J.: Impact of similarity measures on web-page clustering. In: AAAI Workshop (2000)

Handwriting Recognition Using B-Spline Curve

Khoi Nguyen-Tan and Nguyen Nguyen-Hoang

DATIC Lab., DaNang University of Technology
ntkhoi@dut.udn.vn, hoangnguyenbkit@gmail.com

Abstract. This paper aims at presenting novel approach for curve matching and character recognition such as printed writing, handwriting, signatures, etc. based on B-Spline curve. The advantages of the B-Spline that are continuous curve representation and affine invariant, and the robustness. The recognition process is composed of two main steps: sample training and recognition. The computer must be trained with data from bitmap image file. The next step is pre-processing input data from the binary image and finding its skeleton. The reconstruction of a B-Spline curve representing the sample character is applied to find out the control points. Then the sample B-spline curve of each character is stored in a database. For the test character, it has the same process with the sample character. The matching is done by computing the Euclidean distance between the control points of test curve with those of all sample characters to recognize the character. The experimental results show the performance of the proposed algorithm.

Keywords: B-Spline curve, matching curve, handwriting, Optical character, recognition, reconstruction.

1   Introduction

Optical character recognition is a subject that attracts the attention of many researchers but comprehensive solutions for this problem have not been found yet. The key principle of optical character recognition is the description of characters; the result of recognition will be captured by the comparison of these characteristics [1-6]. Speed and accuracy of recognition system depend greatly on the approach, and description of character features. Character recognition is getting more and more useful in daily life for various purposes. During the last few years, researchers have made great efforts on off-line signature recognition. There are many rather effective recognition methods proposed, such as neural network, support vector machine, etc.., and other methods [15, 16]. Character recognition is a form of pattern recognition process. In reality, it is very difficult to achieve 100% accuracy. Many researchers have been done on many types of characters by using different approaches. However, these methods have difficulty recognizing the samples that are larger than the previously studied samples in term of size; the time of training systems are quite large in number; and it is difficult to reconstruct characters.

Major of these researches are about signature verification, however some of them are about character identification. In [1] proposed a wavelet-based offline signature

P.C. Vinh et al. (Eds.): ICCASA 2012, LNICST 109, pp. 335–346, 2013.

verification system that exist within different signatures of the same class and verify whether a signature is a forgery or not. [2] present a signature verification system using Discrete Radon Transform and Dynamic Programming. The author in [3] have used Radon Transform and Hidden Markov Model (HMM) for offline signature verification. Features are extracted by Radon Transform and fed to a HMM classifier.

In [11], the authors compared different statistical methods by using a feature extraction preprocessing, to carry out the recognition of signatures. In [12], the performance of a signature recognition system based on support vector machines (SVM) has been compared with a traditional classification technique, multi-layer perceptrons (MLP). Experimental results show that the performance of SVM is higher than MLP. The common way used for character recognition would be the use of artificial neural networks and feature extraction methods [5]. In [9,10] has proposed an algorithm is based on constructing and comparing B-spline curves of object boundaries.

In this paper, we present a method by using B-splines representation for optical character recognition. The main idea is each character presenting as a curve and its characteristics are described by the control points of B-Spline curve. We combines the advantages of B-spline that are continuous curve representation [7,8] and the robustness of dissimilar matching with respect to noise and affine transformation. It avoids the need for other matching algorithms that have to use the resampled points on the curve. The proposed algorithm has been tested by matching similar shapes from a prototype database. Our experimental results demonstrate that we can achieve good recognizing results.

The rest of this paper is organized as follows: In section 2, overview related works. Section 3 addresses the main steps of our algorithm. In section 4, reconstruction of B-spline curves based on inverse subdivision method are described. Finally, section 5 proposed method for dissimilarity calculations between curves method are described and experimental results are given to demonstrate the usefulness and quality of the approach.

2   Character Recognition Using B-Spline Curve

This section discusses the mathematical formulation of the problem of aligning two curves. We first consider the case of aligning two curve segments and then use this to align two closed curves.

During the process of writing or signing, all characters are formed by certain curves; each word or letter can be considered as a curve. In geometric modeling, B-spline stands as one of the most efficient curve representation. With the property of easy local controlling being invariant under affine transformations such as translation allowed, scales, rotations, B-Spline curve is suitable to simulate handwriting, printed texts or signatures of people with different spellings. The B-spline curve is not uniquely described by a set of control points. The construction of B-Spline curve with each character results in the problem of recognizing the matching set of control points of them.

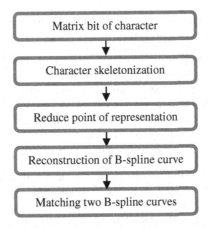

Fig. 1. Steps of handwriting recognition

The main steps of the algorithm are as follows:

1) Scanning and transformation of the document: A printed document is scanned by scanner and can be saved in a bitmap file format. The next, this bitmap file is converted it to monochrome binary image. Now the image is ready to be processed.

2) Segmentation into lines and segments lines into characters: the partitioning of lines from the total document based on thresholding histogram values gathered horizontally. Then characters are segmented from each line by using values of vertical histogram. The next step will process these individual character segmented.

3) Binary the character bitmaps, or transform the image of characters into a bit matrix (convention that black pixel is 0 and white pixels is 1).

4) Finding the skeleton of the characters segmented.

5) Transformation of the bit matrix into the list of co-ordinations

6) Reduction of point number that represents the character skeletonization, retains only main medial axis of a character.

7) Reconstructing B-spline curve from pixel points of the character skeletonization. This process to find the set of control points of B-spline curve.

8) Matching the control points of test B-spline curve and sample B-spline curve to recognize the character corresponding.

These steps are explicitly presented in Figure 1.

2.1 Skeletonization

The objective of skeletonization is to find the medial axis of a character. Skeletonization is the process of thinning of a pattern as many pixels as possible without affecting the general shape of the pattern. After pixels have been thinned, the pattern should still be recognized.

The process of character segmentation is made thin to a unit pixel thickness. There are two main methods of skeletonization:

1) Skeletonization based on smoothing: Considering all the pixels of the object, if it satisfies certain delete conditions, it will be deleted. The skeletonization process is repeated until there is no more pixels which can be deleted.

2) Skeletonization not based on smoothing: Considering at any point of the object, if there are many points of edge which have the same shortest distance to that point; it lies on the median axis. The set of points lying on the median axis of the object forms the skeleton of the character.

We chose the skeletonization based on smoothing algorithm and Hilditch's algorithms [17] for these methods are robust and easy to install. The Figure 2 illustrates a result of skeletonization algorithm for a bitmap character. This algorithm deletes the extra pixels which do not belong to the backbone of the character.

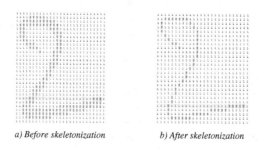

a) Before skeletonization   *b) After skeletonization*

Fig. 2. Result of skeletonization

2.2   Reducing the Number of Data Points

After the skeletonization of character segmented, we obtain a series of consecutive points. The purpose of this step is to minimize the number of point performing the curve and reduce storage space and it is more convenient to find the controlling vector of the characters and to match later.

The curve C(u) consists of n points in the plane $(x_1, y_1), (x_2, y_2)...(x_n, y_n)$. The problem is to remove a number of points on the curve so that a new curve $(x_{i1}, y_{i1}), (x_{i2}, y_{i2})...(x_{im}, y_{im})$ are "nearly identical" to the original curve. Algorithms Bandwidth [17] is used as follow:

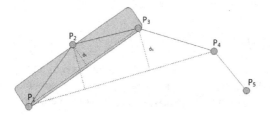

Fig. 3. Result of bandwidth algorithm

1) Identify the first point on the curve and see it as a key point (P_1). The point (P_3) is considered as the variable point. The mid-point (P_2) of the key point and the variable point is intermediate point. The distance between these points is optional.

2) Calculate the distance from the intermediate point to the line connecting the key point and the variable point.

3) Check the distance found. If that distance is smaller than a given threshold θ, the intermediate points can be removed. Otherwise, the key point moves to the intermediate point. In this paper, we chose the value of threshold is *0.4*.

4) The process is repeated, the intermediate point is transferred to the variable point and the next point of the variable one is appointed the new variable point.

The example of this process result is shown in the following Figure 2.

The skeleton hence obtained must have the following properties: as thin as possible, connected, centered. Therefore the result of skeletonization character will be taken as input to the B-spline curve approximation step.

The B-spline curve is considered as an appropriate model for character recognition. In the next section, we present the B-spline mathematical formula and the B-spline curve reconstruction algorithm.

3   B-Spline Curve Approximation

In the following we represent the mathematical formulation of the reconstructing B-spline curve. We shall assume a B-Spline curve $C(u)$ of degree p which is defined by n control points $P = \{P_0, P_1, \ldots, P_{n-1} \mid P_i \in \Re^k\}$. Let a vector known as the knot vector be defined by $\mathbf{U} = \{u_0, u_1, \ldots, u_{n+p}\}$, where U is a nondecreasing sequence that satisfies $u_i \in [0,1]$ and $u_i \leq u_{i+1}$. Then, the B-Spline curve is defined as [7,8]:

$$C(u) = \sum_{i=0}^{n} P_i . N_{i,p}(u)$$

The B-Spline basis functions $N_{i,k}$ are defined as [5]:

$$N_{i,0}(t) = \begin{cases} 1 & u_i \leq t \leq u_{i-1} \\ 0 & otherwise \end{cases}$$

$$N_{i,p}(u) = \frac{u - u_i}{u_{i+p} - u_i} N_{i,p-1}(u) + \frac{u_{i+p+1} - u}{u_{i+p+1} - u_{i+1}} N_{i+1,p-1}(u)$$

The shapes of the $N_{i,k}$ basis functions are determined entirely by the relative spacing between the knot vector U.   B-Splines consist of sections of polynomial curves connected at points called knots. The knot vector defines how the polynomial pieces are blended together with the proper smoothness and determines where and how the control points affect the B-spline curve. If duplication happens at the other knots, we can generate a curve with sharp turns or even discontinuities.

The problem is reconstructing smooth curve from an discrete point data set.

We present in this section a new B-Spline curve reconstruction method based on the non-uniform inverse subdivision scheme (NUISS) [13,14]. As the subdivision scheme is invertible, one can restore recursively all the previous coarser polygon by using the inverse subdivision scheme. Consequently, it also permits to reconstruct the control polygon of a limit parametric curve issued from a nonuniform subdivision curve. After each step of the inverse subdivision, we retrieve curve elements of the previous subdivision curve. The knot intervals are already determined by retaking the information of input polygonal curve.

We propose the formulas to compute the inverse subdivision points based on the formulas of non-uniform cubic B-Spline curve subdivision in [13, 14]. The inverse vertex point P_i^k of polygonal curve P^k (Figure 4) is computed based on the points of polygonal curve P^{k+1} by the following formulas [13,14]:

$$P_i^k = 2P_{2i-1}^{k+1} - \frac{d_i P_{2i-2}^{k+1} + d_{i-1} P_{2i}^{k+1}}{d_{i-1} + d_i} \qquad for\ i = 1...n\text{-}1$$

$$P_i^k = \frac{2(d_{i-1} + d_i + d_{i+1})P_{2i}^{k+1} - (d_i + 2d_{i-1})P_{i+1}^k}{d_i + 2d_{i+1}} \quad for\ i = 1...n\text{-}2$$

$$P_{i+1}^k = \frac{2(d_{i-1} + d_i + d_{i+1})P_{2i}^{k+1} - (d_i + 2d_{i+1})P_i^k}{d_i + 2d_{i-1}} \quad for\ i = n\text{-}2$$

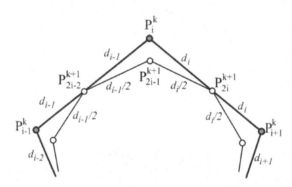

Fig. 4. The relation of inverse points P^k with the points P^{k+1}

For our reconstruction NUISS method, we must determine the knot interval vectors $U = \{u_0, ..., u_{n+p}\}$. As these vectors are computed from knot vectors, we propose to define the knot vector from the input initial polygonal curve. The knot vector greatly affects the shape and parameterization of a B-spline curve. Fundamentally three types of knot vector are used: uniform, open uniform and non-uniform. Different parametric methods have been proposed. We only consider the most widely-used parametric chord length method [5].

Suppose that we are given a set of points $\{P_i\}$ *(i = 0,..., n-1)*, we will find the parametric values $\{u_i \mid 0 \le u_i \le 1, i = 0,...,n-1\}$ associated with these points $\{P_i\}$. Therefore, we use open uniform knot vector and it is defined by the following formula [7,8]:

$$\bar{u}_0 = 0, \quad \bar{u}_{n-1} = 1$$

$$\bar{u}_i = \bar{u}_{i-1} + \frac{\left|P_i - P_{i-1}\right|}{\sum\limits_{j=1}^{n-1}\left|P_i - P_{i-1}\right|} \quad \forall i \in [1,...,n-2]$$

with $\left|P_i - P_{i-1}\right|$ is the length between two consecutive points.

Our goal is to create knot interval vectors for an initial polygonal curve to implement the NUISS scheme, and also to reconstruct the non-uniform B-Spline curve. The knot interval vectors for the initial polygon curve P can be created by using the parametric chord length method. From the initial polygonal curve P with initial knot interval vectors, we can recreate the coarse polygonal curve Q by our NUISS scheme. This coarse curve Q using as a control polygon of the non-uniform B-Spline curve C(u), the knot vectors of which are created from the corresponding knot interval vectors of the polygonal curve. It creates an approximate B-Spline curve reconstruction. The main advantage of our algorithm NUISS is that it can also give us good results for verification purposes and this approach completely avoids the parameterization problem. As the inverse subdivision can be stopped after each step, different approximation curve can be obtained. An interpolation curve is obtained by locally interpolation fitting the given initial data points.

3.1   Matching Using B-Spline Curve

In this step each test character will be recognized and will be identified to a predefined test character. For our algorithm, we made the test character and sample character have the same size. Therefore, it is easily to reconstruct the B-spline curves representing of these characters. All reconstructed B-spline curves have the same degree and number of control points for the matching.

We use the Euclidean distance to evaluate the dissimilarity between two control points set In mathematics. The Euclidean distance or Euclidean metric is the "ordinary" distance between two control points corresponding of two B-spline curves.

With two set of control points $P = (P_1, P_2,...,P_n)$ and $H = (H_1, H_2,...,H_n)$, in N-dimensional Euclidean space, the distance between points P_i and H_i is the length of the line segment connecting them $\overline{P_i H_i}$. Therefore, the Euclidean distance is given by:

$$E(p,q) = \sqrt{\sum_{k=1}^{n}\left(p_i - q_i\right)^2}$$

In the exception case, if the length of two control-point vectors are different, suppose that P has the length n, Q has the length m, with $m>n$, then we need to add $k=m-n$ control points to reconstruct the new B-spline curve for two vectors have the same size.

4   Experimental Results

The test character will be matched with all sample characters. The result of recognition is the studied sample which has the minimal error E with the tested sample.

4.1   Printed Text Recognition

In this experimental, we present an example of recognition a printed text document. Figure 5 shows the training of a test character of number eight in one ten number characters. Curve matching is achieved by computing the Euclidean distances. Also we have tested on different sizes of characters. With the test number character is presented in 14 point Arial font, the accuracy of the recognition process reach 100%. With the 19 point Arial font of size 18, the recognition accuracy is 98%, and with the same Arial font but size 10, the recognition accuracy is 90%.

The recognition result of the large test character is better than that of the small test character. The reason is when using the small size; the character skeletons *should also have a corresponding small size*. Then, the *reconstruction of B-spline curve* from a small point is not well approximated with the initial data points.

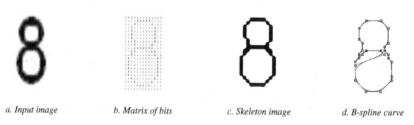

a. Input image   b. Matrix of bits   c. Skeleton image   d. B-spline curve

Fig. 5. The process of recognition of eight font Arial

4.2   Handwriting Recognition

This type of recognition is a function that allows to write onscreen in a small panel, and to recognize characters and other symbols written by hand in natural handwriting. Figures 6(a-d) illustrate our surface reconstruction method applied to the skidoo model. We also present other examples in Figure 3. In order to compare the fitting error across different models, we uniformly scale the data points P to fit within a unit cube.

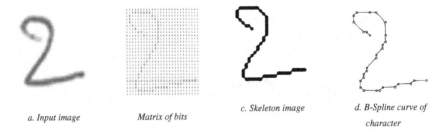

a. Input image	Matrix of bits

c. Skeleton image

d. B-Spline curve of character

Fig. 6. Process of recognition of handwritten

Let the machine learn handwritten digit that has the image size is *40×40px*. The result is as follow (Figure 6).

By computing the Euclidean distances between the sample curves from database and the test B-spline curve reconstructed from the character image, we are able to recognize the character by locating the minimum distance in the table of distances (Table 1).

Table 1. Matching result between sample tests and trained one (handwritten) with the Euclid measure

Sample trained	1 2 3 4 5 6 7 8 9 0									
Sample test	1 2 3 4 5 6 7 8 9 0									
Train Recog.	0	1	2	3	4	5	6	7	8	9
0	**63.73**	114.98	123.23	97.78	122.36	130.28	172.9	161.54	132.29	84.34
1	82.81	**51.75**	81.5	61.23	62.31	71.29	55.54	68.18	107.71	84.83
2	96.04	88.82	**43.69**	129.41	107.33	98.79	155.68	134.38	171.39	178.17
3	81.75	111.58	88.86	**72.91**	110.92	138.25	132.78	87.63	147.84	108.88
4	119.96	76.96	173.73	158.01	**55.56**	116.11	167.26	94.88	185.07	202.79
5	144.68	199.79	139.73	124.12	179.73	**66.34**	145.69	169.94	226.97	191.51
6	103.31	173.64	106.95	80.67	150.66	120.46	**65.29**	146.15	122.56	86.24
7	156.03	206.05	166.55	103.29	136.72	157.35	172.52	**95.33**	189.87	152.28
8	80.09	136.72	89.5	75.34	120.41	119.12	104.45	117.33	**40.84**	113.59
9	130.19	157.74	208.57	104.95	195.96	202.68	199.57	150.13	179.47	**91.11**

Table 1 shows the experimental results where after eight tests, average recognition accuracy of 95 % is obtained. The blue cell illustrated the minimum Euclidean distance in each row of the table. We have set the reference set font as Times New Roman type with size 20.

4.3 Signature Recognition

The signature identification and verification is very important in security and resource access control. Signature recognition examines a person when he signs her name. Many documents such as forms and bank checks necessitate the signing of a signature.

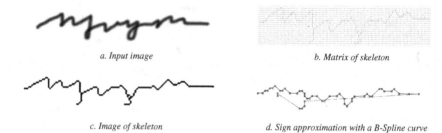

a. Input image   b. Matrix of skeleton

c. Image of skeleton   d. Sign approximation with a B-Spline curve

Fig. 7. Process of recognition of sign

We have to fit a B-Spline curve with sample from a signature image of a person. The sample B-spline curve stored in a database. By computing the differences between the test B-spline curves and all sample curves from database using Euclidean distance, we are able to identify the person by locating the minimum value in all distances.

Let the program learns three sample signatures of three different people (named Long, Nguyen, Yen). The steps of recognition process are illustrated in the Figure 8.

Table 2. Result of matching between sample tests and trained one (signature) with the measure Euclid

Recognize \ Train	(signature 1)	(signature 2)	(signature 3)
(sig a)	**1494.12**	2243.58	9708.1
(sig b)	3153.64	**1236.71**	4333.74
(sig c)	11365.59	10132.86	**7066.92**
	Long	Nguyen	Yen

In the Table 2, the blue cell is the minimum value in each row. The results in Table 1 and Table 2 show that the method of using B-Spline curves to recognize the same sized characters as well as the signature have high percentage of accuracy. Especially, the larger the tested samples are, the more accurate of the recognition is, because the specific deviation and the size are directly proportional. However, when the recognition system recognizes small samples, a specific deviation decreases, it will the resulting in the confusion of the recognition among samples.

5   Conclusions and Further Work

In this paper we deal with the problem of matching and recognizing the optical characters including printed text, handwriting and signature which are modeled as B-splines. The essence of this recognition is comparing the test characters with the sample trained ones. First, the computer must be trained with sample data from bitmap image file. The next step is pre-processing input data including creating the binary image and finding its skeleton. Then the reconstruction of B-Spline curve from skeleton is applied to find out the control points of the character and save them into a sample. The recognition process has the same process. The last step is computation the Euclidean distance between the control points of the test character and the trained samples. The return result is the trained samples that have the smallest Euclidean distance with the control points of the sample character.

The most important part of this recognition method is all the reconstructed B-spline curves from characters have the same degree and number of control points. It makes the identification process easier and less time taken one. Thus, the curve matching error is reduced. The organization of sample data storage is also very important impact on the rate and precision of recognition process. We have run the algorithm to many styles of characters and get high accuracy on those styles. The experimental results showed the robustness and accuracy of the proposed method in B-spline curve matching. The results of recognition characters can be applied in many areas such as text translator, intelligent word recognition, internet search engines…

Further work is improving methods and deploying applications for text recognition. Also parallel approaches may be explored to get the performance of text document recognition process.

References

1. Deng, P.S., Liao, H.-Y.M., Ho, C.W., Tyan, H.-R.: Wavelet–based Off–line Signature Verification. Computer Vision and Image Understanding 76(3), 173–190 (1997)
2. Herbst, B., Coetzer, H.: On An Offline Signature Verification System. In: 9th Annual South African Workshop on Pattern Recognition, pp. 39–43 (1998)
3. Coetzer, J., Herbst, B.M., Du Preez, J.A.: Offline Signature Verification Using the Discrete Radon Transform and a Hidden Markov Model. Eurasip Journal on Applied Signal Processing 4, 559–571 (2004)
4. Basu, J.K., Bhattacharyya, D., Kim, T.-H.: Use of Artificial Neural Network in Pattern Recognition. International Journal of Software Engineering and Its Applications 4(2) (2010)
5. Izakian, H., et al.: Multi-Font Farsi/Arabic Isolated Character Recognition Using Chain Codes. World Academy of Science, Engineering and Technology 43, 67–70 (2008)
6. Pal, U., Dutta, S.: Segmentation of Bangla Unconstrained Handwritten Text. In: ICDAR, 7th, pp. 1128–1132 (2003)
7. Piegl, L., Tiller, W.: The NURBS Book, 2nd edn. Springer (1997)
8. Rogers, D.F.: An Introduction to NURBS With Historical Perspective (2001)
9. Tirandaz, H., Nasrabadi, A., Haddadnia, J.: Curve Matching and Character Recognition by Using B-Spline Curves. IACSIT International Journal of Engineering and Technology 3(2) (2011)
10. Tirandaz, H., Nasrabadi, A., Haddadnia, J.: Curve Matching and Character Recognition by Using B-Spline Curves. IACSIT International Journal of Engineering and Technology 3(2) (2011)

11. Riba, J.R., et al.: Method for invariant signature classification. In: Proceedings of 15th International Conference on Pattern Recognition, vol. 2, pp. 953–956 (2000)

12. Frias-Martinez, E., Sanchez, A., Velez, J.: Support vector machines versus multi-layer perceptrons for efficient off-line signature. Engineering Applications of Artificial Intelligence 19, 693–704 (2006)

13. Nguyen-Tan, K., Le, C.: A method for describing planar cam profile function from a set of digital points. In: Proceedings of the 10th Global Congress on Manufacturing and Management, Thailand, pp. 145–150 (2010)

14. Nguyen-Tan, K., Raffin, R., Daniel, M., Le, C.: B-spline surface reconstruction by inverse subdivisions. In: Proceedings of the 7th International Conference on Computing and Communication Technologies, pp. 336–339 (2009)

15. Mokhtarian, F., Mackworth, A.K.: Scale-Based Description and Recognition of Planar Curves and Two dimensional Shapes. IEEE Trans. PAMI. PAMI-8, 34–43 (1986)

16. Ozdil, M.A., Vural, F.T.Y.: Optical character recognition without segmentation. In: Proceedings of the Fourth International Conference on Document Analysis and Recognition, vol. 2, pp. 483–486. IEEE Computer Society (1997)

17. Cheriet, M., Kharma, N., Liu, C.-L., Suen, C.Y.: Character recognition systems A guide for Students and Practioners. Wiley (2007)

Development of an OPC UA SDK Based WCF Technology and Its Deployment for Environmental Monitoring Applications

Tu Nguyen Thi Thanh and Thang Huynh Quyet

School of Information and Communication Technology,
Hanoi University of Science and Technology, Hanoi, Vietnam
thanhtu@hut.edu.vn, thanghq@soict.hut.edu.vn

Abstract. This paper focuses on a technological innovation that has been applied in many countries and still has continuously been researched to enhance its effectiveness – OPC (Openness, Productivity, and Connectivity) Unified Architecture. OPC Unified Architecture (OPC UA) is new specification used for the connection of accessories, based on open form, and independent of any technological systems. OPC UA gains access to data base and events following its real time or are stored through safe, trustworthy and totally separate connection. The research presented in this paper attempts to introduce the development of an OPC UA SDK based WCF technology and used for monitoring and control systems. The deployment of the proposed OPC UA SDK for an environmental monitoring application (EMA) is also presented as an illustration of the successful development of the proposed OPC UA SDK. This SDK in turn makes system architects and developers easy to design and implement applications in terms of environmental monitoring. In addition, this also reduces the development time and cost for such applications.

Keywords: OPC UA, SDK, XML, WCF technology, web service.

1 Introduction

Extensible Markup Language (XML) is a markup language in which users can define their own tags. XML tags not only show how the data should appear as in HTTP but also convey information about the meaning of data [1, 2]. In order to share information and knowledge among different applications, a shared set of terms describing the application domain with a common understanding is needed. XML concept has been used in the OPC XML-DA specification and the OPC UA specifications. XML based languages provide the means to represent the content, semantics, and schemata of data [3]. By utilizing the exchange of data using a non-proprietary data format, XML is particularly variable in supporting interoperability in distributed heterogeneous environments such as the Internet. XML based languages are used for developing XML based description model as studied and introduced by Wang and Lu [4], Fourer et al. [5], Nugent et al. [6], Wollchlaeger and Bangermann [7], Wollschlaeger et al. [8], etc.

P.C. Vinh et al. (Eds.): ICCASA 2012, LNICST 109, pp. 347–356, 2013.
© Institute for Computer Sciences, Social Informatics and Telecommunications Engineering 2013

Web services technology is software components by describing via Web Services Description Language (WSDL) in which web services are capable of being accessed via standard network protocols such as SOAP over HTTP. Today web services are accepted in practice, industry, and the business [10, 11]. The OPC Foundation now is working on supporting XML and web services as well as proposed in the OPC UA specifications [12]. The greatest advantage of web services is that they allow applications running on different platforms using different architectures and are coded by different program languages. The size of XML messages is very large compared to the size of DCOM messages. However, binary data encoding approach can be used for web services to improve the performance as pointed by Eppler et al. [14], Bayardo et al. [15], etc.

The OPC Foundation in partnership with various industry leaders is publicizing OPC, XML, web services, and openly embracing Microsoft's .NET technology. The OPC UA technology will open much of the business world to process data and distributed information. It will enable management to make informed business decisions faster. The OPC Foundation has clearly indicated that the OPC UA standard intends to enable enterprise interoperability and expects to solve enterprise integration challenges. This is a very ambitious undertaking and has been difficult to determine what elements of enterprise interoperability can actually be standardized. It is clear that the OPC UA standard does not provide everything needed for interoperability from the enterprise IT perspective, but the impact is expected to be considerable.

OPC UA has demonstrated the practicality and effectiveness of it, but in Vietnam the application and studies of OPC UA is very limited, even without any public company research results. On the other hand the specification of the organization of the OPC Foundation OPC UA standard is very flexible and not dependent on any platform, so it is very abstract and elusive. In the SDK was developed by OPC UA standard is either very expensive, not for research purposes (Prosys, UA SDK), or is not fully functional (free version of the Unified Automation), and have the general is closed for application development. Building an SDK in the specification of the OPC Foundation and write applications to illustrate the function has been supported in the SDK, then, using the SDK in the application of information management environment for validating application for practicality and efficiency of the OPC UA standard.

Nowadays, environmental pollution has become one of the hot issues of Vietnam in particular and world in general. Vietnam in the process of modernizing the country, many businesses have very high priority on the issue that returns to the disregard of sustainable development, discharge of untreated wastewater into the environment during produce serious effects on the environment that the violations were the most public concern. In order to prevent acts of unlawful discharge of environmental agencies also frequently measured and the status update in the near industrial areas, but this approach requires officials to make the observation result costly and inefficient. Therefore, the need is to setup a monitoring system/automatic quality monitoring of wastewater from factories and enterprises.

One important application of OPC UA is in the monitoring system control and data acquisition. It is optimized for communication between server and client. The OPC UA systems are used to build the central server application and client application in monitoring stations. Server will model the system's information into the address space, and the client will make the registry change tracking data to continuously update the measured data.

The research attempts to introduce the development of an OPC UA SDK and its deployment for an environmental monitoring application (EMA). This application demonstrates the successful development of the proposed OPC UA SDK. This SDK makes system architects and developers easy to develop their applications and also reduces the development time and cost for this kind of applications.

This paper is organized as follows: The next section provides a background and related work. In Section 3 introduces the design and implementation of an OPC UA SDK. In Section 4, development of an environmental monitoring application is presented. The experiment and discussion is presented in Section 5. Finally, Section 6 concludes some remarks and future works.

2   Related Work

The OPC foundation is an independent, non-profit, industry trade association comprised of more than 470 leading automation suppliers worldwide. In this section, several overviews of related OPC technologies are provided. It is dedicated to ensuring interoperability in automation by creating and maintaining open specifications that standardize the communication of acquired process data, alarms and events, historical data, and batch data to multi-vendor enterprise system and between production devices. The production devices include sensors, instruments, PLCs, RTUs, DCSs, HMIs, historians, trending subsystems, alarm subsystems, etc.

Recently, more than 22000 products are based on the OPC specifications. Current OPC specifications and those being developed include important industrial issues like Data Access (DA), Alarms and Events (AE), Historical Data Access (HDA), Security [13, 14]. The new OPC UA specifications now have been released [9, 16]. This standard is the next generation technology for secure, reliable, and interoperable transport of raw data and preprocessed information from the plant floor (or shop floors) to production planning or the ERP systems. It extends the existing OPC industry standards with fundamental features such as platform independence, scalability, high availability, Internet capability, and much more. In particular, platform independence and scalability allow completely new and cost-effective automation designs to be implemented. The OPC UA technology enables all three types of data - current data, historical data, and alarms and events - to be accessed by a single OPC server, making each type of data relative to each other. Three different types of data with different semantics today have been required in automation systems, for example, to capture the current value of a temperature sensor, an event resulting from a temperature threshold violation, and the historic mean temperature. The OPC Foundation has clearly indicated that the OPC UA standard intends to enable enterprise interoperability and expects to solve enterprise integration challenges. This is a very ambitious undertaking and has been difficult to determine what elements of enterprise interoperability can actually be standardized. It is clear that the OPC UA standard does not provide everything needed for interoperability from the enterprise IT perspective, but the impact is expected to be considerable.

3   Design and Implementation of an OPC UA SDK

To consider the situation of developing an OPC UA client-server application for specific applications, both client and server have specific functionality according to use cases, for example the OPC UA server acquires a data source from devices and the OPC UA client is used to display and draw these data. However, the problems are that trying to separate the functionality into general functionality and dependent functionality for use cases. The general functionality is classified into high-level functionality for connection management, session, etc., and lower-level functionality for data encoding, security, and data transportation, etc. Therefore, the application architecture based on the OPC UA standard can be shown in Fig. 1 (a).

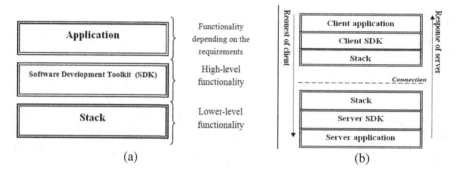

Fig. 1. (a) Application architecture diagram OPC UA standard. (b) Diagram system between server and client.

The system architecture of an OPC UA client-server application can be represented in Fig. 1 (b) including the OPC UA client application and OPC UA server application. It is easy to seem that data from the OPC UA server will pass through OPC UA Client SDK in order to convert into encoded data. The encoded data is transported by the stack in the server side. The goal of this research is only to focus on developing high-level functionality. The lower-level functionality is executed by the use of Windows Communication Foundation (WCF) technology from Microsoft.

3.1   Architecture of the Proposed OPC UA SDK

As aforementioned, the proposed OPC UA SDK has the following functionality:

    i. Connection secure
   ii. Session management, e.g., set timeout for the session, etc.
  iii. Address space management

iv. Subscription management
v. Other functionality like logging, exception handling, etc.

3.2   The Proposed OPC UA SDK and WCF Technology

WCF technology is a platform technology in order to unify interface programming models supported in .NET 2.0. This technology allows developers to implement service solutions to reach stability, flexibility, secure-ability, etc. It reduces the development time and cost for developers [9]. Thus, WCF technology is a compatible technology for developing OPC UA standard and OPC UA SDK.

3.3   The OPC UA Server SDK

The architecture of the proposed OPC UA Server SDK with the mentioned functionality is shown in Fig. 2. The description of each component of OPC UA Server SDK is summarized as follows:

i. ServerBase: This class provides the functions of an OPC UA Server application. The server will start after the function Star() is called.

ii. IServerIntenalData: This is an interface for providing functions that will be called and used by other components in the OPC UA server. For example, SessionManager needs information from NodeManager and SubscriptionManager need to check a session managed by the SessionManager. This interface includes classes as shown like SessionManager, INodeManager, SubscriptionManager, ApplicationDescription, EndpointDescription, and ISecurityHelper.

iii. ServiceHost: This component is included in .NET Framework to create the endpoint of the services.

iv. MasterNodeManager and INodeManager: These components implement services and functions related to address space. The MasterNodeManager consist of CoreNodeManager and might be objects for other INodeManager.

v. CoreNodeManager: This component implements INodeManager Interface. When the object CoreNodeManager is created, it loads standard address space of the OPC UA server from file to memory.

vi. SessionManager: This component implements services and functions related to session management like CreateSession, ActiveSession, CloseSession, etc.

vii. Session: This component stores information for a session between the OPC UA Client application and OPC UA Server application, e.g., the function Activate allows activating a session according to the specific parameters.

viii. SubcriptionManager: This component manages subscriptions and their monitored items. This provides services and functions for subscription management such as AddSubcription, RemoveSubcription, etc.

ix. SessionPublishQueue: A session might have more subscriptions and a list of requests. This component support SubcriptionManager to choose a correspondent subscription to return Notification Messages with storing requests into queue in order to process.

x.   Subcription: This component provides functions and services to manage monitored items such as AddMoniteredItem, RemoveMonitoredItem, etc.

xi.   MonitoredItem: This component contains the parameters of a monitored item. The SubcriptionManager will pass data into monitored item.

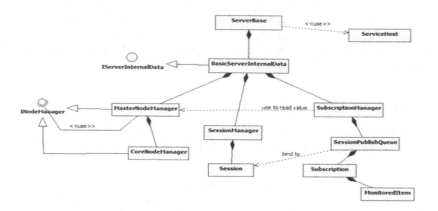

Fig. 2. The architecture of the proposed OPC UA Server SDK based WCF technology

a) Creation of Endpoint

The steps to create an Endpoint can be presented as: The OPC UA server uses ServiceHost from the .NET framework to transfer the description of an Endpoint that depends on each application. ServiceHost calls functions from class BindingFactory in the proposed OPC UA SDK to provide build the bindings for endpoint. Binding often indicates one of three kinds of bindings like WsHttpXMLBinding, UaTcpBinding, or WsHttpBinaryBinding. By the way, the object ServiceHost can create the Endpoint for the OPC UA server.

b) Initialization of the OPC UA Server

The object StandardServer in OPC UA server that provides data and its information to OPC UA client needs to be initialized all parameters. First, it loads the configuration from the file or input-parameters. Then, it initializes the object MasterNodeManager and creates the ServerObject that is a standard object in order to provide the states of the server. Finally, it starts the objects SessionManager and SubcriptionManager in order to create the Endpoint for the OPC UA server.

3.4   The OPC UA Client SDK

The architecture of the proposed OPC UA Client SDK: An OPC UA client calls services and functions that are provided by the OPC UA server by using two objects SessionClientEndpoint and DiscoveryClientEndpoint. In addition, the class ClientBase uses other components such as BindingFactory and ISecurityHelper. The BindingFactory supports the OPC UA client to have correct configurations for connecting to the OPC UA server and ISecurityHelper is used for securing the exchange information between the OPC UA client and OPC UA server.

4   Development of an Environmental Monitoring Application

As the introduction of the proposed OPC UA SDK, the development of an Environmental Monitoring Application (EMA) is implemented by using such an OPC UA SDK. This section presents (i) an overview of EMA system, (ii) devices used for the system, (iii) EMA software analysis and design and system integration.

a) Overview of system architecture

The operation of the proposed system is as follows:

i.   Measurement devices placed on the rivers or lakes will measure the information about the water and this information is sent back to the OPC UA server.

ii.   The OPC UA client in order to monitor such information on the devices requests latest data from the OPC UA server and draws these data in chart format to operators in real-time constraint.

iii.   EMA system can alert events to operators if the mutation of water parameters that support the user to decide his/her decisions timely.

The components of the EMA system can be shown in Fig. 3. These components are divided as: data acquisition module, storage module, and workstation. Data from sensors at the data acquisition module are sent to the OPC UA server through SIM548 based on TCP/IP. The data are stored to database in which the server will provide these data to workstations, i.e., OPC UA client applications. These workstations are located in local area, which show information from sensors and devices to operators in order for representing events and suggestion of these problems.

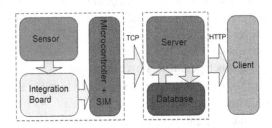

Fig. 3. The components of the EMA system

b) Devices for EMA

Sensors: The sensors are used for the EMA system as the following:

i.   pH sensor (Hana, HI1230): This sensor is widely used in EMA system, which has functionality to convert the pH values into voltage values correspondingly. The voltage values of the sensor are from -414mV to +414mV (in the temperature 25oC).

ii.   DO sensor (Hana, HI76409) is used to measure the concentration of dissolved oxygen in water by using Galvanic method.

iii.   Conductivity sensor is two metal plates placed opposite each other in a certain volume of the water to measure the ability of conducting electricity.

iv.   Light sensor (OPT101) is used to measure the light intensity at the inspection area.

v.   Turbidity sensor is based on the light sensor.

vi.   Depth sensor is used for indirect measurement through the use of pressure sensors by the pressure of a body of water corresponded to the depth of the water mass. The pressure sensor MPXV7035 is used that have output voltage in range from 0.2 to 4.7V.

vii.   Temperature sensor LM35 is used for measuring temperature. The output voltage is compatible with the temperature of the environment.

Microcontroller and SIM: Microcontroller ATmega128 is used because of having potential features: ADC channel with the resolution of 10 bits, two USART blocks for programming, 64 I/O registers, etc. SIM548C is used in the EMA system, which is GSM/GPRS working on 4 bands (EGSM900/DCS1800, GSM850/PCS1900). In addition, SIM supports global positioning system (GPS).

c)   Software Analysis and Design

Functionality Analysis and Design: The intent of the EMA software is to acquire data that come from sensors placed at rivers and lakes in different area through GPRS and TCP/IP protocol, to store these data into database at the center. Each record is marked as a code together with device code, timestamp, etc. Based on these data, operator can make the reports and statistics for environmental situation for rivers and lakes. Form the point of view of the statistics, the operators will have evaluation and solution in order to process timely.

The functionality of the OPC UA server can be summarized as follows:
- F01S: Acquiring and storing data from measurement devices
- F02S: Real-time data query
- F03S: Report query
- F04S: Warning when parameters over threshold

The functionality of the OPC UA client can be summarized as follows:
- F05C: Device information query
- F06C: Real-time data query
- F07C: Warning display
- F08C: Report query

Database Design: The database is designed with three tables: Device table, Location table, and Measurement table. The device information is stored into Device table. Each device is unique. The Location table presents area or river or lake which devices are placed. Lastly, the Measurement table stores data coming from devices.

5   Experimental Result

The EMA (environmental monitoring application) system is basically completed for experiment in order to receiving the monitoring data from sensors to OPC UA Client application. Operators in the client side can monitor these data for their tasks. The experimental setup for environmental application and the interface of the OPC UA Client application can be shown in Fig. 4(a) and Fig. 4(b).

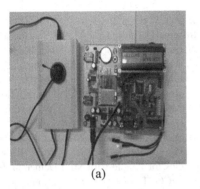
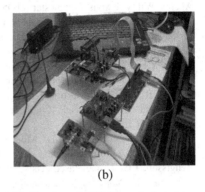

(a)   (b)

Fig. 4. (a) The main of EMA system. (b) The hardware of EMA system.

The EMA system provides functionality for measuring parameters including pH, DO, ORP, temperature, conductivity level, depth level, etc., This information is sent to OPC UA server and then it is represented in the OPC UA client. The experimental results demonstrate the ability of the proposed OPC UA SDK for developing specific application in terms of monitoring and control. These experimental results, however, are initial results for the EMA system. For further experiment, the EMA system should be continuously developed and implemented with the accuracy of measuring parameters, high performance, and alarms and events for operators.

6   Conclusions

This paper has introduced the development of an OPC UA SDK based on the OPC UA specifications that were proposed by the OPC Foundation. The design and implementation for both sides – OPC UA Server SDK and OPC UA Client SDK is based on the Windows Communication Foundation in order to reduce the development time for the proposed SDK. The deployment of the proposed OPC UA SDK has been applied for an environmental monitoring application for acquiring the environmental data from the devices, i.e., sensors, which are placed in the rivers and lakes. This environmental monitoring application demonstrates the successful development of the proposed SDK and the ability of the SDK to real-life applications. The proposed OPC UA SDK in turn makes system architects and developers easy to develop their applications by using the developed components. It also reduces the development time and cost for general monitoring and control systems. In the future work, the system will be continuously developed for both monitoring and control functions, not only for monitoring functions until now. The developed components will be also optimized and the experiments will be conducted for providing more experimental results.

Acknowledgments. The authors would like to thank Nguyen Tri Dung for his support to implement EAM system and Dr. Vu Van Tan for his valuable comments to this paper.

References

1. Singh, M.P., Huhns, M.N.: Service Oriented Computing: Semantics, Processes, and Agents. Wiley & Sons, Chichester (2005)
2. XML Extensible Markup Language, http://www.w3.org/XML/
3. El Gayar, O., Tandekar, K.: An XML Based Schema Definition for Model Sharing and Reuse in a Distributed Environment. Decision Support Systems 43(3), 791–808 (2007)
4. Wang, Y.H., Lu, Y.C.: An XML Based DEVS Modeling Tool to Enhance Simulation Interoperability. In: Pro. of the 14th European Simulation Symposium, pp. 406–410 (2002)
5. Fourer, R., Ma, J., Martin, K.: OSiL – An Instance Language for Optimization, Department of Industrial Engineering and Management Sciences. Northwestern University, Chicago (2006)
6. Nugent, C.D., Mulvenna, M.D., Moelaert, F., Bergvall-Kåreborn, B., Meiland, F., Craig, D., Davies, R., Reinersmann, A., Hettinga, M., Andersson, A.-L., Dröes, R.-M., Bengtsson, J.E.: Home Based Assistive Technologies for People with Mild Dementia. In: Okadome, T., Yamazaki, T., Makhtari, M. (eds.) ICOST. LNCS, vol. 4541, pp. 63–69. Springer, Heidelberg (2007)
7. Wollchlaeger, M., Bangemann, T.: XML based Description Model as a Platform for Web based Maintenance. In: Proc. of the IEEE Conference on Industrial Informatics, pp. 125–130. IEEE Press, Los Alamitos (2004)
8. Wollschlaeger, M., Geyer, F., Krumsiek, D., Wilzeck, R.: XML Based Description Model of a Web Portal for Maintenance of Machines and Systems. In: Proceedings of the 2003 IEEE Conference on Emerging Technologies and Factory Automation, pp. 333–340. IEEE Press, Los Alamitos (2003)
9. Mahnke, W., Leitner, S.-H., Damms, M.: OPC Unified Architecture (2009)
10. Simulation. In: Proceedings of the 7th International Symposium on Distributed Simulation and Real Time Applications, p. 76. IEEE Press, Los Alamitos (2003)
11. Zeeb, E., Bobek, A., Bohn, H., Golatowski, F.: Service Oriented Architectures for Embedded Systems Using Devices Profile for Web Services. In: Proceedings of the 21st International Conference on Advanced Information Networking and Applications Workshops, pp. 956–963. IEEE Press, Los Alamitos (2007)
12. Jammes, F., Smit, H.: Service Oriented Architectures for Devices the SIRENA View. In: Proceedings of the 3rd IEEE International Conference on Industrial Informatics, pp. 140–147 (2005)
13. The OPC Foundation: The OPC Unified Architecture Specifications: Parts 1 11, Version 1.xx (2008), http://www.opcfoundation.org/Downloads.aspx
14. The OPC Foundation: The OPC XML Data Access Specification. Version 1.01 5 (2004), http://www.opcfoundation.org/Downloads.aspx
15. Eppler, W., Beglarian, A., Chilingarian, S., Kelly, S., Hartmann, V., Gemmeke, H.: New Control System Aspects for Physical Experiments. IEEE Transactions on Nuclear Science 51(3), 482–488 (2004)
16. Van Tan, V.: A SOA Based Framework for Building Monitoring and Control Software Systems, Doctoral Dissertation. University of Ulsan, Korea (2010)

Author Index